MINITAB GUIDE
THE IRWIN STATISTICAL SOFTWARE SERIES

Kilman Shin
Ferris State University

IRWIN
Burr Ridge, Illinois
Boston, Massachusetts
Sydney, Australia

Cover Illustration: Boston Graphics, Inc.

©Richard D. Irwin, Inc., 1994

Printed in the United States of America.

ISBN 0-256-15927-0

1 2 3 4 5 6 7 8 9 0 P 1 0 9 8 7 6 5 4

Preface to Minitab Guide

This is a guide to the Minitab system for statistical analysis. In old days, teaching statistics meant showing derivation of formulas and simple numerical examples of hand calculations. However, with the rapid development of popular statistical packages for PC, computer applications has become an important part of statistics courses. More instructors are assigning computer lab work as part of statistics class. This guidebook is designed for such lab work assignments. The Minitab files were written and tested using the Minitab versions 8.0 for DOS and 9.0 for Windows. The topics are arranged in the following order:

1. Quick steps to run Minitab
2. Frequency tables and histograms
3. Measures of central tendency and dispersion
4. Tests for 1-sample
5. Tests for 2-samples (paired and independent samples)
6. Tests for 3 or more samples (ANOVA, MANOVA, ANCOVA)
7. Simple regression and correlation
8. Multiple regression and correlation
9. Autoregression, weighted regression, and ridge regression
10. Use of dummy variables
11. Nonlinear equation and nonlinear estimation
12. Chi-square tests and nonparametric tests
13. Time series analysis and forecasting (moving, exponential, ARIMA)
14. Multivariate analysis (factor, cluster, discriminant, logit, probit, simultaneous equations)
15. Quality control (statistical process control)
16. Data format and generating new variables

To make the guidebook more general to be used with any statistics text, sample problems and data are taken mostly from the solved problems of the following statistics texts (Irwin publications):

Aczel, Complete Business Statistics, 1993
Emory-Cooper, Business Research Methods, 4th ed., 1991 (5th ed., 1994)
Gitlow-Gitlow-Oppenheim-Oppenheim, Tools and Methods for the Improvement of Quality, 1989
Hanke-Reitsch, Understanding Business Statistics, 1991 (2nd ed., 1994)
Mason-Lind, Statistical Techniques in Business and Economics, 8th 1993
Neter-Wasserman-Kutner, Applied Linear Statistical Models, 3rd ed., 1990
Neter-Wasserman-Kutner, Applied Linear Regression Models, 2nd ed., 1989 (NWK)
Siegel, Practical Business Statistics, 1990 (2nd ed., 1994)
Webster, Applied Statistics for Business and Economics, 1992 (2nd ed., 1985)
Wilson-Keating, Business Forecasting, 1990, 2nd ed., 1994

Most sample files are constructed from the solved examples so that readers could refer to the above texts for detailed explanations on the problem, theory, derivation of the formula, solution, and interpretation of the results. The data source is specified in each sample file, and also indicated by the sample file name (abbreviated name of the first author and the textbook page number. The scheduled publication of a new edition is indicated in parentheses).

The following professors reviewed the guide and provided very useful suggestions and comments to improve it:

Amir D. Aczel, Bentley College
Young Sook Chung, Taegu University
Donald R. Cooper, Florida Atlantic University
Joseph Gaffney, University of Connecticut
John Hanke, Eastern Washington University
Barry Keating, University of Notre Dame
Douglas A. Lind, University of Toledo
Benny Lo, Ohlone College
Elan Long, SPSS Corporation
Mahmood Shandiz, Oklahoma City University
Allen Webster, Bradley College
J. Holton Wilson, Central Michigan University

The format of this guide was suggested by Richard D. Irwin editor Dick Hercher, and the following Irwin staff provided various suggestions and support: Heidi Buehre, James Minatel, Colleen Tuscher, Gail Centner, Brian Murray, and Brian Nacik.

This guide is based on the copyrighted publications and software by SPSS Inc. which has provided assistance and cooperation. I would like to acknowledge Marija J. Norusis (author of most SPSS publications), Elan Long, and Ann Glynn of SPSS Corporation. This Guide is dedicated to the people who have developed the SPSS system and work for the SPSS corporation.

I would like to acknowledge Bokman Shin and his family for making available their summer beach house where the earlier manuscripts were written.

Any comments, errors, misprints, and suggestions may be sent to the following address:

Kilman Shin, Professor
College of Business
Ferris State University
Big Rapids, MI 49307

Table of Contents

Chapter 8. Multiple Regression and Correlation Analyses 88

Chapter 9. Autoregression, Weighted Regression, and Ridge Regression 105

Chapter 10. Use of Dummy Variables 126

Chapter 11. Nonlinear Equations and Nonlinear Estimation 135

Chapter 12. Chi-Square Tests and Nonparametric Tests 147

Chapter 13. Time Series Analysis and Forecasting 169

Chapter 14. Multivariate Analysis and Other Miscellaneous Models 195

Chapter 15. Techniques of Quality Control 215

Chapter 1. Quick Steps to Run Minitab

A. Minitab Modules and Programs

The Minitab (Minimum Tabulation) system is one of the most popular and easy-to-run statistical packages and widely used by students of statistics. The advantage of Minitab software is the ease of interactive processing. Minitab consists of 3 modules: (1) Graphics (histograms, stem-and-leaf charts, Box plots, High-low-close), (2) Statistics (descriptive statistics, probability functions, t-tests, ANOVA, MANOVA, ANCOCA, correlation, multiple regression, stepwise regression, principal component analysis, factor analysis, discriminant analysis, nonparametric statistics, time series analysis including ACF, PACF, CCF, and ARIMA models, matrix operation), (3) QC (quality control - statistical process control).

The file format is essentially the same for Minitab for DOS, Minitab for Windows, and Minitab for Mainframe. However, some new features are introduced and minor changes are made in the command structure in Minitab for Windows. Some differences in the command structure are given at the end of this chapter. As for the capacity differences, the mainframe Minitab can handle up to 1,000 columns (variables), but the PC version is limited to 100 columns and 100 constants. Minitab for Windows Release 9 supports worksheet of up to 4 million cells.

B. Quick Steps to Run a Batch File in Minitab for DOS

Step 1: Type a Minitab File

You can type a Minitab program file in the Minitab system as will be explained later. Or, using an external text editor such as MS-DOS Editor or Notepad in the Windows, you can type a file and save it. If you use a wordprocessor such as Wordperfect, Microsoft Word, or Ami Pro, save the file in the ASCII format (DOS text). As an exercise, type the following file using the MS-DOS Editor, and save the file 'income-1.inp' on disk A, B, or hard disk:

```
Note 'Consumption Function: income-1.inp'
Name c1='year' c2='cons' c3='income' c4='interest'
Read c1-c4
1991 200  300  8.0
1992 400  500 10.0
1993 500  600 12.0
1994 550  700  8.0
1995 600  800  7.0
End
Brief 3
Print c1-c4
Describe c1-c4
Regress c2 on 2 c3 c4
```

Note: To write and save a file in the ASCII format (DOS Text file): Wordperfect 5.1: File (CTL/F5) ▶ Save ▶ DOS Text. Wordperfect 5.2 and 6.0: File ▶ Save As ▶ Format ▶ ASCII Text (DOS) ▶ OK. Microsoft Word 5.0: Transfer ▶ Save ▶ Text Only. Microsoft Word for Windows: File ▶ Save As ▶ Save File as Type ▶ DOS Text with Layout (*.ASC) ▶ OK. Ami Pro 3.0: File ▶ Save As ▶ List Files of Type ▶ ASCII ▶ OK

Step 2: Log on Minitab

To log on Minitab, at the Minitab directory prompt, type

C:\Minitab> **Minitab**

Opening Worksheet Screen of Minitab for DOS

```
File  Edit  Calc  Stat  Graph                    F1=Help
Worksheet size: 16174  cells
Press Alt + a highlighted letter to open a menu
MTB >
```

Step 3: Submit the File to Minitab

When you get the Session Window, on the Minitab prompt MTB> line, type the following two commands:

MTB> **Outfile 'a:income-1.out'**
MTB> **Execute 'a:income-1.inp'**

If there is no error in the file, the output will show up on the screen, and will be saved in the file 'income-1.out', which can be printed and edited using a text editor or a wordprocessor. These are the essential steps to run a batch file.

Step 4: To Exit (Quit) Minitab

If you want to quit the Minitab session, on the MTB prompt line, type

MTB> **Stop**

Step 5: To Exit Minitab Temporarily to DOS

On the MTB prompt line, type

MTB> **System**

After you make corrections in the file, to return to Minitab, type

C:\Minitab> **Exit**

C. Quick Steps to Run a Batch File in Minitab for Windows

Step 1: Type a Minitab Batch File

You can type a data set, command set, or a complete input file using the Minitab system as will be explained later in this section. Or, you can type the files using your favorite external text editor such as MS-DOS Editor or Notepad in the Windows. If you use a wordprocessor such as Wordperfect, Microsoft Word, or Ami Pro, save the file in the ASCII format. Type the following file as an exercise and save it in the ASCII format (also called DOS text file) on disk A, B or C.

```
Note 'Consumption Function: Income-1.inp'
Name c1='year' c2='cons' c3='income' c4='interest'
Read c1-c4
1991 200  300  8.0
1992 400  500 10.0
1993 500  600 12.0
1994 550  700  8.0
1995 600  800  7.0
End
Print c1-c4
Describe c1-c4
Regress c2 on 2 c3 c4
```

Step 2: Log on Minitab for Windows

To log on Windows, at the Windows directory, type

C:\Windows> **win**

In the Windows opening menu, double-click the Minitab icon [**Minitab for Windows**] and you will get the Minitab opening windows with the Data Window in front. Click on any place on the **Session Bar** which is located on the top of the Data window, and you will get the Minitab prompt: MTB>

Minitab Opening Windows

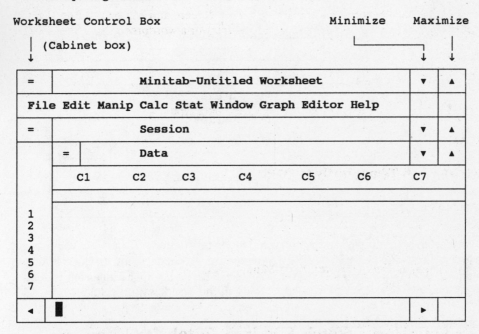

=   Contol box (Worksheet, Session, Data) to get a pull-down menu
▶   Scroll horizontally to the right
◀   Scroll horizontally to the left
↑   Scroll vertically upward (elevator-up button)
↓   Scroll vertically downward (elevator-down button)
▮   Window scroll position indicator.

▼ Minimize .. The window will disappear and it will be reduced to an icon. To return to the initial window, click on the icon to get the pull-down menu, and select Restore.

▲ Maximize .. The window will expand to a larger screen size. To return to the initial window size, click on the Worksheet control box to get the pull-down menu, and click Restore.

In the above screen, there are two types of menus: (1) the cabinet file box menu (control box menu), and (2) the Main Bar Menu in the Minitab Worksheet Window. When you click on each option, you will get a pull-down menu.

File

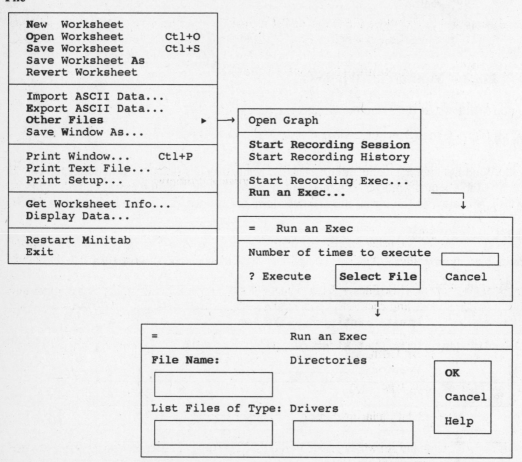

Note: Minitab for Windows must be run in the enhanced mode of Windows. Otherwise, you may get error messages in certain procedures such as ARIMA procedure. To check, in the Program Manager window of Windows, click Help ▶ About Program Manager... If you see [386 Enhanced Mode], it is OK. If you see [Standard Mode], you will need to reinstall the Windows software.

Step 3: Submit the File to Minitab for Windows

On the MTB prompt line, type

MTB> **Outfile 'a:income-1.out'**
MTB> **Execute 'a:income-1.inp'**

The above steps are the simplest method of running a batch file in Minitab for Windows, and they are the same as the operational steps of running Minitab for DOS. The output will show up on the Worksheet Window and at the same time they will be saved in the file 'income-1.out' on Disk A.

Using the Minitab System to Type a File and Execute

To Save the Output:

Before you type anything, on the MTB> prompt line, type

MTB> Outfile 'a:income1.out' or 'a:income1.LIS'.

Output will be saved in the above file in the ASCII format. In the menu system, click Files ▶ Other Files ... ▶ Start Recording Session ▶ Select File. Type the drive and file name to save, and click OK.

To Save Data and Commands (Keyboard Input):

On the MTB prompt line, type

MTB> Journal 'a:income2.inp' or 'a:income2.mtj'

All keyboard input including the data and commands will be saved in the file specified in the ASCII format. At the end of the session, type the Nojournal command otherwise, nothing will be saved:

MTB> Nojournal

You can edit the journal file using an external editor such as MS-DOS Editor since the file will save everything you type including typing errors. This is a good method of interactive processing Minitab.

To use the menu system, click Files ▶ Other Files ▶ Start Recording History. Type the drive and journal file name to save, and click OK. To stop saving the journal, click File ▶ Other Files ▶ Stop Recording History.

To Save a Data Set or Command Set:

On the MTB prompt line, type

MTB> Store 'a:income3.dat', 'a:income3.cmd', or 'a:income3.mtb'.

Either data set or command set will be saved in the ASCII format. You cannot save both files since at the end of the data set, you have to type

MTB> End

By typing End, you meant the end of the data set, but Minitab takes the End command as the end of Store procedure. Also, to run the data set or command set, you have to use the Execute command such as

MTB> Execute 'a:income3.dat', 'a:income3.cmd', or 'a:income3.mtb'

As an example, if you type the following, only the data set will be saved:

```
MTB> Store 'a:income3.dat'
     Storing in File a:income1.dat'
Store> Read c1-c4
Store> 1991 200   300   8.0
Store> 1992 400   500  10.0
Store> 1993 500   600  12.0
```

```
Store> 1994 550   700   8.0
Store> 1995 600   800   7.0

Store> End
MTB> Execute 'a:income1.dat'
```

In the following file, only the command set will be saved:

```
MTB Store 'a:income3.mtb'
    Storing in File a:income1.mtb
Store> Print c1-c4
Store> Describe c1-c4
Store> Regress c2 on 2 c3-c4
Store> End
```

After you have completed typing the data set or command set, you can execute the file by typing

MTB> Execute 'a:income3.mtb'

Step 4: Using the Menu (an alternative method of batch file processing)

An alternative method of executing a batch file is to use the menu system. First, to save the output, in the opening Worksheet Menu, click File ▸ Other Files ▸ Start Recording Session. Specify the output file name to save. Next, to execute a file, in the same pull-down menu, click Run an Exec... You will get the dialog box. Specify: [No. of times to execute]. Then, click [Select File]. In the Dialog Box, specify the file name to execute, and then click OK.

Step 5: To Correct Errors in the File and To Resubmit

Error messages will appear on the worksheet if the file has errors in the data set or in the procedure commands. To make corrections in the data set, on the main bar menu, click Window ▸ Data. Move the cursor to the cell and make corrections.

If the file has errors in the procedure commands, there are 2 methods of correcting and resubmitting the file: (1) Tentatively exit Minitab Worksheet and go to an external text editor. (2) Temporarily exit Minitab Worksheet and go to Windows' Notepad. Retrieve the file and make corrections.

Step 6: To Exit Minitab Temporarily to DOS

To exit Minitab temporarily and go to an external text editor, on the MTB prompt line, type

MTB > System

You will get the Minitab Directory DOS prompt. Use an external text editor and make corrections. To return to Minitab, on the Minitab directory prompt, type

Minitab\Data> Exit

Step 7: To Exit Minitab Temporarily to Windows - Notepad

Assume that you are on the Minitab Worksheet. You got an error message. You want to retrieve a file in the Notepad of the Windows, and make corrections. To exit Minitab Worksheet temporarily and go to the Notepad, take the following steps. Click Control Box ▸ Switch to ▸ Program Manager. In the Task List box, click on Switch to ▸ Accessories ▸ Restore ▸ Notepad.

To retrieve the file into the Notepad, click File ▸ Open. Specify the driver and the file name to retrieve. After making corrections, save the file: File ▸ Save As. Specify the driver and the file name in the dialog box.

To return to Minitab, click Control Box of the Notepad Window ▸ Switch to ▸ Minitab. In the Task List box, click on Switch to. You will be back to the Minitab Worksheet Window.
To submit the corrected file, on the MTB prompt line, type

MTB> Execute 'b:filename'

Step 8: Copying the Output to Notepad or to a Wordprocessor

Text or graph output in the Worksheet may be copied to the Notepad of the Windows or to a wordprocessor for Windows. Take the following steps:

In the Minitab Worksheet Window, click Edit ▸ Select All ▸ Copy. Click Control Box ▸ Switch to ▸ Program Manager ▸ Switch to ▸ Notepad (or Wordperfect or Microsoft Word) ▸ Edit ▸ Paste ▸ File ▸ Save As ▸ Control Box ▸ Switch to ▸ Minitab.

To Save and Retrieve the File

There are two types of files: Minitab system file and ASCII file.

Save - Retrieve	Used for Minitab system files	
Write - Read	Used for ASCII files	
Journal - Nojournal	Saves keyborad input	
Store - End	Saves commands	
Outfile - Nooutfile	Saves output in the ASCII format	

MTB> Save 'b:abc.mtw'   Saves the data set in the Minitab system format in binary code.

MTB> Retrieve 'b:abc.mtb'   Retrieves a Minitab system file.

MTB> Write 'b:abc.dat'   Saves the data set in the ASCII format.
MTB> Read 'b:abc.dat' c1-c3   Retrieves the ASCII data file.

MTB> Store 'b:abc.mtb'   Saves a set of commands in the ASCII format.

MTB> Journal 'b:abc.mtj'   Saves the work file in the ASCII format : Everything you type from the keyboard will be saved including command, data, and typing errors. But, output will not be saved).
MTB> Nojournal   The end of Journal saving. This command is required.

MTB> Outfile 'b:abc.out'   Saves the forthcoming output in the ASCII format. Any extension name can be used (such as out, dat, txt, inp, asc, etc.).

MTB> Nooutfile   End of outfile saving

D. One-File Method and Two-File Method

In the previous sample file 'income-1.inp', Minitab procedure commands and the data set were typed together in one file. However, you can type a Minitab program in two separate files: command file and data file. To run the file, we submit only the command file. Sample files for commands and data set are given below:

Sample Command File: Income-1.cmd

```
Note 'Consumption analysis: Income-1.cmd'
Read 'a:income-1.dat' c1-c4
# Or Read c1-c4 'a:income-1.dat'
Name c1='year' c2='cons' c3='income' c4='interest'
Regress c2 on 2 c3 c4
Describe c2-c4
Print c1-c4
```

Sample Data File: Income-1.dat

```
1986 200  300  8.0
1987 400  500 10.0
1988 500  600 12.0
1989 550  700  8.0
1990 600  800  7.0
```

One-File Method or Two-File Method?

Which method is better, one-file method or two-file method? Particularly when the data size is large, the two-file method is better, because you can retrieve, and edit only the short command file without retrieving the large data file. However, the advantage of using the one-file method in a guide book is that when commands and data set are presented on one page or one screen, it is easier to understand the command and data structure. For this reason, one-file method is used throughout this guide. In running Minitab for Windows, the data entry is the most important part. Once you have entered the data set, the remaining steps are easy because you can select the procedure commands form the menu.

E. Interactive Method of Running Minitab for Windows

There are several methods of running Minitab interactively:

Typing the Data

    (1) Type data in the worksheet,
    (2) Type data in the Data window, or
    (3) Type data using an external editor and retrieve it in Minitab.

Entering Procedure-Commands

    (1) Type procedure commands in the Worksheet, or
    (2) Select procedure commands from the menu.

Thus, running Minitab interactively means combinations of the above methods.

Method 1: Typing the Data and Procedure Commands in the Worksheet

In the Worksheet Window, type both the data and procedure commands as shown below:

```
MTB > Outfile 'a:income-1.out'
```

```
MTB>  Name c1='cons' c2='income'
MTB>  Read c1-c2
DATA> 20  25
DATA> 25  30
DATA> 30  40
DATA> 30  45
DATA> 40  50
DATA> End
MTB>  Describe c1-c2
```

Minitab will produce the output immediately in the same worksheet window, and the output will be saved in the disk file 'income-1.out' on disk A.

Method 2: Type the Data in the Data Window

To get the Data window, if not present in the current window, click Window on the main bar menu. Type the following data in the Data Window:

	c1	c2	c3	c4
	cons	income		
1	20	25		
2	25	30		
3	30	40		
4	30	45		
5	40	50		

Use the Enter and arrow keys to move the cursor. After data entry is completed, to exit the Data window, click the control box of the data window ▸ Next. You will be back to the Session window. Then, type the following commands on the MTB prompt lines:

MTB> Outfile 'a:income1.out'
MTB> Print c1-c2
MTB> Describe c1-c2

The Outfile command saves the output in the file 'income1.out' on disk A. The Print command will print the data set. The Describe command will compute the mean, standard deviation, and other measures.

Method 3: Retrieve a Data File

Instead of typing the data set in the Data Window, if you have a data set typed in the ASCII format on disk A or B, retrieve it as follows:

File ▸ Import ASCII Data.. ▸ [Import ASCII DATA] Store Data in Columns. Type c1-c2 and click OK. Specify the drive and the File Name: income-1.dat. Click OK.

The data set will show up in the Data Window. Since the variable names will not be imported, type each variable name in the top cell of each column: cons and income.

Method 4: Select Procedure Commands from the Menu

Suppose you want to run regression with the current data set in the Worksheet, click **Stat** in the main bar menu. Click Regression ▸ Regression.

Highlight [c1 cons]. Move the cursor to the Response box and click. Click [Select] Response: c1, and click OK. Highlight [c2 income]. Move the cursor to the Predictors box and click. Click [Select] Predictors: c2, and click OK. Click all boxes in the Storage area, and click OK. The output will show up in the Output Window.

To Save the Output

The output can be saved in a disk file. Suppose you are in the Output Window. Click **File ▶ Save Window AS...** In the dialog box, specify the driver and the output file name to save such as b:income-1.out

To Save the Data File

To save the data set, click File ▶ Export ASCII DATA. Highlight all variables and click [Select]. Or, select one variable at a time:

Highlight [c1 cons] and click [Select]. Highlight [c2 income] and click [Select]. In the dialog box, specify the Driver and the Data File Name to save. Click OK.

To Save the Command File (Macro File)

The procedure commands you have selected in the dialog boxes can be saved in an ASCII file: Click Window ▶ History. Next, click File ▶ Save Window As ▶ Save Text [*.txt]. Specify the Driver and the Command File Name, and click OK. For instance, the following macro file can be saved using the regression analysis menu:

```
Read 'B:\REG-1.DAT' c1-c2.
Name c3 = 'SRES1' c4 = 'FITS1' c5 = 'RESI1' c6 = 'COEF1' &
     c7 = 'TRES1' c8 = 'HI1' c9 = 'COOK1' c10 = 'DFIT1' k1 = 'MSE1' &
     m1 = 'XPXI1' m2 = 'RMAT1'
Regress 'cons' 1 'income';
  SResiduals 'SRES1';
  Fits 'FITS1';
  Residuals 'RESI1';
  Coefficients 'COEF1';
  Tresiduals 'TRES1';
  Hi 'HI1';
  Cookd 'COOK1';
  DFits 'DFIT1';
  MSE 'MSE1';
  XPXInverse 'XPXI1';
  RMatrix 'RMAT1'.
```

In the next Minitab session, if you want to run the same program, you can simply submit the macro command file to Minitab. The macro command file can be modified with an external text editor, if you have a different set of data.

To Run Interactively and Save the File in the ASCII Format

You can run Minitab interactively, and copy the file to Windows' Notepad and save the file in the ASCII format. Take the following steps:

Step 1: Click File ▶ Other Files ▶ Start Recording History. Type the drive and file name to save. Click OK.
Step 2: In the Minitab Worksheet, type the following:

```
MTB > Outfile 'a:income1.out'
```

```
MTB>   Name c1='cons' c2='income'
MTB>   Read c1-c2
DATA>  20   25
DATA>  25   30
DATA>  30   40
DATA>  30   45
DATA>  40   50
DATA>  End
MTB>   Describe c1-c2
MTB>   Regress c1 on 1 c2
```

Minitab will produce output immediately at each procedure command, and the output will be saved in the disk file 'income-1.out'.

Step 3: To save the above file in the ASCII format, click on Window ▶ History. You will see the file in the History Window. Click the Control box ▶ Maximize. To copy the current file on the Worksheet to Windows' Notepad, click Edit ▶ Select All ▶ Edit ▶ Copy. Click on the Worksheet Control Box [=] ▶ Switch to ▶ Program Manager ▶ Switch to ▶ Accessories ▶ Restore ▶ Notepad. In the Notepad, click on Edit ▶ Paste. The file will appear in the Notepad Window. Click on File ▶ Save as. Give the drive and file name to save in the dialog box. Click OK. To return to Minitab, click Notepad control box ▶ Switch to ▶ Minitab ▶ Switch to.

F. Differences between Minitab for DOS and Minitab for Windows

Minitab for Windows 9.0 has new features and the command structure is better organized. On the other hand, it is more stringent than Minitab for DOS 8.0 in that Minitab for Windows requires strict command formats. Some examples are given below:

DOS Version 8.0:

```
Plot c1*c2
Plot c1-c2
Plot c1 vs c2
Plot c1 c2
Plot 'income' vs 'cons'
Plot 'income' * 'cons'
G-commands (high-resolution graph)
Gplot c1 vs c2
Ghistogram c1 c2

Regress c1 on 1 c2 &
   St.res c3 fits c4;
   Residuals in c5;
   DW.
Gplot c1  c2;
   Line c4 c2;
   File 'b:Fig1'.
```

Windows Version 9.0:

```
Plot c1*c2
Plot income*cons
Plot 'income'*'cons'


G-commands are abolished
Plot c1*c2
Histogram c1 c2

Regress c1 on 1 c2;
   Sresiduals c3;
   Fits c4;
   Residuals c5;
   DW.
Plot c1*c2;
   Line c4 c2;
   Gsave 'b:Fig1'.
%Fitline c1 c2;
   Gsave 'b:Fig2'.
%Resplot c4 c5;
   Gsave 'b:Fig3'.
```

Note: 'Gsave' is used when you want to save high-resolution graphs in Minitab for Windows, and 'File' is used to save high resolution graphs in Minitab for DOS. Minitab for Windows still accepts the DOS format of Regression. 'Regress c1 on 1 c2 std.resid c3 fits c4' can be still used in the Windows version. %Fitline and %Resplots are new macro files in the Windows version.
St.res = Standardized residuals (Sresiduals), Tresiduals = Studentized residuals.

Data format and methods of generating new variables are explained in chapter 16.

Chapter 2.
Organizing and Presenting the Data

The data sets may be organized and presented in tables and charts that include the following: Tables: Frequency table, Cumulative frequency table, contingency table Charts: Histograms, Cumulative histrogram (cumulative frequency step graph), Frequency polygon, Cumulative frequency polygon (ogive, less than, more than), Stem-and-leaf, Box-chart (Box-and-whisker plot), Dot plot, Hi-low-close time plot, Scatter diagram (X-Y plot), Time series plot, Line chart (single, multiple), Bar chart (vertical, horizontal), Bar chart (clustered, stacked), Block chart, Pie chart, Star chart, Bubble plot, Map (geographical map, choropletch, prism), Surface plot, Contour graph 3D plot (3-dimensional plot), Statistical process chart (quality control chart, Pareto, Cause-and-effect), Normal curve (normal curve, probability plot), Function plot (mathematical functions), Regression fit (with confidence limits, residual plots), Polar coordinate graph, Decision Tree diagram, OC (operating characteristic) curve, Gantt chart, Critical path chart, Network diagram, Flow chart. Many of the above tables and charts are available in Minitab. The major objective of this chapter is to organize and present a data set in terms of tables and charts such as frequency table, cumulative frequency table, histogram, stem-and-leaf chart, Box plot, and high-low-close chart.

Exercise Example 2-1: Frequency Tables and Histograms

A statistician in an airline company was asked to collect, organize, and present the data concerning the number of passengers and miles flown by them. The statistician collected the data for the past 50 days. Run the file and discuss the results. Two sample files are shown below: one for the DOS Version 8.0 and the other for the Windows Version 9.0. File Name: Webst017.inp and Webst17B.inp.

Questions: Run the file and obtain the following:
(1) Frequency table
(2) Cumulative frequency table
(3) Histogram (Frequency polygon)
(4) Cumulative histogram (Cumulative frequency polygon, percent ogive)
(5) Stem-and-leaf plot
(6) Box plot (Box-and-whisker plot)

Minitab File for DOS Version 8.0: Webst017.inp

```
Note 'Frequencies and Histograms: Webst017.inp'
# Webster, p. 17, Tables 2-1, 2-2: DOS Version 8.0
Name c1='month' c2='persons' c3='miles'
Set c1
1:50/1
End
Set c2
68 71 77   83 79 72 74   57 67 69
50 60 70   66 76 70 84   59 75 94
65 72 85   79 71 83 84   74 82 97
77 73 78   93 95 78 81   79 90 83
80 84 91 101 86 93 92 102 80 69
End
Set c3
569.3   420.4   468.5   443.9   403.7
519.7   518.7   445.3   459.0   373.4
493.7   505.7   453.7   397.1   463.9
618.3   493.3   477.0   380.0   423.7
391.0   553.5   513.7   330.0   419.8
```

```
370.7   544.1   470.0   361.9   483.8
405.7   550.6   504.6   343.3   497.9
453.3   604.3   473.3   393.3   478.1
437.9   320.4   473.3   359.3   568.2
450.0   413.4   469.3   383.7   469.1
End
Histogram c2
Histogram c2 c3
Stem-and-leaf in c2
Stem-and-leaf in c3
Boxplot in c2
Boxplot in c3
Dotplot c2 c3
Mplot c2 vs c1, c3 vs c1
Nscore of c2 put in c4
Plot c2*c4
Correlation c2 c4
Nscore of c3 put in c5
Plot c3*c5
Correlation c3 c5
Ghistogram c2;
    File 'b:Pic2-1'.
Ghistogram c3;
    File 'b:Pic2-2'.
Gboxplot in c2
Gboxplot in c3
Gplot c2 * c4
Gplot c3 * c5
```

In the above file, the G-commands do not apply to Minitab for Windows.

Minitab File for Windows Version 9.0: Webst17B.inp

```
Note 'Frequency Tables and Histograms: Webst17B.inp'
# Webster, p. 17, Tables 2-1, 2-2: for Windows Version 9.0
Name c1='month' c2='persons' c3='miles'
Set c1
1:50/1
End
Set c2
68 71 77   83 79 72 74   57 67 69
50 60 70   66 76 70 84   59 75 94
65 72 85   79 71 83 84   74 82 97
77 73 78   93 95 78 81   79 90 83
80 84 91 101 86 93 92 102 80 69
End
Set c3
569.3   420.4   468.5   443.9   403.7
519.7   518.7   445.3   459.0   373.4
493.7   505.7   453.7   397.1   463.9
618.3   493.3   477.0   380.0   423.7
391.0   553.5   513.7   330.0   419.8
370.7   544.1   470.0   361.9   483.8
405.7   550.6   504.6   343.3   497.9
453.3   604.3   473.3   393.3   478.1
437.9   320.4   473.3   359.3   568.2
450.0   413.4   469.3   383.7   469.1
End
Histogram c2;
   Connect;
   Gsave 'b:Fig2-1'.
Histogram c2;
   Cumulative;
   Gsave 'b:Fig2-2'.
Histogram c3

Histogram c3;
```

```
        Cumulative.
Stem-and-leaf in c2
Stem-and-leaf in c3
Boxplot c2
Boxplot c3
Dotplot c2
Dotplot c3
GSTD
Mplot c2 vs c1, c3 vs c1
GPRO
Nscore of c2 put in c4
Plot c2*c4
Correlation c2 c4
Nscore of c3 put in c5
Plot c3*c5
Correlation c3 c5
```

Note: In the above file, the new features are indicated by bold types.

Note: Differences between DOS Version 8.0 and Windows Version 9.0

(1) **G-Commands** such as Gplot and Ghistogram are eliminated in Windows version 9.0. DOS version accepts, for example, both Plot and Gplot commands, but Windows version accepts only the Plot command.

(2) In the Plot procedure for Windows, asterisk * is required in place of 'vs' or '**versus**' which can be used in DOS version. In the DOS version both '*' and 'vs' are valid. However, in the Mplot, Lplot, and Tplot procedures, 'vs' or '**versus**' is still valid, and the asterisk '*' should not be used. In the Windows 9.0 version, extra texts are generally not allowed on the command and subcommand lines.

(3) For character plots, **GSTD** (graph-standard) command is required. To return to high-resolution graphs, **GPRO** command is required.

(4) The subcommand **Cumulative** is a new feature in the Plot procedure.

Edited Partial Output for DOS Version:

```
MTB > Histogram c2 c3
Histogram of persons    N = 50
Midpoint    Count
       50       1  *
       55       1  *
       60       2  **
       65       3  ***
       70       9  *********
       75       7  *******
       80       9  *********
       85       8  ********
       90       3  ***
       95       5  *****
      100       2  **
Histogram of miles    N = 50
Midpoint    Count
      320       2  **
      360       5  *****
      400       9  *********
      440       9  *********
      480      13  *************
      520       5  *****
      560       5  *****
      600       2  **
MTB > Stem-and-leaf in c2
Stem-and-leaf of persons    N  = 50
```

```
Leaf Unit = 1.0
     1      5 0
     3      5 79
     4      6 0
    10      6 567899
    19      7 001122344
   (9)      7 567788999
    22      8 0012333444
    12      8 56
    10      9 012334
     4      9 57
     2     10 12
MTB > Stem-and-leaf in c3
Stem-and-leaf of miles      N  = 50
Leaf Unit = 10
     2      3 23
     4      3 45
     7      3 677
    12      3 88999
    16      4 0011
    19      4 223
    25      4 445555
    25      4 666677777
    16      4 8999
    12      5 00111
     7      5
     7      5 455
     4      5 66
     2      5
     2      6 01

MTB > Boxplot in c2

                            ---------------
            *      ---------------I     +    I-------------------
                            ---------------
         --+---------+---------+---------+---------+---------+----persons
           50        60        70        80        90       100

MTB > Boxplot in c3

                          ------------------
             ---------------I      +      I-------------------
                          ------------------
           +---------+---------+---------+---------+---------+------miles
          300       360       420       480       540       600

MTB > Dotplot c2 c3,                      .   ..
             .         .  ..   ....::::.:...::::...::..   ...:..  .   ..
          -+---------+---------+---------+---------+---------+-----persons
           50        60        70        80        90       100
                                         :
              . . .  : :...:...:.  .:.::::.:.: :.    .: : .    . .
          +---------+---------+---------+---------+---------+------miles
          300       360       420       480       540       600
MTB > Correlation c2 c4
Correlation of persons and C4 = 0.996
```

For normality test, see Example 2-12.

Exercise Example 2-2: Frequency Tables and Histograms

During the last month, 40 new savings accounts were opened with a bank. Mr. Bissey wanted to organize and present the data to the bank president. Run the file and discuss the results. Webst042.inp

Questions: Run the file and obtain the following:

(1) Frequency table

(2) Cumulative frequency table

(3) Histogram (Frequency polygon)

(4) Cumulative histogram (Cumulative frequency polygon, percent ogive)

(5) Stem-and-leaf plot

(6) Box plot (Box-and-whisker plot)

```
Note 'Frequency Tables and Histograms: Webst042.inp'
# Webster, p. 42, ch. 2, Problem 13.
Name c1='savings'
Set c1
  179.80     890.00     712.10     415.00
  112.17    1200.00     293.00     602.02
 1150.00    1482.00     579.00    1312.52
  100.00     695.15     287.00    1175.00
 1009.10     952.51    1112.52     783.00
 1212.43     510.52    1394.05    1390.00
  470.53     783.00    1101.00     666.66
  780.00     793.10     501.01    1555.10
  352.00     937.01     711.11    1422.03
 1595.10     217.00    1202.00    1273.01
End
Tsplot c1
Histogram c1
Dotplot c1
Stem-and-leaf in c1
Stem-and-leaf in c1;
   Increment 100.
Boxplot in c1
Nscore of c1 put in c2
Plot c1*c2
```

Exercise Example 2-3: High-Low-Close Chart

A stock market analyst wanted to present the Dow-Jones stock price indexes in a high-low-close chart. Using the Tsplot command, he wrote the following file. Run the file and find the answer. Webst047.inp

Using Windows Version 9.0

```
Note  'Dow-Jones High-Low-Close Tsplot: Webst047.inp'
# Webster, p. 47, Problem 36.
Name c1='date' c2='high' c3='low' c4='close' c5='day'
Read c1 -c5;
Format (A7, F8.2, F9.2, F9.2, F3.0).
09Jun88 2119.31  2081.79  2093.35  1
10Jun88 2123.58  2084.82  2101.71  2
13Jun88 2144.15  2084.64  2099.40  3
14Jun88 2148.12  2111.13  2124.47  4
End
Tsplot 'close';
   Day;
   Month;
   Year;
   Tdisplay 11 12 13;
   Start 9 7 1988;
   Symbol;
     Type 2;
   Project;
     Base 'low';
   Project;
     Base 'high';
   Minimum 1  0;
```

```
    Maximum 1   15;
    Minimum 2   2000;
    Maximum 2   2200.
# Symbol 2 = +
# Minimum 1 = x-axis
# Mininum 2 = y-axis
```

Using Mplot

```
Note  'Dow-Jones High-Low-Close, Using Mplot: Webs047B.inp'
# Webster, p. 47, Problem 36.
Name c1='date' c2='high' c3='low' c4='close' c5='day'
Read c1 -c5;
Format (A7, F8.2, F9.2, F9.2, F3.0).
09Jun88 2119.31  2081.79  2093.35  1
10Jun88 2123.58  2084.82  2101.71  2
13Jun88 2144.15  2084.64  2099.40  3
14Jun88 2148.12  2111.13  2124.47  4
End
GSTD
# GSTD (graph-standard) command applies to Minitab for Windows
# when character plot is requested.
Mplot c2 vs c5, c3 vs c5, c4 vs c5
Mplot high vs day low vs day close vs day
```

Using Lplot

```
Note  Dow-Jones High-Low-Close, Using Lplot: Webs047C.inp
# Webster, p. 47, Problem 36.
Name c1='price' c2='letter' c3='day'
Set c1
 2119.31   2081.79   2093.35
 2123.58   2084.82   2101.71
 2144.15   2084.64   2099.40
 2148.12   2111.13   2124.47
End
Set c2
8   12 3
8   12 3
8   12 3
8   12 3
End
# 8=High 12=Low 3=Close
Set c3
1   1   1
2   2   2
3   3   3
4   4   4
End
GSTD
# GSTD (graph-standard) applies only to Minitab for Windows
# for character plot.
Lplot 'price' vs 'day' coded in 'letter'
```

Exercise Example 2-4: Frequency Tables and Histograms

Amir Aczel gathered the data on the wealth of 60 wealthiest people. He wanted to construct a frequency table and a histogram: Run the file and discuss the results. ACZEL018.inp

Questions: Run the file and obtain the following:
(1) Frequency table
(2) Cumulative frequency table
(3) Histogram (Frequency polygon)
(4) Cumulative histogram (Cumulative frequency polygon, percent ogive)

(5) Stem-and-leaf plot
(6) Box plot (Box-and-whisker plot)

```
Note ' Frequencies and Histogram - ACZEL018.inp'
# Aczel, p. 18, No. 1-20.
#  Richest 60 people's wealth in billion dollars.
Name c1='wealth'
Set c1
25.0  20.0   8.7  7.5  7.4  6.0  5.7  5.5  5.0  5.0
 4.4   4.0   4.0  3.6  3.4  3.1  3.0  3.0  2.9  2.8
 2.8   2.5   2.5  2.5  2.4  2.4  2.4  2.2  2.0  2.0
 2.0   1.9   1.8  1.7  1.6  1.5  1.5  1.5  1.5  1.4
 1.3   1.3   1.3  1.3  1.2  1.2  1.2  1.2  1.1  1.1
 1.1   1.0   1.0  1.0  1.0  1.0  1.0  1.0  1.0  1.0
End
Tsplot c1
Histogram c1
Dotplot c1
Stem-and-leaf in c1
Boxplot in c1
Nscore of c1 put in c2
Plot c1 * c2
```

Exercise Example 2-5: Frequency Tables and Histograms

Forbes magazine named 50 most powerful corporations in America as Super50. The editor wanted to show net profits of the Super50 in graphs. Run the file and discuss the results. Emory479.inp

Questions: Run the file and obtain the following:
(1) Frequency table
(2) Cumulative frequency table
(3) Histogram (Frequency polygon)
(4) Cumulative histogram (Cumulative frequency polygon, percent ogive)
(5) Stem-and-leaf plot
(6) Box plot (Box-and-whisker plot)

```
Note 'Frequencies and Histogram:Emory479.inp'
#  Emory, p. 479, Table 14-3
#  Net profits of Forbes Super 50 (in million dollars)
Name c1='profit'
# profit = 'net profits of super50'
Set c1
  251.00   498.00   529.00   562.00   584.00   639.40   675.00
  701.00   702.10   740.60   802.00   807.30   807.60   809.00
  820.00   846.00   875.80   900.60   901.40   907.10   922.00
  965.00  1074.50  1075.90  1092.80  1110.70  1157.00  1238.20
 1242.00  1244.00  1367.50  1395.00  1417.30  1508.50  1610.00
 1695.00  1723.80  1809.00  1953.00  2413.00  2480.00  2487.00
 2697.00  2946.00  2975.00  3758.00  3825.00  3939.00  4224.30
End
Tsplot c1
Histogram c1
Dotplot c1
Stem-and-leaf in c1
Boxplot in c1
Nscore of c1 put in c2
Plot c1 * c2
```

Exercise Example 2-6: Frequency Tables and Histograms

Mary Rose, owner of Wilco Vacuum Center, gathered the data on the number of vacuum cleaners sold each day during the last 31 days. She wants to construct a frequency table and a histogram. Run the file and discuss the results. Hanke077.inp

Questions: Run the file and obtain the following:
(1) Frequency table
(2) Cumulative frequency table
(3) Histogram (Frequency polygon)
(4) Cumulative histogram (Cumulative frequency polygon, percent ogive)
(5) Stem-and-leaf plot
(6) Box plot (Box-and-whisker plot)

```
Note ' Frequency Tables and Histograms'
# Hanke, p. 77 Exercise 45
Name c1='sales'
# sales='sales in units of vacuum cleaners'
Set c1
56  89  64  23  45  65  21  78  67  59
85  63  54  21  46  49  78  86  91  65
34  64  67  56  54  23  46  34  37  38  49
End
Histogram c1
Histogram c1;
  Increment 10;
  Start 20;
  Same.
Tally c1;
  All.
Tally in c1;
  Counts;
  Percents;
  Cumcounts;
  Cumpercents;
  Store c1-c5.
Dotplot c1
Stem-and-leaf c1;
    Increment 10.
Boxplot in c1
# For high resolution graphs, G-commands apply
# only to Minitab for DOS
GHistogram c1
GHistogram c1;
  Increment 10;
  Start 20;
  Same.
GDotplot c1
GBoxplot in c1
```

Note: The Tally command works only for integer data.

Exercise Example 2-7: Frequency Tables and Histograms

The manager of Adventure Shops which sells ski equipments and supplies collected the data on purchases by beginning skiers. He wants to represent the data in a frequency table and a histogram. Run the file and discuss the results. Mason058.inp

Questions: Run the file and obtain the following:
(1) Frequency table
(2) Cumulative frequency table
(3) Histogram (Frequency polygon)
(4) Cumulative histogram (Cumulative frequency polygon, percent ogive)
(5) Stem-and-leaf plot

(6) Box plot (Box-and-whisker plot)

```
Note ' Frequencies and Histogram: Mason058.inp'
# Mason, p. 58, No. 25, Adventure Shop sales
Name c1='sales'
#     sales = 'sales per person'
Set c1
140    82   265   168    90   114   172   230   142
 86   125   235   212   171   149   156   162   118
139   149   132   105   162   126   216   195   127
161   135   172   220   229   129    87   128   126
175   127   149   126   121   118   172   126
End
Histogram c1
Histogram c1;
  Increment 40;
  Start 98;
  Same.
Tally c1;
  All.
Tally in c1;
  Counts;
  Percents;
  Cumcounts;
  Cumpercents;
  Store c1-c5.
Set c6;
80:280/40.
Plot c3 * c6.
Plot c5 * c6.
Dotplot c1
Stem-and-leaf c1;
    Increment 10.
Boxplot in c1
```

Exercise Example 2-8: Frequency Tables and Histograms

The quality control manager in the auto assembly line gathered the data on the number of defective cars in each day's production for 15 days. He wants to construct a frequency table and a histogram. Run the following file and discuss your findings. Siege107.inp

Questions: Run the file and obtain the following:
(1) Frequency table
(2) Cumulative frequency table
(3) Histogram (Frequency polygon)
(4) Cumulative histogram (Cumulative frequency polygon, percent ogive)
(5) Stem-and-leaf plot
(6) Box plot (Box-and-whisker plot)

```
Note ' Frequencies and Histogram: Siege107.inp'
#  Siegel, p. 107, Problem 1
#  cars = 'No. of defective cars'
Name c1='cars'
Set c1
30   34    9  14 28  9  23  0
 5   23   25   7  0  3  24
End
Histogram c1
GHistogram c1;
  Increment 5;
  Start 0;
  Same.
Tally c1;
  All.
```

```
Tally in c1;
  Counts;
  Percents;
  Cumcounts;
  Cumpercents;
  Store c1-c5.
Dotplot c1
Stem-and-leaf c1;
    Increment 10.
Boxplot in c1
GBoxplot in c1
```

Exercise Example 2-9: Frequency Tables and Histograms

A computer store manager collected data on computer sales in units for the past 25 cosequtive months. He wants to represent the data in a frequency table and a histogram. File Name: Wils-056.inp

Questions: Run the file and obtain the following:
(1) Frequency table
(2) Cumulative frequency table
(3) Histogram (Frequency polygon)
(4) Cumulative histogram (Cumulative frequency polygon, percent ogive)
(5) Stem-and-leaf plot
(6) Box plot (Box-and-whisker plot)

```
Note 'Frequency Tables and Histograms'
#  Wilson, p. 56, Table 2-1
#  sales = 'computer sales'
Set c1
3   4   5   1   5   3   6   2   7   8   1   13   4
4   7   3   4   2   5   7   4   5   2   6   4
End
Histogram c1
Tally c1;
  All.
Tally in c1;
. Counts;
  Percents;
  Cumcounts;
  Cumpercents;
  Store c1-c5.
Dotplot c1
Stem-and-leaf c1;
    Increment 10.
Boxplot in c1
```

Exercise Example 2-10: Sorting the Data

The following data are the per capita personal incomes in the 50 U.S. states for 1980, 1990, 1992 and family income and the number of tornadoes in each state. Exam2-10.inp

```
Note 'Frequencies and Sorting the Data: Exam2-10.inp'
#                   1980     1990      1990 F   1992     T.
#                   (1)      (2)       (3)      (4)      (5).
Name c1='number' c2='state' c3='income90', c4='income80' &
     c5='family90' c6='income92' c7='tornado'
Read c1-c7;
Format(F3, A16, F5.0, F8.0, F9.0, F8.0, F6.0).
  1. Connecticut    25358    10198     49199    26979     1
  2. New Jersey     24968     9822     47589    26457     3
  3. Massachusetts  22642     8926     44367    24059     3
  4. New York       21974     8966     39741    23534     6
```

```
 5. Maryland        21864     8942    45034    22974      3
 6. Alaska          21761    11572    46581    21603      0
 7. California      20795     9875    40559    21279      5
 8. New Hampshire   20789     8523    41628    22934      2
 9. Illinois        20303     9151    38664    21608     27
10. Hawaii          20254     9065    43176    21218      0
11. Delaware        20039     8259    40252    21451      1
12. Virginia        19746     8296    38231    20629      6
13. Nevada          19416     9714    35837    20266      1
14. Washington      18858     9213    36795    20398      2
15. Rhode Island    18841     8130    39172    20299      0
16. Colorado        18794     8944    35930    20124     26
17. Minnesota       18731     8410    36916    20049     20
18. Pennsylvania    18672     8460    34856    20253     10
19. Florida         18586     8384    32212    19397     53
20. Michigan        18346     8622    36652    19508     19
21. Kansas          17986     8388    32966    19376     40
22. Wisconsin       17503     8315    35082    18727     21
23. Missouri        17497     7954    31838    18835     26
24. Ohio            17473     8275    34351    18624     15
25. Vermont         17436     7410    34780    18834      1
26. Iowa            17249     8012    31659    18267     36
27. Nebraska        17221     7873    31634    19084     37
28. Maine           17200     7218    32422    18226      2
29. Oregon          17156     8304    32336    18202      1
30. Georgia         16944     7088    33529    18130     21
31. Indiana         16864     7874    34082    18043     20
32. Texas           16759     8298    31553    17892    139
33. Wyoming         16398     9420    32216    17423     12
34. Arizona         16297     7943    32178    17119      4
35. North Carolina  16203     6819    31548    17667     15
36. South Dakota    15872     7322    27602    16558     29
37. Tennessee       15798     6991    29546    17341     12
38. Oklahoma        15444     7939    28554    16198     47
39. North Dakota    15255     7339    28707    16854     21
40. Idaho           15160     7451    29472    16067      3
41. Montana         15110     7692    28044    16062      6
42. South Carolina  15099     6505    30797    15989     10
43. Kentucky        14929     6952    27028    16534     10
44. Alabama         14826     6574    28688    16220     22
45. Louisiana       14391     7406    26313    15712     28
46. New Mexico      14228     7138    27623    15353      9
47. Arkansas        14218     6479    25395    15439     20
48. Utah            14083     6874    33246    15325      2
49. West Virginia   13747     6773    25602    15065      2
50. Mississippi     12735     5953    24448    14088     26
51. DC                  *        *    36256        *    -99
End
# income80, income90, income92: per capita personal income.
# family90 ... family income in 1990.
# tornado  ... Average annual number of tornadoes.
# * .... Missing values in Minitab. Below -99 is coded as
#          a missing value:
Code (-99) '*' in c7 put in c7
Histogram c6
Dotplot c6
Boxplot in c6
Stem-and-leaf c6
Sort c6 carry c2, c3-c5 putin c13-c17
Print c14-c17
Sort c2 carry c6 put in c18-c19
Print c18 c19
Sort c2 carry c6 put in c20-c21;
  by c6;
  descending c6.
Print c20-c21
Rank c6 put in c23
Print c2 c6 c23
Nscore of c6 putin c24
```

```
Plot c6 * c24
```

Exercise Example 2-11: Normality Test of a Distribution

Previously, we have examined the frequency distribution using the data on the number of passengers and the miles flown by Pigs and People Airlines. Using the same data, we want to know if the number of passengers and the miles flown are normally distributed. The probability density function of a normal distribution is given by

$$f(x) = \frac{1}{\sigma (2\pi)^{1/2}} \exp^{-(1/2)[(x-\mu)/\sigma]^2}$$

A normal distribution has the following properties:

    1. a bell-shaped
    2. symmetric
    3. the area under the curve is equal to 1.0

If the x-scale is measured in terms of the standardized values, $z = (x-\mu)/\sigma$, the normal distribution is called the standardized normal distribution.

```
Note 'Normality Test: Exam2-11.inp'
# Data:Webster, p. 17, Tables 2-1. 2-2.
Name c1='month' c2='persons' c3='miles'
Set c1
1:50/1
End
Set c2
68 71 77   83 79 72 74   57 67 69
50 60 70   66 76 70 84   59 75 94
65 72 85   79 71 83 84   74 82 97
77 73 78   93 95 78 81   79 90 83
80 84 91 101 86 93 92 102 80 69
End
Set c3
569.3   420.4   468.5   443.9   403.7
519.7   518.7   445.3   459.0   373.4
493.7   505.7   453.7   397.1   463.9
618.3   493.3   477.0   380.0   423.7
391.0   553.5   513.7   330.0   419.8
370.7   544.1   470.0   361.9   483.8
405.7   550.6   504.6   343.3   497.9
453.3   604.3   473.3   393.3   478.1
437.9   320.4   473.3   359.3   568.2
450.0   413.4   469.3   383.7   469.1
End
Nscore of c2 put in c4
Plot c2*c4
Correlation c2 c4
Nscore of c3 put in c5
Plot c3*c5
Correlation c3 c5
# Normal distribution plot for Windows
Set c6
-5:5/0.1
End
PDF c6 c7
Plot c7*c6;
   Connect;
   Axis 1;
   Label 'X-values';
   Axis 2;
   Label 'Probability density';
```

```
     Title 'Normal Curve'.
# Histogram with Normal Curve
Name c8 ='sorted' c9='pdfvalue'
Let k1 = Mean(c2)
Let k2 = Stdev(c2)
Sort c2 put in c8
PDF c8 c9;
   Normal k1 k2.
Let c9 = c9*Count(c2)*5
Histogram c2;
   Cutpoint 50:100/10;
   Line c8 c9.
# Normal distribution plot for DOS Version
Set c6
-5:5/0.1
End
PDF c6 c7
GPlot c7*c6;
   Line c7 c6;
   XLabel 'X-values';
   YLabel 'Probability density';
   Title ' Normal Curve'.
Nsocre of c6 put in c8
Correlation c6 c8
Plot c8*c6
```

Edited Partial Output:

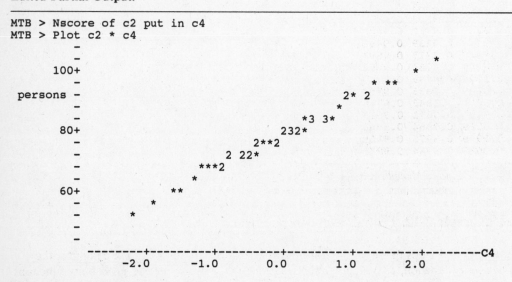

```
MTB > Nscore of c2 put in c4
MTB > Plot c2 * c4
            -
            -                                                    *
     100+                                                    *
            -                                           * **
  persons -                                        2* 2
            -                                     *
            -                               *3 3*
      80+                              232*
            -                        2**2
            -                     2 22*
            -                  ***2
            -                *
      60+             **
            -         *
            -      *
            -
           ---------+---------+---------+---------+---------+--------C4
                  -2.0      -1.0      0.0       1.0       2.0

MTB > Correlation c2 c4
Correlation of persons and C4 = 0.996
MTB > Nscore of c3 put in c5
MTB > Plot c3 * c5
```

```
            -
     600+                                                *
            -                                        *
   miles  -                                  ** **
            -                                 *
            -                              2*
     500+                             **2*
            -                        *22*
            -                    *222*
            -                   2*
            -                 22
     400+            **2*
            -      ****
```

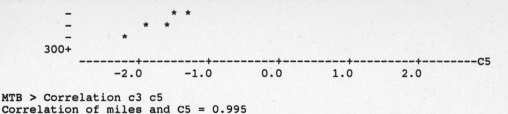

```
MTB > Correlation c3 c5
Correlation of miles and C5 = 0.995
```

In the normality plot, if the normal curve is close to a straight line, the distribution is normal. If the correlation coefficient between the normal score and the initial score is greater than the critical value (Ryan-Joiner test statistic), normality is accepted. This method is equivalent to the Shapiro-Wilk normality test. In the output, both 0.996 and 0.995 are greater than the critical value 0.9764. Thus, we accept the normality of the distribution at the 5 % level.

Ryan-Joiner Test of Normality: Critical Values (R_p)

N	alpha level (α) 0.10	0.05	0.01
4	0.8951	0.8734	0.8318
5	0.9033	0.8804	0.8320
10	0.9347	0.9180	0.8804
15	0.9506	0.9383	0.9110
20	0.9600	0.9503	0.9290
25	0.9662	0.9582	0.9408
30	0.9707	0.9639	0.9490
40	0.9767	0.9715	0.9597
50	0.9807	0.9764	0.9664
60	0.9835	0.9799	0.9710
75	0.9865	0.9835	0.9757
80	0.9871	0.9843	0.9776
100	0.9894	0.9871	0.9818
400	0.9969	0.9964	0.9950
600	0.9979	0.9975	0.9966
1000	0.9987	0.9984	0.9979

Source: *Minitab Reference Manual*, Release 9 for Windows, 1993, p. 13.9.
N = the number of observations, α = significance level.

Exercise Example 2-12. Probability Computation

Minitab has easy steps of computing various probabilities. The following file computes the probability density function, cumulative probability function, and the inverse probability functions are calculated.

```
Note 'Probability Calculation'
# (1) Normal Distribution
Set c1
0:10
End
PDF in c1 put in c2;
Normal mu=5, sigma=2.
CDF in c1 put in c3;
Normal mu=5, sigma=2.
Invcdf in c3 put in c4;
Normal mu=5, sigma=2.
Print c1-c4

# (2) Binomial Distribution
Set c1
0:10
```

```
End
PDF in c1 putin c2;
Binomial N=10, p=0.3.
CDF in c1 putin c3;
Binomial N=10, p=0.3.
Invcdf in c3 put in c4;
Binomial N=10, p=0.3.
Print c1-c4
# (3) Poisson Distribution
set c1
0:15
End
PDF in c1 put in c2;
Poisson mean = 5.
CDF in c1 put in c3;
Poisson mean = 5.
Invcdf in c3 put in c4;
Poisson mean = 5.
Print c1-c4

# (4) Student's t distribution
Set c1
0:3/0.2
End
PDF in c1 put in c2;
   T with v=5.
CDF in c1 put in c3;
   T with v=5.
Print c1-c3

# (5) F distribution
Set c4
1.60:5/0.3
End
PDF in c4 put in c5;
   F with dfa = 3 dfb = 10.
CDF in c4 put in c6;
   F with dfa = 3 dfb = 10.
Print c1 c4-c6

# (6) Chi-square distribution
Set c7
0:20
End
PDF in c7 put in c8;
  Chisquare with df= 8.
CDF in c7 put in c9;
  Chisquare with df=8.
Print c7-c9.

# (7) Exponential distribution
Set c10
0:15
End
PDF in c10 put in c11;
   Exponential b=5.
CDF in c10 put in c12;
   Exponential b=5.
Print c10-c12

 # (8) F distribution
 Set c4
 1.60:5/0.3
 End
 PDF in c4 put in c5;
 F with dfa = 3 dfb = 10.
 CDF in c4 put in c6;
   F with dfa = 3 dfb = 10.
Print c1 c4-c6
```

```
# (9) Chi-square distribution
 Set c7
 0:20
 End
PDF in c7 put in c8;
   Chisquare with df= 8.
   CDF in c7 put in c9;
   Chisquare with df=8.
Print c7-c9.

# (10) Exponential distribution
Set c10
0:15
End
PDF in c10 put in c11;
    Exponential b=5.
    CDF in c10 put in c12;
    Exponential b=5.
Print c10-c12
```

Chapter 3.
Measures of Central Tendency and Dispersion

The objective of this chapter is to compute several measures of central tendency of a distribution. Such measures include mean, median, standard deviation, variance, kurtosis, skewness, percentiles, quartiles, and range. Some of the familiar sample formulas for individual sample data are listed below:

Mean $\qquad\qquad\qquad \bar{X} = \Sigma X/N$

Variance $\qquad\qquad\quad s^2 = \Sigma (X - \bar{X})^2 / (N-1)$

Standard deviations $\qquad s = [\Sigma (X - \bar{X})^2 /(N-1)]^{1/2}$

Skewness $\qquad\qquad\quad s_k = \Sigma (X - \bar{X})^3 / (N-1)$

Kurtosis $\qquad\qquad\quad k_u = \Sigma (X - \bar{X})^4 / (N-1)$

Coefficient of variation $\quad C.V. = s / \bar{X}$

Range $\qquad\qquad\qquad$ Range = Max - Min

Exercise Example 3-1: Mean, Standard Deviation, and Other Measures

Standard deviation of a stock return is used as a measure of total risk of the stock. Mr. Boggs, a stock analyst, gathered the data on the closing prices of a stock for 7 days to compute the return and the risk of the stock. Stock return or the holding period return (HPR) is computed by $R(t)=[price(t) - price(t-1)+ dividend]/price(t-1)$. Run the file and obtain the mean and standard deviation of the holding period returns for each stock. File Name: Webst074.inp

```
Note 'Mean and Standard Deviation: Webst074.inp'
#  Webster, p. 74, Example 3-6; p.89, Example 3-14
Name c1='day' c2='stockA' c3='stockB'
# stockA = price of stock A
# stockB = price of stock B
Read c1-c3
1    87    147
2   120    120
3    54    115
4    92    110
5    73    100
6    80     73
7    63    105
End
Let c4 = Lag(c2)
Let c5 = Lag(c3)
Let c6 = 100*(c2 - c4)/c4
Let c7 = 100*(c3 - c5)/c5
Name c6='return1' c7='return2'
Describe c2-c3, c6-c7
Print c1-c3, c6-c7
# Coefficient of Variation
Let k1=Stdev(c2)/Mean(c2)
Let k2=Stdev(c3)/Mean(c3)
Let k3=Stdev(c6)/Mean(c6)
Let k4=Stdev(c7)/Mean(c7)
Print k1-k4
```

Edited Partial Output:

	N	N*	MEAN	MEDIAN	TRMEAN	STDEV	SEMEAN
stockA	7	0	81.29	80.00	81.29	21.58	8.16
stockB	7	0	110.00	110.00	110.00	22.32	8.43
return1	6	1	3.5	-5.5	3.5	45.4	18.5
return2	6	1	-3.2	-6.7	-3.2	24.7	10.1

	MIN	MAX	Q1	Q3
stockA	54.00	120.00	63.00	92.00
stockB	73.00	147.00	100.00	120.00
return1	-55.0	70.4	-29.7	46.0
return2	-27.0	43.8	-20.5	7.8

```
MTB > Print c1-c3, c6-c7
 ROW   day   stockA   stockB    return1    return2
  1     1      87       147         *          *
  2     2     120       120      37.9310   -18.3673
  3     3      54       115     -55.0000    -4.1667
  4     4      92       110      70.3704    -4.3478
  5     5      73       100     -20.6522    -9.0909
  6     6      80        73       9.5890   -27.0000
  7     7      63       105     -21.2500    43.8356
```

Exercise Example 3-2: Mean, Standard Deviation, and Other Measures

A stock analyst gathered the data on the number of shares for 50 stocks traded on the NYSE and sorted the data in ascending order. She wants to compute means, standard deviations, quartiles, percentiles, and other descriptive statistical measures. Run the file and find the answer. File Name: Webst078.inp

```
Note 'Means and Standard Deviations: Webst078.inp'
# Webster, p. 78, Table 3-6
Name c1='shares'
# shares 'stock shares in 100s'
Set c1
3  10  19  27  34  38  48  56  67  74
4  12  20  29  34  39  48  59  67  74
7  14  21  31  36  43  52  62  69  76
9  15  25  31  37  45  53  63  72  79
10 17  27  34  38  47  56  64  73  80
End
Describe c1
Stdev in c1 putin k1
Zinterval 95 percent with k1 in c1
```

Edited Output:

```
MTB > Describe c1
          N     MEAN   MEDIAN   TRMEAN    STDEV   SEMEAN
shares   50    40.96    38.00    40.89    22.77     3.22
         MIN     MAX      Q1       Q3
shares  3.00   80.00    20.75    62.25
MTB > Stdev in c1 putin k1
   ST.DEV. =       22.768
MTB > Zinterval 95 percent with k1 in c1
THE ASSUMED SIGMA =22.8
          N     MEAN    STDEV   SE MEAN    95.0 PERCENT C.I.
shares   50    40.96    22.77     3.22    (34.64,   47.28)
```

Exercise Example 3-3: Average Annual Growth Rate of GDP

An economics student gathered the GDP data from the Economic Report of the President. He wanted to compute the average annual growth rate of GDP and use it for projection. The annual growth rate of GDP can be computed in 2 ways as shown below. Run the file and find the mean and standard deviation of the GDP growth rate and make projections. File Name: Webst105.inp

growth rate 1 = (income - lagged income) / (lagged income)
growth rate 2 = log(income) - log(lagged income)

```
Note 'Growth rate of GDP: Webst105.inp'
# Webster, p. 105, Problem 16 (data are changed)
Name c1='year' c2='gnp'
# gdp = 'Gross Domestic Product in billions in 1987 prices'
Read c1-c2
1988  4718.6
1989  4838.0
1990  4877.5
1991  4821.0
1992  4927.6
End
Name c3='laggnp' c4='loggnp' c5='laglog' c6='growth1' c7='growth2'
Let c3 = Lag('gnp')
Let c4 = Loge('gnp')
Let c5 = Lag('loggnp')
Let c6 = 100*('gnp'/'laggnp' - 1)
Let c7 = 100*('loggnp' - 'laglog')
Describe c2-c7
Print c1-c7
```

Loge('gnp')   .....   Natural logarithm, base e logarithm
Logten('gnp')   .....   Common logarithms, base 10 logarithm
Lag('gnp')   .....   Lagged by 1 period

Exercise Example 3-4: Mean, Standard Deviation, and Other Measures

Money magazine gathered mortgage rates on 30-year loan of $75,000. The editor wanted to know mean and median mortgage rates. Run the file and find the answer. File Name: ACZEL047.inp

```
Note 'Mean and Standard Deviation: ACZEL047.inp'
# Aczel, p.47. Data: Money Magazine, Feb. 1991, p. 26
Name c1='region' c2='interest' c3='points' c4='monthly'
# interest='interest rate'
# points  ='point payment'
# monthly ='monthly payment'
# total   ='interest + points'
Read c1-c4;
Format(A17, F4.0, F6.0, F10.0;.
Atlanta          9.00  3.25    603.47
Baltimore        9.25  2.50    617.01
Boston           9.13  2.00    610.23
Chicago          9.25  3.00    617.01
Cleveland        9.00  3.00    603.47
Dallas           9.13  3.00    610.23
Denver           8.75  4.00    590.03
Detroit          9.25  2.88    617.01
Houston          9.00  3.38    603.47
Los Angeles      9.38  2.00    623.81
Miami            9.00  3.50    603.47
Minneapolis      9.13  3.25    610.23
New York City    9.25  2.50    617.01
N. New Jersey    9.13  2.75    610.23
Philadelphia     9.13  3.00    610.23
Phoenix          9.13  2.50    610.23
Pittsburgh       9.00  2.75    603.47
San Diego        9.25  2.75    617.01
San Francisco    9.50  2.00    630.64
```

```
Seattle              9.25   2.00    617.01
St. Louis            9.25   2.50    617.01
S.W. Connecticut 9.00      2.75    603.47
Tampa                9.50   1.50    630.64
Washington, D.C. 9.00      3.00    603.47
End
Name c5='total'
Let c5 = 'interest' + 'points'
Describe c2-c5
Print c1-c5
Sort c1 carry c2-c5 putin c6-c10;
   By 'total'.
Print c6-c10
Sort c1 carry c2-c5 put in c11-c15;
   By 'monthly'.
Print c11-c15
Sort c1 carry c2-c5 put in c16-c20;
   By 'interest'.
Print c16-c20
```

Exercise Example 3-5: Mean, Standard Deviation, and Other Measures

The editor of Forbes magazine wanted to compute descriptive statistics for the net profits of Super50 corporations. Run the file and find the answer. File Name: Emor479B.inp

```
Note ' Frequencies and Histogram: Emor479B.inp'
# Emory, p. 479, Table 14-3
# Net profits of Forbes Super 50 (in million dollars)';
# profits = 'net profits of super50';
Set c1
  251.00    498.00    529.00    562.00    584.00    639.40    675.00
  701.00    702.10    740.60    802.00    807.30    807.60    809.00
  820.00    846.00    875.80    900.60    901.40    907.10    922.00
  965.00   1074.50   1075.90   1092.80   1110.70   1157.00   1238.20
 1242.00   1244.00   1367.50   1395.00   1417.30   1508.50   1610.00
 1695.00   1723.80   1809.00   1953.00   2413.00   2480.00   2487.00
 2697.00   2946.00   2975.00   3758.00   3825.00   3939.00   4224.30
End
Describe c1
Stdev in c1 putin k1
Zinterval 95 percent with k1 in c1
```

Exercise Example 3-6: Mean, Standard Deviation, and Other Measures

Bill Emory, director of business research, collected the data on the market value and sales for 50 firms in 10 industrial sectors. He wanted to present the data in summary table forms and histograms, and obtain the mean and standard deviations by sector. Run the file and find the answer. File Name: Emory512.inp

```
Note 'Means, summary, and Tabulate Procedures: Emory512.inp'
# Emory, p. 512, Data Table
Name c1='firm' c2='value' c3='sales' c4='sector'
# firm 'firm id number'
# value 'market value of the firm'
# sales 'sales revenue of the firm'
# sector 'industry sector of the firm'
Read c1-c4
  1   24983.00     8966.00    2
  2   31307.00   126932.00    3
  3   57193.00    54574.00    7
  4   57676.00    86656.00    4
  5   60345.00    62710.00    7
  6   22190.00    96146.00    3
  7   36566.00    39011.00    2
  8   44646.00    36112.00    7
```

```
 9   25022.00    50220.00     4
10   26043.00    25099.00     1
11   13152.00    53794.00     2
12   11234.00    25047.00     5
13   26666.00    23966.00     4
14   20747.00    17424.00     7
15   25826.00    13996.00     7
16   15423.00    32416.00     4
17   15263.00    14150.00     8
18   18146.00    17600.00     1
19   18739.00    15351.00     4
20   23272.00    22605.00     2
21    7875.00    37970.00     5
22    8122.00    11557.00     5
23   18072.00    11449.00     7
24    6404.00    20054.00     8
25   16056.00    13211.00     7
26    9009.00    17533.00     4
27    7842.00    11113.00     2
28    5431.00    19671.00     8
29    5811.00    11389.00     5
30   16257.00    15242.00     2
31   16247.00    10211.00     7
32   18548.00     9593.00     7
33   13620.00     9691.00     7
34   10750.00    12844.00     3
35   12450.00    18398.00     2
36   16729.00    20276.00     7
37   16532.00     8730.00     7
38    5111.00    17635.00    10
39    9116.00     8588.00     4
40   26325.00    25922.00     2
41    8249.00    16103.00     2
42    8407.00    14083.00     3
43   18537.00    11990.00    10
44   23866.00    29443.00     4
45    6872.00    19532.00     7
46    4319.00    10018.00     5
47    9505.00    12937.00     7
48    3891.00    15654.00     8
49    8090.00     7492.00     4
50   11119.00    12345.00     7
End
Histogram in c2
Histogram in c3
Describe c2-c3;
   By c4.
```

Exercise Example 3-7: Mean, Standard Deviation, and Other Measures

June Shapiro wanted to start an advertising agency and gathered the data on the billings of advertising agencies and their employees. She wants to know mean, median, and mode for billings per agency. Run the file and find the answer. File Name: Hanke107.inp

```
Note 'Means and Standard Deviations: Hanke107.inp'
# Data: Hanke, p. 107
Name c1='agency' c2='billing' c3='employ'
# billing 'billings in million $'
Read c1-c3;
Format(A10, F4.0, F4.0).
Wendt        7.4  29
Clark        5.0  31
Coons        3.5  10
Elgeee       2.1   3
Pierce       1.5   8
Robindeaux   1.2  15
Pacific      1.0   4
```

```
Bright      1.0   5
Creative    0.4   1
Degerness   0.3   3
Rasor       0.2   4
End
Describe c2-c3
Print c1-c3
```

Exercise Example 3-8: Mean, Standard Deviation, and Other Measures

USA Today (April 5, 1991) published the data on the salaries of the players of the Cleveland Indians. Bob Mason and Doug Lind want to know the mean and median salaries. Run the file and find the answer. File Name: Mason102.inp

```
Note 'Measures of Central Tendency: Mason102.inp'
# Mason, p. 102, No. 43
# Salaries of the Cleveland Indian players
Name c1='salaries'
Set c1
2500  100   410   2050  1450  115    125  175   900
2025  345   550   100   165   800    100  575   1750
1150  110   102   100   155   100    1368 100   750
End
Describe c1
Let k1=Sum(c1)
Let k2=Mean(c1)
Let k3=Median(c1)
Let k4=Stdev(c1)
Print k1-k4
Zinterval 95 sigma=k4 in c1
```

Exercise Example 3-9: Mean, Standard Deviation, and Other Measures

Planning a world trip for sightseeing, Andy Siegel gathered the data on the price of a roll of film in various cities. He wants to know the average price and standard deviation. Run the file and find the answer. File Name: Siege140.inp

```
Note 'Means and Standard Deviations: Siege140.inp'
#  Siegel, p. 140, Problem 1
Name c1='city' c2='price'
# price = 'price of roll of film'
Read c1-c2;
Format (A10,F6.0).
Cairo       2.95
Hong Kong   3.46
London      5.51
Mexico      3.50
Munich      4.97
Paris       6.86
Sao Paulo   6.25
Tokyo       5.98
End
# (1) Method 1
Describe c2
# (2) Method 2
Let k1=Sum(c2)
Let k2=Mean(c2)
Let k3=Median(c2)
Let k4=Stdev(c2)
Print k1-k4
Zinterval 95 sigma=k4 in c2
```

Exercise Example 3-10: Mean, Standard Deviation, and Other Measures

A computer sales manager gathered the data on the computer sales in units for the past 25 months. He wants to know the monthly mean sales and standard deviation. Run the file and find the answer. File Name: Wils-56B.inp

```
Note 'Means and Standard Deviations: Wils-56B.inp'
#  Wilson, 194 ed., p. 56, Table 2-1
Name c1='sales'
# sales = 'computer sales'
Set c1
3  4  5  1  5  3  6  2  7  8  1  13  4
4  7  3  4  2  5  7  4  5  2  6  4
End
Describe c1
Let k1 = Stdev(c1)
Zinterval 95 sigma=k1 in c1
```

Exercise Example 3-11: Mean, Standard Deviation, and Other Measures

John and Jane Tarzan were doing career planning for their children. They gathered the data on the incomes of medical doctors and salary offers to Ph.D. candidates in 1990. Source: The taxable incomes of medical doctors are from American Medical Association, Annual Compendium of the Social and Economic Characteristics of Medical Practice. The salary offer data are from the Bureau of the Census, Statistical Abstract of the United States, 1991, p. 167. Run the file and find the mean, median, and standard deviation.

```
Note 'Mean, Median and Standard Deviation'
Name c1='medical' c2='income1' c3='engineer' c4='income2'
# income1 'income of medical doctors'
# income2 'income of engineering Ph.D.'
Read c1-c4;
Format(A18, F6.0, A22, F5.0).
Surgeons         236400    Computer Eng      53050
Radiologist      219400    Electrical Eng    52887
Anesthesiologist 207400    Chemical Eng      50570
Obstetricians    207300    Mechanical Eng    48708
Gynecologist     207300    Chemistry         45393
Pediatricians    106500    Civil Eng         43632
General practice 102700    Physics           41361
       *            *      Mathematics       37833
       *            *      Assistant prof    33500
End
Describe c2, c4
Print c1-c4
Let k1=Stdev(c2)
Let k2=Stdev(c4)
Zinterval 95 sigma k1 in c2
Zinterval 95 sigma k2 in c4
```

Chapter 4.
Tests for One Sample: t - Test

Hypothesis test of the mean is a test to infer if a population mean is equal to a specified mean using a sample. Alternatively, it is a test to infer if a sample is taken from a specified population. Hypothesis tests for the mean can be divided into the following categories:

1. One-sample tests (t-test)   ch. 4
2. Two-related sample tests (t-test)   ch. 5
3. Two-independent sample tests (t-test)   ch. 5
4. Three or more sample tests (ANOVA)   ch. 6
5. ANOVA with two or more dependent variables (MANOVA) ch. 6

In t-tests of one sample, the hypothesis statements are:

H_0: $\mu = k$
H_A: $\mu \neq k$

The test statistic is given by:

$$t = (\bar{X} - \mu) / (s/\sqrt{N})$$

where $\bar{X}$ = the sample mean, μ = population mean, $s/\sqrt{N}$ = standard error of the mean, $\sigma_X = \sigma/\sqrt{n}$.

The decision rule is:

Accept H_0 if computed $t \leq$ critical t   at DF = N - 1, α
Accept H_A if computed $t >$ critical t   at DF = N - 1, α

Exercise Example 4-1: Test for One Sample

The sport program manager of NBC wanted to test if the average time length of a football game is exactly equal to 3.1 hours. NBC collected the data on the times (in hours) of 12 professional football games. The hypothesis to test is, if the sample mean is equal to the population mean (μ) 3.1 hours. Run the file and find the answer to NBC's question. File Name: Webst446.inp

H_0: $\mu = 3.1$ or H_0: $\mu - 3.1 = 0$
H_A: $\mu \neq 3.1$ H_A: $\mu - 3.1 \neq 0$

```
Note 't-Test for One Sample Mean: Webst446.inp'
# Webster, p. 446, Problem 19
Name c1='hours' c2='game'
# hours 'time length of a game in hours'
# game  'game number'
Read c1 c2
1  2.91
2  3.19
3  3.05
4  3.21
5  3.09
6  3.19
7  3.12
8  2.98
```

c1 = 'game"   c2 = 'hours'

```
9  3.17
10 2.93
11 2.95
12 3.14
End
Ttest mu=3.1 in c2
Ttest mu=3.1 in c2;
    Alternate = -1.
Ttest mu=3.1 in c2;
    Alternate = +1.
```

Edited Output:

```
MTB > Ttest mu=3.1 in c2
TEST OF MU = 3.1000 VS MU N.E. 3.1000
         N      MEAN    STDEV   SE MEAN       T   P VALUE
game    12     3.0775   0.1102   0.0318    -0.71     0.49
MTB > Ttest mu=3.1 in c2;
SUBC>      Alternate = -1.
TEST OF MU = 3.1000 VS MU L.T. 3.1000
         N      MEAN    STDEV   SE MEAN       T   P VALUE
game    12     3.0775   0.1102   0.0318    -0.71     0.25
MTB > Ttest mu=3.1 in c2;
SUBC>   Alternate = +1.
TEST OF MU = 3.1000 VS MU G.T. 3.1000
         N      MEAN    STDEV   SE MEAN       T   P VALUE
game    12     3.0775   0.1102   0.0318    -0.71     0.75
```

Rules of Decision Making

From the output, what can we conclude? There are two methods of reaching the conclusion. The first method is to compare the computed and critical t values:

If computed t $\leq$ critical t, accept H_0
If computed t $>$ critical t, reject H_0

The computed t value is -0.7072. Compare this t value with the critical value of t for the degrees of freedom DF = N-1 = 12-1 = 11, at α = 0.05 (two-tail test). In the table of t-distribution, the critical value of t is 2.201. Since the absolute value of the calculated t value 0.7072 is less than the critical t-ratio, 2.201 in the table of t-distribution, we accept the null hypothesis. That is, the computed t value is not significantly different from zero.

```
Region of      |   Region of       |   Region of
accepting H_A  |   accepting  H_0   |   accepting H_A

α/2 = 0.025    |   0.475    0.475   |   α/2= 0.025
_____
          - t          0         + t
          critical               critical
          t-value               t-value
          < -2.201 >            < 2.201 >
```

The second method is to compare the significance probability P Value with the "critical probability". The 5% significance level means 0.025 for the two-tail test, and 0.05 for the one-tail test:

Two-tail test   One-tail test

If P value $\geq$ 0.025   Accept H_0 If P value $\geq$ 0.05 Accept H_0
If P value $<$ 0.025   Reject H_0 If P value $<$ 0.05 ~~Accept~~ H_A

Reject.

The P value is the significance probability of rejecting the null hypothesis at the calculated t value. The P value = 0.49 indicates that the critical significance level (alpha level) must be set at $\alpha = 0.49$ to reject the null hypothesis,. Thus, if the computed probability is greater than 0.025 (two-tail test), accept the null hypothesis, and if it is less than $\alpha = 0.05$, reject the null hypothesis.

Exercise Example 4-2: Test for One Sample

For the purpose of hotel room reservation management, the manager of the Hong Kong Hotel wanted to know if the average number of stays in the Hong Kong Hotel is 3.4 days. She gathered the data for the recent 28 guests. Run the file and find the answer. File Name: ACZEL253.inp

```
Note 'T-Test for One Sample: Aczel253.inp'
# Aczel, p 253, Problem 7-15.
Name cl='days'
# days ='days of stay in Hong Kong hotel'
Set cl
5, 4, 3, 2, 1, 1, 5, 7, 8, 4, 3, 3, 2, 5,
7, 1, 3, 1, 1, 5, 3, 4, 2, 2, 2, 6, 1, 7
End
Tinterval 95 % in cl
Ttest mu=3.4 in cl
Ttest mu=3.4 in cl;
  Alternate = -1.
Ttest mu=3.4 in cl;
  Alternate = +1.
```

Exercise Example 4-3: Test for One Sample

A university surveyed salaries of football coaches at 54 colleges to determine a salary contract with a new football coach. John Hanke and Arthur Reitch wanted to know mean salaries. Run the file and find the answer. File Name: Hanke314.inp

```
Note 'T-test for One Sample Mean: Hanke314.inp'
# Hanke, p. 314, Exercise 103
Name cl='salaries'
# salaries ='salaries of football coaches'
Set cl
99541    88946    95292   102677   82200    77331
96805   108830    98584   100358   99326   105207
98957   108827   108239    95867  104182   111255
90446    99483    96166    99956   88452   103121
98897   111854    88209   100381  102281    99076
99802    91353   111597    96003  106994   105967
82139    89856    96377    84055  104997    85154
93206    90775   100276    85210  106501    98986
80008    93535    99385    92242   82518   111352
End
Ttest mu=10000 in cl
Ttest mu=10000 in cl;
  Alternate = -1.
Ttest mu=10000 in cl;
  Alternate = +1.
```

Exercise Example 4-4: Test for One Sample

A quality control manager selected 12 counterbalance bars and measured the length. He wants to test if the mean length is equal to 43 millimeters. Run the file and find the answer. File Name: Mason400.inp

```
Note 'T-Test for One Sample Mean: Mason400.inp'
# Mason, p.400  Example
Name cl='length'
```

```
# length ='length of counterbalance bar'
Set c1
42   39   42   45   43   40   39   41   40   42   43   42
End
Tinterval 95 % in c1
Ttest mu=43 in c1
Ttest mu=43 in c1;
  Alternate = -1.
Ttest mu=43 in c1;
  Alternate = +1.
```

Exercise Example 4-5: Test for One Sample

All mutual funds averaged 9.41% rate of return. A fund manager wanted to test if the mean rate of return for 12 socially aware mutual funds is different from 9.41%. Run the file and find the answer. File Name: Siege388.inp

```
Note 'T-Test of One-Sample Mean: Siege388.inp'
# Siegel p.388, Problem 13
Name c1='fund' c2='return'
# return='return(%)'
Read c1-c2;
Format (A18, F5.0).
Ariel Growth       34.31
Calvert Bond        4.60
Calvert Growth      8.50
Calvert Equity     13.20
Dreyfus Third      14.87
New Alternatives   18.89
Parnassus          36.45
Pax World           7.15
Pioneer            15.63
Pioneer II         17.19
Pioneer Bond        3.85
Pioneer III        26.72
End
Tinterval 95 % in c2
Ttest mean=9.41 in c2
Ttest mean=9.41 in c2;
  Alternate = -1.
Ttest mean=9.41 in c2;
  Alternate = +1.
```

Chapter 5. Tests for Two Samples: t - Test

Hypothesis test for two means is a test to infer if two population means are equal using two samples. Alternatively, it is a test to infer if the two samples are taken from the same population. Two samples can be classified into two types: two-paired (matched, related, dependent) samples and two-independent samples. In two-paired samples, equality of two samples is tested in terms of individual matched pairs. In two-independent samples, equality is tested in terms of two groups as a whole. Thus, in two-independent samples, the order of observations in each sample is not relevant, but in two-related samples, observations should be paired in two samples. In Minitab, different procedures are used depending upon the type of the two samples.

(1) Two-paired samples   ... Ttest procedure
(2) Two-independent samples   ... Twot procedure

A. Tests for Two-Paired Samples

The hypothesis statements for the 2-paired samples are:

H_0: $\mu_1 = \mu_2$ or H_0: $\mu_1 - \mu_2 = 0$
H_A: $\mu_1 \neq \mu_2$ H_A: $\mu_1 - \mu_2 \neq 0$

where μ_1 and μ_2 are the two population means. Letting $\mu_1 - \mu_2 = d$, the two-sample test can be reduced to a one-sample test:

H_0: $d = 0$
H_A: $d \neq 0$

The computed t-value is obtained by:

$$t = \bar{d} / (s_d / \sqrt{n})$$

where $\bar{d}$ = the mean of differences between the paired observations. It is given by

$$\bar{d} = \Sigma\, d_i / n \quad \text{where} \quad d_i = X_{1i} - X_{2i}$$

The standard deviation of differences between the paired observations is given by

$$s_d = [\, \Sigma\, (d_i - \bar{d})^2 / (n-1)\,]^{1/2}$$

where n = the number of paired observations. Since the number of observations for the matched pairs is reduced to n, the degrees of freedom is: DF = n - 1. If each sample has 5 observations, the degrees of freedom DF = 5 - 1 = 4.

Exercise Example 5-1: Test for Two-Paired Samples

There are two types of tracks: turf (grass) track and dirt track. A state horse racing regulation agency wants to know if horses run faster on turf than on dirt tracks. Seven horses were timed in competitive races on each type of track. Run the file and find the answer. File Name: Webst474.inp

```
Note 't-Test for Two-Matched Sample Means: Webst474.inp'
# Webster, p. 474, Table 10-1
Name c1='horse'  c2='timed' c3='timet'
```

```
# timed 'race time on dirt track'
# timet 'race time on turf track'
Read c1-c3;
Format (A19, F5.2, F7.2).
Take your chances    1.82   1.73
Meatball             1.91   1.87
Cross your fingers   1.87   1.82
Jockey's folly       1.73   1.67
Nose knows           1.59   1.63
Boogaloo             1.67   1.72
My mare              1.76   1.65
End
Name c4='gap'
Let c4 = 'timed' - 'timet'
Ttest mu=0 in c4
```

Edited Output:

TEST OF MU = 0.0000 VS MU N.E. 0.0000

	N	MEAN	STDEV	SE MEAN	T	P VALUE
gap	7	0.0371	0.0610	0.0231	1.61	0.16

If the P value is greater than the significance level such as 0.05, the null hypothesis should be accepted. The computed probability is 0.16 in the above output. So, accept the null hypothesis since 0.16 > 0.05. An alternative method is to compare the calculated t value with the critical t value. The critical value is 2.447 for $\alpha = 0.05$ for two-tail test ($\alpha/2 = 0.025$ for each tail) and the degrees of freedom = N - 1 = 7 - 1 = 6. The computed t value is 1.61. Since 2.447 > 1.61. So we accept the null hypothesis. That is, there is no significant difference in the race time of horses between the two types of tracks.

Exercise Example 5-2: Test for Two-Paired Samples

US News and World Report gathered the data on professional incomes at the entry level in the New England area and the Pacific area. Since the problem is concerned with two matched samples, Ttest may be used. Allen Webster wants to know if the salaries differ in the two regions. Run the file and find the answer. File Name: Webst475.inp

```
Note 't-Test for Two Matched Samples: Webst475.inp '
#  Webster, p. 475, Table 10-1
Name c1='job'  c2='salary1' c3='salary2'
# salary1 'salaries in New England'
# salary2 'salaries in Pacific'
Read c1-c3;
Format (A24, F5.0, F7.0).
accountants          22800  26700
computer operator       20300  20700
customer service        19700  20900
financial analyst       28300  29100
programmer           28300  32400
purchasing agent        26700  26500
system analyst          35800  38200
End
Name c4='gap'
Let c4 = 'salary1' - 'salary2'
Ttest mu=0 in c4
```

Exercise Example 5-3: Test for Two-Paired Samples

Industries may be divided into 2 types: one highly concentrated and another less concentrated. An economist selected 9 firms from each type of industry and matched them with respect to foreign competition, and all other factors which can affect industry prices. Allen Webster wanted to know to see if inflation rate is different between the two types of industries due to the market power. Run the file and find the answer. File Name: Webst489.inp

```
Note 't-Test for Two Matched Samples: Webst489.inp'
# Webster, p. 489, Example 11-3
Name c1='industry' c2='inflal' c3='infla2'
# industry 'industry code number'
# infla1 'price increase by firms in concentrated industry'
# infla2 'price increase by firms less concentrated industry'
Read c1-c3
1    3.70  3.20
2    4.10  3.70
3    2.10  2.60
4   -0.9   0.10
5    4.60  4.10
6    5.20  4.80
7    6.70  5.20
8    3.80  3.90
9    4.90  4.60
End
Name c4='gap'
Let c4 = 'infla1' - 'infla2'
Ttest mu=0 in c4
```

Exercise Example 5-4: Test for Two-Paired Samples

Before expanding their services, Home Shopping Network wanted to know if consumers spend more if home shopping network is accessible. The amounts of expenditures were recorded before and after the home shopping network was accessible to 16 households. Run the file and find the answer. File Name: ACZEL308.inp

```
Note 't-Test for 2 Matched Samples: ACZEL308.inp'
# Aczel, p. 308, Example (a)
name c1='shopper' c2='spend1' c3='spend2'
# shopper 'shopper id'
# spend1 'spending before home-shopping TV'
# spend2 'spending after home-shopping TV'
Read c1-c3
 1   334   405
 2   150   125
 3   520   540
 4    95   100
 5   212   200
 6    30    30
 7  1055  1200
 8   300   265
 9    85    90
10   129   206
11    40    18
12   440   489
13   610   590
14   208   310
15   880   995
16    25    75
End
Name c4='gap'
Let c4 = 'spend1' - 'spend2'
Ttest mu=0 in c4
```

Exercise Example 5-5: Test for Two-Paired Samples

An industry analyst wanted to know if sales were significantly different between 2 years, 1993 and 1994. He gathered the data for 10 large corporations. Run the file and find the answer. File Name: Emory544.inp

```
Note 't-Test for Two Matched Sample Means: Emory544.inp'
# Emory, p. 544, Table 15-2
Name c1='firm' c2='sales1' c3='sales2'
# sales1 ='sales in 1993'
# sales2 ='sales in 1994'
Read c1-c3;
Format(A7, F6.0, F8.0).
GM      126932  123505
GE       54574   49662
Exxon    86656   78944
IBM      62710   59512
Ford     96146   92300
ATT      36112   35173
Mobil    50220   48111
DuPont   35099   32427
Sears    53794   49975
Amoco    23966   20779
End
Name c4='gap'
Let c4 = c2-c3
Ttest mu=0 in c4
```

Exercise Example 5-6: Test for Two-Paired Samples

Katrina Bell, analyst for Hexaco Oil, wanted to know if the Hexaco oil prices were higher. She matched Hexaco oil prices with those of independent dealers in each region for 11 regions. Run the file and find the answer. File Name: Hanke348.inp

```
Note 'T-test of 2 Matched Samples: Hanke348.inp'
# Data: Hanke, p.348, Case 3
Name c1='location' c2='hexaco' c3='indep'
# indep='price charged by independent co.'
# hexaco='price charged by Hexaco oil co.'
Read c1-c3
1   90.5  89.9
2   91.9  90.9
3   92.7  90.9
4   91.9  90.9
5   93.6  91.8
6   90.9  90.9
7   90.9  90.9
8   89.8  88.9
9   88.7  88.9
10  87.9  88.6
11  92.7  91.9
End
Let c4 = c2 - c3
Name c4='pricegap'
Ttest mu=0 in 'pricegap'
```

Exercise Example 5-7: Test for Two-Paired Samples

At random 10 persons was selected and they were weighed before and after they joined the Calorie Watchers program. Consumer Agency wanted to test if the Calorie Watchers program worked as claimed. Run the file and find the answer. File Name: Mason413.inp

```
Note 'T-test of Matched Sample Means: Mason413.inp'
# Mason, p. 413. Exercise No. 23
Name c1='name' c2='weight1' c3='weight2'
# weight1 ='weight before diet exercise'
# weight2 ='weight after diet exercise'
Read c1-c3;
Format (A14, F3.0, 2x, F3.0).
Evie Gorky     190  196
Bob Mack       250  240
```

```
Lou Brandon    345   345
Karl Unger     210   212
Sue Koontz     114   113
Pat O'Leary    126   129
KIm Dennis     186   189
Connie Kaye    116   115
Tom Dama       196   194
Maxine Sims    125   124
End
Let c4 = c2 - c3
Name c4='change'
Ttest mu=0 in 'change'
```

Exercise Example 5-8: Test for Two-Paired Samples

Ten experts rated winery's 2 best vintages. They rated wine on a scale from 1 to 20. The winery wants to know if the average ratings are significantly different and which vintage is better. Run the file and find the answer. File Name: Siege390.inp

```
2
Note 'T-test of Matched Sample Means: Siege390.inp'
# Siegel, p.390, Problem 18
Name c1='expert' c2='rating1' c3='rating2'
# rating1 ='rating for chardonnay wine'
# rating2 ='rating for carbernet wine'
Read c1-c3;
Format (A11, F4.0, F6.0).
expert 1    17.8   16.6
expert 2    18.6   19.9
expert 3    19.5   17.2
expert 4    18.3   19.0
expert 5    19.8   19.7
expert 6    19.9   18.8
expert 7    17.1   18.9
expert 8    17.3   19.5
expert 9    18.0   16.2
expert 10   19.8   18.6
End
Let c4 = c2 - c3
Name c4='gap'
Ttest mean=0 in 'gap'
```

B. Test for Two-Independent Samples

The hypothesis statements for the test for two independent samples are:

H_0: $\mu_1 - \mu_2 = 0$
H_A: $\mu_1 - \mu_2 \neq 0$

The test statistic is t ratio:

$$t = (\bar{X}_1 - \bar{X}_2) / s_{X1 - X2}$$

where $s_{X1 - X2}$ is the standard deviation (standard error) of two samples. When sample sizes are small, $N_1 \leq 30$ and $N_2 \leq 30$, the following formulas may be used:

$$s_{X1 - X2} = [s_p (1/N_1 + 1/N_2)]^{1/2}$$

$$s_p = [(N_1 - 1) s^2_1 + (N_2 - 1)s^2_2] / (N_1 + N_2 - 2)]^{1/2}$$

where s_p = the pooled standard deviation of the two samples.

If the sample sizes are large, $N_1 > 30$ and $N_2 > 30$, $s_{X1 - X2}$ can be estimated by

$$s_{X1 - X2} = [\ s^2_1 / N_1 + s^2_2 / N_2\ ]^{1/2}$$

The decision rule is:

$H_0: \mu_1 - \mu_2 = 0$	Accept if $t \leq$ critical t at DF $= N_1 + N_2 - 2$
$H_A: \mu_1 - \mu_2 \neq 0$	Accept if $t >$ critical t at DF $= N_1 + N_2 - 2$

Exercise Example 5-9: Test for Two-Independent Samples

In Exercise Example 5-1, the same set of horses were used to test the turf and dirt tracks. So, it was the case of 2-paired samples. If 2 different sets of horses were used on each track, it would be the case of 2 independent samples. For two independent samples, either Twot command or Twosample commands may be used. Exercise Example 5-9 uses Twot command and Exercise 5-10 uses Twosample command. Run the file and compare the 2 results. File Name: Webs474B.inp

```
Note T-test for Two Independent Sample Means: Webs474B.inp
#  Webster, p. 474 (modified data).
#  group 0 = dirt track
#        1 = turf track
Name c1='horse' c2='group' c3='time'
Read c1 - c3;
Format (A19, F2.0, F7.2).
Take your leaps     0   1.73
Cannonball          0   1.87
Cross your legs     0   1.82
Donkey's belly      0   1.67
Horse nose          0   1.63
Abu dhaby           0   1.72
My hair             0   1.65
Take your chances   1   1.82
Meatball            1   1.91
Cross your fingers  1   1.87
Jockey's folly      1   1.73
Nose knows          1   1.59
Boogaloo            1   1.67
My mare             1   1.76
End
Twot 95 percent in c3 by c2
Twot 95 percent in c3 by groups in c2;
    Alternative=-1.
Twot 95 in c3 by c2;
    Alternative=+1.
Twot 95 in c3 by c2;
    Alternative=-1;
    Pooled.
Twot 95 in c3 groups c3;
    Alternative=+1;
    Pooled.
```

Edited Output:

```
TWOSAMPLE T FOR time
group  N      MEAN     STDEV     SE MEAN
0      7     1.7271   0.0892     0.034
1      7     1.764    0.113      0.043
95 PCT CI FOR MU 0 - MU 1: ( -0.157,  0.082)
TTEST MU 0 = MU 1 (VS NE): T= -0.68  P=0.51  DF=  11

TWOSAMPLE T FOR time
group  N      MEAN     STDEV     SE MEAN
0      7     1.7271   0.0892     0.034
```

```
1       7       1.764       0.113       0.043
95 PCT CI FOR MU 0 - MU 1: ( -0.157,   0.082)
TTEST MU 0 = MU 1 (VS LT): T= -0.68  P=0.25   DF=  11

TWOSAMPLE T FOR time
group  N       MEAN        STDEV    SE MEAN
0      7       1.7271      0.0892     0.034
1      7       1.764       0.113      0.043
95 PCT CI FOR MU 0 - MU 1: ( -0.157,   0.082)
TTEST MU 0 = MU 1 (VS GT): T= -0.68  P=0.75   DF=  11

TWOSAMPLE T FOR time
group  N       MEAN        STDEV    SE MEAN
0      7       1.7271      0.0892     0.034
1      7       1.764       0.113      0.043
95 PCT CI FOR MU 0 - MU 1: ( -0.155,   0.081)
TTEST MU 0 = MU 1 (VS LT): T= -0.68  P=0.25   DF=  12
POOLED STDEV =          0.102
```

If two samples are independent, the degrees of freedom DF = $n_1 + n_2 - 2 = 7 + 7 - 2 = 12$. The computed t value is (-) 0.68 and the critical t value is 2.18 at $\alpha = 0.05$ (two-tail test). So, we accept the null hypothesis that the track time is the same on the two tracks. Alternatively, the significance probability is greater than 0.05, so we accept the null hypothesis.

Exercise Example 5-10: Test for Two-Independent Samples

In Exercise Example 5-2, we have seen the case of wage differences in two regions for the same occupations. If we select random samples of different occupations in each region, the samples can no longer be matched, and the Twosample command may be used. Run the file and find if the salaries are the same in the two regions. File Name: Webs475B.inp

```
Note 't - Test for 2 Independent Sample Means: Webst475B.inp'
Name c1='job1' c2='income1' c3='income2' c4='job2'
# job1 = in the East. job2 = in the West
Read c1-c4;
Format (A17, F5.0, F7.0, A15).
Accountant       22800   26700  Salesman
Comp. operator   20300   28700  Plumber
Service          19700   20900  Teacher
Financial        28300   29100  Stock broker
Programmer       28300   32400  Mechanics
Purchasing       26700   26500  Secretary
System Analyst   35800   38200  Dentist
*                *       98000  Medical doc
End
Twosample 95 percent in c2 c3
Twosample 95 percent in c2 c3;
    Alternative=-1.
Twosample 95 in c2 c3;
    Alternative=+1.
Twosample 95 in c2 c3;
    Pooled;
    Alternative=-1.
Twosample 95 in c2 c3;
    Pooled;
    Alternative=+1.
```

Using the Twot command, the sample file is given below:

```
Note 't-Test for 2 Independent Samples: Webs475C.inp'.
Name c1='job' c2='salary' c3='region'
#  Region 1 'salaries in New England'
#  Region 2 'salaries in Pacific area'
```

```
Read c1-c3;
Format(A17, F5.0, F3.0).
Accountant        22800  1
Comp. operator    20300  1
Service           19700  1
Financial         28300  1
Programmer        28300  1
Purchasing        26700  1
System Analyst    35800  1
Salesman          26700  2
Plumber           28700  2
Teacher           20900  2
Stock broker      29100  2
Mechanics         32400  2
Secretary         26500  2
Dentist           38200  2
Meical doc        98000  2
End
Twot 95 percent in c2 by c3
Twot 95 percent in c2 by groups in c3;
    Alternative=-1.
Twot 95 in c2 by c3;
    Alternative=+1.
Twot 95 in c2 by c3;
    Pooled;
    Alternative=-1.
Twot 95 in c2 groups c3;
    Pooled;
    Alternative=+1.
```

Exercise Example 5-11: Test for Two-Independent Samples

New York Stock Exchange wanted to test if program trading is responsible for stock volatility. It asked its members to cease program trading for 6 working days. It then compared stock price changes during the 8 days before and during the 7 days of suspension of program trading. Run the file and find the answer. File Name: ACZEL347.inp

```
Note 'T-test of 2 Independent Sample Means: ACZEL347.inp'
# Data: Aczel, p. 347, Case 8 - Program trading
Name c1='date'  c2='change' c3='program'
#  change     'Dow-Jones stock price change '
#  program 'program trading' program 1 'prog-on' 2 'prog-off'
Read c1-c3;
Format(A6, F9.0, F4.0).
Jan  5      76.42   1
Jan  6      16.25   1
Jan  7       6.30   1
Jan  8      14.09   1
Jan 11    -140.58   1
Jan 12      33.82   1
Jan 13     -16.58   1
Jan 14      -3.82   1
Jn  15      -8.62   2
Jan 18      39.96   2
Jan 19       7.79   2
Jan 20     -27.52   2
Jan 21     -57.20   2
Jan 22       0.17   2
Jan 25      24.20   2
End
Twot 95 percent in c2 by c3
Twot 95 percent in c2 by program in c3;
    Alternative=-1.
Twot 95 in c2 by c3;
    Alternative=+1.
Twot 95 in c2 by c3;
```

```
    Pooled;
    Alternative=-1.
Twot 95 in c2 by c3;
    Pooled;
    Alternative=+1.
```

Exercise Example 5-12: Test for Two-Independent Samples

Hanke and Reitsch, baseball fans, were arguing whether the teams in the American league had more runs than the teams in the National league. To settle the argument, they gathered the data on the runs. Run the file and settle their dispute. File Name: Hanke351.inp

```
Note 'T-test of 2-Independent Sample Means: Hanke351.inp'
# Hanke, p. 351, Exercise 49.
Name c1='team' c2='runs' c3='league'
# league 1 'American' 2 'National'
Read c1-c3;
Format (A15, F3.0, F3.0).
Boston          842  1
Milwaukee       862  1
Seattle         760  1
Detroit         896  1
toronto         845  1
Texas           823  1
Cleveland       742  1
Kansas          715  1
New York        788  1
Minnesota       786  1
Oakland         806  1
Baltimore       729  1
Chicago         748  1
California      770  1
New York        823  2
Cincinnati      783  2
Montreal        741  2
Pittsburgh      723  2
Chicago         720  2
St. Louis       798  2
San Diego       668  2
San Francisco   783  2
Atlanta         747  2
Philadelphia    702  2
Houston         648  2
Los Angeles     635  2
End
Twot 95 percent in c2 by c3
Twot 95 percent in c2 by league in c3;
    Alternative=-1.
Twot 95 in c2 by c3;
    Alternative=+1.
Twot 95 in c2 by c3;
    Pooled;
    Alternative=-1.
Twot 95 in c2 by c3;
    Pooled;
    Alternative=+1.
```

Exercise Example 5-13: Test for Two-Independent Samples

Commercial Bank and Trust Company wanted to know if younger persons (under age 25) used ATM (automatic teller machine) more often than older persons (over age 60). The bank analyst gathered the data on the number of uses and the age of the user. Run the file and find the answer. File Name: Mason415.inp

```
Note 'T-test of 2 Independent Sample Means: Mason415.inp'
```

```
# Mason, p. 415, Problem 31
# product 1='age 25' 2='age 60'
# use ='no. of uses' age ='age of the user'
Name c1='use' c2='age'
Read c1-c2
10   1
10   1
11   1
15   1
 7   1
11   1
10   1
 9   1
 4   2
 8   2
 7   2
 7   2
 4   2
 5   2
 1   2
 7   2
 4   2
10   2
 5   2
End
Twot 95 percent in c2 by c3
Twot 95 percent in c2 by league in c3;
    Alternative=-1.
Twot 95 in c2 by c3;
    Alternative=+1.
Twot 95 in c2 by c3;
    Pooled;
    Alternative=-1.
Twot 95 in c2 by c3;
    Pooled;
    Alternative=+1.
Anova 'use'='age'
```

Exercise Example 5-14: Test for Two-Independent Samples

The quality control manager of a firm wanted to know whether his firm's product lasts longer than his competitor's product. The data were gathered on the number of days until failure for both products: 12 units were tested for his product and 15 units for his competitor's product. Run the file and find the answer. The following 3 files show different methods of data entry. File Name: Siege391.inp

File 1: Siege391.inp

```
Note 't-Test for 2-Independent Sample Means: Siege391.inp'
# Siegel, p. 391, Problem 19
Name c1='life' c2='type'
# life ='life of product'
# type 1 = 'your product' 2 ='competitors'
Set c1
1.0   8.9   1.2  10.3  4.9  1.8  3.1  3.6
2.1   2.9   8.6   5.3
0.2   2.8   1.7   7.2  2.2  2.5  2.6  2.0
0.5   2.3   1.9   1.2  6.6  0.5  1.2
End
Set c2
12(1) 15(2)
End
# 12(1) means First 12 obs = 1, 15(2) means next 15 obs = 2
# Try 2 methods of one-way analysis of variance
Twot in c1 by c2
Oneway 'life' by 'type'
```

```
Anova  'life'='type'
```

File 2: Sieg391B.inp

```
Note 't-Test for 2 Independent Sample Means: Sieg391B.inp'
# Siegel, p. 391, Problem 19
Name c1='yours' c2='others'
# yours  = life of your product
# others = life of competitor' product
Set c1
1.0    8.9  1.2  10.3  4.9  1.8  3.1
3.6    2.1  2.9   8.6  5.3
End
Set c2
0.2  2.8    1.7   7.2  2.2  2.5  2.6
2.0  0.5    2.3   1.9  1.2  6.6  0.5  1.2
End
Twosample in c1 and c2
Aovoneway for c3 and c4
```

File 3: Sieg391C.inp

```
Title 'T-test of 2-Independent Sample Means: Sieg391C.inp'.
# Siegel, p. 391, Problem 19
Name c1='life' c2='type'
# life ='life of product'. Type 1 ='your product' 2 ='competitors'
Read c1-c2
    1.0    1
    8.9    1
    1.2    1
   10.3    1
    4.9    1
    1.8    1
    3.1    1
    3.6    1
    2.1    1
    2.9    1
    8.6    1
    5.3    1
    0.2    2
    2.8    2
    1.7    2
    7.2    2
    2.2    2
    2.5    2
    2.6    2
    2.0    2
    0.5    2
    2.3    2
    1.9    2
    1.2    2
    6.6    2
    0.5    2
    1.2    2
End
Twot 95 percent in c2 by league in c3;
    Alternative=-1.
Twot 95 in c2 by c3;
    Alternative=+1.
Twot 95 in c2 by c3;
    Pooled;
    Alternative=-1.
Twot 95 in c2 by c3;
    Pooled;
    Alternative=+1.
Twot in c1 by c2
Oneway 'life' by 'type'
Anova  'life'='type'
```

Chapter 6. Tests for 3 or More Samples

ANOVA, MANOVA, ANCOVA

Analysis of variance (ANOVA) is a test to find if 3 or more population means are the same using 3 or more samples or it is a test to find if 3 or more samples are taken from the same population. ANOVA can be divided into the following types:

(1) One-way analysis of variance: One dependent variable and one independent variable (factor)
(2) Two-way analysis of variance: One dependent variable and two independent variables
     1. Two-way ANOVA without replication
     2. Two-way ANOVA with replication
(3) N-way analysis of variance: One-dependent variable and N-independent variables
(4) Multivariate analysis of variance (MANOVA): Two or more dependent variables and one or more independent variables are tested simultaneously.
(5) ANCOVA (analysis of covariance): Independent variables include quantitative variables called covariates as well as the nominal variables. It is a combination of regression analysis and ANOVA.

Assume that there are 3 samples, and there is one-independent variable (factor). The null and alternative hypotheses are:

H_0: $\mu_1 = \mu_2 = \mu_3$ (All population means are equal)

H_A: Not all population means are equal, or
H_A: At least one population mean is not equal to the other population means

where μ_1, μ_2, and μ_3 are the population means.

The formulas for one-way ANOVA may be briefly explained using the following data set:

Samples (k) Observ. (n)	Treatments (k levels of a factor) 1 2 3 .. k					
B 1	X_{11}	X_{12}	X_{13}	.. X_{1k}	ΣX_{1j}	
l 2	X_{21}	X_{22}	X_{23}	.. X_{2k}	ΣX_{2j}	
o 3	X_{31}	X_{32}	X_{33}	.. X_{3k}	ΣX_{3j}	
c .						
k .						
s n	X_{n1}	X_{n2}	X_{n3}	.. X_{nk}	ΣX_{nk}	
Sum	ΣX_{i1}	ΣX_{i2}	ΣX_{i3}	.. ΣX_{ik}	$\Sigma\Sigma X_{ij}$ =	Grand Sum
Mean	$\overline{X}_1$	$\overline{X}_2$	$\overline{X}_3$	.. $\overline{X}_k$	X	Grand Mean

```
Total       =   Variation            +        Variation
Variation       between columns               between rows
                (between samples)             (within samples)
TSS         =   SSC                  +        SSR
(Total Sum      (Sum of Squares               (Sum of Squares
 of Squares)     between Columns)              between Rows)
```

$$\sum_{i}^{n}\sum_{j}^{k}(X_{ij} - X)^2 = \sum_{j}^{k} n\,(X_i - X)^2 + \sum_{j}^{k}\sum_{i}^{n}(X_{ij} - \overline{X}_j)^2$$

The test statistic F-ratio is computed by

$$F = \frac{\text{Population variance estimated using the variance among samples}}{\text{Population variance estimated using the variance within samples}}$$

The underlying idea is that if the samples have come form the same population, the population variances estimated by the two methods should be the same. (1) The first method is to estimate the population variance using the variance among the samples (numerator variance). (2) The second method is to estimate the population variance using each sample variance. If the samples came from different populations with different means, the variability among the sample means should be far greater than the variability within the samples.

Population variance estimated using the sample columns (between-column estimate)

$$V_k = \sigma^2 = \sum_{j}^{k} n\,(\overline{X} - \overline{\overline{X}})^2 / (k - 1)$$

Population variance estimated using each sample (within-column estimate)

$$V_w = \sigma^2 = \sum_{j}^{k} \sum_{i}^{n} (X_{ij} - \overline{X}_j) / (N - k)$$

F-ratio $= V_k / V_w$

where k = the number of samples (columns), n_j = each sample size, N = total number of observations (total sample size $N = \Sigma n_j$). Calculations can be summarized in the following ANOVA table:

Source of variation	Sum of square SS	Degrees of freedom DF	Mean square MS	F-Ratio Pr > F
Model	SSM= $\Sigma\ n(\overline{X} - \overline{\overline{X}})^2$	k-1	SSM/(k-1)	$\dfrac{\text{SSM/(k-1)}}{\text{SSE/(N-k)}}$
Error	SSE= $\Sigma\ \Sigma\ (X - \overline{X})^2$	N-k	SSE/(N-k)	
Total	TSS= $\Sigma\ \Sigma\ (X_{ij} - \overline{\overline{X}})^2$	N-1		

Note: Model (between samples, treatments), Error (within samples)

The decision rule is:

Accept H_0 if computed F $\le$ critical F at DF_1, DF_2, α.
Accept H_A if computed F $>$ critical F at DF_1, DF_2, α.

$DF_1 = k - 1$ and $DF_2 = N - k$

where k = the number of columns, and N = the total number of observations. The above degrees of freedom DF is for the one-way analysis of variance.

Since Minitab provides the significance probabilities for computed F-values, there is no need to look into the F-table to find the critical F-values. If the significance probability is greater than 0.05 for the 5% level, then reject the null hypothesis that all population means are equal.

In MANOVA, 2 or more dependent variables are tested simultaneously:

$$H_0: \quad \begin{bmatrix} \mu_{11} \\ \mu_{21} \end{bmatrix} = \begin{bmatrix} \mu_{12} \\ \mu_{22} \end{bmatrix} = \begin{bmatrix} \mu_{13} \\ \mu_{23} \end{bmatrix}$$

$H_A:$ Not all μ_{ij} are equal

In ANOVA, each dependent variable is tested separately. However, when the dependent variables are correlated to each other, ANOVA can lead to a wrong conclusion, and MANOVA can be used to test the equality of the dependent variables in the system of simultaneous equations.

Exercise Example 6-1: One-Way Analysis of Variance

To test the effectiveness of 3 training programs, 14 employees were divided into 3 groups and each group was assigned to one of the 3 programs. After completion, tests were given. The test scores are given below for each group. The program manager wanted to know if the 3 programs were equally effective.

Person		Program 1	Program 2	program 3
	1	85	80	82
	2	72	84	80
	3	83	81	85
	4	80	78	90
	5	*	82	88

Since there are 3 samples, ANOVA is appropriate for the test of the hypothesis. Run the file and find the answer. File Name: Webst526.inp

```
Note 'One-Way Analysis of Variance! Webst526.inp'
# Webster, p. 526, Table 11-1
Name c1='score' c2='program'
# score 'test score'
# program 'training programs 1, 2, 3'
Read c1 c2
85   1
72   1
83   1
80   1
80   2
84   2
81   2
78   2
82   2
82   3
80   3
85   3
90   3
88   3
End
Oneway in 'score' by 'program'
```

Edited Partial Output:

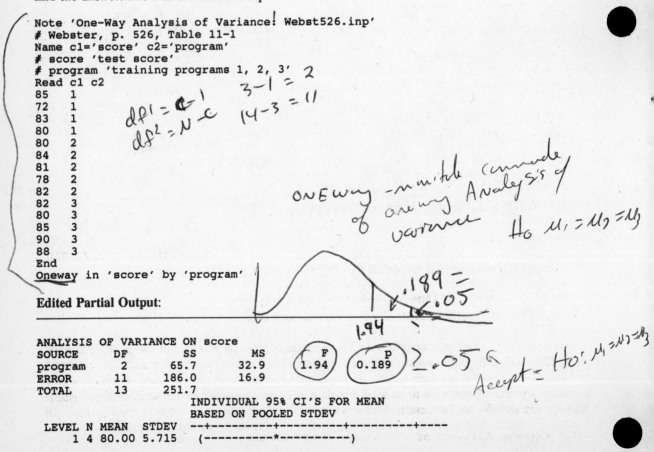

```
ANALYSIS OF VARIANCE ON score
SOURCE     DF      SS       MS        F        p
program     2     65.7     32.9      1.94    0.189
ERROR      11    186.0     16.9
TOTAL      13    251.7
                  INDIVIDUAL 95% CI'S FOR MEAN
                  BASED ON POOLED STDEV
LEVEL N MEAN   STDEV   --+---------+---------+---------+----
      1 4 80.00 5.715    (----------*----------)
```

```
    2 5 81.00 2.236      (----------*-----------)
    3 5 85.00 4.123                  (----------*-----------)
                        --+---------+---------+---------+----
POOLED STDEV = 4.112   76.0       80.0      84.0      88.0
```

Degrees of Freedom for One-Way Analysis of Variance:

In the above output, the computed F value is 1.9432 and significance probability is 0.1894 which is greater than 0.05. So accept the null hypothesis at the 5 % level. Alternatively, at $\alpha = 0.05$, the critical F value is 3.98 in the table of F distribution where the degrees of freedom are:

$$DF_1 = (c-1) = 3-1 = 2, \text{ and } DF_2 = (N-c) = 14-3 = 11.$$

Since $1.94 < 3.98$, we would accept the null hypothesis. That is, the test scores are statistically equal, or the three training programs are not statistically different.

Exercise Example 6-2: One-Way Analysis of Variance
- Tukey, Fisher, Dunnet, MCB Tests for Balanced Design

In Exercise Example 6-1, the main interest was whether the sample means were equal or not. It was not questioned which samples means were different. Minitab has 4 tests: Tukey, Fisher's LSD (Least-Significant-Difference), Dunnet, and Hsu's MCB (Multiple Comparison with Best). Run the file and find which samples are different. File Name: Webst534.inp

```
Note Oneway Anova: Webst534.inp
Name c1='deposits' c2='branch'
# Which two samples are different? Balanced sample sizes
# deposits in $ 100.
# branches 1, 2, 3, 4
# there are 28 customers in total for the 4 bank branches
Set c1
1.3  1.5  0.9  1.0  1.9  1.5  2.1
1.9  1.9  2.1  2.4  2.1  3.1  2.5
3.6  4.2  4.5  4.8  3.9  4.1  5.3
5.1  4.9  5.6  4.8  3.8  5.1  4.8
End
Set c2
7(1)  7(2)  7(3)  7(4)
End
Oneway in c1 levels in c2 put residuals in c3 and fits in c4;
Tukey;
Fisher;
Dunnet  family error rate = 0.05 control level = 1;
MCB family error rate = 0.05 best  = 1.
```

In the above file, 7(1) 7(2) 7(3) 7(4) are code expressions: the first 7 numbers are 1's, the next 7 numbers are 2's, the third 7 numbers are 3's , and the last 7 numbers are 4's.

Exercise Example 6-3: One-Way Analysis of Variance
- Tukey, Fisher, Dunnet, and MCB Tests for Unbalanced Design

Yosemite National Park hired an economist to study financial position of the park. The park receives park revenues from 3 sources: camping fees, fishing licenses, and canoe rentals. He gathered the data on revenues from each source during a weekend: there were 6 camping, 4 fishing, and 5 canoeing activities. He wanted to know if the mean revenues are different in the above 3 activities. Run the file and discuss the results. Webst541.inp

```
Note 'One-Way Analysis of  Variance: Webst541.inp
```

```
# Example 11.4 - ANOVA  for Unbalanced Design (Sample Sizes)
Name c1='revenues' c2 = 'sources'
#  c2 1=camping' 2='fishing' 3='canoeing'
Set c1
47  32  35  25  38  35
30  18  27  35
19  25  20  22  25
End
Set c2
6(1)  4(2)  5(3)
End
Oneway in c1 levels in c2 put residuals in c3 and fits in c4;
Tukey;
Fisher;
Dunnet  family error rate = 0.05 control level = 1
MCB family error rate = 0.05 best  = 1
```

Exercise Example 6-4: Two-Way Analysis of Variance (without Replication)

An accounting firm is considering to select a computer system from 3 models. The system manager selected 5 computer operators with different levels of experiences. The 5 operators produced the following levels of output.

		Computer system 1 day 1	Computer system 2 day 1	Computer system 3 day 1
Experience	1	27	21	25
level	2	31	33	35
	3	42	39	39
	4	38	41	37
	5	45	46	45

Note that in the above table both experience and computer systems are independent variables. So, this is the case of two-way analysis of variance. A two-way analysis of variance model may be expressed in the following equation:

$$Y_{ij} = \mu + A_i + B_j + e$$

With the interactive effect,

$$Y_{ij} = \mu + A_i + B_j + A_i{*}B_j + e$$

where Y = total effect, μ = grand mean, A = the effect of independent variable A; B = the effect of independent variable B, A*B = interactive effect, e = the error term. For the above two-way analysis of variance problem, we have the following 3 sets of hypotheses to test:

For the overall model:

H_0: $\mu_1 = \mu_2 = \mu_3$
H_A: Not all population means are equal.

For variable A (experience levels):

H_0:   A = 0 A's effect is zero.
H_A: A $\neq$ 0 A's effect is not zero.

For variable B (computer systems):

H_0:   B = 0 B's effect is zero.

H_A: $B \neq 0$ B's effect is not zero.

Run the file and find if experience and computer system are significant factors for output determination. File Name: Webst543.inp

```
Note 'Two-Way ANOVA without replication: Webst543.inp'
# Webster, p. 543, Table 11-3
Name c1='output' c2='system' c3='experi'
# output 'level of  output'
# experi 'experience level'
# system 'computer model'
# computer systems 1, 2, 3
# experience levels 1, 2, 3, 4, 5
Read c1-c3
27   1  1
31   1  2
42   1  3
38   1  4
45   1  5
21   2  1
33   2  2
39   2  3
41   2  4
46   2  5
25   3  1
35   3  2
39   3  3
37   3  4
45   3  5
End
Anova c1 = c3 c2
Anova c1 = c3 c2;
 Means c2 c3;
 Fits c5;
 Residuals c6.
```

Edited Partial Output:

Analysis of Variance for output

Source	DF	SS	MS	F	P
experi	4	764.93	191.23	37.25	0.000
system	2	0.93	0.47	0.09	0.914
Error	8	41.07	5.13		
Total	14	806.93			

For the column variable A (computer systems):

$$DF_1 = (c\text{-}1) = (3\text{-}1) = 2$$
$$DF_2 = (r\text{-}1)(c\text{-}1) = (5\text{-}1)(3\text{-}1) = 8$$

For the row variable B (experience levels):

$$DF_1 = (r\text{-}1) = (5\text{-}1) = 4$$
$$DF_2 = (r\text{-}1)(c\text{-}1) = (5\text{-}1)(3\text{-}1) = 8$$

The computed F value is 0.09 for the computer system. The critical F value is 4.46 at $DF_1 = 2$, $DF_2 = 8$, and $\alpha = 0.05$. For the experience level, the computed F value is 37.25. The critical F value is 3.84 at $DF_1 = 4$, $DF_2 = 8$, and $\alpha = 0.05$. In conclusion, the experience level has made the differences in the output, but the computer system has not.

Exercise Example 6-5: Two-Way Analysis of Variance with Replication
- ANOVA with Interactive Effects

To show an example of a two-way ANOVA with replication and interactive effects, the above data are represented below with additional observations for a second group. In each cell, there are two numbers. For instance, there are two observations, 27 and 28 in the first cell: the first number 27 is the output level on day 1 for person p11 with experience level 1 and computer system 1. The second number 28 is the output level on day 2 for person p12 with experience level 1, and the computer system 1. Note that the output levels do not represent the same person's output levels. The same person is not allowed to perform twice in the analysis of variance with replications. When there are two or more observations in one cell, it is the case of ANOVA with replication:

		Computer system 1 group		Computer system 2 group		Computer system 3 group	
		1	2	1	2	1	2
Experience	1	27	28	21	22	25	26
level	2	31	32	33	34	35	36
	3	42	43	39	40	39	40
	4	38	39	41	42	37	38
	5	45	46	46	47	45	46

The ANOVA equation with the interactive effect is given below:

$$Y_{ij} = \mu + A_i + B_j + A_i*B_j + e$$

where Y = total effect, μ = grand mean, A = the effect of independent variable A; B = the effect of independent variable B; e = the error term. In the above equation, there are two independent variables, A and B. The multiplicative portion A*B is an interactive effect of A and B, and the sum A+B is the additive effect of A and B.

The hypothesis statements are the same as in the previous example, except that the interactive effect is added.

For the Interactive Effect:

H_0: A*B = 0
H_A: A*B ≠ 0

Run the file and find if the interactive effect is significant. File Name: Webs543B.inp

```
Note Two-way ANOVA with replication: Webs543B.inp
Name c1='output' c2='system' c3='experi'
# output 'level of  output'
# experi 'experience level'
# system 'computer model'
Read c1-c3
27   1   1
31   1   2
42   1   3
38   1   4
45   1   5
21   2   1
33   2   2
39   2   3
41   2   4
46   2   5
25   3   1
35   3   2
39   3   3
```

```
37   3   4
45   3   5
28   1   1
32   1   2
43   1   3
39   1   4
46   1   5
22   2   1
34   2   2
40   2   3
42   2   4
47   2   5
26   3   1
36   3   2
40   3   3
38   3   4
46   3   5
End
Anova   c1 = c3 c2
Anova   c1 = c3|c2;
   Means c2|c3;
   Fits c5;
   Residuals c6.
```

In the above file, two ANOVA are requested. The first without interactive effects (replication), and the second with replication. The bold faced data are the second observations in each cell. In the second ANOVA statement, the symbol '|' is used to include the interactive effect. c1=c3|c2 is equivalent to c1=c3 c2 c3*c2.

Edited Output:

Source of Variation	Sum of Squares	DF	Mean Square	Signif F	of F
Main Effects	1531.733	6	255.289	510.578	.000
EXPERI	1529.867	4	382.467	764.933	.000
SYSTEM	1.867	2	.933	1.867	.189
2-way Interactions	82.133	8	10.267	20.533	.000
EXPERI SYSTEM	82.133	8	10.267	20.533	.000
Explained	1613.867	14	115.276	230.552	.000
Residual	7.500	15	.500		
Total	1621.367	29	55.909		
Grand Mean =	36.767				

Variable + Category	N	Unadjusted Dev'n	Eta	Adjusted for Independents Dev'n	Beta
EXPERI					
1	6	-11.93		-11.93	
2	6	-3.27		-3.27	
3	6	3.73		3.73	
4	6	2.40		2.40	
5	6	9.07		9.07	
			.97		.97

Grand Mean =   36.767

Variable + Category	N	Unadjusted Dev'n	Eta	Adjusted for Independents Dev'n	Beta
SYSTEM					
1	10	.33		.33	
2	10	-.27		-.27	
3	10	-.07		-.07	
			.03		.03

Multiple R Squared	.945
Multiple R	.972

Exercise Example 6-6: Analysis of Variance

A New York marketing research firm was hired to find consumer preferences for New Coke, Coke Classic, and Pepsi. The firm gathered the data on the number of cans sold in 9 buildings in the city. Run the file and find the answer. File Name: ACZEL408.inp

```
Note 'One-Way and Two-Way ANOVA: ACZEL408.inp'
* Aczel p. 408, Case 9
Name c1='building' c2='cans' c3='brand'
# building 'location'
# cans 'no. of cans sold'
# brand 'brand name'
# brand 1 'newcoke' 2 'clacoke' 3 'pepsi'
Read c1-c3
1    3   1
2    1   1
3   23   1
4   11   1
5    8   1
6   31   1
7   28   1
8    3   1
9    4   1
1    8   2
2    9   2
3   27   2
4   27   2
5   29   2
6   44   2
7   16   2
8    8   2
9    7   2
1    9   3
2    6   3
3   18   3
4   20   3
5   10   3
6   26   3
7   21   3
8    0   3
9    9   3
End
# (1) One-way Anova
ANOVA c2= c3
# (2) ANOVA without interaction
ANOVA   c2 =c1 c3
# (3) ANOVA with interaction
ANOVA   c2 = c1|c2;
    Means c1| c2;
    Fits  c4;
    Residuals  c5.
Print c1-c5
# (4) GLM command
GLM     c2 = c1 c3
# (5) Twoway ANOVA
Twoway c2 by c3 c1
```

Exercise Example 6-7: Analysis of Variance

Best Food grocery chain has 3 stores, and uses 2 advertising campaigns. The marketing analyst wanted to know if the advertising effects were the same. Run the file and find the answer. Hanke411.inp

```
Note 'One-Way and Two-Way Anova: Hanke411.inp'
# Hanke, p. 411, Example 12.7 - sales of 3 stores
```

```
Name c1='store' c2='adtype'  c3='sales'
# adtype 1='advertising method A'
#     2='advertising method B'
# store   1='store 1' 2='store 2' 3='store 3'
Read c1-c3
1  1    12.05
1  1    23.94
1  1    14.63
1  2    25.78
1  2    17.52
1  2    18.45
2  1    15.17
2  1    18.52
2  1    19.57
2  2    21.40
2  2    13.59
2  2    20.57
3  1     9.48
3  1     6.92
3  1    10.47
3  2     7.63
3  2    11.90
3  2     5.92
End
# (1) Oneway
Oneway in c3 by c2
# (2) 2-Way ANOVA with interaction
ANOVA   c3 = c1|c2;
    Means c1| c2;
    Fits  c4;
    Residuals  c5.
Print c1-c5
# (3) 2-Way ANOVA without interaction
ANOVA   c3 =c1 c2
# (4) GLM command
GLM    c3 = c1 c2
# (5) Twoway ANOVA
Twoway c3 by c1 and c2
# (6) Regress command
Regress c3 on 2 c1 c2.
```

Exercise Example 6-8: Analysis of Variance

Martin Motors wanted to know if the gas-mileage varies with the type of gasoline. Four types of gasoline and 3 cars of the same make and model were selected. Since the cars are of the same make and model, and only the gasoline types are different, this should be the case for one-way analysis of variance. If the car type is another factor, it should be the case for two-way analysis of variance. Run the file and find if the gasmileage is the same. File Name: Mason452.inp

```
Note 'One-Way and Two-Way Anova: Mason452.inp'
# Mason, p. 452, Exercise No. 27
Name c1='mileage' c2='gas' c3='car'
# gas 'types of gasoline 1, 2, 3, 4'
# car 'car 1, 2, 3'
Read c1-c3
22.4  1  1
20.8  1  2
21.5  1  3
17.0  2  1
19.4  2  2
20.7  2  3
19.2  3  1
20.2  3  2
21.2  3  3
20.3  4  1
18.6  4  2
```

```
20.4   4   3
End
# (1) Oneway
Oneway in c1 by c2
# (2) 2-Way ANOVA with interaction
ANOVA   c1 = c2|c3;
    Means c1| c2;
    Fits  c4;
    Residuals  c5.
Print c1-c5
# (3) 2-Way ANOVA without interaction
ANOVA   c1 =c2 c3
# (4) GLM command
GLM     c1 = c2 c3
# (5) Twoway ANOVA
Twoway c1 by c2 and c3
# (6) Regress command
Regress c1 on 2 c2 c3.
```

Exercise Example 6-9: Analysis of Variance

The quality assurance department of a firm wanted to evaluate the quality of products of 3 suppliers: Amalgamated, Bipolar, and Consolidated. Quality scores were assigned to each unit of 3 suppliers's products. They want to know if the mean quality scores are different for the 3 suppliers. Run the file and find the answer. File Name: Siege642.inp

```
Note 'One-Way ANOVA: Siege642.inp'
# Siegel, p. 642, Table 15.1.1-quality scores example
Name c1='quality1' c2='quality2' c3='quality3'
# quality1 = quality score of product 1
# quality2 = quality score of product 2
# quality3 = quality score of product 3
Set c1
75   72   87   77   84   82   84   81   78   97
85   81   95   81   72   89   84   73
End
Set c2
94   87   80   86   80   67   86   82   86   82   72
77   87   68   80   76   68   86   74   86   90
End
Set c3
90   86   92   75   79   94   95   85   86   92   92   85
87   86   92   85   93   89   83
End
# (1) Boxplots
Boxplot in c1
Boxplot in c2
Boxplot in c3
Describe c1-c3
# (2) Aovoneway
Aovoneway on c1-c3
# (3) One-Way
Stack c1 c2 c3 into c4;
    Subscripts c5.
Oneway in c4 by c5;
    Tukey;
    Fisher;
    Dunnett 1;
    MCB 1;
    MCB -1.
```

Exercise Example 6-10: Analysis of Variance

Kenton Food Company has 4 different package designs for new cereal. The market research analyst collected the data on sales units for 3 different stores. She wants to know if package designs and stores made differences in sales. Run the file and find the answer. File Name: Neter533.inp

```
Note 'Analysis of Variance: Neter533.inp'
# Neter, p.533, Table 14.1
Name c1='design' c2='case' c3='store'
# design 1 'design 1' 2 'design 2' 3 'design 3'
# store  1 'store  1' 2 'store 2'  3 'store 3'
# design ='type of designs'
# case   ='cereal cases sold'
# store   ='store number'
Read c1-c3
1  12   1
1  18   2
2  14   1
2  12   2
2  13   3
3  19   1
3  17   2
3  21   3
4  24   1
4  30   2
End
# When the sample sizes are unbalanced, use GLM instead of
# ANOVA procedure. GLM procedure works for both balanced and
# unbalanced data.
# (1) Two-Way ANOVA
Brief 3
GLM case = design store
GLM case = design|store;
    Means design|store.
# (2) Try One-Way ANOVA
AOVoneway 'case' by 'design'
AOVoneway 'case' by 'store'
# (3) Try Regression Method
Regress 'case' on 1 'design'
Regress 'case' on 1 'store'
Regress 'case' on 2 'design' 'store'
```

Exercise Example 6-11: ANOVA, MANOVA, ANCOVA

The editor of Air Travel magazine wanted to write a feature story on the quality of airlines. He asked 20 passengers to rate on a scale of 1 to 100 for each of 3 airlines: Pan Am, Delta, and Air France. The results are recorded as rating 1. A week later, the same passengers were asked to rate the airlines again. The results are recorded as rating 2. The editor wanted to know if the 2 ratings are the same for the 3 airlines. Run the file and find if the ratings are different. File Name: Emory550.inp

```
Note 'Title ANOVA, MANOVA, ANCOVA: Emory550.inp'
# MANOVA = Multivariate Analysis of Variance
# ANCOVA = Analysis of Covariance
# Emory, p.550, Table 15-3 (rating 3 is added).
Name c1='sample' c2='rating1' c3='rating2' c4='airline' &
    c5='class'  c6='rating3'
# sample    'sample person ID No.'
# rating1  'first rating of airlines'
# rating2  'second rating of airlines'
# rating3  'third rating of airlines'
# airline 1 'Pan Am' 2 'Delta' 3 'Air France'
# class   1 'economy class' 2 'business class'
Read c1-c6
 1  40  36  1  1  38
 2  28  28  1  1  28
 3  36  30  1  1  33
 4  32  28  1  1  30
 5  60  40  1  1  50
 6  12  14  1  1  13
```

```
 7   32   26   1   1   29
 8   36   30   1   1   33
 9   44   38   1   1   41
10   36   35   1   1   35.5
11   40   42   1   2   41
12   68   49   1   2   58.5
13   20   24   1   2   22
14   33   35   1   2   34
15   65   40   1   2   52.5
16   40   36   1   2   38
17   51   29   1   2   40
18   25   24   1   2   24.5
19   37   23   1   2   30
20   44   41   1   2   42.5
21   56   67   2   1   61.5
22   48   58   2   1   53
23   64   78   2   1   71
24   56   68   2   1   62
25   28   69   2   1   48.5
26   32   74   2   1   53
27   42   55   2   1   48.5
28   40   55   2   1   47.5
29   61   80   2   1   70.5
30   58   78   2   1   68
31   52   65   2   2   58.5
32   70   80   2   2   75
33   73   79   2   2   76
34   72   88   2   2   80
35   73   89   2   2   81
36   71   72   2   2   71.5
37   55   58   2   2   56.5
38   68   67   2   2   67.5
39   81   85   2   2   83
40   78   80   2   2   79
41   92   95   3   1   93.5
42   56   60   3   1   58
43   64   70   3   1   67
44   72   78   3   1   75
45   48   65   3   1   56.5
46   52   70   3   1   61
47   64   79   3   1   71.5
48   68   81   3   1   74.5
49   76   69   3   1   72.5
50   56   78   3   1   67.0
51   88   92   3   2   90
52   79   85   3   2   82
53   92   94   3   2   93
54   88   93   3   2   90.5
55   73   90   3   2   81.5
56   68   67   3   2   67.5
57   81   85   3   2   83
58   95   95   3   2   95
59   68   67   3   2   67.5
60   78   83   3   2   80.5
End
Note '(1) One-way ANOVA'.
Oneway 'rating1' by 'airline'
Note '(2) One-way ANOVA'.
Oneway 'rating1' by 'class'
Note '(3) Two-Way ANOVA for rating 1'.
Twoway 'rating1' by 'airline' 'class'
Note '(4) MANOVA for ratings 1 and 2'.
Note 'MANOVA applies to Minitab for Windows'
ANOVA  'rating1' 'rating2' = 'airline' 'class';
   Manova;
   Eigen;
   SSCP;
   Partial.
Note '(5) ANCOVA (ANOVA with Covariate)'
```

```
ANCOVA rating3 = airline|class;
   Covariates rating1 rating2;
   Means airline|class.
Note '(6) ANCOVA with GLM command'
GLM rating3 = airline class airline*class;
   Covariates rating1 rating2.
```

* Note: A covariate is a continuous variable used as an independent variable.

Exercise Example 6-12: ANOVA, MANOVA, and ANCOVA

An economist has collected the following data to examine if the wage rate varies with sex, race, education, and experience. (1) State the hypotheses. (2) Run the file. (3) Discuss the results.

		Race 0 Education			Race 1 Education		
		1	2	3	1	2	3
Experi	1	100	200	300	120	220	320
	2	110	220	310	140	230	340
	3	120	230	320	160	250	360
	4	130	240	340	180	280	390

```
Note 'ANOVA and ANCOVA'
Name c1='income' c2='experi' c3='educate' c4='race' c5='wealth'
# income = 'wages'
# experi = 'experience'
# educate= 'education level'
# race 0='black' 1='white'
# wealth = 'savings + property'
Read c1-c5
100 1 1 0   1200
110 2 1 0   1300
120 3 1 0   1400
130 4 1 0   1400
200 1 2 0   1800
220 2 2 0   2300
230 3 2 0   1700
240 4 2 0   2500
300 1 3 0   3200
310 2 3 0   3100
320 3 3 0   3500
340 4 3 0   3300
120 1 1 1   1500
140 2 1 1   1600
160 3 1 1   1800
180 4 1 1   1900
220 1 2 1   2100
230 2 2 1   2400
250 3 2 1   2000
280 4 2 1   2100
320 1 3 1   3200
340 2 3 1   3500
360 3 3 1   3700
390 4 3 1   4100
End
Note '(1) One-Way ANOVA'.
Oneway 'income' by 'race'
Note '(2) One-Way ANOVA'.
Oneway 'income' by 'race'
Note '(3) 3-Way ANOVA for income'.
ANOVA 'income'= 'race' 'educate' 'experi'
Note '(4) MANOVA for income and wealth'
Note '*** MANOVA Applies to Minitab for Windows ***'
ANOVA income wealth = educate experi race;
   Manova;
   Eigen;
```

```
     SSCP;
     Partial.
Note '(5) ANCOVA (ANOVA with Covariate)'
ANCOVA income = experi educate race;
     Covariates wealth;
     Means experi educate race.
Note '(6) ANCOVA with GLM command'
GLM income = educate experi race;
     Covariates wealth.
```

Exercise Example 6-13: ANOVA, MANOVA and ANCOVA

Australian mineral drink Koala Springs is sold in the 3 North American market regions in 2 flavors: lemon-lime and orange-mango. The importer wanted to know if the drink sales are the same in the 3 regions. The importer selected 20 stores in each region and gathered the data on 20 weekly sales. Run the file and find the answer. File Name: ACZEL779.inp

In the case of univariate analysis of variance, there is only one dependent variable. In MANOVA, there are two or more dependent variables. In this case, the dependent variables are the sales of the lemon-lime and orange-mango drink. The hypotheses statements are:

$$H_0: \quad \begin{bmatrix} \mu_{11} \\ \mu_{21} \end{bmatrix} = \begin{bmatrix} \mu_{12} \\ \mu_{22} \end{bmatrix} = \begin{bmatrix} \mu_{13} \\ \mu_{23} \end{bmatrix}$$

$H_A:$ Not all μ_{ij} are equal

where i = region, 1, 2, 3; j = drink type, 1, 2.

```
Note 'MANOVA and ANCOVA: ACZEL779.inp'.
# Aczel, p. 779, Example (b) - population data is added.
Name c1='region' c2='store' c3='lemon' c4='orange' c5='popula'
# region 'region of sales'
# store 'store type'
# lemon 'lemon drinks'
# orange 'orange drinks'
# popula 'population in 1000'.
# region 1 'north' 2 'west' 3 'south'
# store  1 'super' 2 'conve'
Read c1-c5
1   1   22   34   100
1   1   23   35   110
1   1   24   32   120
1   1   25   30   130
1   1   27   33   140
1   1   23   30   100
1   1   24   32   120
1   1   26   34   120
1   1   24   29   130
1   1   27   31   140
1   2   28   33   150
1   2   29   35   100
1   2   25   36   90
1   2   21   30   80
1   2   20   35   110
1   2   22   33   130
1   2   20   34   120
1   2   18   28   70
1   2   19   29   80
1   2   20   30   140
2   1   41   44   130
2   1   42   43   120
2   1   43   45   110
```

```
2   1   42  50  130
2   1   43  48  120
2   1   41  47  140
2   1   45  51   80
2   1   46  53   90
2   1   47  49  110
2   1   48  50   70
2   2   50  53   80
2   2   42  40   90
2   2   41  46  120
2   2   42  47  130
2   2   39  42   90
2   2   41  43  120
2   2   40  42  130
2   2   45  51  120
2   2   44  50  120
2   2   48  54  140
3   1   61  60  150
3   1   62  65   80
3   1   62  64   90
3   1   60  60   60
3   1   64  69  120
3   1   65  69  130
3   1   66  70  140
3   1   61  65  120
3   1   56  60   80
3   1   55  61  120
3   2   62  63  110
3   2   68  73   80
3   2   63  67   90
3   2   66  68   50
3   2   65  72   80
3   2   66  68  140
3   2   57  61  140
3   2   55  62  120
3   2   59  68  110
3   2   60  66  100
End
Note '*** MANOVA works for Minitab Versions 9.0 '
Note '(1) MANOVA for orange and lemon'
ANOVA 'orange' 'lemon' = 'region' 'store';
   Manova;
   Eigen;
   SSCP;
   Partial.
Note '(2) ANCOVA (ANOVA with Covariate)'
ANCOVA orange lemon = region|store;
   Covariates popula;
   Means region|store.
Note '(3) ANCOVA with GLM command'
GLM orange lemon = region|store;
   Covariates popula.
```

Exercise Example 6-14: ANOVA with Repeated Measures

Six judges were selected to rate 4 Chardonnay wines. They rated the wines on a scale of 0 to 40. The wine company wanted to know if the 4 ratings are all equal. The effects of judges are considered random and the effects of wines (treatment) are considered fixed. The winery wanted to know if the 4 ratings were the same. Run the file and find the answer. File Name: Nete1041.inp

```
Note 'ANOVA - Repeated Measures: Nete1041.inp'
# Neter, p. 1041, Table 28.3
Name c1='rating' c2='judge' c3='wine'
Set c1
20  24  28  28
15  18  23  24
```

```
18   19   24   23
26   26   30   30
22   24   28   26
19   21   27   25
End
# S: 6 Judges for 4 wines (total 24 numbers)
# (1:6)4
Set c2
1 1 1 1 2 2 2 2 3 3 3 3
4 4 4 4 5 5 5 5 6 6 6 6
End
# A: 4 wines for 6 judges (total 24 numbers)
# 6(1:4)
Set c3
1 2 3 4 1 2 3 4 1 2 3 4 1 2 3 4 1 2 3 4 1 2 3 4
End
ANOVA rating = judge
ANOVA rating = wine
ANOVA rating = judge wine;
   Random judge;
   EMS;
   Restricted;
   Fits c4;
   Residuals c5.
Nscores c5 c6
Plot c5*c6
Correlation c5 c6
Histogram c5
Dotplot c5
Dotplot c5;
   By 'wine'.
Dotplot c5;
   By 'judge'.
Histogram c6
Dotplot c6
Dotplot c6;
   By 'wine'.
Dotplot c6;
   By 'judge'.
```

Exercise Example 6-15: ANOVA with Repeated Measures

A clinician selected 12 persons to test the effects of 2 drugs A and B on the blood flow. He applied the following 4 types of treatments:

A1B1: Neither A nor B is used   A1B2: Only B is used
A2B1: Only A is used   A2B2: Both A and B are sued

He measured the blood flow after each treatment. A negative number indicates a decrease in blood flow. He wanted to know if the effects of the treatments were significant. Run the file and find the answer. File Name: Nete1054.inp

```
Note 'ANOVA - Repeated Measures: Nete1054.inp'
# Neter, p. 1054, Table 28.9
Name c1='blood' c2='subject' c3='A' c4='B'
# blood   = 'blood flow'
# subject = 'patients'
# A       = 'treatment: drug A and drug B'
# a negative number indicates a decrease in blood flow
Set c1
   2   10   9   25
  -1    8   6   21
   0   11   8   24
   3   15  11   31
   1    5   6   20
```

```
   2  12   9  27
  -2  10   8  22
   4  16  12  30
  -2   7   7  24
  -2  10  10  28
   2   8  10  25
  -1   8   6  23
End
# S: 12 Subjects: 4 treatments for each subject (total 48)
# (1:12)4
Set c2
 1  1  1  1  2  2  2  2  3  3  3  3  4  4  4  4  5  5  5  5
 6  6  6  6  7  7  7  7  8  8  8  8  9  9  9  9 10 10 10 10
11 11 11 11 12 12 12 12
End
# A drug: (A1 A1 and A2 A2) for 12 subjects (total 48)
# 12(1:2)2
Set c3
1 1 2 2 1 1 2 2 1 1 2 2 1 1 2 2 1 1 2 2 1 1 2 2
1 1 2 2 1 1 2 2 1 1 2 2 1 1 2 2 1 1 2 2 1 1 2 2
End
# B drug: (B1 B2 and B1 B2) for 12 subjects (total 48)
# 24(1:2)
Set c4
1 2 1 2 1 2 1 2 1 2 1 2 1 2 1 2 1 2 1 2 1 2 1 2
1 2 1 2 1 2 1 2 1 2 1 2 1 2 1 2 1 2 1 2 1 2 1 2
End
ANOVA blood = c2 c3 c4 c3*c4;
    Random c2;
    EMS;
    Restricted;
    Fits c5;
    Residuals c6.
Nscores c6 c7
Plot c6*c7
Correlation c6 c7
Histogram c6
Dotplot c6
Dotplot c6;
  By c2.
Dotplot c6;
  By c3.
Histogram c7
Dotplot c7;
  By c2.
Dotplot c7;
  By c3.
```

Exercise Example 6-16: ANOVA with Repeated Measures

A national retail shoe store selected 5 chain stores (subjects) to test 2 advertising campaigns (factor A). The sales data (dependent variable) were collected for three 2-week periods (factor B): 2-weeks before the advertising, 2-weeks during the advertising, and 2-weeks after the advertising. They wanted to know if the advertising effects were significant. Run the file and find the answer. File Name: Nete1063.inp

```
Note 'ANOVA - Repeated Measures: Nete1063.inp'
# Neter, p. 1063, Table 28.13
Name c1='sales' c2='market' c3='A' c4='B'
# sales   = 'shoe sales'
# Subject = '10 markets'
# A       = 'advertising A1 and A2'
# B       = 'time 1, 2, 3'
Set c1
 958  1047   933
```

```
1005   1122    986
 351    436    339
 549    632    512
 730    784    707
 780    897    718
 229    275    202
 883    964    817
 624    695    599
 375    436    351
End
# S: market 2(1:5)3 (total 30 numbers)
Set c2
1 1 1 2 2 2 3 3 3 4 4 4 5 5 5
1 1 1 2 2 2 3 3 3 4 4 4 5 5 5
End
# A: adverting (1:2)15 (total 30 numbers)
Set c3
1 1 1 1 1 1 1 1 1 1 1 1 1 1 1
2 2 2 2 2 2 2 2 2 2 2 2 2 2 2
End
# B: time periods 10(1:3) (total 30 numbers)
Set c4
1 2 3 1 2 3 1 2 3 1 2 3 1 2 3
1 2 3 1 2 3 1 2 3 1 2 3 1 2 3
End
ANOVA sales = A market(A) B A*B;
   Random market(A);
   EMS;
   Restricted;
   Fits c5;
   Residuals c6.
Nscore of c6 c7
Plot c6*c7
Correlation c6 c7
```

Chapter 7.
Simple Regression and Correlation Analyses

Regression and correlation analyses can be divided into two categories: (1) simple regression and correlation, and (2) multiple regression and correlation. Simple correlation analysis measures the degree (intensity) and direction of a linear relationship (association) between two variables, whereas simple regression analysis measures the pattern (direction and size or slope) of a linear relationship between two variables. Multiple correlation and regression analyses are discussed in chapter 8.

Simple Regression and Correlation

A simple linear regression equation takes the following form:

$$Y = a + bX + e$$

where a = intercept constant, b = regression slope coefficient, Y = dependent (explained) variable, X = independent (explanatory) variable, e = the error term. For the above simple regression equation, the parameters are estimated by the following formulas:

Regression coefficients:

Slope $b = \Sigma (X-\bar{X})(Y-\bar{Y}) / \Sigma(X-\bar{X})^2$

Intercept $a = \bar{Y} - b\bar{X}$

Coefficient of determination:

$$r^2 = \Sigma(\hat{Y} - \bar{Y})^2 / \Sigma(Y-\bar{Y})^2 = 1 - [\Sigma(Y-\hat{Y})^2 / \Sigma(Y-\bar{Y})^2]$$

where $\Sigma(Y-\hat{Y})^2$ = SSE (sum of squared errors), $\Sigma(Y-\bar{Y})^2$ = SST (total sum of squares).

Correlation coefficient:

$$r = \Sigma (X-\bar{X})(Y-\bar{Y}) / [\Sigma(X-\bar{X})^2\Sigma(Y-\bar{Y})^2]^{1/2}$$

Adjusted correlation coefficient $\bar{r}$ and Adjusted coefficient of determiantion $\bar{r}^2$:

$$\bar{r}^2 = 1 - (1 - r^2)(N-1)/(N-K)$$

Standard error of the estimate (SEE) and Root mean squared error (RMSE):

$$s_{y.x} = [\Sigma(Y-\hat{Y})^2 / (N-k)]^{1/2}$$

where N = the number of observations, k = number of constants to estimate, including the intercept (k = the number of total variables, including the independent and dependent variables. In the simple regression equation, k = 2).

Standard error of the forecast:

$$s_F = S_{y.x} [1 + 1/N + (X_i - \bar{X})^2/ \Sigma(X - \bar{X})^2]^{1/2} \quad /5$$

Confidence interval of the forecast:

$$\hat{Y} - z S_F \leq Y \leq \hat{Y} + z S_F \qquad /5$$

where z = 1.96 for the 95% confidence interval if the degrees of freedom DF = N-2 $\geq$ 30. If DF = N - 2 < 30, then t value is used. If DF = 29 and the confidence level is 95%, then t = 2.045.

Standardized regression coefficients (Beta coefficients):

$$Y^* = \beta_0 + \beta_1 X^*$$

where $Y^* = (Y-\bar{Y})/s_Y$ and $X^* = (X-\bar{X})/s_x$. Y^* and X^* are called standardized variables, and s_y and s_x are standard deviations of Y and X respectively. Since the variables are measured in standardized units, the standardized regression coefficients (beta coefficients) can be used for the purpose of comparing the size of regression coefficients.

Significance Tests

The significance of the regression and correlation coefficients are tested by the following t ratios: The standard errors of the regression coefficients

$$s_a = s_{y.x} [\Sigma X^2/(N\Sigma(X-\bar{X})^2]^{1/2}$$

$$s_b = s_{y.x} / [\Sigma(X-\bar{X})^2]^{1/2}$$

The t - ratios for the intercept and slope coefficients are given by the following.

For the intercept a:

$$t = a / s_a \quad DF = N-k, \text{ i.e., } DF = N-2 \text{ for the simple regression.}$$

For the slope b:

$$t = b / s_b \quad DF = N-k, \text{ i.e., } N-2$$

For the correlation coefficient r, the standard error of the correlation coefficient, t-ratio, and the F ratio are:

$$s(r) = [(1 - r^2) / (N - k)]^{1/2}$$

$$t = \frac{r}{(1 - r^2) / (N-k)]^{1/2}} \quad DF = N-k, \text{ i.e., } N-2$$

$$F = [\Sigma (\hat{Y} - \bar{Y})^2/ (k-1)] / [\Sigma(Y - \hat{Y})^2 / (N-2)]$$

$$F = t^2, DF_1 = k - 1 = 2 - 1 = 1, DF_2 = N - k = N-2$$

The hypothesis statements and the decision rules are:

$$H_0: \beta = 0 \quad \text{Accept } H_0 \quad \text{if } t < \text{critical t at given DF and } \alpha$$
$$H_A: \beta \neq 0 \quad \text{Accept } H_A \quad \text{if } t \geq \text{critical t}$$

$$H_0: \alpha = 0 \quad \text{Accept } H_0 \quad \text{if} \quad t < \text{critical } t$$
$$H_A: \alpha \neq 0 \quad \text{Accept } H_A \quad \text{if} \quad t \geq \text{critical } t$$

$$H_0: \rho = 0 \quad \text{Accept } H_0 \quad \text{if} \quad t < \text{critical } t$$
$$H_A: \rho \neq 0 \quad \text{Accept } H_A \quad \text{if} \quad t \geq \text{critical } t$$

General Assumptions of OLS Method

In estimating the simple and multiple regression coefficients, the OLS (ordinary least squares method) method is often used. The OLS method is based on the following assumptions:

1. The mean value of the error terms is zero: $E(e) = 0$
2. The error terms are independent (absence of serial correlation): $cov(e_i, e_j) = 0$
3. The variance of the error terms is constant (condition of homoscedasticity, i.e., absence of heteroscedasticity): $Var(e_i) = \sigma^2$
4. The error term and the independent variable are independent: $cov(e_i, X_i) = 0$
5. The independent variables are independent of each other (absence of multicollinearity): $Cov(X_i, X_j) = 0$
6. The dependent variable is not correlated to the error term (absence of simultaneous equation bias): $Cov(e_i, Y_i) = 0$
7. The model is correctly specified (All relevant variables are included in the model, and the functional relationship is correctly expressed.)
8. The independent variable is a fixed (deterministic) variable, but the dependent variable Y is a random (stochastic) variable.
9. The dependent and independent variables are measured without errors (absence of measurement errors)
10. The relationship between the dependent and independent variables is linear.

If the above assumptions do not hold, the parameters estimated by the OLS method are either inefficient, biased, or inconsistent. That is, the estimation results will be unreliable. These problems are discussed in chapter 9. The OLS estimators are said BLUE (best linear estimator), if the following conditions are met: (y = an estimator)

1. An estimator is unbiased if $E(\hat{y}) = y$
2. An estimator is efficient if it has a minimum variance as compared with any other estimate obtained using any other econometric methods. $Var(\hat{y}) < Var(\hat{y}) < Var(\ddot{y})$....
3. An estimator is a linear estimator if it is a linear function of the sample observations.

$$\bar{Y} = \Sigma Y/N = (1/N)(Y_1 + Y_2 + ...) = Y_1/N + Y_2/N + ...$$

Exercise Example 7-1: Simple Regression and Correlation

A computer hard disk manufacturer wanted to establish the relationship between the number of hard disk produced and total cost. The head financial analyst gathered the data on the number of hard disks produced and total cost during the recent 5 days. Two files are presented below: one for the DOS version and the other for the Windows version. Webs587A.inp and Webs587B.inp

Questions: Run the file and find the following:
(1) Scatter diagram
(2) Total cost function (regression equation)
(3) Total fixed cost (intercept constant)
(4) Marginal cost (regression slope coefficient)
(5) Average cost (y/x)

(6) R^2 and adjusted R^2
(7) F-ratio
(8) Is R significant?
(9) Standard error of the estimate (root mean saquared error)
(10) Standard error of the regression coefficient
(11) t-ratios of the regression coefficients
(12) Are the regression coefficients significant?
(13) Regression line (chart)

test [handwritten bracket by (9) and (10)]

14) Find Standard error of farcast. 15) confidence Interval of - farcast. [handwritten]

Minitab File for DOS: Webs587A.inp

```
Note 'Simple Regression for DOS Version: Webs587A.inp'
# Webster, p. 587, Table 12-1
Name c1='day' c2='drive' c3='cost'
# day   'day of observation'
# drive 'number of hard disk drives'
# cost  'cost of production'
Read c1-c3
1  50   450
2  40   380
3  65   540
4  55   500
5  45   420
End
Note '(1) Plots'
Plot c3*c2;
   Xincrement = 10;
   Xstart =30;
   Yincrement = 100;
   Ystart =300.
Gplot c3*c2;
   File 'b:Fig1'.
Note '(2) Correlation'
Correlation c2 c3
Note '(3) Simple Regression'
Brief 3
Regress c3 on 1 c2  Std.resid c4 Fits c5;
   Residuals in c6;
   DW.
Tsplot c6
Plot c6*c5
Note '(4) Drawing a Fitted Line'
Regress c3 on 1 c2 std.resid c7 fits c8;
   Residuals = c9;
   DW.
Gplot c3*c2;
   Line c5 c2;
   File 'b:Pic2'.
Note '(5) Residual Plots'
Plot c6*c5
Plot c9*c8
```

[handwritten left margin: All output]
[handwritten left margin: Not 1, 2, 3. all output]

Minitab File for Windows: Webst587.win

```
Note 'Simple Regression for Windows Version: Webs587B.inp'
# Webster, p. 587, Table 12-1
Name c1='day' c2='drive' c3='cost'
# day   'day of observation'
# drive 'number of hard disk drives'
# cost  'cost of production'
Read c1-c3
1  50   450
2  40   380
3  65   540
4  55   500
5  45   420
```

```
End
Note '(1) Plots'
Plot c3*c2;
   Xincrement = 10;
   Xstart =30;
   Yincrement = 100;
   Ystart =300.
Plot c3*c2;
   Gsave 'b:Fig1'.
Note '(2) Correlation'
Correlation c2 c3
Note '(3) Regression Format for DOS version 8.0'
Brief 3
Regress c3 on 1 c2 Std.resid c4 fits c5;
   Residuals in c6;
   DW.
Tsplot c6
Plot c6*c5
Note '(4) Regression format for Windows version 9.0'
Regress c3 on 1 c2;
   Sresiduals c7;
   Fits c8;
   Residuals = c9;
   DW.
Note
Plot c3*c2;
   Line c5 c2;
   Gsave 'b:Fig2'.
Note '(5) Drawing a Confidence Interval'
%Fitline c3*c2;
   Gsave 'b:Fig3'.
Note '(5) Residual Plots'
%Resplots c8 c9;
   Gsave 'b:Fig4'.
```

(1) The **G-commands** such as Gplot and Ghistogram are no longer used in the Windows version. Instead of using Gplot or Ghistogram commands, simply Plot and Histogram will produce high-resolution graphs in the Windows version.

(2) In saving a high-resolution graph, **File** command is used in the DOS version. However, **Gsave** command is used in the Windows version.

(3) In the Windows version 9.0, the Plot command requires an asterisk "*" between the variables names as in Plot c3*c2. In the DOS version, the following formats are all valid: Plot c3 vs c2, Plot c3-c2, Plot c3*c2, etc.

(4) In the Regression procedure for DOS, the **Std.resid** (standardized residual values) and **Fits** options (fitted values, predicted values) are specified all on one Regress command line. However, in the Windows version, they are now read as subcommands, and must be specified in separate lines. But, the DOS format is still accepted in the Windows version 9.0. Since some users may be still using Minitab for DOS version, the DOS format is used in the following sample files.

(5) In the Windows version, a macro command is indicated by prefix %.

   %Fitline is used to draw a regression fit line and the 95% confidence interval. Gsave 'filename' will save the high resolution graph in the specified file with the default extension MGF(Minitab graph). In the DOS version a high-resolution graph is saved with extension **PRN** for printer, and **COM1** for plotter.

   %Resplot is used to produce residual model diagnostics.

Edited Partial Output for DOS:

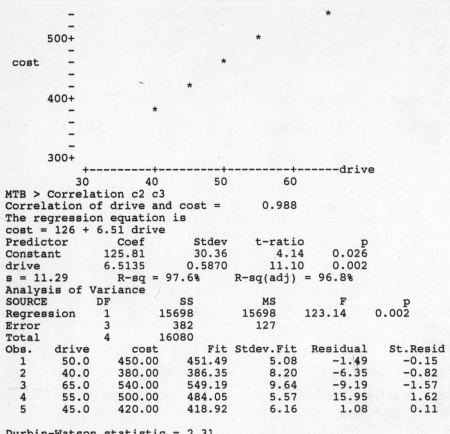

```
          -                                        *
          -
     500+                             *
          -
 cost     -                     *
          -
          -              ~    *
     400+
          -         *
          -
          -
          -
     300+
          +---------+---------+---------+------drive
           30        40        50        60
MTB > Correlation c2 c3
Correlation of drive and cost =      0.988
The regression equation is
cost = 126 + 6.51 drive
Predictor       Coef        Stdev      t-ratio          p
Constant      125.81        30.36         4.14      0.026
drive         6.5135        0.5870       11.10      0.002
s = 11.29        R-sq = 97.6%      R-sq(adj) = 96.8%
Analysis of Variance
SOURCE         DF           SS           MS          F         p
Regression      1         15698        15698     123.14     0.002
Error           3           382          127
Total           4         16080
Obs.    drive       cost       Fit  Stdev.Fit   Residual   St.Resid
  1      50.0     450.00     451.49      5.08      -1.49      -0.15
  2      40.0     380.00     386.35      8.20      -6.35      -0.82
  3      65.0     540.00     549.19      9.64      -9.19      -1.57
  4      55.0     500.00     484.05      5.57      15.95       1.62
  5      45.0     420.00     418.92      6.16       1.08       0.11

Durbin-Watson statistic = 2.31
```

1. Regression Summary

The important statistical results to study are the intercept, regression coefficient, correlation coefficient (R), coefficient of determination (R^2), adjsuted R^2, F-ratio, standard error of the estimate (SEE), and the DW statistic. The above statistics can be summarized in the following format:

$$y = 125.8108 + 6.5135\ x \quad R^2 = 0.9762 \quad \bar{R}^2 = 0.9683 \quad DW = 2.317$$
$$(4.14)^* \quad (11.10)^* \quad F = 123.14 \quad SEE = 11.2906$$

where y = total cost, x = number of hard disks produced. The numbers in the parentheses are the t-ratios. The asterisk * indicates that the regression coefficient is significant at the 5 % level.

2. Correlation Coefficient R, R^2, and $\bar{R}^2$

The correlation coefficient R and the coefficient of determination R^2 are both very high and statistically significant since the computed F-value 123.14 is greater than the critical F-value 12.71 in the F-table (the numerator degrees of freedom = 2-1 =1, and the denominator degrees of freedom = 5-2=3, α = 5% for the two-tail test, i.e., $\alpha/2$ = 0.025). Alternatively, there is no need to look into the F table since Minitab output shows the rejection probability for the F-value: signi F = 0.0016. Since the rejection probability is less than, say, the alpha level 0.05, we reject the null hypothesis of no significance. That is, the R^2 is significant at the 5% level. R^2 0.9762 indicates that

97.62% of total variation in the dependent variable (total cost) is explained by the independent variable (the number of hard disks produced). The adjusted R^2 is used to compare regression equations with different numbers of independent variables. It is discussed in detail in chapter 8.

3. Regression Coefficients

The intercept constant is 6.5135 and the slope coefficient is 6.5135. Are they significant? The corresponding t values are 4.144 and 11.097 respectively. They are significant at the 5 % level since the computed t-values are greater than the critical t-value 3.182 in the t-table (DF = 5-2=3, $\alpha/2$ = 0.025). Alternatively, without looking into the t-table, we see the rejection probabilities that are given below the heading Sig T. They are 0.0255 and 0.0016 respectively. Since the rejection probabilities are less than 0.05 (α = 0.05), we reject the null hypothesis of no significance. That is, the intercept and regression coefficient are both significant at the 5% level.

What is the meaning of the regression coefficient? The slope regression coefficient is a marginal effect of a change in the independent variable on the dependent variable (dy/dx). In the case of the hard disk production, the regression coefficient 6.51 indicates that if one more hard disk is produced the cost will rise by $6.51. In economics, it is the marginal cost of the hard disk. What does the intercept constant mean? It indicates that if no hard disk is produced (x=0), the total cost will be $ 125.81. Thus, it is equivalent to total fixed cost. If 100 hard disks are produced the total cost is y = 125.8108 + 6.5135 (100) = 777.16 ($). Can you find the average total cost ? Dividing the total cost equation by quantity (x), average cost y/x = 125.8108/x + 6.5135. As x increases, the average cost falls. If x = 100, total cost y = 125.8108/100 + 6.5135 = 7.77 ($).

4. Standard Error of Estimate (SEE)

Standard error of the estimate is 11.2906. SEE is an overall measure of the goodness of fit. The smaller the SEE, the better is the regression equation. It is also used to find the confidence interval of the forecast.

5. Durbin-Watson Statistic

Durbin-Watson statistic is used to test the significance of serial correlation of the error terms usually for the time series data. The computed DW statistic is 2.317. The critical upper limit of the Durbin-Watson statistic is 1.400 found in the table of the Durbin-Watson statistic (For N=5, DW statistic is not available. So N=6 is used. Critical values or significance probabilities for DW statistics are not provided by Minitab or any other statistical package). Since the computed DW statistic is greater than the critical value, we conclude that serial correlation of the error term is not significant. If the serial correlation is significant, it implies that regression results are not reliable in the sense that R^2 is overestimated and the standard errors of regression coefficients are underestimated. That is, R^2 and t ratio are overestimated and thus not reliable. If the serial correlation is not significant, it means that the results, i. e., R^2 and t ratios are reliable. The problems of serial correlation, heteroscedasticity, and multicollinearity are discussed in detail in chapter 9.

Regress Subcommands

```
Regress c1 on 2  c2  c3;
   Noconstant;              No intercept constant
   Weights      c4;
   Sresiduals   c5;         Standardized residuals (Std.resid)
   Tresiduals   c6;         Studentized residuals
   Residuals    c7;
   Fits         c8;         Fitted (predicted) values
```

```
Coefficients c9;          Regression coefficients
Hi          c10;          Leverage
CookD       c11;          Cook's distance
Dfits       c12;
XPXinv      M1;           Inverse matrix
Rmatrix     M2;
Predict for E1 E2;        E1, E2 ... values for predictors
MSE         k1;           Mean squared error
Tolerance   k2;
VIF;                      Variance inflation factor
DW;                       Durbin-Watson statistic
Pure;                     Pure error lack-of-fit test
XLof;                     Experimental lack-of-fit test
```

Exercise Example 7-2: Simple Regression and Correlation

The management of Hop Scotch Airlines wanted to know if there is a relationship between the number of passengers and the advertising expenditures. Monthly advertising expenditures and the number of passengers are collected for 15 most recent months. Run the file and find the answer. File Mame: Webst591.inp

```
Note 'Hop Scotch Airlines: Webst591.inp'
# Webster, p. 591, Table 12-2'
Name c1='month' c2='persons' c3='adver'
# month    'month of  observation'
# persons 'number of passengers'
# adver    'advertising'
Read c1 - c3
 1   15   10
 2   17   12
 3   13    8
 4   23   17
 5   16   10
 6   21   15
 7   14   10
 8   20   14
 9   24   19
10   17   10
11   16   11
12   18   13
13   23   16
14   15   10
15   16   12
End
Plot c2*c3
Correlation c2 c3
Regress c2 on 1 c3;
   DW.
Regress c2 on 1 c3;
   Sresiduals c4;
   Fits c5;
   Residuals c6;
   DW.
Tsplot c6
Plot c6*c5
# For Windows
%Resplot c5 c6
```

Exercise Example 7-3: Simple Regression and Correlation

A stock market analyst collected the data on the January stock price change (%) and yearly stock price change (%) using the Standard and Poor's 500 Index for 1950-87. He wanted to know if January stock price change can be used as a predictor of yearly stock price change. Run the file and find the answer. File Name: ACZEL460.inp

```
Note 'Simple Regression and Correlation: ACZEL460.inp'
# Aczel, p.460 Case 10: stock price changes
Name c1='year' c2='jchange' c3='ychange'
Note jchange 'January change'
Note ychange 'yearly change'
Read c1-c3
1950    1.7    21.8
1951    6.1    16.5
1952    1.6    11.8
1953   -0.7    -6.6
1954    5.1    45.0
1955    1.8    26.4
1956   -3.6     2.6
1957   -4.2   -14.3
1958    4.3    38.1
1959    0.4     8.5
1960   -7.1    -3.0
1961    6.3    23.1
1962   -3.8   -11.8
1963    4.9    18.6
1964    2.7    13.0
1965    3.3     9.1
1966    0.5   -13.1
1967    7.8    20.1
1968   -4.4     7.7
1969   -0.8   -11.4
1970   -7.6     0.1
1971    4.0    10.8
1972    1.8    15.6
1973   -1.7   -17.4
1974   -1.0   -29.7
1975   12.3    31.5
1976   11.8    19.1
1977   -5.1   -11.5
1978   -6.2     1.1
1979    4.0    12.3
1980    5.8    25.8
1981   -4.6    -9.7
1982   -1.8    14.8
1983    3.3    17.3
1984   -0.9     1.4
1985    7.4    26.0
1986    0.5    14.9
1987   13.2     2.0
End
Plot c2*c3
Correlation c2 c3
Regress c3 on 1 c2;
   Sresidual in c4;
   Fits c5;
   Residuals c6;
   DW.
Tsplot c6
Plot c6*c5
# For Windows
%Resplots c6 c5
```

Exercise Example 7-4: Simple Regression and Correlation

Ashenfleter wanted to predict the price of wine using average growing-season temperatures and rainfall. Run the file and find if the relationship is significant. File Name: Emory600.inp

```
Note 'Simple Regression and Correlation: Emory600.inp'.
# Emory, p. 600.
# No data on rain fall.
Name c1='year' c2='temp' c3='price'
# temp   'temperature'
```

```
# price   'price of wine per case'
Read c1-c3
  1   11.80   1813.00
  2   15.70   2558.00
  3   14.00   2628.00
  4   22.90   3217.00
  5   20.00   3228.00
  6   20.10   3629.00
  7   17.90   3886.00
  8   23.40   4897.00
  9   24.60   4933.00
 10   25.70   5199.00
End Data.
Note '(1) Plots'
Plot c3*c2
Note '(2) Correlation'
Correlation c2 c3
Note '(3) Simple Regression'
Brief 3
Regress c3 on 1 c2;
   Sresiduals c4;
   Fits c5;
   Residuals c6;
   CookD c7;
   DW.
Note '(4) Residual Plots'
Tsplot c6
Plot c6*c5
# For Windows
%Resplots c6 c5
```

Exercise Example 7-5: Simple Regression and Correlation

Donna Pico, director of research, wanted to defend her budget request. She gathered the data on annual profits and research and development expenditures for 8 pharmaceutical companies to investigate the relationship between the 2 variables. If her company profit is 60 (million dollars), how much would be the 'justifiable' research budget request? Run the file and find the answer. File Name: Hanke447.inp

```
Note 'Simple Regression: Hanke447.inp'
# Hanke, p. 447, Exercise 8 - profit and research
Name c1='company' c2='profit' c3='research'
# research = 'research expenditures in million dollars'
# profit   = 'annual profit in million dollars'
Read c1-c3
1    25    5
2    30    7
3    20    4
4    50   10
5    40    8
6    60   12
7    50    6
8    35   11
End
Plot 'research' * 'profit'
Correlation 'research' 'profit'
# Regress c3 on 1 c2;
    Sresiduals c4;
    Fits c5;
    Residuals c6;
    DW.
Tsplot c6
Plot c6*c5
# For Windows
%Resplots c6 c5
```

Exercise Example 7-6: Simple Regression and Correlation

A sociologist gathered the data on the birth rate and suicide rate for 10 countries from the UN Statistical Yearbook to investigate a possible causal relationship between the 2 variables. Run the file and find the answer. File Name: Mason489.inp

```
Note 'Simple Regression: Mason489.inp'
# Mason-Lind text (ch. 13, p. 489, Exercise No. 28)
#  birth = 'birth rate per 1000'
#  suicide= 'suicide rate per 1000'
Name  c1='country' c2='birth' c3='suicide'
Read c1-c3;
Format (A17, F4.0, 3X, F4.0).
Australia        15.7   11.1
Czechoslovakia   18.4   21.9
Finland          13.5   25.1
Germany          13.9   30.5
Italy            12.5    5.8
Mexico           35.3    2.1
Poland           19.0   12.1
Singapore        17.0   11.3
Spain            17.2    4.0
United States    15.3   12.7
End
Ploct c2 * c3
Plot 'birth' * 'suicide'
Correlation 'birth' 'suicide'
Brief 3
Regression 'suicide' on 1 'birth';
   Sresiduals c4;
   Fits c5;
   Residuals c6;
   DW.
Tsplot c6
Plot c6*c5
# For Windows
%Resplots c6 c5
```

Exercise Example 7-7: Simple Regression and Correlation

A TV producer wanted to know if the Nielson rating and People Meters rating give the similar rating of TV programs. She collected the ratings data for 10 most popular shows. Run the file and find the answer. File Name: Siege404.inp

```
Note 'Simple Regression: Siege404.inp'
# Siegel, p. 404, Example
Name c1='tvshow' c2='nielson' c3='people'
# nielson='Nielson rating'
# people='People rating'
Read c1-c3;
Format (A20, F5.0, F6.0).
Cosby show           27.4  24.4
Family ties          27.2  25.5
Cheers               24.1  25.5
Moonlighting         22.7  20.2
Night court          22.1  20.1
Growing pains        18.3  17.5
Who's the boss       17.5  16.1
Family ties special  17.5  18.3
Murder she wrote     16.8  14.7
60 Minutes           16.5  13.6
End
Plot 'nielson' * 'people'
Correlation 'nielson' 'people'
Regression 'nielson' on 1 'people';
```

```
      Sresiduals c4;
   Fits c5;
   Residuals c6;
   DW.
Tsplot c6
Plot c6*c5.
# For Windows
%Resplots c6 c5
```

Exercise Example 7-8: Simple Regression and Correlation

Westwood Company wanted to establish the relationship between the units of production and the man-hours required. They gathered the data on the units of production and the man-hours used during the past 10 production days. Run the file and find the answer. File Name: Neter044.inp

```
Note 'Simple Regression: Neter044.inp'
# Neter, p. 44, Table 2-2: Westwood Company
Name c1='manhour' c2='output'
# output='units of production'
Read c1-c2
 73   30
 50   20
128   60
170   80
 87   40
108   50
135   60
 69   30
148   70
132   60
End
# '(1) Simple Plot'.
Plot  'output' * 'manhour'
# '(2) Correlation Analysis'
Correlation 'manhour' 'output'
# '(3) Regression Analysis'
Brief 3
Regress 'output' on 'manhour';
    Sresiduals c3;
   Fits c4;
   Residuals in c5;
   DW.
Tsplot c5
Plot c5*c4
For Windows
%Resplots c5 c4
```

Exercise Example 7-9: Simple Regression and Correlation

A transit authority distributed transit maps in 8 cities, and examined the number of ridership. The economist at the transit authority wanted to know if map distribution increased ridership. Run the file, study scatter and residual plots, and discuss the results. File Name: Neter119.inp

```
Note 'Simple Regression: Neter119.inp'
# Neter, p. 119, Table 4-1: Transit Example
Name c1='map' c2='rider'
# map   'maps distributed(1000)'
# rider 'increase in ridership(1000)'
Read c1-c2
 0.60    80
 6.70   220
 5.30   140
 4.00   120
 6.55   180
 2.15   100
```

```
  6.60   200
  5.75   160
End
# '(1) Simple Plot'.
Plot  'rider'*'map'
GPlot  'rider'*'map'
# '(2) Correlation Analysis'
Correlation 'map' 'rider'
# '(3) Regression Analysis'
Brief 3
Regress 'rider' on 1 'map';
  DW;
  Residuals c3.
Set c4
1:8
End
Plot c3*c4
Gplot c3*c4
# (4) Regression in Log
Let  c5=Loge(c2)
Let  c6=Loge(c1)
Regress c5 on 1 c1;
    DW.
Name c5='logride'
Plot c5*c1
Gplot c5*c1
# (5) Regression in quadratic form
Let c7=c1*c1
Name c7='map2'
Regress c2 on 2 c1 c7;
  Sresiduals c8;
  Fits c9;
  Residuals c10;
  DW.
Tsplot c10
Plot c10*c9
For Windows
%Resplots c10 c9
```

Exercise Example 7-10: Simple Regression and Correlation

The Charles Plumbing Supplies Company wanted to know the relationship between the work units performed and total variable cost. Run the file and find the answer. File Name: Neter169.inp

```
Note 'Simple Regression: Neter169.inp'
# Neter, p. 169, Table 5-2: Warehouse Example
Name c1='work' c2='cost'
# work   'work units performed'
# cost   'variable labor cost'
Read c1-c2
  20   114
 196   921
 115   560
 122   575
 100   475
  33   138
 154   727
  80   375
 147   670
 182   828
 160   762
End
# '(1) Simple Plot'
Plot 'cost'*'work'
# '(2) Correlation Analysis'
Correlation 'cost' 'work'
# '(3) Regression Analysis'
```

```
Brief 3
Regress 'cost' on 1 'work';
   Sresiduals c3;
   Fits c4;
   Residuals c5.
Plot c4*'work'
Plot c5*'work'
Regress 'cost' on 1 'work';
   Sresiduals c6;
   Fits c7;
   Noconstant;
   Residuals in c8.
# (4) Plots
Tsplot c5.
Plot c8*c7
# For Windows
%Resplots c7 c8
```

Exercise Example 7-11: Simple Regression and Correlation

Economists Wilson and Keating wanted to forecast housing starts. They gathered the quarterly data for private new housing starts and the mortgage rate for 1980-1990. Run the file and find the regression equation. Make forecast for each quarter when interest rate is 9.32%. File Name: Wils -235.inp

```
Note 'Simple Regression and Correlation: Wils-235.inp'
# Wilson, pp. 235, Tables 5-6
Name c1='time' c2='yearq' c3='house' c4='rate'  &
     c5='q1' c6='q2' c7='q3'
# yearq      'year and quarter'
# house      'housing starts'
# rate       'mortgage rate, %'
# q1         'quarter 1'
# q2         'quarter 2'
# q3         'quarter 3'
Read c1-c7;
Format (F2.0, A7, F7.0, F10.0, 3F3.0).
 1 1980q1   159.9    13.7300    0  0  0
 2 1980q2   203.3    14.4333    1  0  0
 3 1980q3   272.6    12.6500    0  1  0
 4 1980q4   225.3    14.2633    0  0  1
 5 1981q1   166.5    15.1433    0  0  0
 6 1981q2   229.9    16.2267    1  0  0
 7 1981q3   184.8    17.4267    0  1  0
 8 1981q4   124.1    17.7333    0  0  1
 9 1982q1   113.6    17.4167    0  0  0
10 1982q2   178.2    16.7567    1  0  0
11 1982q3   186.7    16.1733    0  1  0
12 1982q4   184.1    14.0200    0  0  1
13 1983q1   202.9    13.0500    0  0  0
14 1983q2   322.3    12.7600    1  0  0
15 1983q3   307.5    13.6533    0  1  0
16 1983q4   234.8    13.4667    0  0  1
17 1984q1   236.5    13.3300    0  0  0
18 1984q2   332.6    14.0033    1  0  0
19 1984q3   280.3    14.4967    0  1  0
20 1984q4   234.7    13.6500    0  0  1
21 1985q1   215.3    13.0567    0  0  0
22 1985q2   317.9    12.7767    1  0  0
23 1985q3   295.0    12.1367    0  1  0
24 1985q4   244.1    11.7267    0  0  1
25 1986q1   234.1    10.5567    0  0  0
26 1986q2   371.4    10.2533    1  0  0
27 1986q3   325.4    10.2400    0  1  0
28 1986q4   250.6     9.6600    0  0  1
29 1987q1   241.4     9.1433    0  0  0
```

```
30 1987q2   346.5    10.3233   1  0  0
31 1987q3   321.3    10.5000   0  1  0
32 1987q4   237.1    10.8533   0  0  1
33 1988q1   219.7    10.0833   0  0  0
34 1988q2   323.7    12.3067   1  0  0
35 1988q3   293.4    10.5033   0  1  0
36 1988q4   244.6    10.3933   0  0  1
37 1989q1   212.7    10.8033   0  0  0
38 1989q2   302.1    10.6733   1  0  0
39 1989q3   272.1    10.0000   0  1  0
40 1989q4   216.5     9.8200   0  0  1
41 1990q1   217.0    10.1233   0  0  0
42 1990q2   271.3    10.3367   1  0  0
43 1990q3   233.0    10.1067   0  1  0
44 1990q4   173.6     9.9533   0  0  1
End
# '(1) Correlation Analysis'
Correlation 'house'  'rate'
# '(2) Regression Analysis'
Brief 3
Regress 'house' on 1 'rate';
   Sresiduals  c8;
   Fits c9;
   Residuals c10;
   DW.
Plot c10 * 'time'
Plot c10 * c9
# '(3) Regression Analysis'
Regress 'house' on 1 'rate';
   Sresiduals c11;
   Fits c12;
   Noconstant;
   Residuals in c13;
   DW.
Tsplot c13.
Plot c13*c12
For Windows
%Resplots c13 c2
```

Exercise Example 7-12: Simple Regression and Correlation

The Phillips curve is an inverse relationship between the rate of unemployment and the rate of inflation, which is expressed in the following function:

$$U = a - b\,p \quad \text{or} \quad U = a + b\,1/p$$

where U = unemployment rate, p = inflation rate. On the other hand, the rational expectationists presented the following hypothesis:

$$U = a - b\,(p - p^e) + e$$

where p^e = expected inflation rate. To test the above hypotheses, the following file was written. Run the file and find if the Phillips relation is significant.

```
Note 'Inflation and Unemployment: Shin7-12.inp'
Name c1='year' c2='gnp' c3='cons' c4='interest' c5='unemp' &
    c6='infla' c7='invest' c8='income'
# invest 'gross domestic investment'
# income 'disposable income'
# gnp    'GNP'
# all variables in 1982 prices
Read c1-c8
1970 2416.2  1492.0   8.04   4.8   5.7  381.5 1668.1
1971 2484.8  1538.8   7.39   5.8   4.4  419.3 1728.4
1972 2608.5  1621.9   7.21   5.5   3.2  465.4 1797.4
1973 2744.1  1689.6   7.44   4.8   6.2  520.8 1916.3
1974 2729.3  1674.0   8.57   5.5  11.0  481.3 1896.6
1975 2695.0  1711.9   8.83   8.3   9.1  383.3 1931.7
1976 2826.7  1803.9   8.43   7.6   5.8  453.5 2001.0
1977 2958.6  1883.8   8.02   6.9   6.5  521.3 2066.6
1978 3115.2  1961.0   8.73   6.0   7.6  576.9 2167.4
1979 3192.4  2004.4   9.63   5.8  11.3  575.2 2212.6
1980 3187.1  2000.4  11.94   7.0  13.5  509.3 2214.3
1981 3248.8  2024.2  14.17   7.5  10.3  545.5 2248.6
1982 3166.0  2050.7  13.79   9.5   6.2  447.3 2261.5
1983 3279.1  2146.0  12.04   9.5   3.2  504.0 2331.9
1984 3501.4  2249.3  12.71   7.4   4.3  658.4 2469.8
1985 3618.7  2354.8  11.37   7.1   3.6  637.0 2542.8
1986 3717.9  2446.4   9.02   6.9   1.9  639.6 2635.3
1987 3845.3  2515.8   9.38   6.1   3.6  669.0 2670.7
1988 4016.9  2606.5   9.71   5.4   4.1  705.7 2800.5
1989 4117.7  2656.8   9.26   5.2   4.8  716.9 2869.0
1990 4155.8  2682.2   9.32   5.4   5.4  690.3 2893.3
End
Name c9='infla1' c10='infla2' c11='laggnp' c12='gnp1' &
    c13='growth'
Let 'infla1' = Lag('infla')
Let 'infla2' = Lag('infla1')
Let 'laggnp' = Lag('gnp')
Let 'gnp1'   = Lag('gnp')
Let 'growth' = 100*('gnp'/'gnp1'-1)
Note '(1) Plot'.
Plot 'unemp'*'infla'
Note '(2) Simple Correlation'
Correlation 'unemp' 'infla'
Note '(3) Simple Regression for DOS'
Regress 'unemp' on 1 'infla' stfd.resid in c14 fits in c15;
    Residuals c16;
    DW.
Plot 'unemp'*'infla';
    Line 'infla' c15.
Plot c16*'infla'
Plot c16*c15
```

```
Note '(4) Simple regression for Windows'
Regress 'unemp' on 1 'growth';
    Sresiduals c17;
    Fits c18;
    Residuals c19;
    DW.
Tsplot c19
Plot c19*c18
%Resplots c19 c18
```

Edited Partial Output:

```
MTB > Note '(1) Plot'
MTB > Plot 'unemp' vs 'infla'
         -          *            *
         -
     9.0+
         -
 unemp   -                            *
         -
         -
     7.5+              *     *              *
         -          *
         -      *                  *              *
         -
     6.0+          *          *
         -              *
         -          *  *    *              *
         -              *                *
         -              * *
         --------+---------+---------+---------+---------+--------infla
               2.5       5.0       7.5      10.0      12.5
```

```
MTB > Note '(2) Simple Correlation'
MTB > Correlation 'unemp' 'infla'
Correlation of unemp and infla = 0.007
MTB > Note '(3) Simple Regression'
MTB > Regress 'unemp' on 1 'infla' std.resid in c14 fits in c15;
SUBC>           Residuals in c16;
SUBC>      DW.
The regression equation is
unemp = 6.55 + 0.003 infla
```

Predictor	Coef	Stdev	t-ratio	p
Constant	6.5506	0.7113	9.21	0.000
infla	0.0033	0.1021	0.03	0.974

s = 1.421   R-sq = 0.0%   R-sq(adj) = 0.0%

Analysis of Variance

SOURCE	DF	SS	MS	F	p
Regression	1	0.002	0.002	0.00	0.974
Error	19	38.361	2.019		
Total	20	38.363			

Unusual Observations

Obs.	infla	unemp	Fit	Stdev.Fit	Residual	St.Resid
11	13.5	7.000	6.595	0.800	0.405	0.34 X
13	6.2	9.500	6.571	0.310	2.929	2.11R
14	3.2	9.500	6.561	0.441	2.939	2.18R

Durbin-Watson statistic = 0.61

Exercise Example 7-13: Systematic Risk Beta

A stock analyst wanted to calculate systematic risk for General Motors. In the Value Line Investment Survey, the systematic risk (ß) for GM was listed as 1.10 which was calculated using the weekly data for 5 years. He wanted to see if the results are different with annual data. He gathered high-low prices and annual dividend. From the Economic Indicators, he was able to obtain Standard and Poor's stock price index and the annual dividend yield. Run the file and find systematic risk.

In the file, the following formulas are used:

$$R_i = \alpha + \beta R_m$$

where R_i = holding period return on stock i, R_m = holding period return on the market portfolio, β = systematic risk beta, α = intercept constant (return when $R_m = 0$).

Average price = (high price + low price)/2
Holding period return for GM: $R_{GM} = (P_t - P_{t-1} + D_t)/P_{t-1}$

Dividend for SP stocks (diviSP) = $100(D_t/P_t)/P_t$
Holding period return on the market $R_{SP} = 100(SP_t - SP_{t-1} + DiviSP)/SP_{t-1}$

File for Minitab for Windows

```
Note 'Systematic Risk Beta: Shin7-13.win'
# File for Minitab for Windows
Name c1='year' c2='high' c3='low' c4='divi' c5='sp' c6='yieldSP'
# high     'high price of the year for GM'
# low      'low price of the year for GM'
# divi     'annual dividend for GM'
# sp       "Standard and Poor's index"
# yieldSP 'dividend yield (D/P)'
# diviSP  'dividend on SP stocks'
# hprGM   'holding period return on GM (%)'
# market  'holding period return on market (%)'
Read c1-c6
1983  40.0  28.0  1.40  160.41  4.40
1984  41.4  30.5  2.38  160.46  4.64
1985  42.5  32.1  2.50  186.84  4.25
1986  44.3  32.9  2.50  236.34  3.49
1987  47.1  23.4  2.50  286.83  3.08
1988  44.1  30.0  2.50  265.79  3.64
1989  50.5  39.1  3.00  322.84  3.45
1990  50.5  33.1  3.00  334.59  3.61
1991  44.4  26.8  1.60  376.18  3.24
1992  44.4  28.8  1.40  415.74  2.99
End
Name c7='price' c8='price1' c9='hprGM' c10='diviSP' &
     c11='sp1' c12='market'
Let 'price'    = ('high'+'low')/2
Let 'price1'   = Lag('price')
Let 'hprGM'    = 100*('price'-'price1'+'divi')/ 'price1'
Let 'diviSP'   = 'yieldSP'*'sp'/100
Let 'sp1'      = Lag('sp')
Let 'market'   = 100*('sp'-'sp1'+'diviSP')/'sp1'
Print c1-c12
Describe c2-c12
Correlation c2-c12
Name c13='resid1' c14='fits1'
Brief 3
Plot 'hprGM'*'market'
Regress  'hprGM' on 1 'market';
   Residuals c13;
   Fits       c14;
   DW.
%Fitline 'hprGM' 'market'
%Resplots 'fits1' 'resid1'
Regress  'hprGM' on 1 'market';
   Noconstant;
   Residuals c15;
   Fits       c16;
```

DW.

File for Minitab for DOS

```
Note 'Systematic Risk Beta: Shin7-13.inp'
# File for Minitab for DOS
# Hewlett-Packard Corporation: Value Line beta = 1.35
Name c1='year' c2='high' c3='low' c4='divi' c5='sp' c6='yieldSP'
# high      'high price of the year for HP'
# low       'low price of the year for HP'
# divi      'annual dividend for HP'
# sp        "Standard and Poor's index"
# yieldSP   'dividend yield (D/P)'
# diviSP    'dividend on SP stocks'
# hpr       'holding period return on HP (%)'
# market    'holding period return on market (%)'
Read c1-c6
1983   48.3   34.3    0.16   160.41   4.40
1984   45.5   31.1    0.20   160.46   4.64
1985   38.9   28.8    0.22   186.84   4.25
1986   49.6   35.8    0.22   236.34   3.49
1987   73.6   39.3    0.23   286.83   3.08
1988   65.5   43.8    0.28   265.79   3.64
1989   61.5   40.3    0.36   322.84   3.45
1990   50.4   24.9    0.42   334.59   3.61
1991   57.4   29.9    0.48   376.18   3.24
1992   85.0   50.4    0.73   415.74   2.99
End
Name c7='price' c8='price1' c9='hpr' c10='diviSP' &
     c11='sp1' c12='market'
Let 'price'    = ('high'+'low')/2
Let 'price1'   = Lag('price')
Let 'hpr'      = 100*('price'-'price1'+'divi')/ 'price1'
Let 'diviSP'   = 'yieldSP'*'sp'/100
Let 'sp1'      = Lag('sp')
Let 'market'   = 100*('sp'-'sp1'+'diviSP')/'sp1'
Print c1-c12
Describe c2-c12
Correlation c2-c12
Name c13='resid1' c14='fits1'
Brief 3
Plot 'hpr'*'market'
Regress  'hpr' on 1 'market' std.resid in c13 fits in c14;
   Residuals c13;
   DW.
```

Chapter 8.
Multiple Regression and Correlation Analyses

A multiple regression model is used to examine the relationship between one dependent variable and 2 or more independent (explanatory, predictor) variables. The general form of a linear multiple regression equation can be expressed in the following form:

$$Y = b_1 + b_2 X_2 + b_3 X_3 + b_4 X_4 + \ldots + e$$

where Y = dependent (explained) variable, X_i = independent (explanatory, predictors) variables. $b_1, b_2, b_3 \ldots$ = regression coefficients, and e = the error term.

The regression coefficients $b_2, b_3, b_4, \ldots$ measure the net relationship between the dependent variable and the each of the independent variables. The multiple correlation coefficient R measures the degree of total relationship (correlation) between the dependent variable and the independent variables as a group. The partial correlation coefficients $r_{1,234..}$, $r_{2.132,..}$ measure the degree of net relationship between the dependent variable and each of the independent variables holding all other independent variables, that are included in the model, constant.

Multiple Regression and Correlation Coefficients

To show some formulas used to compute a multiple regression equation, consider the following multiple regression equation with 2 independent variables:

$$Y = b_1 + b_2 X_2 + b_3 X_3 + e$$

Letting $y = Y - \bar{Y}$, $x_2 = X_2 - \bar{X}_2$, $x_3 = X_3 - \bar{X}_3$

Multiple regression coefficients:

$$b_2 = \frac{(\Sigma yx_2)(\Sigma x_3{}^2) - (\Sigma yx_3)(\Sigma x_2 x_3)}{(\Sigma x_2{}^2)(\Sigma x_3{}^2) - (\Sigma x_2 x_3)^2}$$

$$b_3 = \frac{(\Sigma yx_3)(\Sigma x_2{}^2) - (\Sigma yx_2)(\Sigma x_2 x_3)}{(\Sigma x_2{}^2)(\Sigma x_3{}^2) - (\Sigma x_2 x_3)^2}$$

$$b_1 = \bar{Y} - b_2 \bar{X}_2 - b_3 \bar{X}_3$$

Multiple coefficient of determination:

$$R^2 = \Sigma(\hat{Y} - \bar{Y})^2 / \Sigma(Y - \bar{Y})^2 = 1 - [\Sigma(Y - \hat{Y})^2 / \Sigma(Y - \bar{Y})^2]$$

where $\Sigma(Y - \hat{Y})^2$ = SSE (sum of squared errors), $\Sigma(Y - \bar{Y})^2$ = SST (total sum of squares).

Multiple correlation coefficient:

$$R = \Sigma(X - \bar{X})(Y - \bar{Y}) / [\Sigma(X - \bar{X})^2 \Sigma(Y - \bar{Y})^2]^{1/2}$$

Adjusted multiple correlation coefficient $\bar{R}$ and Adjusted multiple coefficient of determination $\bar{R}^2$:

$$\bar{R}^2 = 1 - (1 - R^2)(N-1)/(N-k)$$

Standard error of the estimate (SEE) and Root mean squared error (RMSE):

$$s_{y.x} = [\ \Sigma(Y-\hat{Y})^2 / (N-k)\ ]^{1/2}$$

where N = no. of observations, k = the number of constants to estimate, including the intercept (k = the number of total variables, including the independent and dependent variables. In the simple regression equation, k = 2).

Standardized regression coefficients (Beta coefficients):

$$Y^* = \ss_0 + \ss_1 X_1^* + \ss_2 X_2^* + ...$$

where $Y^* = (Y-\bar{Y})/s_Y$, $X_1^* = (X_1-\bar{X}_1)/s_{x1}$, $X_2^* = (X_2 - \bar{X}_2)/s_{x2}$. Y^* and X_i^* are called standardized variables. s_y and s_x are standard deviations of Y and X respectively. Since the variables are measured in standardized units, the standardized regression coefficients (beta coefficients) can be used for the purpose of comparing the size of regression coefficients.

Significance Tests

For the significance tests of the regression and correlation coefficients, the following statistics are needed:

The standard errors of the regression coefficients:

$$s(b_1) = s_{y.x} \left[\frac{1}{N} + \frac{\bar{X}_2^2\ \Sigma x_3^2 + \bar{X}_3\ \Sigma x_2 - 2\ \bar{X}_2\ \bar{X}_3\ \Sigma x_2 x_3}{[\ \Sigma x_2^2 \Sigma x_3^2 - (\Sigma x_1 x_2)^2]} \right]^{1/2}$$

$$s(b_2) = s_{y.x}\ \Sigma x_3^2 / [\ \Sigma x_2^2 \Sigma x_3^2 - (\Sigma x_2 x_3)^2]$$

$$s(b_3) = s_{y.x}\ \Sigma x_2^2 / [\ \Sigma x_2^2 \Sigma x_3^2 - (\Sigma x_2 x_3)^2]$$

The multiple regression coefficients are tested by the following t-ratios:

$$t_{b1} = b_1 / s(b_1)\ \text{ for DF} = N-k \text{ and } \alpha$$

$$t_{b2} = b_2 / s(b_2)$$

$$t_{b3} = b_3 / s(b_3)$$

The multiple correlation coefficient R is tested by the following F-ratio:

$$F = \frac{R^2/ (k-1)}{(1-R^2)/ (N-k)}$$

where k-1 is numerator degrees of freedom, N-k is the denominator degrees of freedom, and k is the number of parameters to be estimated.

Partial Correlation Coefficients

The partial correlation coefficient is a measure of net correlation when other variables are held constant. Assume that there are 3 variables in a regression equation (one is the dependent variable):

$$Y_1 = b_1 + b_2 X_2 + b_3 X_3 + e$$

The partial correlation coefficients are calculated by the following formulas:

$$r_{12.3} = [\ r_{12} - r_{13}\ r_{23}\ ] / [\ (1-r^2_{13})(1-r^2_{23})\ ]^{1/2}$$

$$r_{13.2} = [\ r_{13} - r_{12}\ r_{23}\ ] / [\ (1-r^2_{12})(1-r^2_{23})\ ]^{1/2}$$

$$r_{23.1} = [\ r_{23} - r_{12}\ r_{13}\ ] / [\ (1-r^2_{12})(1-r^2_{13})\ ]^{1/2}$$

Significance of partial correlation coefficients is evaluated using the t test:

$$t = \frac{r_{12.3}}{[\ (1 - r^2_{12.3})\ /(\ N - k\ )\ ]^{1/2}}$$

H_0: $\rho_{12.3} = 0$ Accept H_0 if t $\leq$ critical t   at DF = N-k, and α
H_A: $\rho_{12.3} \neq 0$ Accept H_A if t $>$ critical t   at DF = N-k, and α

The problems of serial correlation, multicollinearity and heteroscedasticity are discussed in chapter 9.

Exercise Example 8-1: Multiple Regression and Correlation

Hop Scotch Airlines hired Ace Rickenbacker as a management consultant. His first task was to form a prediction equation for the number of passengers. In addition to advertising expenditures, he included national income as another predictor. File Name: Webs666A.inp and Webs666B.inp

Questions: Run the file and find the following:
(1) Multiple regression equation
(2) Is R^2 significant at the 5% level ?
(3) Are advertising and income significant ?

Minitab File for DOS Version: Webs666A.inp

```
Note 'Multiple Regression Analysis: Webs666A.inp'
# Webster, p. 666, Table 13-1
Name c1='month' c2='persons' c3='adver' c4='income'
# persons    'number of passengers'
# adver    'advertising'
# income  'national income'
Read c1-c4
  1   15   10   2.40
  2   17   12   2.72
  3   13    8   2.08
  4   23   17   3.68
  5   16   10   2.56
  6   21   15   3.36
  7   14   10   2.24
  8   20   14   3.20
  9   24   19   3.84
 10   17   10   2.72
 11   16   11   2.07
 12   18   13   2.33
 13   23   16   2.98
 14   15   10   1.94
 15   16   12   2.17
```

```
End
Note (1) Correlation
Correlation c2-c4
Brief 3
Note (2) Regression
Regress c2 on 2 c3 c4 std.resid in c5 fits in c6;
    Residuals in c7;
    VIF;
    DW.
Plot c6 * c1
Plot c7 * c6
Tsplot c7
Note (3) Stepwise regression
Stepwise c2 on c3 c4
Note (4) Regression for prediction
Set c8
20 30 40 50
End
Set c9
3.0 4.0 5.0 6.0
End
Name c8='x1' c9='x2'
Regress c2 on 2 c3 c4 Std.resid c10 Fits c11;
    VIF;
    DW;
    Predict for 'x1' 'x2'.
```

Minitab File for Windows Version 9.0: Webs666B.inp

```
Note 'Multiple Regression Analysis: Webs666B.inp'
# Webster, p. 666, Table 13-1
Name c1='month' c2='persons' c3='adver' c4='income'
# persons   'number of passengers'
# adver     'advertising'
# income    'national income'
Read c1-c4
  1  15  10  2.40
  2  17  12  2.72
  3  13   8  2.08
  4  23  17  3.68
  5  16  10  2.56
  6  21  15  3.36
  7  14  10  2.24
  8  20  14  3.20
  9  24  19  3.84
 10  17  10  2.72
 11  16  11  2.07
 12  18  13  2.33
 13  23  16  2.98
 14  15  10  1.94
 15  16  12  2.17
End
Note (1) Correlation
Correlation c2-c4
Brief 3
Note (2) Regression
Regress c2 on 2 c3 c4;
    Residuals c5;
    Fits c6;
    VIF;
    DW.
Note (3) Stepwise regression
Stepwise c2 on c3 c4
Note (4) Regression for prediction
Set c8
20 30 40 50
End
Set c9
```

```
3.0 4.0 5.0 6.0
End
Name c8='x1' c9='x2'
Regress c2 on 2 c3 c4;
   VIF;
   DW;
   Predict for 'x1' 'x2'.
Note (5) Graph (placed at the end of the file)
%Resplots c5 c6;
   Gsave 'b:Fig8-1'.
Plot c7*c6
Tsplot c7
```

Edited Partial Output:

```
MTB > Correlation c2-c4
        persons     adver
adver    0.968
income   0.903     0.870
The regression equation is
persons = 3.53 + 0.840 adver + 1.44 income

Predictor      Coef       Stdev     t-ratio       p     VIF
Constant      3.5284     0.9994        3.53     0.004
adver         0.8397     0.1419        5.92     0.000     4.1
income        1.4410     0.7360        1.96     0.074     4.1

s = 0.8217      R-sq = 95.3%      R-sq(adj) = 94.5%
Analysis of Variance
SOURCE       DF         SS         MS         F        p
Regression    2     163.632     81.816     121.18    0.000
Error        12       8.102      0.675
Total        14     171.733
SOURCE       DF       SEQ SS
adver         1     161.044
income        1       2.588
Obs.   adver   persons      Fit  Stdev.Fit  Residual   St.Resid
  1    10.0    15.000    15.383     0.289    -0.383      -0.50
  2    12.0    17.000    17.524     0.230    -0.524      -0.66
  3     8.0    13.000    13.243     0.392    -0.243      -0.34
  4    17.0    23.000    23.105     0.419    -0.105      -0.15
  5    10.0    16.000    15.614     0.346     0.386       0.52
  6    15.0    21.000    20.965     0.332     0.035       0.05
  7    10.0    14.000    15.153     0.275    -1.153      -1.49
  8    14.0    20.000    19.895     0.304     0.105       0.14
  9    19.0    24.000    25.015     0.506    -1.015      -1.57
 10    10.0    17.000    15.844     0.428     1.156       1.65
 11    11.0    16.000    15.748     0.360     0.252       0.34
 12    13.0    18.000    17.802     0.392     0.198       0.27
 13    16.0    23.000    21.257     0.393     1.743       2.42R
 14    10.0    15.000    14.721     0.367     0.279       0.38
 15    12.0    16.000    16.731     0.387    -0.731      -1.01
R denotes an obs. with a large st. resid.
Durbin-Watson statistic = 1.95
```

1. Regression Summary

From the above regression results, we can write the following regression equation:

$$Y = 3.5285 + 0.8397\, X_1 + 1.4410\, X_2 \qquad R^2 = 0.9530 \quad \bar{R}^2 = 0.945 \quad F = 121.18$$
$$\quad\ (13.53)^* \ \ (5.92)^* \qquad\quad (1.96) \qquad\ \ SEE = 0.8217 \quad DW = 1.95$$

where Y = persons, X_1 = advertising, and X_2 = income. The numbers in parentheses are the t-values. The asterisk * indicates that the regression coefficient is significant at the 5 % level.

2. Simple Correlation Coefficient r

The simple correlation matrix shows the following:

(1) The r between persons and advertising = 0.968
(2) The r between persons and income = 0.903
(3) The r between income and advertising = 0.870

Are the above simple correlation coefficients significant ? The simple correlation coefficients can be evaluated in terms of the t value:

$$t = r / [(1 - r^2)/(N-k)]^{1/2}$$

where N = number of observations, r = simple correlation coefficient. DF = N - k = the degrees of freedom, where k is the number of regression constants including the intercept constant. Thus it is equal to the total number of variables in the regression including the dependent variable. If the computed t is grater than the critical t value in the table of t-distribution for the given α level and degrees of freedom, the correlation coefficient is significant:

$H_0: r = 0$ Accept if $t_{N-3} <$ critical t
$H_A: r \neq 0$ Accept if $t_{N-3} >$ critical t

All the simple correlation coefficients are significant either at the 0.1 % level.

3. Partial Correlation Coefficients

The partial correlation coefficient is a measure of net correlation when the other variables are held constant. In Minitab, partial correlation coefficients are not available. Using SAS or SPSS, the following partial correlations are obtained:

$r_{12.3} = 0.86298$ between persons and advertising, holding income constant
$r_{13.2} = 0.49201$ between persons and income, holding advertising constant

The t-ratio formula is the same for the partial correlation coefficient as that for the simple correlation coefficient:

$$t = r / [(1 - r^2)/(N-k)]^{1/2}$$

where N = number of total observations, k = total number of variables included in the calculation of partial correlation coefficients. Thus, in the multiple regression equation, it is equal to the total number of coefficients to estimate including the constant intercept, or the total number of variables in the multiple regression equation including the dependent variable. In this case, there are 3 total variables.

For $r_{12.3}$, $t = 0.86298 / [(1 - 0.86298^2)/(15-3)]^{1/2} = 5.917$
For $r_{13.2}$, $t = 0.49201 / [(1 - 0.49201^2)/(15-3)]^{1/2} = 1.958$

The degrees of freedom is DF = N-k = 15-3 = 12. the critical t value is 2.179 for $\alpha = 0.05$ (two-tail test). In effect, the $r_{12.3}$ is significant, but $r_{13.2}$ is not.

4. Multiple Correlation Coefficient R and Multiple Coefficient of Determination R^2

Multiple correlation coefficient (R) measures the degree of correlation between the dependent variable and the set of the independent variables as a whole. R^2 is called the coefficient of determination. The significance of R is tested using the F test. The computed F value is 121.18, but the critical F value is 3.88 at the 5 % level for the denominator degrees of freedom $DF_1 = K-1 = 3 - 1 = 2$ and the numerator degrees of freedom $DF_2 = N-K = 15 - 3 = 12$. Since the computed F value is greater than the critical F value, we conclude that the R^2 is significant at the 5 % level.

An alternative method is to use the significance probability associated with the computed F value. The number below the heading Prob > F, i.e., 0.0083, is the significance probability under the null hypothesis that the multiple correlation coefficient is equal to zero. Since the significance probability is 0.0001 which is less than 0.05, we accept the alternative hypothesis that R^2 is significant at the 0.0001 level (0.01 %).

$H_0: R = 0$　　　Accept if　computed $P \geq 0.05$
$H_A: R \neq 0$　　　Accept if　computed $P < 0.05$

5. Adjusted R^2　($\bar{R}^2$)

In the regression results, R^2 is 0.9528, and the adjusted R^2 is 0.9450. The adjusted R^2 is usually less than R^2. What is the use of the adjusted R^2? As stated before, R^2 measures the percentage of total variation in the dependent variable Y in terms of the estimated regression equation. In a multiple regression equation, as the number of independent variables increases the R and R^2 values always increase even by 0.0000001 regardless of the significance of the additional independent variable (explanatory variable), and you could increase the R^2 value virtually to 1.0 by merely increasing the number of independent variables.

So it appears that the more independent variables you include in a multiple regression equation, the higher is R^2, and the better. However, if you conclude that a regression model with a larger R^2 is better than another regression model with a lower R^2, the evaluation could be wrong and misleading since R^2 will increase even if the additional independent variable may not be significant. A fair method of comparing two regression models is to compare R^2, when the number of independent variables are the same in the two models. When the number of independent variables are not the same, this factor should be used to adjust the R^2 values. Indeed, the adjusted R-square (R-Bar-Square) is devised for this purpose, and it is an R^2 adjusted for the number of independent variables. The relationship between the R^2 and the adjusted R^2 is given by the following equation:

$$\bar{R}^2 = 1 - [(1-R^2) (N-1) / (N-k)]$$

In the above equation, N-k is the denominator. As k increases, the term $(1-R^2)(N-1)/(N-k)$ increases, and thus the adjusted R^2 will fall, since $1-R^2 \geq 0$. And it is possible that the adjusted R^2 will be negative if $(1-R^2) (N-1)/(N-k) > 1.0$

For instance, if $R^2 = 0.2$, N=20, k = 6, then

$$\bar{R}^2 = 1 - [(1-0.2) (20-1)/(20-6)] = 1 - 1.03 = -0.03$$

6. Multiple Regression Coefficients

A regression coefficient of a multiple regression equation is called a partial regression coefficient in the sense that it measures the net effect of the independent variable on the dependent variable holding other independent variables constant. In the regression results, we have 0.3528, 0.8397 and 1.4410. Are they significant? The significance of a regression coefficient can be evaluated using the t test:

$$t = b / s_b$$

where b = regression coefficient, s_b =the standard error of the regression coefficient. If the computed t ratio is compared with the critical t value in the table of t distribution for the degrees of freedom DF = N-K and the given α level. For the DF = 15-2 = 13, and α = 0.05 (each tail 0.05/2), the critical t-value is 2.160

H_0: b = 0   Accept if $t_{N-K} \leq$ critical t
H_A: b $\neq$ 0   Accept if $t_{N-K} >$ critical t

An alternative method is to use the significance probabilities associated with the computed t values of the regression coefficients. In the regression output, a number in the column of Prob > |T| is the significance probability under the null hypothesis that the regression coefficient is zero:

H_0: b = 0   Accept if   computed P $\geq$ 0.05
H_A: b $\neq$ 0   Accept if   computed P < 0.05

The regression coefficients, t-ratios, and the significance probabilities are represented below:

```
Predictor      Coef       Stdev      t-ratio        p
Constant      3.5284     0.9994        3.53      0.004
adver         0.8397     0.1419        5.92      0.000
income        1.4410     0.7360        1.96      0.074
```

First, to apply the t-ratios decision rule, the t ratio is greater than the critical t value 2.160 for intercept and advertising. But the t-ratio for income is less than the critical t value. So, we conclude that intercept and advertising are significant but income is not. Second, to apply the significance probability decision rule, the significance probabilities are less than 0.05 for the intercept and advertising, but it is greater than 0.05 for income. So, we conclude that intercept and advertising are significant but income is not. "Significant" means that the regression coefficient is significantly different from zero.

In interpreting the size of the slope regression coefficient, it is equal to the marginal effect of a change in the independent variable on the dependent variable ($\partial Y / \partial X_i$). For example, the advertising expenditure is 0.8397. It implies that if the advertising expenditures increase by 1 dollar, the number of passengers would increase by 0.8397 persons (both units are measured in 1000 units in the Webster text). The regression coefficient of income is 1.4410. It implies that if national income increases by 1 \$ (in trillion dollars), the number of passengers will increase by 1.4410 persons (in 1000 persons). However, this prediction is not reliable since the regression coefficient is not significant. Finally, what is the meaning of intercept constant? The intercept constant is 0.3528. It means and if both advertising and income are zero, the number of passengers is equal to 0.3528 persons (in 1000 persons). If it is significant, it usually implies that some other explanatory variables are missing in the model.

7. Standard Error of the Estimate (SEE) and Root Mean Squared Error (RMSE)

The standard error os the estimate is an overall measure of the goodness-of-fit of the regression model. The smaller the SEE, the better is the regression model. The SEE is also used to compute the standard error of the forecast.

8. Durbin-Watson Statistic

Durbin-Watson statistic is used to test the significance of serial correlation of the error terms usually for the time series data. The DW statistic is 1.952. The critical upper limit of the Durbin-Watson statistic is 1.952 found in the table of the Durbin-Watson statistic. Since the computed DW statistic is greater than the critical value, we conclude that serial correlation of the error term is not significant. Critical values or significance probabilities for DW statistics are not provided by Minitab or any other statistical package. If the serial correlation is significant, it implies that regression results are not reliable in the sense that R^2 is overestimated and the standard errors of regression coefficients are underestimated. That is, R^2 and t ratio are overestimated and thus not reliable. If the serial correlation is not significant, it means that the results, i. e., R^2 and t ratios are reliable. The problems of serial correlation, heteroscedasticity, and multicollinearity are discussed in detail in chapter 9.

Exercise Example 8-2: Multiple Regression and Correlation

Lisa Clucksman of Prudential Edna Kranz Real Estate wanted to build a prediction equation for price of condominiums, and gathered the data for 25 condominiums. Run the file and obtain the regression equation. File Name: ACZEL553.inp

```
Note 'Multiple Regression and Correlation: ACZEL553.inp'
# Aczel, p. 553, Problem 11-114
Name c1='price' c2='rooms' c3='bedrooms' c4='baths'  &
     c5='age' c6='assessed' c7='area'
#   price     'price of condominium ($1,000)'
#   rooms     'number of rooms'        bedrooms 'number of bedrooms'
#   baths     'number of bathrooms'      age   'age of condominium'
#   assessed  'assessed value($1,000)'   area  'square feet'
Read c1-c7
145     4   1   1   69  116.5   790
144.9   4   2   1   70  127.2   915
145.9   3   1   1   78  127.6   721
146.5   4   1   1   75  121.7   800
146.9   4   2   1   40   94.8   718
147.9   4   1   1   12  169.7   915
148     3   1   1   20  151.8   870
148.9   3   1   1   20  147.8   875
149     4   2   1   70  140.5  1078
149     4   2   1   60  120.4   705
149.9   4   2   1   65  160.8   834
149.9   3   1   1   20  135.9   725
149.9   4   2   1   65  125.4   900
152.9   5   2   1   37  134.5   792
153     3   1   1  100  132.1   820
154     3   1   1   18  140.8   782
158     5   2   1   89  158.0   955
158     4   2   1   69  127.6   922
159     4   2   1   60  152.8  1050
159     5   2   2   49  157.0  1092
179.9   5   2   1   90  165.8  1180
179.9   6   3   1   89  158.3  1328
179.5   5   2   1   60  148.1  1175
179     6   3   1   87  158.5  1253
175     4   2   1   80  158.9   650
End
Note '(1) Correlation'
Correlation c1-c7
Note '(2) Regression'
Brief 3
Regress 'price' on 6 'rooms' 'bedrooms' 'baths' 'age' &
  'assessed' 'area';
   Residuals c8;
   VIF;
   DW.
Title '(3) Stepwise Regression'
Stepwise 'price' 'rooms' 'bedrooms' 'baths' 'age' 'assessed' 'area';
   Fenter = 4;
```

```
    Noconstant.
Title '(4) Best Regression'
Breg 'price' 'rooms' 'bedrooms' 'baths' 'age' 'assessed' 'area';
    Best 3.
```

Exercise Example 8-3: Multiple Regression and Elasticity

Diamond State Telephone Company sent a questionnaire to randomly selected 62 new firms. It asked the total number of telephone lines they would demand at alternative sets of line installation charge, monthly charge per line, and rotary discount. The survey results are summarized in the data set. Run the file and find the price elasticities. File Name: ACZEL554.inp

```
Note 'Multiple Regression: ACZEL554.inp'
# Aczel, p. 554, Case 11
Name c1='demand' c2='charge1' c3='charge2' c4='discount'
# demand    'demand for telephone lines'
# charge1   'installation charge'
# charge2   'monthly charge'
# discount  'rotary discount'
Read c1-c4
201   12.50   10.32   4.55
199   12.50   10.32   3.05
195   12.50   10.32   1.50
196   18.60   10.32   4.55
187   18.60   15.65   4.55
190   12.50   15.65   3.05
181   18.60   15.65   1.50
167   18.60   20.82   4.55
165   18.60   20.92   3.05
166   25.12   15.65   3.05
150   25.12   20.92   4.55
147   25.12   20.92   1.50
140   37.10   20.92   1.50
121   37.10   27.18   4.55
120   37.10   27.18   3.05
125   25.12   27.18   1.50
145   18.60   27.18   4.55
114   18.60   34.00   4.55
113   18.60   34.00   1.50
108   25.12   34.00   1.50
105   37.10   34.00   3.05
End
Name c5='logdeman' c6='logchar1' c7='logchar2' c8='logdis'
Let 'logdeman' = Loge(demand)
Let 'logchar1' = Loge(charge1)
Let 'logchar2' = Loge(charge2)
Let 'logdis'   = Loge(discount)
Correlation 'demand' 'charge1' 'charge2' 'discount'
Brief 3
Regress 'demand' on 3 'charge1' 'charge2' 'discount';
    Sresiduals c9;
    Fits c10;
    Residual c11;
    DW.
Tsplot c11
Plot c11 * c10
Regress 'logdeman' on 3 'logchar1' 'logchar2' 'logdis';
    Sresid c12;
    Fits c13;
    Residual c14;
    DW.
Tsplot c14
Plot c14 * c13
Stepwise 'demand' 'charge1' 'charge2' 'discount'
```

Exercise Example 8-4: Multiple Regression and Correlation

A merger-acquisition specialist wanted to predict the market value of the stock. He collected the data for 10 large corporations. Run the file and find significant variables. File Name: Emory622.inp

```
Note 'Multiple Regression and Correlation: Emory622.inp'
* Emory, p. 622
Name c1='company' c2='assets' c3='sales' c4='value' c5='profit'  &
    c6='cash' c7='employee'
# assets 'total assets'
# sales  'net sales'
# value  'market value of the stock'
# profit 'net profits'
# cash   'cash flows'
# employee 'no. of employees'.
# dollars in millions, employees in thousands.
Read c1-c7
    1    1034.00   1510.00    697.00    82.60   126.50   16.60
    2     956.00    785.00   1271.00    89.60   191.20    5.00
    3    1890.00   2533.00   1783.00   176.00   267.00   44.00
    4    1133.00    532.00    752.00    82.30   137.10    2.10
    5   11682.00   3790.00   4149.00   413.50   806.80   11.90
    6    6080.00    635.00    291.00    18.10    35.20    3.70
    7   31044.00   3296.00   2705.00   337.30   425.50   20.10
    8    5878.00   3204.00   2100.00   145.80   380.00   10.80
    9    1721.00    981.00   1573.00   172.60   326.60    1.90
   10    2135.00   2268.00   2634.00   247.20   355.50   21.20
End
# (1) Correlation analysis
Correlation 'assets' 'sales' 'value' 'profit' 'cash' 'employee'
# (2) Regression- Stepwise
Stepwise 'assets' 'sales' 'value' 'profit' 'cash' 'employee'
# (3) Regression
Brief 3
Regress 'assets' on 5 'sales' 'value' 'profit' 'cash' 'employee';
    Sresiduals c8;
    Fits in c9;
  Residuals = c10;
    VIF;
    DW.
Tsplot c10
Plot c10 * c9
```

Exercise Example 8-5: Multiple Regression and Correlation

Amy Green wanted to predict weekly sales of garden supplies. As independent variables she included the number of TV ads and the average high temperature during a week. She gathered the data for 8 recent weeks. Run the file and find if the variables are significant. File Name: Hanke499.inp

```
Note 'Multiple Regression and Correlation: Hanke499.inp'
# Hanke, p. 499, Example 14.2 - TVads, temperature and sales
Name c1='week' c2='sales' c3='tvads' c4='temp'
# sales = 'sales in 1000 $'
# tvads = 'no. of TV ads.'
# temp  = 'average temperature'
Read c1-c4
1    125    3    41
2    152    5    86
3    131    4    33
4    133    4    47
5    142    5    64
6    116    3    22
7    127    3    55
```

```
8    163    6    84
End
Plot c2 * c3
Plot c2 * c4
Correlation c2-c4
Brief 3
Regress c2 on 2 c3 c4;
  VIF;
  DW.
Regress c2 on 2 c3 c4;
  Noconstant;
  CookD in c5;
  Predict for 7 80.
Name c5='CookD'
Print c2-c5
```

Exercise Example 8-6: Multiple Regression and Correlation

The human resource director of a firm wanted to know if weekly sales are related to sales-people's test score and achievement rating. He gathered the data on 5 sales-persons. Run the file and find the answer. File Name: Mason534.inp

```
Note 'Multiple Regression and Correlation: Mason534.inp'
Name c1='person' c2='score' c3='rating' c4='sales'
# persons = 'sales persons'
# test    = 'test score'
# rating  = 'achievement rating'
# sales   = 'weekly sales';
Read c1-c4;
Format (A18, F2.0, F3.0, F4.0).
Mr. Amber          4   2    5
Mr. Archer         7   5   12
Ms. Smith          3   1    4
Mr. Malcolm        6   4    8
Ms. Goodwin       10   6   11
End
Brief 3
Plot 'sales' * 'score'
Correlation c2-c4
Brief 3
Regress 'sales' on 2 'score' 'rating'
```

Exercise Example 8-7: Multiple Regression and Correlation

The marketing manager of Zarthan Company gathered the data on sales, target population, and per capita disposable income to form a prediction equation for sales. Run the file and find if the variables are significant. File Name: Neter249.inp

```
Note 'Multiple Regression: Neter249.inp'
# Neter, p. 249, Table 7-2: Zarthan Company Example
Name c1='district' c2='sales' c3='popu' c4='income'
# sales   'jars in gross'
# popu    'population 1000'
# income  'per capita income'
Read c1-c4
  1   162   274   2450
  2   120   180   3254
  3   223   375   3802
  4   131   205   2838
  5    67    86   2347
  6   169   265   3782
  7    81    98   3008
  8   192   330   2450
  9   116   195   2137
 10    55    53   2560
```

```
11   252   430   4020
12   232   372   4427
13   144   236   2660
14   103   157   2088
15   212   370   2605
End
# '(1) Correlation Analysis'
Correlation 'sales' 'popu' 'income'
# '(2) Regression Analysis'
Brief 3
Regress 'sales' on 2 'popu' 'income';
   Sresiduals c5;
   Fit c6;
   Residuals c7;
   DW.
# '(3) Plots
Plot c7 * c6
Tsplot c7
```

Exercise Example 8-8: Multiple Regression and Correlation

For a study of body fat, a medical researcher gathered data on triceps, thigh, and midarm for 20 healthy females 25-34 years old. Run the file and find if the variables have expected signs. File Name: Neter272.inp

```
Note 'Multiple Regression: Neter272.inp'
# Neter, p. 272, Table 8-1: Body Fat Example
Name c1='subject' c2='triceps' c3='thigh' c4='midarm' &
     c5='bodyfat'
# triceps='skinforld thickness'
# thigh  ='thigh circumference'
# midarm ='midarm circumference'
# bodyfat='body fat'
Read c1-c5
  1   19.5   43.1   29.1   11.9
  2   24.7   49.8   28.2   22.8
  3   30.7   51.9   37.0   18.7
  4   29.8   54.3   31.1   20.1
  5   19.1   42.2   30.9   12.9
  6   25.6   53.9   23.7   21.7
  7   31.4   58.5   27.6   27.1
  8   27.9   52.1   30.6   25.4
  9   22.1   49.9   23.2   21.3
 10   25.5   53.5   24.8   19.3
 11   31.1   56.6   30.0   25.4
 12   30.4   56.7   28.3   27.2
 13   18.7   46.5   23.0   11.7
 14   19.7   44.2   28.6   17.8
 15   14.6   42.7   21.3   12.8
 16   29.5   54.4   30.1   23.9
 17   27.7   55.3   25.7   22.6
 18   30.2   58.6   24.6   25.4
 19   22.7   48.2   27.1   14.8
 20   25.2   51.0   27.5   21.1
End
Note '(1) Correlation Analysis'
Correlation 'triceps' 'thigh' 'midarm' 'bodyfat'
Note '(2) Regression Analysis'
Brief 3
Regress 'bodyfat' on 3 'triceps' 'thigh' 'midarm';
Sresiduals c6;
   Fits c7;
   Residuals c8;
   VIF.
Tsplot c8
Plot c8 * c7
```

```
Stepwise 'bodyfat' on 'triceps' 'thigh' 'midarm' ;
   Fenter=4.0.
```

Exercise Example 8-9: Multiple Regression and Correlation

The market value of stocks is equal to the stock price times the number of outstanding shares of stock. Siegel, merger-acquisition specialist, gathered the data on assets, sales and employees to form a prediction equation. Run the file and find significant variables. File Name: Siege506.inp

```
Note 'Multiple Regression: Siege505.inp'
# Siegel, 505, Example
Name c1='firm' c2='value' c3='assets' c4='value' c5='employ'
# value 'market value of the firm'
# employ 'no. of employees'
Read c1-c5;
Format (A20, F4.0, F6.0, F7.0, F8.0).
Goodyear          3023    8610   10328    121586
Firestone         1386    2593    3712     55000
Gencorp           1949    2119    3099     26700
Goodrich          1319    1820    2553     11914
Premark            867    1407    1959     21900
Dayco              254     511     911      4000
Armstrong          191     521     800      7505
Rubblemaid        1969     579     795      6103
Cooper             375     368     578      5398
Dorsey             159     190     527      4400
Danaher            252     741     524      6950
Carlisle           314     322     466      4949
Millipore         1778     398     443      4868
Standard Products  468     199     443      5700
lancaster Colony   267     250     423      5100
End
Correlation 'value' 'assets' 'sales' 'employ'
Regress 'value' on 3 'assets' 'sales' 'employ' std.resid c6 fits c7;
   Residuals c8;
     VIF;
     DW.
Tsplot c8
Plot c8 * c7.
Stepwise 'value' 'assets' 'sales' 'employ' std.resid c6 fits c7
```

Exercise Example 8-10: Multiple Regression and Correlation

An economist at GM wanted to predict quarterly sales of cars and parts. Run the file and obtain the regression equation. File Name: Wils-171.inp

```
Note 'Multiple Regression: Wils-171.inp'
# Wilson, 1990 ed., pp. 118, 124, 171, Tables 4-1, 4-2, 5-1
Name c1='time' c2='yearq' c3='income' c4='cars' &
     c5='interest' c6='q1' c7='q2' c8='q3'
# yearq    = 'year and quarter'
# income   = 'personal disposable income'
# cars     = 'motor vehicle and parts sales'
# interest = 'prime interest rate, %'
# q1       = 'quarter 1'
# q2       = 'quarter 2'
# q3       = 'quarter 3'
Read c1-c8;
Format(F2.0, A7, F8.0, F9.0, F9.0, 3F3.0).
 1 1976q1   70.20   1983.10   6.83333   1  0  0
 2 1976q2   71.40   1992.80   6.90000   0  1  0
 3 1976q3   73.00   2005.90   7.08667   0  0  1
 4 1976q4   76.30   2022.20   6.54000   0  0  0
 5 1977q1   84.00   2026.90   6.25000   1  0  0
 6 1977q2   84.40   2049.60   6.47000   0  1  0
```

```
 8 1977q4    87.60   2120.80   7.67333   0  0  0
 9 1978q1    86.30   2128.20   7.97667   1  0  0
10 1978q2    98.10   2167.70   8.30000   0  1  0
11 1978q3    97.20   2176.40   9.14000   0  0  1
12 1978q4    98.70   2202.00  10.8100    0  0  0
13 1979q1    99.00   2216.60  11.7500    1  0  0
14 1979q2    93.70   2206.50  11.7167    0  1  0
15 1979q3    98.90   2213.60  12.1167    0  0  1
16 1979q4    95.90   2213.60  15.0800    0  0  0
17 1980q1    98.30   2225.60  16.3967    1  0  0
18 1980q2    80.10   2185.60  16.3233    0  1  0
19 1980q3    89.60   2207.10  11.6100    0  0  1
20 1980q4    93.20   2238.70  16.7333    0  0  0
21 1981q1   103.20   2242.90  19.2133    1  0  0
22 1981q2    97.10   2235.00  18.9300    0  1  0
23 1981q3   106.50   2262.90  20.3233    0  0  1
24 1981q4    95.40   2253.70  17.0133    0  0  0
25 1982q1   105.70   2245.70  16.2700    1  0  0
26 1982q2   105.70   2260.90  16.5000    0  1  0
27 1982q3   108.30   2263.40  14.7167    0  0  1
28 1982q4   115.70   2271.10  11.9567    0  0  0
29 1983q1   115.00   2288.40  10.8800    1  0  0
30 1983q2   128.50   2311.10  10.5000    0  1  0
31 1983q3   133.70   2335.40  10.9767    0  0  1
32 1983q4   144.40   2392.70  11.0000    0  0  0
33 1984q1   150.40   2446.90  11.0700    1  0  0
34 1984q2   155.80   2460.30  12.3067    0  1  0
35 1984q3   154.40   2481.90  12.9900    0  0  1
36 1984q4   157.60   2493.10  11.8033    0  0  0
37 1985q1   162.30   2495.70  10.5367    1  0  0
38 1985q2   165.30   2550.80  10.1967    0  1  0
39 1985q3   182.80   2524.70   9.50000   0  0  1
40 1985q4   166.40   2540.70   9.50000   0  0  0
End
Correlation 'time' 'income' 'cars' 'interest'
Regress 'cars' on 2 'income' 'interest' std.resid c8 fits c9;
   Residuals c10;
     VIF;
     DW.
TSplot c10
Plot c10 * c9
Regress 'cars' on 2 'income' 'interest' c6-c8;
   Sresiduals c11;
     Fits c12;
   Residuals c13;
     VIF;
     DW.
TSplot c13
Plot c13 * c12
```

Exercise Example 8-11: Import Function of Cars

An economist at GM Corporation wanted to estimate the demand functions for US cars and imported cars. Run the file and obtain the import function.

```
Note 'Import Function of Cars: Exam8-11.inp'
Name c1='year' c2='cars' c3='popu' c4='cons' c5='gnp'  &
    c6='interest' c7='unemp' c8='imports'
# cars      'passenger car production in USA 1000 units'
# imports  'imports of cars and trucks in 1000 units'
# interest 'interest rate (Baa, Moody's)'
# unemp      'unemployment rate (%)'
# popu       'population in millions'
#    Consumption and GNP ... in billion dollars, 1982 prices
#    Cars     popu    Cons     GNP     i     U   Imports
Code (-99) '*' c1-c8 c1-c8
# Value -99 is coded as missing values.
```

```
# Value -99 is coded as missing values.
# An asterisk '*' represents also a missing value.
Read c1-c8
1981 6673.32   230.138   2024.2    3248.8    16.04  7.5 2774.85.
1982 5157.48   232.520   2050.7    3166.0    16.11  9.5 2633.89
1983 5683.20   234.799   2146.0    3279.1    13.55  9.5 2850.29
1984 8147.85   237.001   2249.3    3501.4    14.19  7.4 3046.60
1985 7817.42   239.279   2354.8    3618.7    12.72  7.1 3606.08
1986 7910.05   241.625   2446.4    3717.9    10.39  6.9 4162.19
1987 7388.69   243.942   2515.8    3845.3    10.58  6.1 4020.94
1988 6973.64   246.307   2606.5    4016.9    10.83  5.4 3706.25
1989 7112.46   248.762   2656.8    4117.7    10.18  5.2 3338.95
1990  -99      251.394   2682.2    4155.8    10.36  5.4 *
End
Correlation 'cars' 'popu' 'cons' 'gnp' 'interest' 'unemp' 'imports'
Brief 3
Regress 'cars' on 5 'popu' 'gnp' 'interest' 'unemp' 'imports';
   Sresiduals c9;
   Fits c10;
     Residuals c11;
     VIF;
     DW.
TSplot c11
Plot c11 * c10
Regress 'imports' on 4  'popu' 'gnp' 'interest' 'unemp';
   Sresiduals c12;
   Fits c13;
   Residuals c14;
   VIF;
   DW.
TSplot c14
Plot c14 * c13
```

Note: The car data are from *Wards's Automotive Yearbook*, 1990.
Other data are from *Economic Report of the President*, 1991.

Exercise Example 8-12: Consumption and Investment Functions

An economic student gathered data on macroeconomic variables to obtain consumption function, investment function and other macroeconomic functions.

Questions: Run the file and evaluate the following:
(1) Consumption function with absolute income
(2) Consumption function with expected income (permanent income)
(3) Investment function with GDP and interest rate
(4) Unemployment rate and unanticipated inflation rate (rational expectations
   hypothesis)

```
Note 'Inflation and Unemployment'
Name c1='year' c2='gnp' c3='cons' c4='interest' &
    c5='unemp' c6='infla' c7='invest' c8='income'
# invest 'gross domestic investment'
# income 'disposable income'
# gnp    'GNP'
# UAI    'unanticipated inflation rate'
# all values in 1982 prices
Read c1-c8
1970 2416.2   1492.0   8.04   4.8   5.7   381.5 1668.1
1971 2484.8   1538.8   7.39   5.8   4.4   419.3 1728.4
1972 2608.5   1621.9   7.21   5.5   3.2   465.4 1797.4
1973 2744.1   1689.6   7.44   4.8   6.2   520.8 1916.3
1974 2729.3   1674.0   8.57   5.5  11.0   481.3 1896.6
1975 2695.0   1711.9   8.83   8.3   9.1   383.3 1931.7
1976 2826.7   1803.9   8.43   7.6   5.8   453.5 2001.0
```

```
1977    2958.6    1883.8    8.02    6.9    6.5    521.3  2066.6
1978    3115.2    1961.0    8.73    6.0    7.6    576.9  2167.4
1979    3192.4    2004.4    9.63    5.8   11.3    575.2  2212.6
1980    3187.1    2000.4   11.94    7.0   13.5    509.3  2214.3
1981    3248.8    2024.2   14.17    7.5   10.3    545.5  2248.6
1982    3166.0    2050.7   13.79    9.5    6.2    447.3  2261.5
1983    3279.1    2146.0   12.04    9.5    3.2    504.0  2331.9
1984    3501.4    2249.3   12.71    7.4    4.3    658.4  2469.8
1985    3618.7    2354.8   11.37    7.1    3.6    637.0  2542.8
1986    3717.9    2446.4    9.02    6.9    1.9    639.6  2635.3
1987    3845.3    2515.8    9.38    6.1    3.6    669.0  2670.7
1988    4016.9    2606.5    9.71    5.4    4.1    705.7  2800.5
1989    4117.7    2656.8    9.26    5.2    4.8    716.9  2869.0
1990    4155.8    2682.2    9.32    5.4    5.4    690.3  2893.3
End
Name c9='infla1' c10='infla2' c11='infla3' c12='income1' &
     c13='income2' c14='income3' c15='gnp1' c16='growth'
Let 'infla1' = Lag('infla')
Let 'infla2' = Lag('infla1')
Let 'infla3' = Lag('infla2')
Let 'income1'= Lag('income')
Let 'income2'= Lag('income1')
Let 'income3'= Lag('income2')
Let 'gnp1'   = Lag('gnp')
Let 'growth' = 100*('gnp'/'gnp1' - 1)
# (1) Consumption function with absolute income and interest
Regress 'cons' on 3 'income' 'interest';
    Sresiduals c17;
    Fits c18;
    Residuals c19;
    VIF;
    DW.
# (2) Consumption function with expected income'
Regress 'income' 3 'income1' 'income2' 'income3';
    Sresiduals c20;
    Fits c21;
    Residuals c22;
    VIF;
    DW.
Regress 'cons' on 1 c21 std.resid c22 fits c23;
    Residuals c24;
    DW.
# '(3) Inflation and Unemployment'
Regress 'infla' on 3 'infla1' 'infla2' 'infla3';
    Sresiduals c25;
    Fits c26;
    Residuals c27;
    DW.
Let c28='infla' - c26
Name c28='UAI'
Regress 'unemp' on 1 'uai';
    DW.
# (4) Investment function with GDP and interest
Regress 'invest' on 2 'gdp' 'interest';
    DW.
```

Concept

Chapter 9. Autoregression, Weighted Regression, and Ridge Regression: Serial Correlation, Heteroscedasticity, and Multicollinearity

General Assumptions of OLS Method

In this chapter, we discuss the problems of (1) serial correlation, (2) heteroscedasticity, and (3) multicollinearity. In estimating the simple and multiple regression coefficients, the OLS (ordinary least squares) method is usually used. As stated before in chapter 7, the ordinary least-squares (OLS) method is based on the following assumptions:

1. The mean value of the error terms is zero: $E(e) = 0$
2. The error terms are independent (absence of serial correlation): $cov(e_i, e_j) = 0$
3. The variance of the error terms is constant (condition of homoscedasticity, i.e., absence of heteroscedasticity): $Var(e_i) = \sigma^2$
4. The error term and independent variable are independent: $cov(e_i, X_i) = 0$
5. The independent variables are independent of each other (absence of multicollinearity): $Cov(X_i, X_j) = 0$
6. The dependent variable is not correlated to the error term (absence of simultaneous equation bias): $Cov(e_i, Y_i) = 0$
7. The model is correctly specified (All relevant variables are included in the model, and the functional relationship is correctly expressed.)
8. The independent variable is a fixed (deterministic) variable, but the dependent variable Y is a random (stochastic) variable. The dependent variable should not be a categorical variable (in such a case, use discriminant, logit, or probit models)
9. The dependent and independent variables are measured without errors (absence of measurement errors)
10. The relationship between dependent and independent variables is linear.

If one of the above assumptions is not met, the OLS estimators may be biased, inconsistent, or inefficient. Desirable properties of an estimator is given below. OLS estimators are said BLUE (best linear estimator), if the first 3 conditions are met: ($\hat{y}$ = an estimator):

1. An estimator (estimating formula) is unbiased if the estimate (estimated value) is equal to the unknown parameter: $E(\hat{y}) = y$.
2. An estimator is efficient if the estimate has a minimum variance as compared with any other estimates obtained using any other econometric methods: $Var(\hat{y}_1) < Var(\hat{y}_2) < Var(\hat{y}_3)$ ...
3. An estimator is a linear estimator if the estimate is a linear function of the sample observations.

$$\bar{Y} = \Sigma Y/N = (1/N)(Y_1+Y_2+...) = Y_1/N + Y_2/N + ...$$

4. An estimator is consistent if the estimate approaches the true value as the sample size increases:

A. Serial Correlation and Autoregression

Use of DW Statistic

Autocorrelation is a correlation between successive values of the same variable. In practice, serial correlation and autocorrelation are synonymously used, though serial correlation can mean corre-lation with other lagged time series variables. If autocorrelation of the error term is significant, it can be an indication of misspecification of the model. That is, an important variable may be missing, or a functional relationship may be wrong. In such cases, if the OLS method is used, the estimated standard error of the regression will be biased downward, and incorrect conclusions can be derived as to the significance of variables.

The DW statistic is used to detect an autocorrelation. The first order autocorrelation (serial correlation) is the regression coefficient ρ in the following function of successive residuals:

$$e_t = \rho \, e_{t-1} + v_t$$

where $\rho = \sum_{t=2}^{n} e_t \, e_{t-1} / \sum_{t=2}^{n} e_{t-1}^2$.

The DW statistic is calculated by the following:

$$DW = \sum_{t=2}^{n} (e_t - e_{t-1})^2 / \sum_{t=1}^{n} e_t^2 \approx 2(1-\rho)$$

The relationship between the autocorrelation and the DW statistic is given by:

$$DW = \sum (e_t - e_{t-1})^2 / \sum e_t^2 = (\sum e_t^2 - 2 \sum e_t \, e_{t-1} + \sum e_{t-1}^2) / \sum e_t^2$$

Since $\sum_{t=1}^{n} e_t^2$ is very close to $\sum_{t=2}^{n} e_{t-1}^2$,

$$DW \approx (2 \sum e_t^2 - 2 \sum e_t \, e_{t-1}) / \sum e_t^2 = 2 (1 - \sum e_t \, e_{t-1} / \sum e_t^2) \approx 2 (1 - \rho)$$

where $\rho = \sum e_t \, e_{t-1} / \sum e_t^2$.

So, if the autocorrelation coefficient ρ is zero, DW is 2.0. If $\rho \neq 0$, DW will diverge from 2. For instance, if DW = 1.935, which is very close to 2.0.

The decision rule is:

$H_0: \rho = 0$ Accept   if $4-d_U < DW < d_L$
                      if $d_U < DW < 2$

$H_A: \rho \neq 0$ Accept   if $4-d_L < DW < 4$ (negative ρ)
                      if $0 < DW < d_L$ (positive ρ)

Indeterminate   if $d_L < DW < d_U$
                      if $4-d_U < DW < 4 - d_L$

where d_L = the lower limit, d_U = the upper limit of the significance points in the table of critical DW statistics. The lower and upper limits of the DW statistic varies with the number of observations and the number of independent variables. If the number of observation is 15, and the number of independent variables is 2, $d_L = 0.95$, and $d_U = 1.54$. So, we should conclude that the serial correlation is not significant.

If an independent variable is the lagged dependent variable, instead of Durbin-Watson statistic, Durbin's h statistic is used to test the significance of serial correlation:

$$h = \rho \, [n/(1-n \, Var(b))]^{1/2}$$

where ρ = serial correlation, $Var(b)$ = variance of the coefficient of the lagged dependent variable, n = sample size, h = Durbin's h, which is tested with the z value for the null hypothesis of no serial correlation, if the sample size is large.

Autoregression (Generalized Difference Equation) Method

When the successive error terms are correlated each other, the OLS (ordinary least squares) estimators of regression coefficients are still unbiased and consistent. But it affects efficiency. That is, if the serial correlation is positive, OLS tends to underestimate the true standard error of the estimate. As a result, the true R^2 is overestimated and the standard error of the regression coefficients will be underestimated. In such a case, a variable may be wrongly concluded as significant. Thus, the t-test and F test will no longer be valid.

The serial correlation is detected in terms of the Durbin-Watson test statistic. The first order and second order serial correlations are expressed in the following equations:

(1) $e_t = \rho \, e_{t-1} + u_t$, where $u_t = 0$
(2) $e_t = \rho_1 \, e_{t-1} + \rho_2 \, e_{t-2} + u_t$

The Durbin-Watson test statistic is given by:

(3) $$DW = \sum_{t=2}^{n} (e_t - e_{t-1})^2 \, / \, \sum_{t=1}^{n} e_t^2$$

When the serial correlation coefficient ρ is significant, GLS (Generalized Least Squares) method may be used to remove the effect of serial correlation. There are the following methods:

1. Cochrane-Orcutt two-step procedure (CO2)
2. Iterative Cochrane-Orcutt procedure (COi)
3. Durbin's two-step procedure — *and serial levels*
4. Hildreth-Lu Procedure
5. Prais-Winsten method (PW)
6. Theil-Nagar modification
7. Bayesian method
8. Maximum likelihood procedure (ML)
9. Unconditional least-squares method (ULS, nonlinear least-squares method)
10. Yule-Walker method (YW, two-step full transform method)
11. Iterative Yule-Walker procedure (YWi)

Since the two-step Cochrane-Orcutt procedure is simple and easy to understand, it is explained below:

Given the regression equation,

(4) $Y_t = b_0 + b_1 \, X_t + e_t$

For the period t-1,

(5) $Y_{t-1} = b_0 + b_1 \, X_{t-1} + e_{t-1}$

Multiply (5) by ρ (absolute value if $\rho < 0$),

(6)　　$\rho\ Y_{t-1} = \rho b_0 + \rho\ b_1\ X_{t-1} + \rho\ e_{t-1}$

Subtracting (6) from (5),

(7)　　$\dot{Y}_t - \rho\ Y_{t-1} = (b_0 - \rho b_0) + b_1(X_t - \rho\ X_{t-1}) + (e_t - \rho\ e_{t-1}) = (1-\rho)\ b_0 + b_1(\ X_t - \rho\ X_{t-1}) + e_t - \rho\ e_{t-1}$

which can be rewritten as

(8)　　$Y_t^* = b_0^* + b_1\ X_t^* + u_t$

where $Y_t^* = Y_t - \rho\ Y_{t-1}$, $b_0^* = (1-\rho)\ b_0$, $X^* = X_t - \rho\ X_{t-1}$, and $u_t = e_t - \rho\ e_{t-1}$, where $E(u_t)=0$

By the assumption of Equation (1), the error term is no longer correlated in Equation (7), and OLS can be applied to estimate Equation (8). Equation (7) is the generalized difference equation, and applying the OLS method to Equation (8) is equivalent to using the GLS method.

Minitab does not have a procedure command to estimate the autoregressive models. But, you could do the following: First, use other statistical packages that have such estimation procedures (SPSS, SAS, SHAZAM, Systat, Soritec, Limdep, RATS). Second, using Minitab, you could run the OLS regression on the first differenced variables:

$$Y_t - Y_{t-1} = a + b\ (X_t - X_{t-1})$$

Third, you can write a macro file to do the 2-step Cochrane-Orcutt procedure using Minitab. It takes the following 3 steps:

Step 1: Compute a regression equation and obtain residuals.
Step 2: Compute a regression equation using the residuals to obtain the serial correlation coefficient or regression coefficient of residuals.
Step 3: Using the serial correlation coefficient of the residuals, apply the Cochrane-Orcutt procedure. That is, obtain the generalized differences of variables, and run the OLS regression on the transformed variables.

Exercise Example 9-1: Serial Correlation and Autoregression

The market analyst of Blaisdell Company wants to compute a regression equation to predict company sales with industry sales. File Names: Neter493.inp and Neter493.win

Questions: Run the file and answer the following:
(1) Regression equation (OLS model)
(2) Is the serial correlation significant?
(3) Autoregression equations
(4) Compare the two regression results (OLS and autoregression models)

Minitab File for DOS: Neter493.inp

```
Note 'Serial Correlation Analysis: Neter493.inp'
# Neter, p. 493, Table 13-2, Blaisdell Company Example
Name c1='date' c2='time' c3='company' c4='industry'
# company  'company sales'
# industry 'industry sales'
Read c1-c4;
Format(A6, F4.0, 2F7.0).
1983:1   1   20.96   127.3
     2   2   21.40   130.0
```

```
        3    3   21.96   132.7
        4    4   21.52   129.4
   1984:1    5   22.39   135.0
        2    6   22.76   137.1
        3    7   23.48   141.2
        4    8   23.66   142.8
   1985:1    9   24.10   145.5
        2   10   24.01   145.3
        3   11   24.54   148.3
        4   12   24.30   146.4
   1986:1   13   25.00   150.2
        2   14   25.64   153.1
        3   15   26.36   157.3
        4   16   26.98   160.7
   1987:1   17   27.52   164.2
        2   18   27.78   165.6
        3   19   28.24   168.7
        4   20   28.78   171.7
End
# (1) Step 1: Regression of company sales on industry sales
Regress 'company' on 1 'industry' std.resid c5 fits c6;
   Residuals in c7;
   DW.
Name c7='residual'
Tsplot c7
Plot c7 * c6
# (2) Step 2: Find serial correlation of residuals
Let c8 = Lag(c7)
Correlation c7-c8
Regress c7 on 1 c8;
   Noconstant;
   Coefficient c9.
Print c9
# (3) Step 3: Apply the Cochrane-Orcutt procedure:
#      Obtain the generalized difference equation.
Name c10='complag' c11='indlag'
Let c10=Lag(c3)
Let c11=Lag(c4)
Name c12='compdif' c13='inddif'
Let c12=c3 - c9*c10
Let c13=c4 - c9*c11
Regress c12 on 1 c13 std.resid c14 fits c15;
   Residuals c16;
   DW.
Plot c16 * c15
Tsplot c14
Print c3-c4 c8-c9 c10-c11 c12-c13
# (4) OLS using the First Differences
Let c16 = c3-c10
Let c17 = c4-c11
Name c16='y-dif' 'c17='x-dif'
Regress c16 on 1 c17 std.resid in c18 fits in c19;
   Residuals c20;
   DW.
TSplot c20
Plot c20 * c19
```

Minitab File for Windows: Neter493.win

```
Note 'Serial Correlation Analysis: Neter493.win'
# Neter, p. 493, Table 13-2, Blaisdell Company Example
Name c1='date' c2='time' c3='company' c4='industry'
# company   'company sales'
# industry 'industry sales'
Read c1-c4;
   Format(A6, F4.0, 2F7.0).
1983:1    1   20.96   127.3
     2    2   21.40   130.0
```

```
         3    3   21.96   132.7
         4    4   21.52   129.4
   1984:1    5   22.39   135.0
         2    6   22.76   137.1
         3    7   23.48   141.2
         4    8   23.66   142.8
   1985:1    9   24.10   145.5
         2   10   24.01   145.3
         3   11   24.54   148.3
         4   12   24.30   146.4
   1986:1   13   25.00   150.2
         2   14   25.64   153.1
         3   15   26.36   157.3
         4   16   26.98   160.7
   1987:1   17   27.52   164.2
         2   18   27.78   165.6
         3   19   28.24   168.7
         4   20   28.78   171.7
End
Regress 'company' on 1 'industry';
   Sresiduals c5;
   Fits c6;
   Residuals in c7;
   DW.
Name c7='residual'
TSplot c7
%Resplots c6 c7
Let c8 = Lag(c7)
Correlation c7-c8
Regress c7 on 1 c8;
   Noconstant;
   Coefficient c9.
Print c9
Name c10='complag' c11='indlag'
Let c10=Lag(c3)
Let c11=Lag(c4)
Name c12='compdif' c13='inddif'
Let c12=c3 - c9*c10
Let c13=c4 - c9*c11
Regress c12 on 1 c13;
   Sresiduals c14;
   Fits c15;
   Residuals c16;
   DW.
TSplot c14
%Resplots c14 c15
Let c16 = c3-c10
Let c17 = c4-c11
Name c16='y-dif' 'c17'='x-dif'
Regress c16 on 1 c17;
   Sresiduals c18;
   Fits in c19;
   Residuals c20;
   DW.
TSplot c20
%Resplots c19 c20
```

Note: The regression results have to be converted to the original form. This is explained at the end of the following output.

Edited Partial Output

```
MTB > # (1) Step 1: Regression of company sales on industry sales
MTB > Regress 'company' on 1 'industry' std.resid c5 fits c6;
SUBC>    Residuals in c7;
SUBC>    DW.
The regression equation is
```

```
company = - 1.45 + 0.176 industry
Predictor       Coef        Stdev       t-ratio        p
Constant       -1.4548      0.2141       -6.79      0.000
industry       0.176283     0.001445    122.02      0.000
s = 0.08606      R-sq = 99.9%      R-sq(adj) = 99.9%
Analysis of Variance
SOURCE         DF         SS          MS          F          p
Regression      1        110.26      110.26    14888.15    0.000
Error          18          0.13        0.01
Total          19        110.39
Durbin-Watson statistic = 0.73
MTB > Name c7='residual'
MTB > Tsplot c7

residual-
        -           4
        -
  0.125+
        -                            4   6
        -                              5
        -           5 6 7                      8
        -         3                         7
  0.000+
        - 1                         3            0
        -    2              8           2            9
        -                       9
        -
  -0.125+
        -                    0  1
        -
        -
        -
          +---------+---------+---------+---------+
          0         5        10        15        20
```

MTB > # (2) Step 2: Find serial correlation of residuals
```
MTB > Let c8 = Lag(c7)
MTB > Correlation c7-c8
Correlation of residual and C8 = 0.630
MTB > Regress c7 on 1 c8;
SUBC>    Noconstant;
SUBC>    Coefficient c9.
The regression equation is
residual = 0.631 C8
19 cases used 1 cases contain missing values
Predictor   Coef   Stdev    t-ratio   p
Noconstant
    C8     0.6312  0.1833    3.44     0.003
s = 0.06665
Analysis of Variance

SOURCE       DF        SS          MS          F          p
Regression    1      0.052669    0.052669    11.86     0.003
Error        18      0.079955    0.004442
Total        19      0.132624
MTB > Print c9
    c9  0.631163
```
MTB > # (4) Step 3: Apply Cochrane-Orcutt procedure
```
MTB > Let c10=Lag(c3)
MTB > Let c11=Lag(c4)
MTB > Name c10='complag' c11='indlag' c12='compdif' c13='inddif'
MTB > Let c12=c3 - c9*c10
MTB > Let c13=c4 - c9*c11
MTB > Regress c12 on 1 c13 std.resid c14 fits c15;
SUBC>    Residuals c16;
SUBC>    DW.
The regression equation is
compdif = - 0.394 + 0.174 inddif
Predictor       Coef        Stdev       t-ratio        p
Constant       -0.3941      0.1672       -2.36      0.031
```

```
inddif        0.173758      0.002957        58.77      0.000
s = 0.06715      R-sq = 99.5%      R-sq(adj) = 99.5%
Analysis of Variance
SOURCE        DF          SS          MS          F          p
Regression    1        15.575      15.575    3453.65      0.000
Error         17        0.077       0.005
Total         18       15.652
Durbin-Watson statistic = 1.65
```

Regression Summary:

The above results show the following regression equation:

$$Y_t - 0.6312\, Y_{t-1} = -0.3941 + 0.17376\, (X_t - 0.6312\, X_{t-1}) \qquad (1)$$

To convert the above regression equation to the original form:

Since $-0.3941 = b_0\, (1 - 0.6312)$, $b_0 = -0.3941/(1-0.6312) = -1.0686$.

Equation (1) can be rewritten as $Y_t = -1.0686 + 0.17376\, (X_t - 0.6312\, X_{t-1}) + 0.6312\, Y_{t-1}$ $\qquad (2)$

Ignoring the X_{t-1} and Y_{t-1} terms: $Y_t = -1.4548 + 0.17376\, X_t$ (Neter-Wasserman-Kutner, pp. 498-499)

Also, $s(b_0) = s(b_0')/(1-\rho) = 0.1672/(1-0.6312) = 0.4534$, and $s(b_1) = s(b_1') = 0.0030$.

The following results are obtained using SAS (2 - 5) and SPSS (6 - 8):

```
(1) OLS    Y = -1.4548 + 0.1763 X    DW = 0.735     R²=0.9988   RMSE= 0.0861
(2) ULS    Y = -1.2550 + 0.1749 X    DW = 1.7026    R²=0.9965   RMSE= 0.0682
(3) ML     Y = -1.2877 + 0.1751 X    DW = 1.6604    R²=0.9969   RMSE= 0.0683
(4) YW     Y = -1.2903 + 0.1751 X    DW = 1.6563    R²=0.9970   RMSE= 0.0683
(5) YW(i)  Y = -1.2679 + 0.1750 X    DW = 1.6878    R²=0.9967   RMSE= 0.0682
(6) ML     Y = -1.2876 + 0.1751 X                               SEE=0.0682
(7) PW     Y = -1.2679 + 0.1750 X              Adj R²=0.9967    SEE=0.0682
(8) COi    Y = -0.4883 + 0.1702 X              Adj R²=0.9873    SEE=0.0684
```

Exercise Example 9-2: Serial Correlation and Autoregression

Several economic variables are collected to compute a consumption function and other macroeconomic functions. Run the file and determine if the serial correlation is significant.

```
Note 'Autoregression Analysis'
Name c1='year' c2='gnp' c3='cons' c4='interest' c5='unemp' &
     c6='infla' c7='invest' c8='income'
# invest 'gross domestic investment'
# gnp 'GNP (gross national product)'
# income 'disposable personal income'
Read c1-c8
1970  2416.2   1492.0    8.04   4.8    5.7   381.5  1668.1
1971  2484.8   1538.8    7.39   5.8    4.4   419.3  1728.4
1972  2608.5   1621.9    7.21   5.5    3.2   465.4  1797.4
1973  2744.1   1689.6    7.44   4.8    6.2   520.8  1916.3
1974  2729.3   1674.0    8.57   5.5   11.0   481.3  1896.6
1975  2695.0   1711.9    8.83   8.3    9.1   383.3  1931.7
1976  2826.7   1803.9    8.43   7.6    5.8   453.5  2001.0
1977  2958.6   1883.8    8.02   6.9    6.5   521.3  2066.6
1978  3115.2   1961.0    8.73   6.0    7.6   576.9  2167.4
1979  3192.4   2004.4    9.63   5.8   11.3   575.2  2212.6
1980  3187.1   2000.4   11.94   7.0   13.5   509.3  2214.3
1981  3248.8   2024.2   14.17   7.5   10.3   545.5  2248.6
1982  3166.0   2050.7   13.79   9.5    6.2   447.3  2261.5
```

```
1983    3279.1    2146.0    12.04    9.5    3.2    504.0  2331.9
1984    3501.4    2249.3    12.71    7.4    4.3    658.4  2469.8
1985    3618.7    2354.8    11.37    7.1    3.6    637.0  2542.8
1986    3717.9    2446.4     9.02    6.9    1.9    639.6  2635.3
1987    3845.3    2515.8     9.38    6.1    3.6    669.0  2670.7
1988    4016.9    2606.5     9.71    5.4    4.1    705.7  2800.5
1989    4117.7    2656.8     9.26    5.2    4.8    716.9  2869.0
1990    4155.8    2682.2     9.32    5.4    5.4    690.3  2893.3
End
# (1) Step 1: Regression of company sales on industry sales
Regress 'cons' on 2 'income' 'interest' std.resid c9 fits c10;
    Residuals in c11;
    VIF;
    DW.
Name c11='residual'
Tsplot c11
Plot c11 * c10
# (2) Step 2: Find serial correlation of residuals
Let c12 = Lag(c11)
Correlation c11-c12
Regress c11 on 1 c12;
    Noconstant;
    Coefficient c13.
Print c13
# (3) Step 3: Apply the Cochrane-Orcutt procedure:
#     Obtain the generalized difference equation.
Name c14='cons1' c15='income1' c16='inter1'
Let 'cons1'  = Lag('cons')
Let 'income1'= Lag('income')
Let 'inter1' = Lag('interest')
Name c17='cons2' c18='income2' c19='inter2'
Let c17= 'cons' - c13*'cons1'
Let c18= 'income' - c13*'income1'
Let c19= 'interest' - c13*'inter1'
Regress c17 on 2 c18 c19 std.resid c20 fits c21;
    Residuals c22;
    DW.
Plot c22 * c21
Tsplot c22
# (4) OLS using the First Differences
Let c23 = 'cons'- 'cons1'
Let c24 = 'income' - 'income1'
Let c25 = 'interest' - 'inter1'
Name c23='cons3' c24='income3' c25='inter3'
Regress c23 on 2 c24 c25 std.resid in c26 fits in c27;
    Residuals c28;
    DW.
TSplot c28
Plot c28 * c27
```

Minitab File for Windows: Exam9-2.win

```
Note 'Autoregression Analysis'
Name c1='year' c2='gnp' c3='cons' c4='interest' c5='unemp'  &
    c6='infla' c7='invest' c8='income'
# invest 'gross domestic investment'
# gnp 'GNP (gross national product)'
# income 'disposable personal income'
Read c1-c8
1970    2416.2    1492.0    8.04    4.8     5.7    381.5  1668.1
1971    2484.8    1538.8    7.39    5.8     4.4    419.3  1728.4
1972    2608.5    1621.9    7.21    5.5     3.2    465.4  1797.4
1973    2744.1    1689.6    7.44    4.8     6.2    520.8  1916.3
1974    2729.3    1674.0    8.57    5.5    11.0    481.3  1896.6
1975    2695.0    1711.9    8.83    8.3     9.1    383.3  1931.7
1976    2826.7    1803.9    8.43    7.6     5.8    453.5  2001.0
1977    2958.6    1883.8    8.02    6.9     6.5    521.3  2066.6
1978    3115.2    1961.0    8.73    6.0     7.6    576.9  2167.4
```

```
1979  3192.4   2004.4    9.63   5.8  11.3   575.2 2212.6
1980  3187.1   2000.4   11.94   7.0  13.5   509.3 2214.3
1981  3248.8   2024.2   14.17   7.5  10.3   545.5 2248.6
1982  3166.0   2050.7   13.79   9.5   6.2   447.3 2261.5
1983  3279.1   2146.0   12.04   9.5   3.2   504.0 2331.9
1984  3501.4   2249.3   12.71   7.4   4.3   658.4 2469.8
1985  3618.7   2354.8   11.37   7.1   3.6   637.0 2542.8
1986  3717.9   2446.4    9.02   6.9   1.9   639.6 2635.3
1987  3845.3   2515.8    9.38   6.1   3.6   669.0 2670.7
1988  4016.9   2606.5    9.71   5.4   4.1   705.7 2800.5
1989  4117.7   2656.8    9.26   5.2   4.8   716.9 2869.0
1990  4155.8   2682.2    9.32   5.4   5.4   690.3 2893.3
End
Regress 'cons' on 2 'income' 'interest';
    Tresidual c9;
    Fits c10;
    Residuals in c11;
    VIF;
    DW.
Name c11='residual'
Tsplot c11
%Resplots c9 c11
Let c12 = Lag(c11)
Correlation c11-c12
Regress c11 on 1 c12;
    Noconstant;
    Coefficient c13.
Print c13
Name c14='cons1' c15='income1' c16='inter1'
Let 'cons1'  = Lag('cons')
Let 'income1'= Lag('income')
Let 'inter1' = Lag('interest')
Name c17='cons2' c18='income2' c19='inter2'
Let c17= 'cons' - c13*'cons1'
Let c18= 'income' - c13*'income1'
Let c19= 'interest' - c13*'inter1'
Regress c17 on 2 c18 c19
    Tresidual c20;
    Fits c21;
    Residuals c22;
    DW.
Tsplot c22
%Resplots c21 c22
Let c23 = 'cons'- 'cons1'
Let c24 = 'income' - 'income1'
Let c25 = 'interest' - 'inter1'
Name c23='cons3' c24='income3' c25='inter3'
Regress c23 on 2 c24 c25;
    Tresidual c26;
    Fits in c27;
    Residuals c28;
    DW.
TSplot c28
%Resplots c17 c28
```

B. Heteroscedasticity and Weighted Regression

The OLS regression method assumes that the variance of dependent variable remains constant regardless of the values of independent variables. This condition of constant variance is called homoscedasticity (homoskedasticity), and denoted by a constant variance of the error term, which is equal to the conditional variance of the dependent variable: $Var(e_i) = \sigma^2$. If the variance of dependent variable increases or decreases when independent variables change, the condition is called heteroscedasticity (heteroskedasticity).

In the presence of heteroscedasticity, the OLS regression method leads to unbiased and consistent estimates but leads to inefficient parameter estimates and inconsistent covariance matrix, That is, the variance of the estimated parameter is not a minimum. As a result, statistical tests of the significance may lead to an incorrect conclusion. Heteroscedasticity usually does not occur in the time series data when both independent and dependent variables tend to change in the same magnitude. For instance, both income and consumption change about at the same rate. But heteroscedasticity can occur more often in the cross section data. There are several tests of detecting heteroscedasticity (Gujarati, 1988; Greene, 1990; Pindyck and Rubinfeld, 1991).

1. Graphic method
2. Goldfield-Quandt test
3. Breusch-Pagan-Godfrey test
4. Park test
5. Glejser test
6. Spearman's rank correlation test
7. White's NR^2 test (chi-square test).

In Minitab for Windows, the new macro command "%Resplots" provides residual model diagnostics. However, there is no procedure command for the test of heteroscedasticity. One method is to write a macro file of computing White's NR^2 statistic.

White's Heteroscedasticity Test

The method of computing White's test statistic NR^2 is explained in Webster (1992, p. 722). Assume that there are 2 independent variables:

Step 1: Run the OLS regression on the initial equation, and obtain the residuals (e_i).

$$Y = a_0 + a_1X_1 + a_2X_2 + e_i \qquad (1)$$

Step 2: Square each residual and regress it on the initial independent variables and their cross products, and obtain R^2:

$$e_i^2 = b_0 + b_1X_1 + b_2X_2 + b_3X_1^2 + b_4X_2^2 + b_5X_1X_2 + v \quad (2)$$

Step 3: Multiply R^2 by N (the number of observations) to get NR^2.

White's test statistic is NR^2 which is chi-square distributed. The degrees of freedom is DF = k-1, where k = the number of constants in the auxiliary equation including the intercept constant. In Equation (2), DF = k -1 = 6 - 1 = 5.

The decision rule is:

H_0: $\sigma_i^2 = \sigma^2$ Accept if $NR^2 \leq \chi^2_{\alpha,N}$
H_A: $\sigma_i^2 \neq \sigma^2$ Accept if $NR^2 > \chi^2_{\alpha,N}$

If NR^2 is less than or equal to the critical value of chi-square, accept the null hypothesis of homoscedasticity. Otherwise, accept the alternative hypothesis of heteroscedasticity.

If heteroscedasticity is significant, instead of OLS, we can use WLS (weighted least-squares method), which is a special case of GLS (generalized least squares) method. Under the WLS method, if heteroscedastic variances σ_i^2 are known, the variance can be used as weights to

standardize the dependent and independent variables, and OLS is applied. In Minitab, weighted regression can be obtained using the Weight subcommand in the Regression procedure. The following sample file performs White's test and weighted regression.

Exercise Example 9-3: Heteroscedasticity and Weighted Regression

A health researcher wanted to know the relationship between diabolic blood pressure and age, and collected the data for healthy adult women 20 to 60 years old. The following file checks heteroscedasticity and performs the weighted regression. File Name: Neter421.inp

Questions: Run the file and answer the following:
(1) Obtain the OLS regression.
(2) Is heteroscedasticity significant?
(3) Compare the OLS and weighted regression results.

Minitab File for DOS: Neter421.inp

```
Note 'Weighted Regression: Neter421.inp'
# Neter, p. 421, Table 11-7, Diastolic Blood Pressure Example
Name c1='subject' c2='age' c3='blood'
# blood='diastolic blood pressure'
Read c1-c3
    1   27   73
    2   21   66
    3   22   63
    4   26   79
    5   25   68
    6   28   67
    7   24   75
    8   25   71
    9   23   70
   10   20   65
   11   29   79
   12   24   72
   13   20   70
   14   38   91
   15   32   76
   16   33   69
   17   31   66
   18   34   73
   19   37   78
   20   38   87
   21   33   76
   22   35   79
   23   30   73
   24   37   68
   25   31   80
   26   39   75
   27   46   89
   28   49  101
   29   40   70
   30   42   72
   31   43   80
   32   46   83
   33   43   75
   34   49   80
   35   40   90
   36   48   70
   37   42   85
   38   44   71
   39   46   80
   40   47   96
   41   45   92
   42   55   76
   43   54   71
```

```
44   57   99
45   52   86
46   53   79
47   56   92
48   52   85
49   57  109
50   50   71
51   59   90
52   50   91
53   52  100
54   58   80
End
# (1) Graphic method of checking heteroscedasticity
Plot 'blood' * 'age'
# (2) Weighted regression by Weights subcommand
Regress 'blood' on 1 'age' std.resid in c4 fits in c5;
   Weights are 'age';
   Residuals are in c6;
   DW.
Plot c6 * c5
TSplot c6
# (3) Weighted regression by manual method
Let c7='blood'/'age'
Let c8=1/'age'
Regress c7 on 1 c8 std.resid c9 fits c10;
    Residuals c11;
    DW.
Tsplot c11
Plot c11 * c10
# (4) NR-square Test
# First, run Y = a0 + a1 X + e
# Second, run e² = b0 + b1 X + b2 X² + v and get R²
Regress 'blood' on 1 'age' std.resid c12 fits c13;
    Residuals in c14;
    DW.
Let c15='age'**2
Name c15='agesq'
Let c16=c14**2
Name c16='residsq'
Regress c16 on 2 'age' 'agesq' std.resid c17 fits c18;
   Residuals in c19;
   DW.
```

Minitab Command File for Windows: Neter421.win

```
Note 'Weighted Regression: Neter421.win'
# Neter, p. 421, Table 11-7, Diastolic Blood Pressure Example
Name c1='subject' c2='age' c3='blood'
# blood='diastolic blood pressure'
# Assume the Data File is Neter421.dat on disk A.
Read 'a:Neter421.dat' c1-c3
Plot 'blood'* 'age'
# (1) Regression 1
Regress 'blood' on 1 'age';
   Sresiduals c4;
   Fits c5;
   Weights  'age';
   Residuals c6;
   DW.
Let c7='blood'/'age'
Let c8=1/'age'
Name c7='bloodage' c8='agerecip'
# (2) Regression 2
Regress c7 on 1 c8;
   Sresiduals c9;
   Fits c10;
   Residuals c11;
   DW.
```

```
# (3) Regression 3
Regress 'blood' on 1 'age';
   Sresiduals c12;
   Fits c13;
   Residuals in c14;
   DW.
Let c15='age'**2
Name c15='agesq'
Let c16=c14**2
Name c16='residsq'
# (4) Regression 4
Regress c16 on 2 'age' 'agesq';
   Sresiduals c17;
   Fits c18;
   Residuals in c19;
   DW.
%Resplots c5 c6
%Resplots c10 c11
%Resplots c18 c19
```

In the regression results for Equation (4), find R^2 and multiply it with N to get NR^2 which is chi-square distributed with the degrees of freedom DF = k-1, where k = the number of constants including the intercept constant in the regression equation of the squared errors. In the output, the residual model's $R^2=0.234$, and N = 53, so $NR^2= 12.402$. It is greater than the critical chi-square value 5.99 for the 2 degrees of freedom. So we reject the null hypothesis of homoscedasticity.

Exercise Example 9-4: Heteroscedasticity and Weighted Regression

A student of consumption economics collected the data on consumption and income for 15 male and female consumers. She wanted to compute consumption function but wanted to know if heteroscedasticity is significant. Run the file and find the answer. File Name: Webs712A.inp

In the sample file, White's NR^2 is computed and then weighted regression is performed. The consumption function is

$$C = a + bY + cS + e \qquad (1)$$

Next, to compute White's NR^2, the squared error term is regressed on the intercept constant b_0, and cross products of independent variables, i.e., Y, Y^2, S, S^2, and YS. But $S^2 = S$, so the S^2 term is dropped. But YS term is not dropped since YS is not equal to Y.

$$e^2 = b_0 + b_1 Y + b_2 S + b_3 Y^2 + b_4 YS + u \qquad (2)$$

```
Note 'Weighted Regression - Heteroscedasticity: Webs712A.inp'
# Webster, p. 712, Table 14-1
Name c1='person' c2='cons' c3='income' c4='sex'
# cons    'consumption in $'
# income 'personal income in $1000'
# sex 1 = 'male' 0 ='female'
Read c1-c4
1   51   40   1
2   30   25   0
3   32   27   0
4   45   32   1
5   51   45   1
6   31   29   0
7   50   42   1
8   47   38   1
9   45   30   0
10  39   29   1
End
Brief 3
```

```
# '(1) Step 1: Regression: C = a0 + a1 Y + a2 S + e'
Regress 'cons' on 2 'income' 'sex' Std.resid in c5 and fits in c6;
    Residuals in c7;
    DW.
Tsplot c7
Plot c7 * c6
# '(2) Step 2: Auxiliary regression: '
#   e² = b0 + b1 Y + b2 S + b3 Y² + b4 YS + u
Let c8 = c7**2
Let c9 = 'income'**2
Let c10 = 'income' * 'sex'
Name c8 = 'e**2'  c9 = 'Y**2'  c10 ='Y*S'
Regress c8 on 4 'income' 'sex' c9 c10 std.resid c11 fits c12;
    Residuals c13;
    DW.
Tsplot c13
Plot c13 * c12
# (3) Weighted regression
Regress 'cons' on 2 'income' sex std.resid c14 fits c15.
    Weights 'income';
    Residuals c16;
    DW.
Tsplot c16
Plot c16 * c15
```

In the output, you will find that for the auxiliary regression equation, $R^2 = 0.2151$, N = 15. So, $NR^2 = 15(0.2151) = 3.2265$, and the critical chi-square is 9.4877 for $\alpha=0.05$ and DF = 5-1 = 4. Since the calculated $\chi^2 <$ table χ^2, we accept the null hypothesis: H_0: $\sigma^2_i = \sigma^2$. That is, heteroscedasticity is not significant. So, weighted regression is not needed. For the purpose of illustration, however, a weighted regression is requested in (3) and (4) in the above file.

Exercise Example 9-5: Heteroscedasticity and Weighted Regression

A student of housing economics wanted to compute a demand function for housing. Also, she wants to test if heteroscedasticity is significant. Run the file, evaluate if heteroscedasticity is significant, and obtain the weighted regression.

Minitab has a procedure for weighted regression. The following file shows 3 regression results: (1) Minitab weighted regression, (2) OLS regression, and (3) Weighted regression with transformed data. The method of using transformed data is explained below:

The demand function for housing is given by

$$H = a + b\,Y + e \qquad (1)$$

where H= housing expenditures, Y = income, e = the error term. The transformed function using income with weights is given by

$$H/Y = 1/Y + b + e/Y \qquad (2)$$

Assume that $V(e)=cY^2$, where c = a constant. Then,

$$Var(e/Y) = (1/Y^2)\,Var(e) = (1/Y^2)\,cY^2 = c \quad (3)$$

Since the variance of the error term is now a constant (homoscedastic) in the above transformed equation, the OLS method can be applied to Equation (2).

```
Note 'Weighted Regression:
#  Pindyck-Rubinfeld, p. 131, Tab6-1.dat'
```

```
Name c1='group' c2='housing' c3='income'
# housing 'expenditures on housing(in $1000)'
# income 'national income (in $1000)'
Read c1-c3
1    1.8   5
1    2.0   5
1    2.0   5
1    2.0   5
1    2.1   5
2    3.0   10
2    3.2   10
2    3.5   10
2    3.5   10
2    3.6   10
3    4.2   15
3    4.2   15
3    4.5   15
3    4.8   15
3    5.0   15
4    4.8   20
4    5.0   20
4    5.7   20
4    6.0   20
4    6.2   20
End
Name c4 ='house2' c5='income2' c6='incomesq'
Let  c4 = 'housing'/'income'
Let  c5 = 1/'income'
Let  c6 = 'income'**2
# (1) Weighted regression with Weight subcommand:
Regress 'housing' on 1 'income';
   Weights are 'income';
   DW.
# (2) OLS regression
Regress 'housing' on 1 'income';
   Residuals in c7;
   DW.
Let c8 = c7**2
# (3) For White's heteroscedasticity test
Regress c8 on 2 'income' 'incomesq';
   DW.
# (4) Weighted regression with transformed data:
Regress c4 on 1 c5;
   DW.
```

In the output, we will see the following regression results:

$H = 1.0040 + 0.2296\ Y$ ... Weighted regression
$H = 0.8900 + 0.2372\ Y$ ... OLS regression

Using the transformed data, the OLS regression equation is:

$$H/Y = 0.2495 + 0.7529\ 1/Y + e \qquad \bar{R}^2 = 0.7523$$
$$\quad\ (21.28)^* \quad (7.66)^*$$

To convert to the original form, multiply the above equation by Y to get

$$H = 0.7529 + 0.2495\ Y + e/Y \text{ ... OLS with transformed data}$$

C. Multicollinearity and Ridge Regression

The Problem of Multicollinearity

The condition of high correlation between independent variables is called collinearity or multicollinearity. The existence of multicollinearity can generate the following problems. (Gujarati, 1988, ch. 10, pp. 279-309).

1. In the presence of perfect multicollinearity, the OLS regression coefficients are indeterminate and their standard errors are infinite.
2. In the presence of high multicollinearity, the OLS method tends to increase the variance and covariance of the regression coefficients.
3. As a result of including 2 or more independent variables, R^2 can be large, but none of the related independent variables can be significant, or very few variables can be significant.
4. Some of the related variables can have 'wrong' signs.

If the independent variables are highly correlated, you have to remove some independent variables. But which variables? Also, it can cause an error called the specification error. A specification error means that the estimated regression coefficients can be biased if important variables are not included in a model. Thus, there is no simple rule to apply in including or removing independent variables.

Methods of Detecting Multicollinearity: VIF and CI

There are several methods of detecting multicollinearity:

1. Examine the simple correlation matrix. By definition, if the simple correlation coefficients are significant between the independent variables multicollinearity exists. However, the existence of a significant correlation does not always cause a problem. Lawrence Klein's rule is that if the simple correlation coefficient r is less than the multiple correlation coefficient R, it may not cause a problem.

2. Examine the increases in R^2 when additional independent variables are added. If R^2 does not improve too much, there may exist multicollinearity. In a stepwise regression, ΔR^2 may be negligible when an additional variable is added.

3. Examine the partial correlation coefficients. When the simple correlation coefficient is significant, but the partial correlation coefficient is not significant, it may indicate a significant multicollinearity between the variables. However, the partial correlation test is not always effective in that partial correlation coefficients can be high and yet the problem of multicollinearity can exist.

4. Calculate the VIF (Variance Inflation Factor). Assume that there are 3 independent variables:

$$Y = b_0 + b_1X_1 + b_2X_2 + b_3X_3 + e.$$

To calculate the VIF take the following steps:

First, for variable X_1, calculate R^2 by regressing X_1 on other independent variables, i.e., X_2 and X_3, the VIF for X_1 is given by $VIF(X_1) = 1/(1-R_1^2)$.

Second, regress X_2 on X_1 and X_3, and obtain R^2, and the VIF for X_2 is $VIF(X_2) = 1/(1-R_2^2)$.

Third, regress X_3 on X_1 and X_2, and the VIF for X_3 is $VIF(X_3) = 1/(1-R_3^2)$.

If the independent variable is not related to other independent variables, $R^2 = 0$, and thus VIF = 1. If there is a perfect correlation, $R^2 = 1$, and VIF = ∞. If $R^2 = 0.9$, VIF = $1/(1-0.9) = 10$. Webster (p. 683-684) states that the general rule of thumb is: if VIF = 10 or above, the multicollinearity can be a significant problem. In the sample output, VIF = 4.108, which is far below 10. The Tolerance Value (TV) is defined as $TV = 1 - R_i^2$. Thus the smaller the TV, the larger is VIF. In Minitab, the subcommand VIF will produce VIF values.

5. Calculate the F ratio using the auxiliary regression equations.

Assume there are 3 independent variables:

$$Y = b_0 + b_1X_1 + b_2X_2 + b_3X_3$$

Regress each independent variable on the rest of the other independent variables, and obtain $R^2_{1.23}$, $R^2_{2.13}$, $R^2_{3.12}$.

For instance, the F ratio for independent variable X_1 is calculated by:

$$F_{1.23} = \frac{R^2_{1.23}/(k-2)}{(1-R^2_{1.23})/(N-k+1)}$$

where N = the number of observations, k = the number of independent variables.

The calculated F ratio is compared with the critical value of F distribution with $DF_1 = k-2$ and $DF_2 = N-k+1$. If the $F_{1.23}$ is greater than the critical F value, the independent variable X_1 is significantly correlated with the other independent variables, X_2 and X_3.

6. Calculate the CI (Condition Index)

The condition index (condition number) is given by:
CI = [Maximum Eigenvalue/Eigenvalue of a variable]$^{1/2}$

If the condition index lies between 10 - 30, there is moderate to strong collinearity; and if it exceeds 30, there is severe multicollinearity. (Gurjarati, p. 301). For example, if 3 eigenvalues are given, the Condition Indexes are

$\checkmark$ [2.96138/0.03218] = 9.59
$\checkmark$ [2.96138/0.00644] = 21.4504

The above index 21.4504 indicates a moderate to strong collinearity. As explained in Gujarati, each of the above methods has drawbacks, and we can not tell which method should be used in any particular case.

Remedial Measures for Multicollinearity

Some of the remedial measures are given below (Gujarati, 1988, pp. 302-307; Neter-Wasserman-Kutner, 1990, p. 411-412):

1. One or more independent variables may be dropped from the model. But which variables? It can cause specification errors.
2. Transform variables in the forms of differences. But this can cause the error term serially

correlated.

3. In polynomials, express the variables in the form of deviations from the mean, If the problem persists, try orthogonal polynomials. Under the method of orthogonal polynomials, instead of raw values, a vector of coded coefficients (orthogonal polynomials) that reflect the various degrees of polynomials are used as independent variables (see Exercise Example 11-6).

4. Add new data (observations), and multicollinearity may be reduced. But it is not always possible to add more data.

5. Combine correlated variables into one new variable.

6. Use cross section and time series data to estimate certain coefficients.

7. Use ridge regression method which is a modified OLS method. It estimates ridge-standardized regression coefficients

8. Use the stepwise regression method. It will remove the variables whose contribution to R^2 is negligible.

9. Use factor analysis or principal component analysis to find variables that are closely related.

The underlying idea of ridge regression method may be briefly discussed. The OLS estimator is an unbiased estimator under the required assumptions. However, in the presence of multicollinearity the OLS estimator increases the variances and covariances of the regression coefficients. Is it possible to the variances of the regression coefficients? Ridge regression aims to reduce the variance by including some bias in the OLS estimator. That is, the side effect of reducing the variance is to increase a bias in the estimator. Thus, you have two choices: unbiased estimator and large variance or biased estimator and smaller variance. Given the regression equation $y = \beta X + e$ in matrix form, under the OLS method, the regression coefficient ß is computed by

$$\beta = (X'X)^{-1} X'Y$$

Under the ridge regression method, the ridge standardized regression coefficient ß* is estimated by

$$\beta^* = (X'X + kI)^{-1} X'Y$$

where k is the bias parameter which ranges between 0 and 1. As k increases, the bias in the parameter value increases but the variance falls. The ridge standardized regression coefficients can be plotted against the k value. This plot is called a ridge trace or ridge plot. When the ridge regression coefficient stabilizes at a smallest k value, it can be chosen as an optimal value of k.

The ridge regression method is not available in Minitab (available in SAS, SPSS, Statgraphics, Rats, Shazam, Limdep). The following file deals with the detection of multicollinearity using VIF subcommand.

Exercise Example 9-6. Multicollinearity and Ridge Regression

In Minitab, ridge regression is not available. The following file is to obtain VIF data. A health researcher collected data to study the relation of bodyfat to other variables. The file deals with the detection of multicollinearity. Run the file and evaluate the multicollinearity in terms of the VIF. File Names: Neter412.inp and Neter412.win

Minitab File for DOS: Neter412.inp

```
Note 'Multiple Regression with VIF: Neter412.inp'
# Neter, pp. 412-414: Data are in p. 272, Table 8-1,
# Body Fat Example
Name c1='subject' c2='triceps' c3='thigh' c4='midarm' c5='bodyfat'
# triceps 'skinfold thickness'
# thigh   'thigh circumference'
# midarm  'midarm circumference'
```

```
# bodyfat 'body fat'
Read c1-c5
    1   19.5   43.1   29.1   11.9
    2   24.7   49.8   28.2   22.8
    3   30.7   51.9   37.0   18.7
    4   29.8   54.3   31.1   20.1
    5   19.1   42.2   30.9   12.9
    6   25.6   53.9   23.7   21.7
    7   31.4   58.5   27.6   27.1
    8   27.9   52.1   30.6   25.4
    9   22.1   49.9   23.2   21.3
   10   25.5   53.5   24.8   19.3
   11   31.1   56.6   30.0   25.4
   12   30.4   56.7   28.3   27.2
   13   18.7   46.5   23.0   11.7
   14   19.7   44.2   28.6   17.8
   15   14.6   42.7   21.3   12.8
   16   29.5   54.4   30.1   23.9
   17   27.7   55.3   25.7   22.6
   18   30.2   58.6   24.6   25.4
   19   22.7   48.2   27.1   14.8
   20   25.2   51.0   27.5   21.1
End
Note '(1) Correlation Analysis'
Correlation c2-c5
Note '(2) Regression Analysis'
Regress 'triceps' on 3 'thigh' 'midarm' 'bodyfat' &
      std.res c6 fits c7;
   Residuals c8;
   CookD c9;
   VIF;
   DW.
Note '(3) Stepwise regression'
Stepwise 'bodyfat' 'triceps' 'thigh' 'midarm';
   Fenter = 4;
   Best = 2.
```

Minitab Command File for Windows: Neter412.win

```
Note 'Multiple Regression with VIF: Neter412.inp'
# Neter, p. 412-414: Data p. 272, Table 8-1, Body Fat Example
Name c1='subject' c2='triceps' c3='thigh' c4='midarm' &
      c5='bodyfat'
# triceps 'skinfold thickness'
# thigh   'thigh circumference'
# midarm  'midarm circumference'
# bodyfat 'body fat'
Read 'b:Neter412.dat' c1-c5
Note (1) Correlation
Correlation c2-c5
Note (2) Regression
Regress 'bodyfat' on 3 'triceps' 'thigh' 'midarm';
   Sresiduals c6;
   Fits c7;
   Residuals c8;
   CookD c9;
   VIF;
   DW.
Note (3) Stepwise regression
Stepwise 'bodyfat' 'triceps' 'thigh' 'midarm';
   Fenter = 4;
   Best   = 2.
Note (4) Graphs ... graph commands should be placed last
%Resplots c7 c8
Plot c7*c8
Tsplot c8
```

Edited Partial Output:

```
   (1) Correlation
          triceps     thigh    midarm
thigh      0.924
midarm     0.458     0.085
bodyfat    0.843     0.878     0.142
   (2) Regression
* NOTE *   triceps is highly correlated with other  predictor variables
* NOTE *     thigh is highly correlated with other  predictor variables
* NOTE *    midarm is highly correlated with other  predictor variables
The regression equation is
bodyfat = 117 + 4.33 triceps - 2.86 thigh - 2.19 midarm
Predictor      Coef      Stdev     t-ratio        p        VIF
Constant     117.08      99.78        1.17     0.258
triceps       4.334      3.016        1.44     0.170      708.8
thigh        -2.857      2.582       -1.11     0.285      564.3
midarm       -2.186      1.595       -1.37     0.190      104.6

s = 2.480       R-sq = 80.1%      R-sq(adj) = 76.4%

Analysis of Variance

SOURCE        DF          SS          MS         F         p
Regression     3       396.98      132.33     21.52     0.000
Error         16        98.40        6.15
Total         19       495.39

SOURCE        DF       SEQ SS
triceps        1       352.27
thigh          1        33.17
midarm         1        11.55
Durbin-Watson statistic = 2.24
   (3) Stepwise regression
 Stepwise regression of bodyfat  on  3 predictors, with N =    20
     STEP        1
CONSTANT    -23.63
thigh         0.86
T-RATIO       7.79
S             2.51
R-SQ         77.10
  best alt.
VARIABLE    triceps
T-RATIO       6.66
VARIABLE    midarm
T-RATIO       0.61
   (4) Graphs
Omitted.
```

In the OLS regression results, VIF values indicate significant multicollinearity. The thigh size has a wrong negative sign. Minitab also produced warnings on the collinearity. In the ridge regression results (obtained by SPSS and SAS) for k=0.02 as selected by Neter (1990, p. 414), the improper negative sign is changed to a positive sign.

OLS: $Y = 117.08 + 4.33411 X_1 - 2.85689 X_2 - 2.18606 X_3$ Adj. $R^2 = 0.7641$

Ridge: $\hat{Y} = -7.403 + 0.55535 X_1 + 0.36814 X_2 - 0.19163 X_3$ Adj. $R^2 = 0.7409$

Chapter 10.
Use of Dummy Variables

Types of Measurement and Variables

Dummy variables can be used as independent variables in regression analysis. For the cases where dummy variables are used as dependent variables, see chapter 14 (discriminant, logit, and probit models). To understand the meaning of dummy variables, we start with the types of variables or measurement. Measurement means an assignment of numbers to any events, objects, or things. There are four types of measurements.

1. Ratio level of measurement (Ratio variables)

Numbers are assigned to measure both the "interval" and the "intensity" (ratio) of objects, events, or things. To be called as the ratio level of measurement, it must meet 2 conditions: (1) the number 0 must have an absolute meaning, and (2) the ratio of 2 numbers must measure the intensity of the 2 numbers. Examples are income, consumption, saving, height, length, interest rate, unemployment rate, and inflation rate. The distance (interval) between the two numbers is constant, and the ratio of the two numbers measures "intensity". For the ratio level of measurement, number zero must mean absence of an object or an event. For instance, 20 cm means that it is longer than 5 cm by 4 times, and 0 cm means that there is no length. The ratio level of measurement is also called the cardinal level of measurement. Examples: \$1, \$2; 1 meter, 2 meters; 1 km, 2 km; 1 foot, 2 feet; 1 acre, 2 acres; 1 year, 2 years;... For instance, 5 years is 2.5 times as long as 2 years, and 7 km is 3.5 times as long as 2 km.

2. Interval level of measurement (Interval variables)

Numbers are assigned to measure a constant interval of an object, but it does not measure the intensity of an object. In interval measures, (1) the number zero does not represent an absence of the event, and (2) the ratio of 2 numbers does not represent an intensity. All ratio measures are both ratio measures and interval measures, but not all interval measures are ratio measures. Examples of 'pure' interval measures include the following: measurement of temperature (Fahrenheit and Celsius), test scores, IQ scores, and preference order scale. These measurements are not ratio measures because the 0 and ratio have no meaning fixed meaning. The zero degree does not mean absence of temperature. The 0, 50 and 100 degrees in Celsius correspond to 32, 122, and 212 degrees in Fahrenheit [C=(5/9)(F-32)]. But, the ratio is 100/50 = 2.0 in centigrade, but 212/122 = 1.738 in Fahrenheit.

3. Ordinal level of measurement (Ordinal level or rank order variables)

Numbers are assigned to measure ranks or order of sizes. For example, if there are 3 students, numbers 1, 2, and 3 may be assigned to rank the performance of the 3 students. The rank numbers are ordinal measures, because the rank numbers do not tell how many times, and how much No. 1 is smarter than No. 2. Examples: low income, middle income, high income; young, middle age, old age; elementary education, secondary education, college education. For instance, you can assign numbers 1, 2, and 3 to low, middle, and high income consumers. But, the intervals between the income levels are not necessarily constant. That is, the income gap between the low and middle, and the income gap between the middle and high income levels are not necessarily the same.

4. Nominal level of measurement (Nominal variables)

Under nominal measurement, arbitrary numbers are assigned to distinguish variables. Such variables are called nominal variables, dummy variables, indicator variables, categorical variables, qualitative variables, binary variables, binomial variables, dichotomous variables, multinomial variables, and label variables. For example, you can assign a number 0 to a female consumer and a number 1 to male consumer to distinguish the two groups of consumers, or you can assign a 0 to a male and a 1 to female. Such measurement need not binomial but can be multinomial. Examples are: black and white; liberal, conservative, mediocre, progressive, and opportunist; war time and peace time; inflationary period and deflationary period; married, divorced, widowed, never married; dead and alive; smoker and non-smoker; own a video-phone and do not own a video-phone; bad and good; south, west, north, and east; democrats, republicans, and independent; atheist, buddhist, catholic, jew, moslem, and protestant; first quarter, second quarter, third quarter, and fourth quarter; spring, summer, autumn, and winter.

Dummy variables can be used either as a dependent variable or an independent variable. The cases where dummy variables are used as dependent variables are discussed in chapter 15 (multivariate analysis - discriminant, logit, probit). The cases where dummy variables are used as independent variables are discussed in this chapter. In using dummy variables for regression analysis, the level values and the variable name must not be confused. For example, in case of male and female consumers, there should only one dummy variable called sex with 2 levels (0, 1). In case of seasonal quarters, there should be only 3 dummy variables, each dummy variable with 2 levels (0, 1). That is, it is not the case of one variable with 4 levels or 4 variables with 2 levels as will be seen later in the following examples.

Exercise Example 10-1: Dummy Variables as Independent Variables

The regional manger of a department store wanted to know if consumer expenditures are different with income and sex of the consumer. File Name: Webs712B.inp

Questions: Run the file and obtain the following consumption functions:
(1) $C_3 = c_0 + c_1 Y_3$ for both male and female
(2) $C_4 = d_0 + d_1 Y + d_2 S$ for both male and female with sex dummy variable
(3) $C_1 = a_0 + a_1 Y_1$ for male only
(4) $C_2 = b_0 + b_1 Y_2$ for female only

Minitab File for DOS: Webst712.inp

```
Note 'Dummy Variable to represent sex: Webst712.inp'
# Webster, p. 712, Table 14-1
Name c1='person' c2='cons' c3='income' c4='sex'
# cons    'consumption in $'
# income 'personal income in $1000'
# sex 1 'male' 0 'female'
Read c1-c4
  1  51  40  1
  2  30  25  0
  3  32  27  0
  4  45  32  1
  5  51  45  1
  6  31  29  0
  7  50  42  1
  8  47  38  1
  9  45  30  0
 10  39  29  1
 11  50  41  1
 12  35  23  1
 13  40  36  0
 14  45  42  0
 15  50  48  0
```

```
End
Brief 3
# (1) Consumption function without sex
Regress 'cons' on 1 'income';
   Residuals in c5;   VIFj
   DW.
# (2) Consumption function with dummy variable
Regress 'cons' on 2 'income' 'sex';
   Residuals in c6;   VIFj
   DW.
# (3) Consumption function for male only
Copy 'cons' 'income' c7-c8;
   Use 'sex'=1.
Regress c7 on 1 c8;
   Residuals in c9;   VIFj
   DW.
# (4) Consumption function for female only
Copy 'cons' 'income' c10-c11;
   Use 'sex'=0.
Regress c10 on 1 c11;
   Residuals c12;   VIFj
   DW.
```

Minitab Command File for Windows: Webst712.win

```
Note 'Dummy Variable to represent sex: Webst712.inp'
# Webster, p. 712, Table 14-1
Name c1='person' c2='cons' c3='income' c4='sex'
# cons   'consumption in $1000'
# income 'personal income in $1000'
# sex 1 'male' 0 'female'
Read 'b:Webst712.dat' c1-c4
Brief 3
Regress 'cons' on 1 'income';
   Residuals c5;
   Fits c6;
   DW.
Regress 'cons' on 2 'income' 'sex';
   Residuals c7;
   Fits c8;
   DW.
Copy 'cons' 'income' c9-c10;
   Use 'sex' = 1.
Regress c9 on 1 c10;
   Residuals c11;
   Fits c12;
   DW.
Copy 'cons' 'income' c13-c14;
   Use 'sex' = 0.
Regress c13 on 1 c14;
   Residuals c15;
   Fits c16;
   DW.
%Resplots   c5 c6
%Resplots   c7 c8
%Resplots   c11 c12
%Resplots   c15 c16
```

Edited Partial Output:

```
MTB > # (1) Consumption function without sex
MTB > Regress 'cons' on 1 'income';
The regression equation is
cons = 13.1 + 0.845 income
Predictor      Coef      Stdev      t-ratio      p
Constant      13.053     5.031       2.59      0.022
income        0.8448     0.1400      6.03      0.000
s = 4.086       R-sq = 73.7%      R-sq(adj) = 71.7%
```

```
Durbin-Watson statistic = 1.67
MTB > # (2) Consumption function with dummy variable
MTB > Regress 'cons' on 2 'income' 'sex';
The regression equation is
cons = 12.2 + 0.791 income + 5.11 sex
Predictor        Coef        Stdev      t-ratio        p
Constant       12.211        3.938         3.10    0.009
income         0.7912       0.1107         7.15    0.000
sex             5.107        1.672         3.05    0.010
s = 3.191        R-sq = 85.2%      R-sq(adj) = 82.7%
Durbin-Watson statistic = 2.18
```

Exercise Example 10-2: Seasonal Dummy Variables

Economists Wilson and Keating wanted to forecast new housing starts. They gathered quarterly data on the private new housing starts and mortgage interest rates for 1980-90. Run the file and make forecast for each quarter when the mortgage interest rate is 9.32 %. File Name: Wils235B.inp

```
Note 'Dummy Variables to represent seasons: Wils235B.inp'
# Wilson, p. 235, Table 5-6
Name c1='time' c2='yearq' c3='house' c4='rate'
     c5='q2' c6='q3' c7='q4'
#  yearq       'year and quarter'
#  house       'housing start'
#  rate        'mortgage interest rate, %'
#  q2          'quarter 2'
#  q3          'quarter 3'
#  q4          'quarter 4'
Read c1-c7;
Format(F2.0, A7, F7.0, F10.0, 3F3.0).
 1 1980q1  159.9    13.7300  0  0  0
 2 1980q2  203.3    14.4333  1  0  0
 3 1980q3  272.6    12.6500  0  1  0
 4 1980q4  225.3    14.2633  0  0  1
 5 1981q1  166.5    15.1433  0  0  0
 6 1981q2  229.9    16.2267  1  0  0
 7 1981q3  184.8    17.4267  0  1  0
 8 1981q4  124.1    17.7333  0  0  1
 9 1982q1  113.6    17.4167  0  0  0
10 1982q2  178.2    16.7567  1  0  0
11 1982q3  186.7    16.1733  0  1  0
12 1982q4  184.1    14.0200  0  0  1
13 1983q1  202.9    13.0500  0  0  0
14 1983q2  322.3    12.7600  1  0  0
15 1983q3  307.5    13.6533  0  1  0
16 1983q4  234.8    13.4667  0  0  1
17 1984q1  236.5    13.3300  0  0  0
18 1984q2  332.6    14.0033  1  0  0
19 1984q3  280.3    14.4967  0  1  0
20 1984q4  234.7    13.6500  0  0  1
21 1985q1  215.3    13.0567  0  0  0
22 1985q2  317.9    12.7767  1  0  0
23 1985q3  295.0    12.1367  0  1  0
24 1985q4  244.1    11.7267  0  0  1
25 1986q1  234.1    10.5567  0  0  0
26 1986q2  371.4    10.2533  1  0  0
27 1986q3  325.4    10.2400  0  1  0
28 1986q4  250.6     9.6600  0  0  1
29 1987q1  241.4     9.1433  0  0  0
30 1987q2  346.5    10.3233  1  0  0
31 1987q3  321.3    10.5000  0  1  0
32 1987q4  237.1    10.8533  0  0  1
33 1988q1  219.7    10.0833  0  0  0
34 1988q2  323.7    12.3067  1  0  0
35 1988q3  293.4    10.5033  0  1  0
36 1988q4  244.6    10.3933  0  0  1
```

```
37 1989q1  212.7   10.8033   0  0  0
38 1989q2  302.1   10.6733   1  0  0
39 1989q3  272.1   10.0000   0  1  0
40 1989q4  216.5    9.8200   0  0  1
41 1990q1  217.0   10.1233   0  0  0
42 1990q2  271.3   10.3367   1  0  0
43 1990q3  233.0   10.1067   0  1  0
44 1990q4  173.6    9.9533   0  0  1
End, Data.
# '(1) Correlation'
Correlation 'time' 'house' 'rate' c5-c7
# '(2) Regression for DOS'
Regress 'house' on 4 'rate' c5-c7; std.resid c9 fits c10;
      Residuals c11;
      Fits c12;
      DW.        UIF;
Tsplot c11
Plot c11 * c12
# '(3) Regression for Windows'
Regress 'house' on 4 'rate' c5-c7;
      Residuals c8;
      Fits c9;
      DW.
Tsplot c15
Plot c15*c16
%/Resplots c8 c9
```

Exercise Example 10-3: Testing Supply-Side Economic Policy Years

The supply-side economics argues that if tax rate is reduced, the incentive to work will increase, and so GNP will rise. As a result, tax revenue will increase. To test the effect of supply-side policies, the dummy variable 1 is assigned to the Reagan period, 1981-1990, and 0 is assigned to the other period (Reagan administration ended in 1988, but there was no policy change during 1989-92). You can type the dummy data values for each year in the data set, or you can add statements for the dummy values as shown in the following file. That is, two statements are used for the dummy values. Federal taxes and government expenditures are in current values, so they are adjusted by GNP deflator to obtain real tax revenue and real expenditures. Run the file and find if the supply-side economic policy years are different from the other years.

```
Note 'Budget and Trade Deficits'
# Using dummy variables for 1981-90.
Name c1='year' c2='gnp' c3='cons' c4='interest' c5='unemp' &
     c6 ='infla' c7='invest' c8='income' c9='tax' c10='expend' &
     c11='export' c12='import' c13='price'
# invest 'gross domestic investment'
# income 'disposable personal income'
# gnp     'GNP'
# tax     'federal revenue'
# expend 'federal expenditure'
# price   'implicit GNP deflator'
# except tax and expenditures, all values are in 1982 prices
Read c1-c13;
Format (F4.0, 2F8.0, F7.0, F8.0, 2F7.0, F8.0/   &
          F12.0, F8.0, F7.0, F8.0, F7.0).
1970  2416.2  1492.0    8.04     4.8     5.7   381.5  1668.1
       195.4   207.8  178.3   208.3    42.0
1971  2484.8  1538.8    7.39     5.8     4.4   419.3  1728.4
       202.7   224.8  179.2   218.9    44.4
1972  2608.5  1621.9    7.21     5.5     3.2   465.4  1797.4
       232.2   249.0  195.2   244.6    46.5
1973  2744.1  1689.6    7.44     4.8     6.2   520.8  1916.3
       263.7   269.3  242.3   273.8    49.5
1974  2729.3  1674.0    8.57     5.5    11.0   481.3  1896.6
       293.9   305.5  269.1   268.4    54.0
1975  2695.0  1711.9    8.83     8.3     9.1   383.3  1931.7
```

```
           294.9    364.2    259.7    240.8    59.3
1976      2826.7   1803.9     8.43      7.6     5.8    453.5   2001.0
           340.1    393.7    274.4    285.4    63.1
1977      2958.6   1883.8     8.02      6.9     6.5    521.3   2066.6
           384.1    430.1    281.6    317.1    67.3
1978      3115.2   1961.0     8.73      6.0     7.6    576.9   2167.4
           441.4    470.7    312.6    339.4    72.2
1979      3192.4   2004.4     9.63      5.8    11.3    575.2   2212.6
           505.0    521.1    356.8    353.2    78.6
1980      3187.1   2000.4    11.94      7.0    13.5    509.3   2214.3
           553.8    615.1    388.9    332.0    85.7
1981      3248.8   2024.2    14.17      7.5    10.3    545.5   2248.6
           639.5    703.3    392.7    343.4    94.0
1982      3166.0   2050.7    13.79      9.5     6.2    447.3   2261.5
           635.3    781.2    361.9    335.6   100.0
1983      3279.1   2146.0    12.04      9.5     3.2    504.0   2331.9
           659.9    835.9    348.1    368.1   103.9
1984      3501.4   2249.3    12.71      7.4     4.3    658.4   2469.8
           726.0    895.6    371.8    455.8   107.7
1985      3618.7   2354.8    11.37      7.1     3.6    637.0   2542.8
           788.7    985.6    367.2    471.4   110.9
1986      3717.9   2446.4     9.02      6.9     1.9    639.6   2635.3
           827.9   1034.8    397.1    526.9   113.8
1987      3845.3   2515.8     9.38      6.1     3.6    669.0   2670.7
           913.8   1071.9    451.8    570.3   117.4
1988      4016.9   2606.5     9.71      5.4     4.1    705.7   2800.5
           972.4   1114.2    534.7    610.6   121.3
1989      4117.7   2656.8     9.26      5.2     4.8    716.9   2869.00
          1052.9   1187.2    593.3    647.4   126.3
1990      4155.8   2682.2     9.32      5.4     5.4    690.3   2893.3
          1111.7   1273.0    630.3    667.8   131.5
End
Name c14='tax1' c15='expend1' c16='tax2' c17='expend2' &
     c18='import2' c19='export2' c20='dummy1'
Let 'tax1' = 100*'tax'/'price'
Let 'expend1' = 100*'expend'/'price'
Let 'tax2'    = Lag('tax1')
Let 'expend2' = Lag('expend1')
Let 'import2' = Lag('import')
Let 'export2' = Lag('export')
Let 'dummy1'  = (c1 >= 1981)
# dummy variable dummy 1 is generated with value 1 for period 1981-90 and
# values 0 for the period 1970-80.
Name c21='govdef1' c22='imdef1' c23='govdef2' c24='imdef2'
Let 'govdef1' = 'expend1' - 'tax1'
Let 'imdef1'  = 'import' - 'export'
Let 'govdef2' = Lag('govdef1')
Let 'imdef2'  = Lag('imdef1')
Brief 3
Regress 'tax1'    on 3 'gnp' 'tax2'    'dummy1';
   DW.
Regress 'expend1' on 3 'gnp' 'expend2' 'dummy1';
   DW.
Regress 'import'  on 3 'gnp' 'import2' 'dummy1';
   DW.
Regress 'export'  on 3 'gnp' 'export2' 'dummy1';
   DW.
Regress 'govdef1' on 3 'gnp' 'govdef2' 'dummy1';
   Dw.
Regress 'imdef1'  on 3 'gnp' 'imdef2'  'dummy1';
   DW.
```

Exercise Example 10-4: Chow Test Using a Dummy Variable

The Chow test is used to evaluate if 2 samples are different or they can be combined into one pooled sample. The test can be used for both time series data and cross section data. If the 2 samples are different, it means that regression equations from 2 samples should have significantly different parameters. If the 2 samples are from the same population, the regression parameters should not be significantly different. There are 2 methods.

Method 1: Chow test

Step 1: Calculate 3 regression equations in total: for samples 1 and 2, and for the pooled sample.

Regression for sample 1	$y_1 = a_0 + a_1 x_1 + e_1$	Find ESS_1
Regression for sample 2	$y_2 = b_0 + b_1 x_1 + u_1$	Find ESS_2
Regression for pooled sample	$y_p = c_0 + c_1 x_1 + v_1$	Find ESS_p

where ESS_i = Error Sum of Squares (Sum of Squared Residuals) for samples 1, 2 and the pooled sample.

Step 2: Substitute the ESS_i values in the following F-ratio:

$$F = \frac{(ESS_p - ESS_1 - ESS_2) / k}{(ESS_1 + ESS_2) / (N-2k)}$$

where $N = n_1 + n_2$, total number of observations in the pooled sample, k = the number of coefficients to estimate in each regression equation (including the intercept constant).

Step 3: Compare the above computed F value with the critical value of F.
The degrees of freedom are : $v_1 = k$ and $v_2 = N - 2k$

If the computed $F \leq$ critical value of F, accept the null hypothesis that the 2 samples are the same. If the computed $F >$ critical value of F, accept the alternative hypothesis that the 2 samples are significantly different.

For instance, If $N = 80$, $k = 4$, $\alpha = 0.05$, then the critical $F = 2.4859$

Method 2: Dummy Variable Method

An alternative method is to use the dummy variable.

Step 1:   Estimate the regression equation for the pooled sample:

$Y_1 = a_0 + a_1 X_1 + a_2 X_2 + e_1$ Find ESS_p

Step 2:   Estimate the regression equation with a dummy variable and obtain ESS_d.

$Y_2 = a_0 + a_1 X_1 + a_2 X_2 + b_1 D X_1 + b_2 D X_2 + e_2$ Find ESS_d

where ESS_p = Error Sum of Squares for the pooled sample, ESS_d = Error Sum of Squares for the pooled sample with dummy variable. D = dummy variable: $D = 1$ for sample 1, and $D = 0$ for sample 2.

Step 3: Substitute the ESS_i values in the following F-ratio:

$$F = \frac{(ESS_p - ESS_d) / k}{ESS_d / (N-2k)}$$

where $N = n_1 + n_2$, total number of observations in the pooled sample, k = the number of coefficients to estimate in each regression equation (including the intercept constant).

Step 4: Compare the above computed F value with the critical F value. The degrees of freedom are: $\nu_1 = k$ and $\nu_2 = N - 2k$.

If the computed $F \leq$ critical value of F, accept the null hypothesis that the 2 samples are the same. If the computed $F >$ critical value of F, accept the alternative hypothesis that the 2 samples are significantly different

For instance, If $N = 80$, $k = 4$, $\alpha = 0.05$, then the critical $F = 2.4859$.
(For details, see Dougherty,1992; Gujarati, 1988; Ramanathan, 1992).

The following sample file tests if the male wage rate is significantly different from female wage rate. The dependent variable is log wage rate, and the independent variables are years of experiences and years of education. Run the file, compute the F ratio, and determine if the 2 regressions are different.

```
Note 'Wage study for male and female'
# Cross section data for 1990
# N = 22 workers: male = 11, female = 11
Name c1='code' c2='age' c3='experi' c4='hours'
Name c5='wage' c6='educa' c7='sex'  c8='bonus'
# wage 'wage rate per month in 1000 Won'
Read c1-c8
    1  16.6  0.3  219.2   275.090   9   1    121589
    2  18.5  0.8  225.1   299.292  10   1    278561
    3  22.3  1.2  227.4   368.865  11   1    414678
    4  27.4  2.3  226.0   448.900  12   1    771220
    5  32.0  3.5  226.5   495.813  13   1   1002888
    6  36.9  4.9  228.0   533.899  14   1   1220818
    7  41.9  6.0  228.3   543.966  15   1   1334290
    8  47.0  7.3  229.3   551.458  16   1   1406293
    9  51.8  7.2  231.9   515.045  16   1   1223433
   10  56.5  5.2  229.8   447.131   9   1    830416
   11  63.4  4.6  214.8   413.319   9   1    613080
    1  16.4  0.9  222.4   228.032   9   0    333968
    2  18.5  1.7  227.2   259.593  10   0    561106
    3  21.7  2.5  231.0   298.661  11   0    562650
    4  26.9  2.2  228.8   308.456  12   0    428318
    5  32.2  2.0  226.4   297.776  13   0    459936
    6  37.0  2.4  227.7   295.459  14   0    531433
    7  41.9  3.0  230.4   295.411  15   0    548194
    8  47.0  3.5  230.4   297.887  16   0    530522
    9  51.7  3.5  230.1   288.548   9   0    475656
   10  56.5  2.9  229.6   278.225   9   0    362022
   11  62.8  2.5  231.1   260.393   9   0    265367
End
Name c9 ='Logwage'
Let  c9 = Loge('wage')
# (1) Pooled data for both male and female
Regress 'logwage' on 2 'experi' 'educa';
    DW.
# (2) For male data only
Copy c9  c3  c6 into c10 c11 c12;
    Use c7=1.
Regress c10 on 2 c11 c12;
    DW.
# (3) For female data only
Copy c9  c3  c6 into c13 c14 c15;
    Use c7=0.
Regress c13 on 2 c14 c15;
    DW.
# (4) Sex dummy variable method
Name c16 ='sexexp' c17='sexedu'
```

```
Let   c16 = c3*c7
Let   c17 = c6*c7
Regress 'logwage' on 5 'experi' 'educa' 'sex' 'sexexp' 'sexedu';
  DW.
```

Chapter 11.
Nonlinear Equations and Nonlinear Estimation

The relationship between variables may not necessarily be linear, but nonlinear. Examples are cost curves (total, marginal, average), revenue curves (total, marginal, average), the Cobb-Douglas production function, CES production function, the Phillips curve, population growth curve, income growth, etc. Nonlinear equations may be converted to linear equations, and they can be estimated by the OLS method. However, certain nonlinear equations cannot be transformed to linear equations. Such nonlinear equations may be estimated by the method of NLLS (Nonlinear Least Squares Method, such as Maximum Likelihood Method).

Linear Transformation and Linear Estimation

Many nonlinear equations can be transformed into a linear equation in terms of logarithms. In such a case, OLS can be applied. As an example, the Cobb-Douglas production function is given by:

$$Q = A L^{\alpha} K^{\beta} e$$

where Q = output, A = technological coefficient (efficiency parameter), L = labor, K = capital, and e = the error term. The above Cobb-Douglas production function can be transformed into a linear equation in terms of logarithms:

$$\ln Q = \ln A + \alpha \ln L + \beta \ln K + \ln e$$

Since the above equation is a linear multiple regression equation, the OLS method can be applied.

Nonlinear Equation and Nonlinear Least-Squares Estimation

Some nonlinear equations cannot be easily transformed into a linear equation, and in such cases, nonlinear least squares (NLLS) method may be used. Consider the following equation:

$$\ln Q = \ln \gamma - (\nu/\rho) \ln [\delta K^{-\rho} + (1-\delta) L^{-\rho}] + \epsilon$$

The above equation is a CES (Constant Elasticity of Substitution) production function. Nonlinear estimation methods include direct search, direct optimization, and iterative linearization method. The iterative linearization method uses the property that "any nonlinear function can be expressed as a Taylor series expansion" (Pindyck and Rubinfeld, 1991; Greene, 1990, p. 256)

A 'nonlinear equation' and a 'nonlinear least squares method' (NLLS) should be distinguished. The former refers to a functional relationship, whereas the latter refers to a method of estimation. Not all nonlinear equation needs to be estimated by the method of nonlinear least squares or the maximum likelihood method. In this chapter, we will discuss the methods of estimating nonlinear equations using OLS.

Exercise Example 11-1: Loglinear Equations

The CEO of Black Jack Coal Company noticed that monthly sales curve was not linear but convex. So he asked the quantitative analysis section to fit the following model for trend projection of the monthly sales. Consider an exponential equation

$$y = a\, b^x$$

where y = monthly sales, x = month. In terms of logarithms, the exponential function can be transformed into a linear equation:

$$\ln y = \ln a + (\ln b)\, x$$

As another example, consider $y = a\, X^b$. In logarithms,

$$\ln y = \ln a + b \ln X$$

Run the file and compare the regression results. File Name: Webst725.inp

```
Note 'Loglinear Equation: Webst725.inp'
# Webster, p. 725, Example 14-1
Name c1='month' c2='sales'
# sales 'monthly sales'
Read c1-c2
  1    31
  2    43
  3    61
  4    85
  5   118
  6   164
  7   228
  8   316
  9   444
 10   611
End
Name c3='logsale' c4='logmonth'
Let 'logsale' = Loge('sales')
Let 'logmonth'= Loge('month')
End
# (1) Regression
Regress 'sales' on 1 'month' Std.resid c5 fits in c6;
   Residuals c7;
   DW.
Plots c7*c6
Tsplot c7
# (2) Regression in Log.
Regress 'logsale' on 1 'logmonth' std.resid c8 fits in c9;
   Residuals c10;
   DW.
Plots c10*c9
Tsplot c10
%Resplots c6 c7
%Resplots c9 c10
```

(handwritten annotations:) let C3 = loge(c2)
(1) Regression
Regress C3 on 1 c1;
DW.
plot C2*C1
plot C3*C1

Note: The macro file command **%Resplots** is applicable only in Minitab for Windows.

Edited Partial Output:

```
MTB > Plots 'sales'*'month'
 Sales
 600+
   -
   -                                          *
   -
   -                                     *
 400+
   -
   -                              *
   -
   -                        *
```

```
200+
  -                                               *
  -                                       *
  -                               *       *
  -               *       *
 0+
 --+---------+---------+---------+---------+---------+----month
  0.0       2.0       4.0       6.0       8.0      10.0
```

```
MTB > # (2) Regression in raw data
MTB > Regress 'sales' on 1 'month' Std.resid c5 fits in c6;
SUBC>      Residuals c7;
SUBC>      DW.
The regression equation is
sales = - 116 + 59.3 month
Predictor       Coef      Stdev      t-ratio        p
Constant      -115.80      51.68       -2.24      0.055
month          59.255       8.329       7.11      0.000
s = 75.65       R-sq = 86.4%      R-sq(adj) = 84.6%
Analysis of Variance
SOURCE        DF         SS          MS         F        p
Regression     1       289666      289666      50.61    0.000
Error          8        45787        5723
Total          9       335453
Durbin-Watson statistic = 0.51
MTB > Tsplot c7
    150+
      -                                      0
C7    -
      -
      -     1
    75+
      -
      -        2
      -                                  9
      -
     0+          3
      -
      -             4
      -                           8
      -              5
   -75+                     6   7
      -
       +-----+-----+-----+-----+-----+
       0     2     4     6     8    10
MTB > # (3) Regression in Log.
MTB > Regress 'logsale' on 1 'logmonth' std.resid c8 fits in c9;
SUBC>      Residuals c10;
SUBC>      DW.
The regression equation is
logsale = 2.96 + 1.30 logmonth
Predictor       Coef      Stdev      t-ratio        p
Constant       2.9609     0.2438      12.15      0.000
logmonth       1.3046     0.1466       8.90      0.000
s = 0.3224      R-sq = 90.8%      R-sq(adj) = 89.7%
Analysis of Variance
SOURCE        DF         SS          MS         F        p
Regression     1        8.2311      8.2311     79.19    0.000
Error          8        0.8316      0.1039
Total          9        9.0627
Durbin-Watson statistic = 0.58
MTB > Tsplot c10
C10    -    1                           0
       -
       -
  0.300+
       -                                  9
       -
       -
```

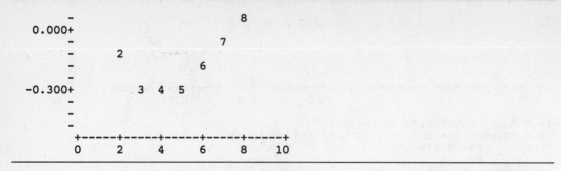

```
          -                                    8
   0.000+
          -                              7
          -          2
          -                         6
          -
  -0.300+          3   4   5
          -
          -
          -
          +-----+-----+-----+-----+-----+
          0     2     4     6     8     10
```

Exercise Example 11-2: Polynomial Equations

    In addition to the loglinear models, the quantitative department of Black Jack Coal Company tried linear, loglinear, and polynomial equations to project monthly sales. Run the file and compare the results. Webs725B.inp

(1) $Y = b_0 + b_1 X + e$

(2) $\ln y = \ln b_0 + b_1 \ln X + e$

(3) $Y = b_0 + b_1 X + b_2 X^2 + e$

(4) $Y = b_0 + b_1 X + b_2 X^2 + b_3 X^3 + e$

```
Note 'Loglinear Equation: Webs725B.inp'
# Webster, p. 725, Example 14-1
Name c1='month' c2='sales'
# sales 'monthly sales'
Read c1-c2
  1    31
  2    43
  3    61
  4    85
  5   118
  6   164
  7   228
  8   316
  9   444
 10   611
End
Name c3='logsale' c4='logmonth' c5='month2' c6='month3'
Let 'logsale'  = Loge('sales')
Let 'logmonth' = Ln('month')
Let 'month2'   = 'month'**2
Let 'month3'   = 'month'**3
Note '(1) Regression'
Regress 'sales' on 1  'month'
     std.resid in c7 fits in c8;
     Residuals c9;
     DW.
Note '(2) Regression'
Regress 'sales' on 3  'month' 'month2' 'month3'
     std.resid in c10 fits in c11;
     Residuals c12;
     DW.
Tsplot c9
Tsplot c12
%Resplot c8 c9
%Resplot c11 c12
```

Exercise Example 11-3: Equations with Square Roots and Reciprocals

A personnel manager wanted to know if training increases sales-person's performance. The firm selected 10 sales trainees, and collected data on the number of days of training received and performance score. Run the file and find the answer. File Name: Neter143.inp

```
Note 'Nonlinear Equations: Neter143.inp'
# Neter, p. 143, Table 4-8: Sales Training Example
Name c1='days' c2='score'
# days= 'days of training' score= 'test score'
Read c1-c2
0.5   46
0.5   51
1.0   71
1.0   75
1.5   92
1.5   99
2.0  105
2.0  112
2.5  121
2.5  125
End
# (1) Plot of the data
Plot c2* c1
Tsplot c1
Tsplot c2
MTsplot c2 c1
# (2) Regression
Brief 3
Regress c2 on 1 c1 std.resid c3 fits c4;
   Residuals c5.
Tsplot c5
Plot c5*c4
# (3) Other regression models
Let c6  = c1**2
Let c7  = Sqrt(c2)
Let c8  = Loge(c2)
Let c9  = 1/Sqrt(c2)
Let c10 = 1/c1
Regress c6  on 2 c1 c6
Regress c7  on 1 c1
Regress c8  on 1 c1
Regress c9  on 1 c1
Regress c10 on 1 c1
Exponentiate c1 putin c11
Regress c2 on 1 c11
```

Exercise Example 11-4: Quadratic Equations

A staff analyst for a cafeteria thinks that the number of self-service coffee dispensers in a cafeteria line is related to the sales of coffee. She tried linear and quadratic forms of relationships between the 2 variables. Run the file and compare the two regression equations. File Name: Neter321.inp

```
Note 'Quadratic Equation: Neter321.inp'
# Neter, p. 321, Table 9-1: Cafeteria Coffee Sales Example
Name c1='cafe' c2='dispens' c3='sales'
# cafe     ='cafeteria'
# dispens  ='no. of dispensers'
# sales    ='coffee sales'
Read c1-c3
 1  0  508.1
 2  0  498.4
 3  1  568.2
 4  1  577.3
```

```
     5   2   651.7
     6   2   657.0
     7   3   713.4
     8   3   697.5
     9   4   755.3
    10   4   758.9
    11   5   787.6
    12   5   792.1
    13   6   841.4
    14   6   831.8
End
Let c4='dispens'**2
Name c4='dispens2'
Plot 'sales'* 'dispens'
Gplot 'sales'* 'dispens'
Regress 'sales' on 1 'dispens'
Regress 'sales' on 2 'dispens' 'dispens2' std. res. in c5 fits in c6;
   Residuals in c7;
   DW.
Name  c6='predict' c7='residual'
Let k1 =Mean('dispens')
Let c8='dispens' - k1
Plot 'sales' * c8
Tsplot c7
Plot  c7 * c6
# For Windows
%Resplots c7 c6
```

Exercise Example 11-5: Polynomial Equations - 2 Independent Variables

A researcher thinks the life of a new power cell depends upon the charge rate and temperature. In his experiment, the charge rate was controlled at 3 levels (0.6, 1.0, 1.4 amperes) and the temperature was controlled at 3 levels (10, 20, 30 °C). The researcher is interested in interaction effects and curvature effects. Run the file and determine if such effects are significant. File Name: Neter330.inp

```
Note 'Quadratic Equation with 2 Ind. Var.: Neter330.inp'
# Neter, p. 330, Table 9-4: Power Cells Example
Name c1='cell' c2='charge' c3='temp' c4='cycle'
# cell  ='cell no.'
# charge= 'charge rate'
# temp  ='temperature'
# cycle ='no. of cycles'
Read c1-c4
    1   0.6   10    150
    2   1.0   10     86
    3   1.4   10     49
    4   0.6   20    288
    5   1.0   20    157
    6   1.0   20    131
    7   1.0   20    184
    8   1.4   20    109
    9   0.6   30    279
   10   1.0   30    235
   11   1.4   30    224
End
Let c5='charge'**2
Let c6='temp'**2
Let c7='charge'*'temp'
Name c5='charge2' c6='temp2' c7='chartem'
Regress 'cycle' on 2 'charge' 'temp'
Regress 'cycle' on 5 'charge' 'temp' 'charge2' 'temp2' 'chartem'
Let k1=Mean('charge')
Let k2=Mean('temp')
Let c8=('charge' - k1)/0.4
Let c9=('temp' - k2)/10
```

```
Name c8='chargec' c9='tempc' c10='chargec2' c11='tempc2'
Let c10= 'chargec'**2.
Let c11='tempc'**2.
Let c12= c10*c11
Name c12='chartemc'
Regress  'cycle' on 5 'chargec' 'tempc' 'chargec2' 'tempc2' 'chartemc' &
    std. resid put in c13 fits in c14;
    Residuals in c15;
    DW.
Plot c15 * c14
# Normal Probability Plot
Nscore of c15 put in c16
Plot c15 * c16
Correlation c15 c16
# For Windows
%Resplots c15 c14
```

Exercise Example 11-6: Orthogonal Polynomials

In polynomial regression, a problem is high multicollinearity. To reduce multicollinearity, the following methods can be used: (1) Transform the independent variables to deviations from the mean: x = X - Mean. (2) Transform to z values (standardized values). (3) Use orthogonal polynomials. Orthogonal polynomials are uncorrelated. Under the method of orhtogonal polynomials, instead of raw values, a vector of coded coefficients (orthogonal polynomials) that reflect the various degrees of polynomials are used as independent variables. The method of deriving the coefficients of orthogonal polynomials are explained in Myers (1979, pp.435-445) and Draper and Smith (1981, pp. 266-274), and the orthogonal coefficients are found in the appendix tables of Winer (1971, 1991), Myers (1979), Draper and Smith (1981) and Pedhazur (1982). In the following sample file, polynomial regressions are carried out in raw data, deviations and orthogonal polynomials (Pedhazur, 1982, pp. 415-416). A researcher wanted to know the effect of practice on visual discrimination. Run the file and compare the results.

```
Note 'Orhtogonal Polynomials'
# Pedhazur, Multiple Regression in Behavioral Research
# 2nd ed., 1982, pp. 407-417
Name c1='visual' c2='practice' c3='op1' c4='op2' c5='op3'  &
    c6='op4'    c7='op5'
#    visual          = 'visual discrimination score'
#    practice        = 'no. of practices'
#    op1             = 'orthogonal polynomials degree 1'
#    op2             = 'orthogonal polynomials degree 2'
Read c1-c7
4    2   -5    5   -5    1  -1
6    2   -5    5   -5    1  -1
5    2   -5    5   -5    1  -1
7    4   -3   -1    7   -3   5
10   4   -3   -1    7   -3   5
10   4   -3   -1    7   -3   5
13   6   -1   -4    4    2 -10
14   6   -1   -4    4    2 -10
15   6   -1   -4    4    2 -10
16   8    1   -4   -4    2  10
17   8    1   -4   -4    2  10
21   8    1   -4   -4    2  10
18  10    3   -1   -7   -3  -5
19  10    3   -1   -7   -3  -5
20  10    3   -1   -7   -3  -5
19  12    5    5    5    1   1
20  12    5    5    5    1   1
21  12    5    5    5    1   1
End
Name c8 = 'prac2' c9 ='prac3'    c10='prac4' c11='prac5'
Name c12= 'vmean' c13='pracmean' c14='vdev'  c15='pdev1'
Name c16= 'pdev2' c17='pdev3'    c18='pdev4' c19='pdev5'
```

```
Let 'prac2' = 'practice'**2
Let 'prac3' = 'practice'**3
Let 'prac4' = 'practice'**4
Let 'prac5' = 'practice'**5
Let 'vmean' = Mean('visual')
Let 'pracmean' = Mean('practice')
Let 'vdev'    = 'visual' - 'vmean'
Let 'pdev1'   = 'practice' - 'pracmean'
Let 'pdev2' = 'pdev1'**2
Let 'pdev3' = 'pdev1'**3
Let 'pdev4' = 'pdev1'**4
Let 'pdev5' = 'pdev1'**5
Note '(1) Correlation'
Correlation  'visual' 'practice' 'prac2' 'prac3' 'prac4' 'prac5'
Correlation  'visual' c2-c5
Correlation  'vdev'   'pdev1' 'pdev2' 'pdev3' 'pdev4' 'pdev5'
Note '(2) Plot'
Plot 'visual'*'practice'
Note '(3) Polynomial regression'
Regress 'visual' on 5 'practice' 'prac2' 'prac3' 'prac4' 'prac5'
Note '(4) Polynomial regression in deviations:x=X-Mean'
Regress 'visual'   on 5 'pdev1' 'pdev2' 'pdev3' 'pdev4' 'pdev5'

Note '(5) Polynomial regression in deviations: x and y'
Regress 'vdev'   on 5 'pdev1' 'pdev2' 'pdev3' 'pdev4' 'pdev5'
Note '(6) Orthogonal polynomials regression'
Regress 'visual' on 5 c3-c7
```

Exercise Example 11-7: Cobb-Douglas Production Function

A production manager at GM wants to form a relationship between output, labor and capital. He wants to estimate the following Cobb-Douglas production function:

$$Q = AL^{\alpha} K^{\beta} e$$

where Q = output, A = technological coefficient (efficiency parameter), L = labor, K = capital, and e = the error term. The parameters α and ß are the relative labor and capital shares respectively. They also represent the partial elasticities of labor and capital respectively. If α + ß = 1, it signifies constant returns to scale; if α + ß > 1, increasing returns to scale; and if α + ß < 1, decreasing returns to scale. To estimate the exponents α and ß, rewriting it in logarithms,

$$\ln q = \ln A + \alpha \ln K + \beta \ln L + \ln e$$

Run the file and estimate the parameters.

```
Note 'Cobb-Douglas Production Function'
Note c1='firm' c2='output' c3='capital' c4='labor'
Read c1-c4
1    220  20  10
2    240  15  20
3    250  10  25
4    300  15  30
5    150   5  10
6    200  12  15
7    300  16  30
8    350  20  25
9    500  35  30
10   600  40  45
End
Name c5='output1'  c6='capital1' c7='labor1'
Let c5=Ln('output')
Let c6 = Loge('capital')
Let c7 = Loge('labor')
Note '(1) production function - additive model'
Regress 'output' on 2 'capital' 'labor' std.resid c8 fits c9;
```

```
      Residuals c10;
      DW.
Tsplot c10
Note '(2) production function - Cobb-Douglas model'.
Regress 'output1' on 2 'capital1' 'labor1' &
      std.resid c11 fits c12;
      Residuals c13
      DW.
Tsplot c11
```

Exercise Example 11-8: CES Production Functions
- Nonlinear Least-Squares Estimation Method

An economist at Boma Industry wanted to predict output in terms of a CES (constant elasticity of substitution) production function:

$$\ln q = b + a \ln [d\ L^s + (1-d)\ K^s]$$

where q = output, L = labor, K = capital; b, a, d, s = parameters to be estimated: d = distribution share parameter, s = substitution parameter. Since the above equation cannot be transformed to a linear equation in terms of logarithms, the nonlinear least squares method (iterative numerical method) can be used. Since Minitab does not have the NLLS procedure, an SPSS sample file is given below. Run the file using SPSS and find the parameters.

SPSS File:
```
Title 'Nonlinear Least-Squares Regression'.
* CES Production Function Model.
* Log q = A  + B*Log(C*L**D + (1-C)*K**D).
* z = (d*L**s + (1-d)*K**s).
* d  = distribution share parameter.
* s  = substitution parameter.
* a, b, d, s = parameters to estimate.
* A, B, C, D = parameters to estimate.
* L = labor, K = capital ... variable names.
Data List Free/ L K Q.
Variable Labels  L 'labor'/ K 'capital'/ Q 'output'.
Compute logq = Ln(q).
Begin Data.
10   20   100
12   21   110
15   22   120
16   23   125
17   25   130
End Data.
Model Program  A=0 B=-1 C= 0.5  D =-1.
Compute Pred = A + B*Ln(C*L**D + (1-C)*K**D).
NLR logq.
```

Edited Partial SPSS Output:

```
All the derivatives will be calculated numerically.
  Iteration  Residual SS          A           B           C           D

      1       18.62563840  .000000000  -1.0000000  .500000000  -1.0000000
      1.1     2958.525145  2.94414604  2.07725693  .163602391  -3.6909366
Run stopped after 400 model evaluations and 176 derivative evaluations.
The iterations limit has been reached.
```

Nonlinear Regression Summary Statistics   Dependent Variable LOGQ

Source	DF	Sum of Squares	Mean Square
Regression	4	113.22765	28.30691
Residual	1	4.093456E-05	4.093456E-05
Uncorrected Total	5	113.22769	
(Corrected Total)	4	.04448	

R squared = 1 - Residual SS / Corrected SS =   .99908

```
                                      Asymptotic 95 %
                         Asymptotic   Confidence Interval
Parameter    Estimate    Std. Error   Lower          Upper
A          2.955753172   .227898008   .060034415    5.851471930
B          -.154970131   .188804278  -2.553955939   2.244015677
C           .181865391   .354437368  -4.321688378   4.685419161
D         -3.994648257  4.718864535 -63.95350723   55.964210712
Asymptotic Correlation Matrix of the Parameter Estimates
                   A          B          C          D
A            1.0000     -.0211      .3332      .1089
B            -.0211     1.0000     -.9482     -.9961
C             .3332     -.9482     1.0000      .9718
D             .1089     -.9961      .9718     1.0000
```

Exercise Example 11-9: Nonlinear Least-Squares Estimation Method (NLLS)

A medical student wanted to develop a regression model for predicting the degree of long-term recovery with the number of days of hospitalization. The degree of recovery is measured by the index of prognosis for long-term recovery. The higher index reflects a good prognosis. He wanted to fit the following model:

$$Y = b_0 \exp(b_1 X) + e$$

where Y = the index of prognosis for long-term recovery, X = days of hospitalization, e = the error term. Since the above model is a nonlinear model and cannot be transformed to a linear equation, the nonlinear least-squares method may be applied. Run the file using SPSS and find the Parameters. NWK-552.inp.

SPSS File:

```
Title 'Nonlinear Least-Squares: NWK-552.inp'.
* neter-Wasserman-Kutner, 1989.
* Exponential Equation y = b0 exp(b1*X)+e .
*   y = b0*exp(b1*X) + e.
Data List Free/ patient days index.
Variable Labels
    Patient   'Patient id'
    days      'days hospitalized'
    index     'prognosis index'.
Begin Data.
 1   2  54
 5   5  50
 3   7  45
 4  10  37
 5  14  35
 6  19  25
 7  26  20
 8  31  16
 9  34  18
10  38  13
11  45   8
12  52  11
13  53,  8
14  60   4
15  65   6
End Data.
List All.
Title '(1) Nonlinear regression'.
Model Program b0=0.1 b1=-0.1.
Compute Pred = b0*exp(b1*days).
NLR index.
Title '(2) Nonlinear regression'.
* NonLinear Regression.
MODEL PROGRAM B0=1 B1=-1 .
```

```
COMPUTE PRED2 = B0 * EXP(B1 * days).
NLR index
  /OUTFILE='C:\WINDOWS\TEMP\SPSSFNLR.TMP'
  /PRED PRED2
  /Save pred2 resid(resid2)
  /CRITERIA SSCONVERGENCE 1E-8 PCON 1E-8.
Title '(3) Plots'.
Plot Plot Resid2 with days.
Plot Format = Overlay
  /Plot index Pred2 with days.
Title '(4) Nonlinear regression with derivatives'.
Model Program b0=0.1 b1=-0.1.
   Compute Pred3 = b0*exp(b1*days).
   Derivatives.
   Compute Der.b0 = exp(b1*days).
   Compute Der.b1 = b0*days*exp(b1*days).
NLR index
   /Pred pred3
   /Save=Resid(Resid3) Derivatives Pred3
   /Outfile= 'b:nonlin.out'.
Title '(5) Plots'.
Plot Plot Resid3 with days.
Plot Format = Overlay
   /Plot index Pred3 with days.
```

Exercise Example 11-10: Nonlinear Least-Squares Estimation Method (NLLS)

An electronic product manufacturer started to produce a new product in 2 locations A (1) and B (0). Plant B has more modern facilities and hence was expected to have a higher efficiency than plant A. During the early weeks of production of new products, the learning curve effect was expected to work. That is, for the early weeks, efficiency improves and then stabilizes. The plant manager wanted to fit the following model:

$$Y = b_o + b_1 X_1 + b_3 \exp(b_2 X_2)$$

where Y = relative efficiency, X_1 = location of the plant, X_2 = time in weeks, and b_i = parameters to be estimated. Time (week) is included as an independent variable to see the learning curve effect. The data were gathered for 90 weeks for each plant, but only selected weeks were included in the data set. Since the model cannot be transformed to a linear equation, the nonlinear least squares method (iterative numerical method) should be applied. Run the file using SPSS and find the parameters. File Name: NWK-569.inp

SPSS File:
```
Title 'Nonlinear Least-Squares: NWK-569.inp'.
* Neter-Wasserman-Kutner, 1989.
* Exponential Equation y = a + b*X1 + d*exp(c*X2) + e.
Data List Free/ obs location week effi.
Variable Labels
     obs 'observation'
     location 'plant location'
     week 'week of production'
     effi 'realtive efficiency'.
Begin Data.
  1  1   1   0.483
  5  1   2   0.539
  3  1   3   0.618
  4  1   5   0.707
  5  1   7   0.762
  6  1  10   0.815
  7  1  15   0.881
  8  1  20   0.919
  9  1  30   0.964
 10  1  40   0.959
```

```
11   1   50    0.968
12   1   60    0.971
13   1   70    0.960
14   1   80    0.967
15   1   90    0.975
16   0   1     0.517
17   0   2     0.598
18   0   3     0.635
19   0   5     0.750
20   0   7     0.811
21   0   10    0.848
22   0   15    0.943
23   0   20    0.971
24   0   30    1.012
25   0   40    1.015
26   0   50    1.007
27   0   60    1.022
28   0   70    1.028
29   0   80    1.017
30   0   90    1.023
End Data.
Title '(1) Nonlinear Regression'.
MODEL PROGRAM A=1 B=0 C=-1 D=0 .
COMPUTE PRED1 = a+b*location+d*exp(c*week).
NLR effi
   /OUTFILE='c:nwk569.out'
   /PRED pred1
   /SAVE PRED1 RESID DERIVATIVES
   /CRITERIA SSCONVERGENCE 1E-8 PCON 1E-8 .
Title '(2) Nonlinear Regression with Derivatives'.
MODEL PROGRAM A=1 B=0 C=-1 D=0 .
COMPUTE PRED2 = a+b*location+d*exp(c*week).
Derivatives.
Compute D.a = 1.
Compute c.b = location.
Compute D.d = exp(c*week).
Compute D.c = d*week*exp(c*week).
NLR effi
    /Save=Resid(Reffi2) Derivatives Pred2
    /Outfile 'c:nwk569.out'.
Title '(3) Plots'.
Plot plot Reffi2 With week.
Plot Format=Overlay
    /Plot effi Pred2 With week.
Title '(4) Another model'.
Model Program k=1.3 b=0.5 c=1 d= 0.5.
Compute Pred3 = k/ (1+ b*location+c*d**week).
NLR effi
    /Pred=pred3
    /Save=Resid(Reffi3) Pred3
    /Outifle ='c:nwk570.out'.
Title '(5) Plots'.
Plot Plot Reffi3 With week.
Plot Format=Overlay
    /Plot effi Pred3 With week.
```

Chapter 12.
Chi-Square Tests and Nonparametric Tests

Statistical tests of hypotheses may be divided into two types: (1) parametric tests and (2) nonparametric tests. The differences between parametric and nonparametric tests are summarized below:

Parametric Tests

Parametric tests are used in two cases: (1) when the data variables are measured in the ratio or interval levels, and (2) when the samples are assumed to have been drawn from a certain mathematical population distribution. When the data are interval and ratio variables, the mean and standard deviation have meaning for the specified population distribution. For instance, the z-test assumes that the population is normally distributed. The t-test assumes that the population has the t-distribution, and the F test assumes that the population has the F distribution. The shape and probability are determined by the mean and standard deviation.

Nonparametric Tests

Nonparametric tests are used in two cases. (1) When the data values are measured on the nominal (categorical) level or ordinal level (ranks). If the data are ordinal or nominal, the mean and standard deviation are generally meaningless. That is, nonparametric tests are often used when the mean and standard deviation have no meaning. (2) When there is no specific assumption on the distribution of the population from which the sample data have been drawn. That is, even if the data are interval or ratio variables and thus the mean and standard deviation have meaning, if no specific assumption is made on the distribution of the population from which the samples have been drawn, nonparametric tests can be applied.

Thus, the hypotheses to be tested by nonparametric tests are usually not concerned with specific parameter values. That is, whether the population means are equal or not is not the question. In nonparametric tests, the question is whether two or more medians are equal, whether a sample is a random sample, whether a sample has been drawn from a particular population distribution, or whether two or more samples have been drawn from the same population, or whether 2 or more samples are related or independent.

In effect, nonparametric tests can be used (1) when data values are nominal or ordinal, and (2) when the population distribution is not normal, the sampling distribution does not follow the t distribution or F distribution. Chi-square tests are included in nonparametric tests if the data are nominal or ordinal variables. On the other hand, parametric tests are used (1) when the data are interval or ratio variables, and (2) when the population distribution is normal or has a mathematical distribution.

Types of Parametric and Nonparametric Tests

The parametric tests include:

(1) z-test (for one-mean, two-means, $N \geq 30$)
(2) t-test (for one-mean, two-means, $N < 30$)
(3) F-test (for 3 or more means, for two-variances)

(4) χ^2-test (for one-variance)

The nonparametric tests include:

(1) Chi-square (χ^2) test for the goodness-of-fit
(2) Chi-square (χ^2) test for independence of 2 samples
(3) Chi-square (χ^2) test for equality of population proportions
(4) Chi-square (χ^2) test for population variance
(5) Wilcoxon Signed Rank test for 1 sample
(6) Wilcoxon Signed Rank test for matched samples
(7) Mann-Whitney U test for 2 independent samples
(8) Kruskal-Wallis test for 3 or more independent samples
(9) Friedman test for matched (paired) samples
(10) Spearman rank correlation coefficient
(11) Sign test for 1 sample
(12) Sign test for matched (paired) samples
(13) Runs test for randomness for 1 sample
(14) Kolmogorov-Smirnov test for the goodness-of-fit

Nonparametric Tests in Minitab

The following nonparametric tests are available in Minitab:

(1) Runs	Runs test
(2) Test	Sign test
(3) Sinterval	Sign confidence interval
(4) Wtest	1 sample Wilcoxon signed rank test
(5) Winterval	1 sample Wilcoxon confidence interval
(6) Mann-Whitney	2 sample Mann-Whitney-Wilcoxon rank sum test
(7) Kruskal-Wallis	k-independent sample test
(8) Mood	Mood median test
(9) Friedman	Test for randomized blocks
(10) Walsh	Walsh averages of all pairs
(11) Wdiff	Differences in all pairs
(12) Wslope	All pair slopes
(13) Chisquare	Chi-square test of independence
(14) Chi-square test	For the goodness-of-fit .....

Exercise Example 12-1: Chi-Square Test for the Goodness-of-Fit

Seven Seas, Inc. sells 4 types of boats. Chris Columbus, marketing director, wanted to know if the demand for each type of boat is uniform. He selected a sample of 48 boats sold during the past several months, as shown in the following file. This is a problem which can be solved by the chi-square test for the goodness-of-fit. The null and alternative hypotheses are:

H_0: All boat sales are uniform.
H_A: All boat sales are not uniform.

The chi-square test statistic is computed by:

$$\chi^2 = \Sigma \left[(O - E)^2/E \right]$$

where χ^2 = chi-square statistic, O = observed value, E = expected value. The degrees of freedom DF = k-1, where k = the number of cells. Run the file and find if the boat sales are equal. File

Name: Webst747.inp

```
Note 'Chi-Square Test for the Goodness of Fit: Webst747.inp'
# Webster, p. 747, Table 15-1
Name c1='boat' c2='sale' c3='expected'
# boat   'type of  boats sold'
# sales 'sales of  boats'
# expected ' value of  sales'
Read c1-c3;
Format (A20, F4.0, F4.0).
Pirates Revenge        15  12
Jolly Roger            11  12
Bluebeard's Treasure   10  12
Ahab's Quest           12  12
End
Note (1) Chi-square statistic = k1
Let k1 = Sum((c2-c3)**2/c3)
Count c2 put in k2
Let k3 = k2-1
Note Chi-square statistic is k1:
Note (2) Degrees of Freedom  = K3
Print k1, k3
Note (3) Chi-square cumulative probability (alpha level) = k5
CDF value=k1 putin k4;
 Chisquare DF = k3.
Print k3
Let k5 = 1- k4
Print k5
Note Significance level = k5
```

Edited Partial Output:

```
(1) Compute chi-square statistic  = k1
(2) Degrees of Freedom  = K3
K1      1.16667
K3      3.00000
(3) Chi-square cumulative probability (alpha level ) = k5
K3      3.00000
K5      0.761010
Significance level = k5
```

Since the calculated chi-square, 1.167, is less than the critical chi-square, 7.815 for DF = 4-1 = 3, and α = 0.05, we accept the null hypothesis. Alternatively, the significance level is 0.761 which is greater than 0.05. So we accept the null hypothesis that the boat sales are uniformly distributed.

Exercise Example 12-2: Chi-Square Test for the Goodness of Fit

O'Hare International Airport hired an economist to investigate traffic patterns. The past records of several years showed that there were 3.2 landings per minute on average. The economist wanted to test if the landings are Poisson distributed. Run the file and find the answer. File Name: Webst751.inp

The null and alternative hypotheses are:

H_0: The airplane arrivals are Poisson distributed.
H_A: The airplane arrivals are not Poisson distributed.

The Poisson distribution is given by:
$$P(x) = \mu^x e^{-\mu} / x!$$

where μ = mean= $E(x)$, e = the base of natural logarithm, 2.7182818. Since the mean is given as

$\mu = 3.2$, the Poisson probability is calculated as a function of x (the number of arrivals) (Webster, p. 751, Table 15-1)

x	0	1	2	3	4	5 and over	Total
P(x)	.0408	.1304	.2087	.2226	.1781	.2194	1.0
E_i	8.16	26.08	41.74	44.52	35.62	43.88	200
O_i	10	23	45	49	32	41	200

The Poisson probability for 5 and over is found as follows: Add up all the probabilities for x=0 ~ 4, and subtract the sum from 1.0: $P(x \geq 5) = 1 - P(x \leq 4) = 1 - 0.7806 = 0.2194$. The expected values of x (the number of arrivals) are found by multiplying the total number of arrivals (N=200) with each probability. Given the actual observed and expected values, the remaining step is to calculate the χ^2

$$\chi^2 = \Sigma \left[(O\text{-}E)^2 / E \right]$$

```
Note 'Chi-square test for the goodness of fit: Webst751.inp '
# Webster, p. 751, Table 15-2
Name c1='location' c2='landing' c3='freq' c4='Poisson'
#   location 'data location number'
#   landing 'no. of landing'
#   freq 'frequencies'
#   Poisson 'Poison probability'.
Read c1-c4
1  0  10  0.0408
2  1  23  0.1304
3  2  45  0.2087
4  3  49  0.2226
5  4  32  0.1781
6  5  41  0.2195
End
Name c5='expected'
Set c5
8.16 26.08 41.74 44.52 35.62 43.90
End
Note (1) Chi-square value = k1
Let k1 = Sum((c3-c5)**2/c5)
Count c3 put in k2
Let k3 = k2-1
Note chi-square value k1
Print k1
Note (2) Degrees of freedom = k3
Print k3
Note (3) Significance level (alpha) = k5
CDF value=k1 putin k4;
   Chisquare DF = k3.
Print k4
Let k5=1-k4
Print k5
Note Significance level = k5
```

Exercise Example 12-3: Chi-Square Test for the Goodness of Fit

Dick and Fred wanted to start a membership dining club near the campus of Big University. They interviewed 200 students on the intention to join such a club. The results were classified into 4 categories of living arrangements (type and location of housing and eating arrangements). They wanted to know if the intended club membership is related to the living arrangements. Run the file and find the answer. File Name: Emory538.inp

```
Note 'Chi-Square Test for the Goodness-of-Fit: Emory538.inp'
# Emory p. 538.
Name c1='living' c2='number' c3='actual' c4='cell'
# living 'living arrangements'
```

```
# number 'number interviewed'
# actual 'intended club membership'  cell  'cell number'.
Read c1-c4;
Format (A9, F2.0, F4.0, F3.0).
Dorm      90  16  1
Apart1    40  13  2
Apart2    40  16  3
Home      30  15  4
End
Name c5='expected'
Let 'expected' = ('number'/200)*60
Note (1) Compute chi-square value = k1
Let k1 = Sum((c3-c5)**2/c5)
Count c3 put in k2
Let k3 = k2-1
Note chi-square value k1
Print k1
Note (2) Degrees of freedom = k3
Print k3
Note (3) Significance level (alpha) = k5
CDF value=k1 putin k4;
  Chisquare DF = k3.
Print k4
Let k5=1-k4
Print k5
Note Significance level is k5
```

Example 12-4: Chi-Square Test for the Goodness of Fit

The assembly line of a firm produces 3 components: chip, soldering joint, and circuit board. During the previous week, defective units were 8 chips, 35 soldering joints, and 7 bad boards. During the previous year, when the assembly line was under control, 15.2% of chips, 60.5% of soldering joints, and 24.3% of boards were defective. The quality manager wanted to know if the assembly line is under control during the previous week. Run the file and find the answer. File Name: Siege707.inp

```
Note 'Goodness-of-Fit Test: Chi-Square Test: Siege707.inp'
# Siegel, 707, p. 707, Example
Name c1='part' c2='observed' c3='expected'
# observed='observed number of defective items'
Read c1-c3;
Format(A8, F2.0, F7.0).
chip     8   7.60
solder  35  30.25
board    7  12.15
End
Note (1) Chi-square = k1
Let k1=Sum((c2-c3)**2)
Note (2) Degrees of freedom = k3
Count c2 put in k2
Let k3= k2 - 1
Print k3
Note (3) Significance level (alpha) = k5
CDF value=k1 putin k4;
  Chisquare DF = k3.
Print k4
Let k5=1-k4
Print k5
Note Significance level is k5
```

Exercise Example 12-5: Chi-Square Test for Independence

Wilma Keeto, director of product research at Dow Chemical, wanted to test the effectiveness of insecticides. One insecticide contains dichlorovinyl, and another does not. Wilma distributed the dichlorovinyl-product to 75 consumers and non-dichlorovinyl product to 25 consumers and asked to

rate the effectiveness of the product on a scale: above average, average, and below average.
File Name: Webst757.inp

	dichlorovinyl	non-dichlorovinyl
Above average	20	11
Average	40	40
Below average	15	80

Wilma wanted to know if the two types of insecticides were equally rated. The hypotheses are:

H_0: The rating and dichlorovinyl are independent (not correlated), $O_{ij} = E_{ij}$.
H_0: The rating and dichlorovinyl are dependent (correlated), $O_{ij} \neq E_{ij}$.

The problem of independence or dependence can be solved using the chi-square test of independence. The chi-square statistic is given by:

$$\chi^2 = \sum_{i=1}^{r} \sum_{j=1}^{c} (O_{ij} - E_{ij}) / E_{ij}$$

where the degrees of freedom is: DF= (c-1)(r-1), r = the number of rows, and c = the number of columns, O = observed frequencies, and E = expected frequencies. The expected value of a cell is determined by:

$$\sum r_{ij} \cdot \sum c_{ij} / N$$

where N = total number of frequencies.

The decision rule is:

H_0 Accept if calculated $\chi^2 \leq$ critical χ^2 at DF - (c-1)(r-1), α
H_A: Accept if calculated $\chi^2 >$ critical χ^2 at DF - (c-1)(r-1), α

```
Note 'Chi-Square Test for Independence: Webst757.inp '
# Webster, p. 757, Table 15-5
Name c1='rating' c2='dichlo' c3='nondichlo'
#   dichlo 'no. of persons voted for dichlorovinyl'
#   nondichlo 'no. of persons voted for nondichlorovinyl'
Read c1-c3;
Format(A9, F2.0, F4.0).
Above     20   11
Average   40    8
Below     15    6
End
Chisquare c2-c3
```

Edited Partial Output:

```
Expected counts are printed below observed counts
          dichlo        C3      Total
    1         20         11        31
           23.25       7.75
    2         40          8        48
           36.00      12.00
    3         15          6        21
           15.75       5.25
Total         75         25       100
ChiSq =   0.454 +   1.363 +
          0.444 +   1.333 +
          0.036 +   0.107 = 3.738
df = 2
```

In the above output, the computed chi-square is 3.738. Is it significant ? Minitab does not provide the associated significance level. In the table of chi-square distribution, the critical value of chi-square in the table is 4.605 for the degrees of freedom DF = (c-1)(r-1) = (3-1)(2-1) = 2, and at α = 0.05. Since 3.378 < 4.605, we accept the null hypothesis. That is, there is no correlation between customer rating and the dichlorovinyl.

To compute the significance level, run the following macro file, which will produce the significance level = 0.1543. Since it is greater than 0.05 accept the null hypothesis. k1 (chi-square), k2 (degrees of freedom) are obtained from the above output.

```
Note 'Title Chi-Square Significance Level'
# Required Data: k1 and k3
# k1 = chi-square, k3 = degrees of freedom
Let k1 = 3.738
Let k3 = 2
Note (3) Significance level (alpha) = k5
CDF value=k1 putin k4;
   Chisquare DF = k3.
Print k4
Let k5=1-k4
Print k5
Note Significance level is k5
```

Exercise Example 12-6: Chi-Square Test for Independence

The marketing manger of Hedonistic Auto Sales wanted to know if the rich people think the price of a car is an important factor in purchasing decision. She divided customers into 3 income groups (low, medium, and high), and their opinions were rated on 3 levels (great, moderate, and little). The question is whether the rating of importance of car price is related to income levels. Run the file and find the answer. File Name: Webst759.inp

```
Note 'Chi-Square Test for Independence: Webst759.inp'
#  Webster, p. 759, Example 15-2
Name c1='rating' c2='low' c3='medium' c4='high'
# rating   'Rating of importance '
# income levels 'low'  'medium'  'high'
# Cell numbers are the number of persons
Read c1-c4;
Format (A12,F2.0,2F4.0).
Great       83  62  37
Moderate    52  71  49
Little      63  58  63
End
Chisquare c2-c4
```

Exercise Example 12-7: Chi-Square Test for Independence

A plant manager wanted to know if smoking is related to on-the-job accidents. He gathered the data for 34 workers who had accidents and 32 workers without accidents, and the smokers were divided into heavy and moderate smokers. Run the file and find the answer. File Name: Emory541.inp

```
Note 'Chi-Square Test of Independence: Emory541.inp'.
# Emory, p. 541, ch. 15, Example.
Name c1='smoking' c2='accident' c3='noaccident'
# smoking   'status of smoking'.
# accident 'on-the-job accident'
Read c1-c3;
Format (A10, F2.0, F3.0).
heavy      12  4
moderate    9  6
```

```
nonsmoker 13 22
End
Chisquare c2-c3
Table c2-c3;
  Chisquare 3.
```

Note: The number 3 in the Chisquare subcommand indicates an output level (all).

Exercise Example 12-8: Chi-Square Test for Independence

A male released from federal prison may return to his home town to live or he may go elsewhere. The Federal Correction Agency wanted to know which makes the better adjustment to civilian life. The data are presented in the following file. Run the file and find the answer. File Name: Mason593.inp

	Outstanding	Good	Fair	Unsatisfactory
Hometown	27	35	33	25
Other towns	13	15	27	25

```
Note 'Chi-Square Test of Independence: Mason593.inp'
# Mason, p. 593, Example
Name c1='town' c2='excell' c3='good' c4='fair' c5='unsat'
# unsat = 'unsatisfactory'
Read c1-c5;
Format(A12, F2.0, 3F4.0).
home town    27 35 33 25
other town   13 15 27 25
End
Chisquare c2-c5
```

Exercise Example 12-9: Chi-Square Test for Independence

A firm produces 3 models of rowing machines: basic, designer, and complete. To start a new sales campaign the marketing manager wanted to know if consumer types are related to product types. He divided consumers into two types: practical and impulsive. The data were gathered in a small test market. Run the file and find the answer. File Name: Siege713.inp

```
Note 'Chi-Square Test of Independence: Siege713.inp'
* Siegel, p. 713, Example
Name c1= 'model' c2='practical' c3='impulsive'
#   model 'rowing machine models'
# practical 'practical buyer'
# impulsive 'impulsive buyer'
Read c1-c3;
Format (A11, F2.0, F4.0).
basic       22  25
designer    13  88
complete    54  19
End
Chisquare c2-c3
Table c2-c3;
   Chisquare 3.
```

Exercise Example 12-10: Sign Test for 2-Paired Samples

A market analyst was hired by a retail chain to measure the effectiveness of a promotional game. He selected 12 retail stores, and monthly sales were recorded before and during the promotional game. He wanted to know if the promotional game increased sales. Run the file and find the answer. File Name: Webst762.inp

```
Note 'Sign Test for Two-Paired Samples: Webst762.inp'
# Webster, p. 762, Table 15-7
Name c1='store' c2='before' c3='during'
#  before='sales before the game'
#  during='sales during the game'
Read c1-c3
1     42   40
2     57   60
3     38   38
4     49   47
5     63   65
6     36   39
7     48   49
8     58   50
9     47   47
10    51   52
11    83   72
12    27   33
End
Let c4=c3-c2
Name c4='gap'
Stest mean=0 in c4;
    Alternative +1.
Stest median= 0 in c4;
    Alternative=-1.
Stest median=0 in c4
Sinterval confidence=95 in c4
```

Exercise Example 12-11: Sign Test for 2-Paired Samples

At Samuelson Chemicals, a computer competency test was given to 15 managers before and after a computer training session. Bob Mason wants to know if the computer training session was effective. Run the file and find the answer. File Name: Mason607.inp

```
Note 'Sign Test for Two Paired Samples: Mason607.inp'
# Mason, p. 607, Example.
Name c1='name' c2='before' c3='after' c4='word1' 'word2'
# before='rating before training' after='rating after training'
# word1 ='rating in word' word2= 'rating in word'
# before 1 'poor'  2 'fair'  3 'good'  4 'excel'  5 'outst'
# after  1 'poor'  2 'fair'  3 'good'  4 'excel'  5 'outst'
Begin Data.
Read c1-c5;
Format(A15, F1.0, F4.0, A6, A8).
T.J. Bowers      3    5    good    outst
Sue Jenkins      2    4    fair    excel
James Brown      4    3    excel   good
Tad Jackson      1    3    poor    good
Andy Love        4    4    excel   excel
Sarah Truett     3    5    good    outst
John Sinshi      1    2    poor    fair
Jean Unger       4    5    excel   outst
Coy Farmer       3    1    good    poor
Troy Archer      1    3    poor    good
V.A. Jones       3    5    good    outst
Coley Casper     2    4    fair    excel
Candy Fry        3    2    good    fair
Arthur Seiple    3    5    good    outst
Sandy Gumpp      1    3    poor    good
End
Let c6=c3-c2
Name c6='gap'
Stest mean=0 in c6;
  Alternative +1.
Stest median= 0 in c6;
  Alternative=-1.
Stest median=0 in c6
```

```
Sinterval confidence=95 in c6
```

Exercise Example 12-12: Sign Test for 2-Paired Samples

An advertising agency showed two advertisements to 17 persons. Each person was asked to rate each advertisement on a scale from 1 to 5. The agency wanted to know if the 2 advertisements are significantly different in ratings. Run the file and find the answer. File Name: Siege682.inp

```
Note 'Sign test of 2-Paired Samples: Siege682.inp'
# Data: Siegel, p. 682, Example
Name c1='person' c2='rating1' c3='rating2'
# rating1='rating on ad 1' rating2='rating on ad 2'
Read c1-c3
  1  4  2
  2  2  4
  3  4  5
  4  4  4
  5  4  4
  6  2  5
  7  3  3
  8  4  5
  9  3  5
 10  5  4
 11  3  4
 12  3  5
 13  4  5
 14  5  5
 15  4  5
 16  5  4
 17  2  5
End
Let c4=c2-c3
Name c4='gap'
Stest median= 0 in c4
Stest median= 0 in c4;
    Alternative=-1.
Stest median= 0 in c4;
    Alternative=+1.
Sinterval confidence=95 in c4
Stem-and-Leaf in c4
```

Exercise Example 12-13: Sign Test for One Sample: Mean and Median Tests

Beverly Lundquist, manager of Sandwich Garden Restaurant, measured waiting time for 27 customers. She wanted to know if the mean waiting time is more than 30 minutes. Run the file and find the answer. File Name: Hanke781.inp

```
Note 'Sign Test for One Sample, Median Test: Hanke781.inp'
# Hanke, p.781, Example 20.2
Name c1='time'
# time 'waiting time for lunch'
Set c1
22  33  25  34  36  29  30  27  31
23  30  32  28  32  40  29  31  35
26  34  33  26  27  37  38  32  34
End
Name c2 ='mean1'
Let  c2 = c1-30
Stest median= 0 in c2
Stest median= 0 in c2;
    Alternative=-1.
Stest median= 0 in c2;
    Alternative=+1.
Sinterval confidence=95 in c2
```

Exercise Example 12-14: Mann-Whitney Test for 2 Independent Samples

The Mann-Whitney U test (Wilcoxon Rank Sum test, Mann-Whitney-Wilcoxon test) deals with 2 independent samples. It tests if the two samples have been drawn from an identical population distribution based on rank numbers. On the other hand, the Wilcoxon test (Wilcoxon Signed-Rank test) deals with 2 related (matched pair) samples or 1 sample. It tests if the median of differences between the 2 population distributions is zero, or if the median of a distribution is zero.

The hypotheses are:

H_0: The two samples are from the same population;
The two samples have the same population medians, or the two population medians are equal, $M_{d1} - M_{d2} = 0$.

H_A: The two samples are from different populations;
The two samples do not have the same population medians; or the two population medians are not equal, $M_{d1} - M_{d2} \neq 0$.

The decision rule is:

H_0: Accept if computed z $\leq$ critical z   at α
H_A: Accept if computed z $>$ critical z   at α

A pottery factory manager experimented 2 firing methods. He applied the firing method 1 to 12 clay pieces, and the firing method 2 to 10 clay pieces. He measured the cooling time for the clay pieces. He wanted to determine if the two methods are different in cooling time. The Mann-Whitney test is used since there is no assumption of normality as to the distribution of cooling time. Run the file and find the answer. File Name: Webst773.inp

```
Note 'Mann-Whitney U Test: Webst773.inp'
# Webster, p. 773, Section 15.5: 2-independent samples
Name c1='Method1'  c2='Method2'
# method1 'cooling time with method 1'
# method2 'cooling time with method 2'
Set c1
27  31 28 29 39 40 35 33 32 36 37 43
End
Set c2
34  24 38 28 30 34 37 42 41 44
End
Mann-Whitney confidence 95 in c1 c2
Mann-Whitney confidence 97.5 in c1 c2;
   Alt=-1.
Mann-Whitney confidence 97.5 in c1 c2;
   Alt=+1.
```

Edited Partial Output

```
Mann-Whitney Confidence Interval and Test
Method1    N =  12     Median =      34.000
Method2    N =  10     Median =      35.500
Point estimate for ETA1-ETA2 is      -1.000
95.6 pct c.i. for ETA1-ETA2 is (-7.000,4.999)
W = 130.0
Test of ETA1 = ETA2  vs.  ETA1 n.e. ETA2 is significant at 0.6209
The test is significant at 0.6206 (adjusted for ties)
Cannot reject at alpha = 0.05
```

In the above results, the Wilcoxon 2-sample test (Mann-Whitney U test) statistic is 0.4950. The critical z value is 1.65 for the 10% level (two-tail test). So, we accept the null hypothesis. Alternatively, the significance probability is 0.6209 (or 0.6206) which is greater than 0.1. So, we accept the null hypothesis that the two firing methods are the same. In the above output, Sum of Scores 130.00 and is the sums of rank numbers in sample 1.

Exercise Example 12-15: Mann-Whitney Test for 2 Independent Samples

A training manager in a large chain store divided 22 sales employees into 2 groups, and applied 2 training methods. The training manager wanted to know which training method was better to increase sales. She gathered the sales data for the 22 employees in the 2 training group. Run the file and find the answer. File Name: Emory576.inp

```
Note 'Mann-Whitney U Test for 2 Independent Samples: Emory576.inp'.
# Emory, p. 576.
Name c1='sample' c2='sales1' c3='sales2'
# sample   'sample number'
# sales1   'sales with training method 1'
# sales2   'sales with training method 2'
Read c1-c3
  1    1500    1340
  2    1540    1300
  3    1860    1620
  4    1230    1070
  5    1370    1210
  6    1550    1170
  7    1840    1770
  8    1250     950
  9    1300    1380
 10    1350    1460
 11    1710    1030
End
Mann-Whitney confidence = 95 in c2 c3
Man-Whitney confidence = 97.5 in c2 c3;
    Alternative=-1.
Man-Whitney confidence = 90 in c2 c3;
    Alternative=+1.
```

Exercise Example 12-16: Mann-Whitney Test for 2 Independent Samples

A mechanical aptitude test was given to 9 male and 5 female assembly line workers. The plant manager wants to know if there are differences in the test scores between male and female workers. He assumes that the test scores are not normally distributed. Run the file and find the answer. File Name: Mason618.inp

```
Note 'Mann-Whitney U Test: Mason618.inp'.
# Mason, p. 618, ch. 17, p. 618, Example.
Name c1='score1' c2='score2'
# score1 'male score'
# score2 'female score'
Set c1
1500 1600  670  800  1100  800  1320  1150  600
End
Set c2
1400 1200 780 1350 890
End
Mann-Whitney confidence 95 in c1 c2
Mann-Whitney confidence 97.5 in c1 c2;
    Alt=-1.
Mann-Whitney confidence 97.5 in c1 c2;
    Alt=+1.
```

```
Mann-Whitney confidence 97.5 in c1 c2;
   Alt=+1.
```

Exercise Example 12-17: Mann-Whitney Test for 2 Independent Samples

A Savings and Loan Association wants to know if high income people prefer fixed-rate mortgage loans to variable-rate mortgage loans. In the recent mortgage loan applications, 16 applied for the fixed rate and 14 applied for variable rate. Their income data were given in the application forms. Run the file and discuss if income levels are significantly different between the 2 types of loan applicants. File Name: Siege686.inp

```
Note 'Mann-Whitney test for 2 independent samples: Siege686.inp'
# Siegel, p. 686, Example
Name c1='incomef' c2='incomev'
# incomef 'income of fixed rate group'
# incomev 'income of variable rate group'
Set c1
34   25    41  57  79  22.5  30  17
36   28   240  22  57  68.0  58  49
End
Set c2
37.5  86.5  36.5  65.5  21.5  36.5  99.5
36    91    59.5  31    88    35.5  72
End
Mann-Whitney confidence = 95 in c1 c2
Man-Whitney confidence = 97.5 in c1 c2;
    Alternative=-1.
Man-Whitney confidence = 90 in c1 c2;
    Alternative=+1.
```

Exercise Example 12-18: Wilcoxon Test for 2-Paired Samples

The Wilcoxon test (Wilcoxon matched-pair signed-rank test) deals with 2 paired samples (matched pair) or 1 sample. It tests if the 2 population medians are equal or if the difference between the two population medians is zero. Note that t-test is used to find if the two population means are equal.

Sunglass Hut, Inc. has 16 stores that sell two types of sunglasses: violet and pink. Sanford Ziff, owner of the Hut, wanted to know whether violet and pink sales are the same. He gathered sales data for the 16 stores during the first month of operation. Run the file and find the answer. File Name: Aczel652.inp

```
Note 'Wilcoxon Matched-Pair Signed Rank Test: ACZEL652.inp'.
# Aczel, p. 652, Example (i).
# want to know if violet sold and pink sold are the same.
Name c1='store' c2='violet' c3='pink'
# violet 'violet color sun glasses sold'
# pink   'pink color sun glasses sold'
Read c1-c3
1    56   40
2    48   70
3   100   60
4    85   70
5    22    8
6    44   40
7    35   45
8    28    7
9    52   60
10   77   70
11   89   90
12   10   10
13   65   85
```

```
Name c4='gap'
Let c4 = c2-c3
Note (1) Wilcoxon test for matched 2 samples
Wtest on c4
Wtest on c4;
   Alternative= +1.
Wtest on c4;
   Alternative= -1.
Winterval on c4
Note (2) Mann-Whitney test for 2 independent samples
# For the purpose of comparison
Mann-Whitney c2-c3
Mann-Whitney c2-c3;
   Alternative=+1.
Mann-Whitney c2-c3;
   Alternative=-1.
```

Exercise Example 12-19: Wilcoxon Test for 2-Paired Samples

A market researcher wanted to test the effect of brand name on quality perception. Ten consumers were selected and asked to rate 2 samples of products on an ordinal scale 1 to 100. They were told that one product is a well-known drink and the other is a new product. In truth, however, the two samples were identical. Run the file and find the answer. File Name: Emory572.inp

```
Note 'Wilcoxon test: Emory572.inp'
# Emory, p. 572, Example
Name c1='branded' c2='unbranded'
# branded='branded product'
# unbranded='unbranded product'
Set c1
52   37   50   45   56 51
40   59   38   40
End
Set c2
48   32   52   32   59  50
29   54   38   32
End
Name c3='gap'
Let c3 = c1-c2
Note (1) Wilcoxon test for matched 2 samples
# For the purpose of comparison
Wtest on c3
Wtest on c3;
   Alternative= +1.
Wtest on c3;
   Alternative= -1.
Winterval on c3
```

Exercise Example 12-20: Wilcoxon Test for One Sample

The average number of messages transmitted by a private communications satellite was 149 per hour. The management selected a random sample of 25 operation hours in the recent month and gathered the number of messages transmitted. The management wants to know if the demand for communications by their satellite has declined recently. Run the file and find the answer. File Name: ACZEL653.inp

```
Title 'Wilcoxon Matched-Pair Signed Rank Test: ACZEL653.inp'
# Aczel, p. 653, Example(i)
Name c1='message'
# message='number of messages transmitted'
Set c1
151   144   123   178   105   112   140   167   177   185   129   160
110   170   198   165   109   118   155   102   164   180   139   166   182
End
```

```
Name c2='gap'
Let c2=c1-149
Note Wilcoxon test for 1 sample
Wtest on c2
Wtest on c2;
  Alternative= +1.
Wtest on c2;
  Alternative= -1.
Winterval on c2
```

Exercise Example 12-21: Kolmogorov-Smirnov Test for 1 Sample

The Kolmogorov-Smirnov D test for 1 sample is used to test if an observed sample distribution is the same as a theoretical distribution, and the Kolmogorov-Smirnov test for k-independent samples is used to test if the k-samples are drawn from the same population. Kolmogorov-Smirnov tests use the cumulative distributions for both 1 sample and k samples.

To find student interest in joining a membership-dining club, 60 students were interviewed from each class of freshmen, sophomore, junior, senior, and graduates. The dining club manager wanted to know if there are differences among students in various classes as to their intention of joining the dining club. The theoretical distribution in this case is a uniform distribution. Since Minitab does not have a procedure command for K-S tests, an SPSS sample file is given. Run the file and find the answer. File Name: Emory570.inp (SPSS File)

SPSS File:
```
Title 'Kolmogorov-Smirnov Test of 1 Sample: Emory570.inp'.
* Emory, p. 570.
Data List Free / number.
Variable Labels  number 'no. of students who will join the club'.
Begin Data.
5  9  11  16  19
End Data.
Npar Tests K-S (uniform) = number
    /Statistics=All.
```

Exercise Example 12-22: Kolmogorov-Smirnov Test for 2 Samples

A plant manager wanted to know if on-the-job accident rate is higher among smokers. So, 34 workers with accidents and 34 workers without accidents were selected and they were classified to heavy and moderate smokers. Since Minitab does not have a procedure command for K-S tests, below is given a file for SPSS.

* SPSS File:
```
Title 'Kolmogorov-Smirnov Test of 2 Samples: Emory574.inp'.
* Emory, p. 574.
Data List Free /group accident smoke.
Variable Labels
     group 'accident or no accident'
     /accident 'number of accidents'
     /smoke 'smoking status'.
Value Labels
     group 1 'accident-yes' 2 'accident-no'
     /smoke 1 'heavy smoker' 2 'moderate smoker' 3 'non-smoker'.
Begin Data.
1  12  1
1   9  2
1  13  3
2   4  1
2   6  2
2  24  3
```

```
End Data.
Weight By accident.
Npar Tests K-S = accident By smoke (1, 3).
```

Exercise Example 12-23: Kruskal-Wallis Test, Friedman Test, and Mood Median Test

The Kruskal-Wallis test is used to compare 3 or more independent samples when the data are ordinal data. It is equivalent to One-Way ANOVA in rank. In ANOVA, the k-distributions are assumed to be normal with equal variance. In the Kruskal-Wallis test, such assumptions are not required.

Friedman test is used to test if k-related samples have been drawn from the same population. It is equivalent to Two-Way ANOVA in rank. Mood median test is used to test if 2 or more population distributions have the same medians.

The hypotheses of the Kruskal-Wallis test are:

H_0: All k samples have the same population distribution.
H_A: Not all k samples have the same population distribution.

The decision rule is:

Accept H_0: if computed K $\leq$ critical χ^2 value at DF = k - 1, and α.
Accept H_A: if computed K > critical χ^2 value at DF = k - 1, and α.

The account manager of a store randomly selected 3 customers. She wanted to know if the 3 customers have the same collection period. Run the file and find the answer. File Name: Webst785.inp

```
Note (1) Kruskal-Wallis Test (One-Way ANOVA): Webst785.inp
Note (2) Friedman test (Two-Way ANOVA)
Note (3) Mood median test
# Webster, p. 785, Table 15-11'
name c1='sample' c2='buyer' c3='days'
# days 'collection period'
# buyer 1 'customer 1' 2 'customer 2'
#        3 'customer 3'
Read c1-c3
1  1  28
2  1  19
3  1  13
4  1  28
5  1  29
6  1  22
7  1  21
1  2  26
2  2  20
3  2  11
4  2  14
5  2  22
6  2  21
1  3  22
2  3  17
3  3  16
4  3  15
5  3  29
End
Note (1) Kruskal-Wallis test
Kruskal-Wallis in c3 by c2
Note (2) Friedman test
```

```
Friedman for c3 by c2 blocked by c1
Note (3) Mood test - Mood median test
Mood in c2 by c1
```

Edited Output:

```
MTB > Note (1) K-S test
MTB > Kruskal-Wallis in c2 by c1
LEVEL     NOBS     MEDIAN   AVE. RANK    Z VALUE
    1        7      22.00       11.3       1.13
    2        6      20.50        7.9      -0.89
    3        5      17.00        8.9      -0.30
OVERALL     18                   9.5
H = 1.37   d.f. = 2   p = 0.503
H = 1.38   d.f. = 2   p = 0.501 (adj. for ties)
MTB > Note (2) Mood test - Mood median test
MTB > Mood in c2 by c1
Mood median test of days
Chisquare = 0.80    df = 2    p = 0.671
                                    Individual 95.0% CI's
buyer N<= N> Median  Q3-Q1  ------+---------+---------+---------+
   1   3   4  22.0    9.0            (--------+------------)
   2   4   2  20.5    9.8   (----------------+-------)
   3   3   2  17.0   10.0        (---+-----------------------)
                            ------+---------+---------+---------+
                            15.0      20.0      25.0      30.0

Overall median = 21.0
* NOTE * Levels with < 6 obs. have confidence < 95.0%
```

In the above output, the Kruskal-Wallis test statistic K is represented by the Chisq = 1.38. which is not significant. In the Mood median test, chi-square value is 0.80 with 2 degrees of freedom, which is not significant.

Exercise Example 12-24: Kruskal-Wallis Test for 3 or More Independent Samples
- One-Way ANOVA by Ranks

The pricing manager of the Big Top Supermarket wanted to determine the best price differential between Big Top's brand of canned green beans and the national brands. She divided Big Top's 18 stores into 3 groups, and experimented 3 price differentials: 1 cent, 3 cents, and 5 cents. She gathered gross profits for each store in the 3 groups. She wanted to know if the gross profits are different among the 3 groups of stores due to different discount policies. Run the file and find the answer. File Name: Emory578.inp

```
Note 'Kruskal-Wallis Test: Emory578.inp'
# and Mood Median test
# One-way analysis of variance by ranks
# Emory, p. 578, p. 433, Exhibit 15-1
Name c1='sample' c2='discount' c3='profit'
#   sample 'sample no.'
# discount 'discount policy'
# profit 'gross profit'.
# discount 1 'discount 1' 2 'discount 2' 3 'discount 3'.
Read c1-c3
1   1    6
2   1    7
3   1    8
4   1    7
5   1    9
6   1   11
1   2    8
2   2    9
3   2    8
4   2   10
```

```
5    2    11
6    2    13
1    3     9
2    3     9
3    3    11
4    3    10
5    3    14
6    3    13
End
Note (1) Kruskal-Wallis test: One-way ANOVA
Kruskal-Wallis for c3 by c2
Note (2) Mood median test
Mood for c3 by c2
Note (3) Friedman test:Two-way ANOVA
Friedman c3 by c2
```

Exercise Example 12-25: Kruskal-Wallis Test for 3 or More Samples
- One-Way ANOVA by Ranks

A management seminar leader gave a test to 3 groups of executives from manufacturing, finance, and trade. He wants to know if the 3 groups are equally knowledgeable. If not, he wanted to give 3 separate seminar sessions. He assumes that the test scores are not normally distributed and that the population variances are not the same. Run the file and find the answer. File Name: Mason623.inp

```
Note 'Kruskal-Wallis Test: Mason623.inp'
# and Mood median test
# Mason, p. 623, ch. 17, Example.
Name c1='person' c2='industry' c3='score'
# person 'executives'
# industry 'industry'
# score 'test score'
Read c1-c3
1    1    51
2    1    32
3    1    17
4    1    69
5    1    86
6    1    62
7    1    96
1    2    14
2    2    31
3    2    68
4    2    87
5    2    20
6    2    28
7    2    77
8    2    97
1    3    89
2    3    20
3    3    60
4    3    72
5    3    56
6    3    22
End
Note (1) Kruskal-Wallis test: One-way ANOVA
Kruskal-Wallis for c3 by c2
Note (2) Mood median test
Mood for c3 by c2
Note (3) Friedman test:Two-way ANOVA
Friedman c3 by c2
```

Exercise Example 12-26: Runs Test for Randomness

A set of time series data is a random walk if $E(y_t - y_{t-1}) = E(e_t) = 0$.

Three sets of data are used to test randomness: In the first data set, male and female employees are selected for training purpose. Is the selection random? In the second data set, there is another series of male and female selection for the same question. In the third data set, the daily outputs of coal production are examined. Daily outputs vary. Using the median or the mean value, the production manager wants to know if the daily outputs are random. These 3 data series are represented below:

```
              1   2   3   4   5   6   7   8   9  10  11  12 13 14
```


```
              1   2   3   4   5   6   7   8   9  10  11  12 13 14
─────────────────────────────────────────────────────────────────
Series 1   M   F   M   F   M   F   M   F   M   F   M   F
Runs (r)   1   2   3   4   5   6   7   8   9  10  11  12
r  = 12
n₁ =  6  (number of occurrence of event M)
n₂ =  6  (number of occurrence of event F)
N  = 12 (total observations)
─────────────────────────────────────────────────────────────────
Series 2   M   F   F   F   M   M   M   F   F   M   M   M
Runs (r)   1   2           3           4       5
r  = 5
n₁ =  7  (number of occurrence of event M)
n₂ =  5  (number of occurrence of event F)
N  = 12 (total observations)
─────────────────────────────────────────────────────────────────
Series 3  31  57  52  22  24  59  25  29  27  44  43  32 40 60
           B   A   A   B   B   A   B   B   B   A   A   B  A  A
Runs (r)   1   2       3   4   5               6       7  8
r  = 8
n₁ =  7  (number of occurrence of event B)
n₂ =  7  (number of occurrence of event A)
N  = 14 (total observations)
─────────────────────────────────────────────────────────────────
```

The hypotheses are:

H_0: The data series is random.
H_A: the data series is not random.

If either n_1 or n_2 is less than 20, use the Webster Tables M1 and M2, for instance. Table M1 shows the minimum critical number of runs for $\alpha = 0.05$. Table M2 shows the critically high values for runs.

If either n_1 or n_2 is greater than 20, the normal distribution is a good approximation to sampling distribution of r (Siegel and Castellan, 1988, p. 62).

$$z = \frac{[\, r + h - 2\, n_1\, n_2\, /\, N - 1\,]}{\sqrt{[2\, n_1\, n_2\, (2 n_1\, n_2 - N) / [N^2(N-1)]}}$$

where h is a correction factor: $h = 0.5$ if $r < 2 n_1 n_2 / N - 1$, and $h = -0.5$ if $r > 2 n_1 n_2 / N - 1$

Accept H_0 if computed $z \leq 1.96$ at $\alpha = 0.05$
Accept H_A if computed $z > 1.96$ at $\alpha = 0.05$

File Name: Webst768.inp

```
Note 'Runs test for Randomness: Webst768.inp'
#  Webster, pp. 768-770
# data 1 = 'employee selection'
# data 2 = 'employee selection'
# data 3 = 'coal production'
# data 4 = 'errors of prediction'
Name c1='data1' c2='data2' c3='data3' c4='data4'
# data 1 and 2: 1 'male' 0 'female'
```

```
# data 3: coal production
# data 4: prediction errors 1 'over' 0 'under'
Set c1
1 0 1 0 1 0 1 0 1 0 1 0
End
Set c2
1 0 0 0 1 1 1 0 0 1 1 1
End
Set c3
31 57 52 22 24 59 25 29 27 44 43 32 40 60
End
Set c4
1 1 1 1 1 1 0 0 0 0 0 1 1 1 1 1 0 0
End
Runs c1
Runs c2
Runs c3
Runs c4
```

Edited Output:

```
data1
   K =      0.5000
   The observed no. of runs =  12
   The expected no. of runs =   7.0000
    6 Observations above K     6 below
 * N Small -- Following approx. may be invalid
            The test is significant at  0.0025
   data2
   K =      0.5833
   The observed no. of runs =   5
   The expected no. of runs =   6.8333
    7 Observations above K     5 below
 * N Small -- Following approx. may be invalid
            The test is significant at  0.2524
            Cannot reject at alpha = 0.05
   data3
   K =     38.9286
   The observed no. of runs =   8
   The expected no. of runs =   8.0000
    7 Observations above K     7 below
 * N Small -- Following approx. may be invalid
            The test is significant at  1.0000
            Cannot reject at alpha = 0.05
   data4
   K =      0.5882
   The observed no. of runs =   4
   The expected no. of runs =   9.2353
   10 Observations above K     7 below
 * N Small -- Following approx. may be invalid
            The test is significant at  0.0068
```

Exercise Example 12-27: Rank Correlation - Spearman and Kendall

A correlation coefficient measures the degree (intensity) and the direction of a linear relationship between two variables. A simple correlation coefficient is calculated using an interval or ratio data values, whereas a rank correlation coefficient is calculated when the data values are ordinal values to measure the degree and direction of correlation.

The Spearman rank correlation coefficient r_s is calculated by:

$$r_s = 1 - 6(\Sigma \, d_i^2) \, / \, [\, n(n^2-1) \,]$$

where $\Sigma \, d_i^2$ = the sum of squared differences between the paired rank numbers, n = the number of pairs of observations.

The hypotheses are:

H_0: $r_s = 0$
H_A: $r_s \neq 0$

The significance of a rank correlation coefficient is tested by the z statistic when the sample size N > 30:

$z = r_s / [1 / \sqrt{(N-1)}] = r_s \sqrt{(N-1)}$

The decision rule is:

H_0: Accept if computed z $\leq$ critical z at α
H_A: Accept if computed z > critical z at α

If the sample size N $\leq$ 30, then the special table is used to find the critical values for the Spearman rank correlation coefficients (It is not the t table. For instance, see Webster, 1992, p. 973, Appendix Table N).

Amco Tech, a manufacturer of computer microcopies, hired 7 computer technicians and gave a test to measure their basic skills. After one year, their job performance was expressed by the rank numbers. The firm wanted to determine if there is a significant correlation between the test scores and the job performance. In Minitab, rank the variables first, and use the Correlation command. The rank correlation coefficient can be computed by the Correlation command. Run the file and find the answer. File Name: Webst780.inp

```
Note 'Rank and Rank Correlation: Webst780.inp'
# Webster, p. 780, Table 15-9
Name c1='name' c2='test' c3='perform1' c4='perform2'
# name 'technician'
# test 'test score'
# perform1  'top performance is ranked as No. 1'
# perform2  'top performance is ranked as No. 7'
Read c1-c4;
Format (A18, F2.0, F6.0, F5.0).
J. Smith          82      4      4
A. Jones          73      7      1
D. Boone          60      6      2
M. Lewis          80      3      5
G. Clark          67      5      3
A. Lincoln        94      1      7
G. Washington     89      2      6
End
Note '(1) Ordinary Correlation (Pearson)'
Correlation c2-c3
Correlation c2-c4
Note '(2) Rank correlation (Spearman)'
# In Minitab ranking, the smallest number is always ranked as No. 1
# In performance ranking 1, the top is ranked as No. 1.
# So, the rank correlation coefficient will be negative if test score and
# performance are in fact positively correlated.
Rank c2 put in c5
Correlation c3 c5
Print c1-c5
Note '(3) Rank correlation (Spearman)'
# In Minitab ranking, the smallest number is always ranked as No. 1
# in performance ranking 2, the top is ranked as No. 7.
Correlation c5 c4
```

Exercise Example 12-28: Rank Correlation - Spearman and Kendall

A market researcher wanted to know if there is a correlation between population and per capita expenditures for a new food product. Since the variables are not normally distributed, he wanted to use the rank correlation analysis. Run the file and find the answer. File Name: NWK-541.inp

```
Note 'Rank Correlation and Ranking: Nwk-541.inp'
# Neter-Wasserman-Kutner, 1989, p. 541
Name c1='market' c2='popu' c3='spending'
# market = 'test market'
# popu   ='population'
# spending ='per capita spending'
Read c1-c3
 1     29  127
 2    435  214
 3     86  133
 4   1090  208
 5    219  153
 6    503  184
 7     47  130
 8   3524  217
 9    185  141
10     98  154
11    952  194
12     89  103
End
Note '(1) Ordinary Correlation (Pearson)'
Correlation c2-c3
Note '(2) Rank correlation (Spearman)'
# The smallest number is always ranked as No. 1 in Minitab.
Rank c2 put in c4
Rank c3 put in c5
Correlation c4 c5
```

Chapter 13.
Time Series Analysis and Forecasting:
Moving Average, Exponential Smoothing, ARIMA, and Index Numbers

There are many forecasting methods including the following:

Minitab Command

(1) Subjective method

(2) Survey method *−Top economist*

(3) Repeated survey method (Delphi method)

(4) Random walk model

(5) Constant growth model   %Trend

(6) Simple moving average

(7) Double moving average

(8) Trend, cycle, season, and irregular   %Trend, %Decomp

(9) Single (simple) exponential smoothing   %Ses

(10) Brown's double exponential smoothing   %Des

(11) Holt's exponential smoothing   %Des

(12) Winters' exponential smoothing   %Wintmult, %Wintadd

(13) ARIMA models   ARIMA

(14) Regression models   Regress

(15) Spectral analysis

Lots are on Diskette

In this chapter, seasonal index, moving average, exponential smoothing, ARIMA models, and index numbers are discussed. Regression models are discussed in chapters 7-11, and spectral analysis is not available in Minitab (available in SPSS and SAS).

A. Moving Average and Exponential Smoothing

In the above list, Minitab's ARIMA and Regression models are excellent and easy to use and available for both Minitab for DOS version 8.0 and Minitab for Windows versions 9.0. Minitab for Windows has the following macro files: (1) %Trend (quadratic, growth and S curves), (2) Decomp (decomposition of time series data, additive and multiplicative), (3) %SES (single exponential smoothing), (4) %DES (Holt or Brown double exponential smoothing), (5) %Wintmult (Holt-Winters multiplicative seasonal exponential smoothing), and (6) %Wintadd (Holt-Winters additive seasonal exponential smoothing). In these macro files, if the weight values are not specified, Minitab finds the optimal weight values. The time series macro file formats are summarized below. k is a constant, and c is a column number.

Macro Commands and Optional Subcommands for Time Series Analysis

Trend Fitting of Time Series Data
%Trend c1;
Quadratic, Growth or Scurve; Optional, default is a linear trend
   Forecast k1;   Forecast for k1 values
   Origin k2;   Forecasts start on the smoothed value in period k2
   Trstore c2;   Fitted trend line is stored
   Residuals c3;   Residuals are stored
   Fostore c4;   Forecast values are stored
   Noplot;   Default plot is turned off

Table;   Table of data, trend line and detrended data
Title 'This is Trend Analysis'.

Linear trend: $y_t = b_0 + b_1 T + e$
Quadratic trend: $y_t = b_0 + b_1 T + b_2 T^2 + e$
Growth: $y_t = b_0(b_1{}^T)e$
Scurve (Pearl-Reed logistic) $y_t = (10^a)/[b_0 + b_1(b_2{}^T)]$

Decomposition of Time Series Data
%Decomp c1 k1;   k1 is the length of the seasonal pattern such as 4, 12
     Multiplicative (or Additive);   Optional, default is multiplicative

     Start k2;   If the monthly data starts with July, k2=7
     Forecasts k3;   Forecast k3 values
     Origin k4;   Forecasts start on the smoothed value in period k4
     Sestore c2;   Seasonal component is stored
     Trstore c3;   Trend component is stored
     Detstore c4;   Detrended data is stored
     Desstore c5;   Seasonally adjusted data is stored
     Fostore c6;   Forecast values are stored
     Residuals c7;   Residuals are stored
     Notrend;   Trend is not included
     Noplot;   No plot is requested, default is plot
     Table;   Table of data and fitted values
     Title 'Decomposition Analysis'.

Single Exponential Smoothing
%SES c1;
     Weight k1;   Optional, weight value $0 < k1 < 1$, default is optimal search
     Forecasts k2;   Forecast k2 values
     Origin k3;   Forecasts start on the smoothed value in period k3
     Smstore c2;   Smoothed values are stored
     Fostore c3;   Forecast values are stored
     Upstore c4;   95 % upper limit values are stored
     Lostore c5;   95 % lower limit values are stored
     Residuals c6;   Residuals are stored
     Noplot;   No plot is requested, default is plot
     Table;   Table of data and fitted values
     Title 'Single Exponential Smoothing'.

Double Exponential Smoothing (Holt, Brown)
%DES c1;
     Weight K1 K2;   Optional weight values (k1=level, k2=trend), default is optimal search
     Forecasts k3;   Forecast k3 values
     Origin k4;   Forecasts start on the smoothed value in period k4
     Smstore c2;   Smoothed values are stored
     Lestore c3;   Level component is stored
     Trstore c4;   Trend component is stored
     Fostore c5;   Forecast values are stored
     Upstore;   95 % upper limit values are stored
     Lostore c6;   95 % lower limit values are stored
     Residuals c5;   Residuals are stored
     Noplot;   No plot is requested, default is plot

Table;   Table of data and fitted values
Title 'Double Exponential Smoothing'.

Winters' Multiplicative Exponential Smoothing

%Wintmult c1 k1;   k1 is the length of seasonal pattern such as 4 and 12
Weight K2 K3 K4;   Optional weight values (k2=level, k3=trend, k4=seasonal),
                          default is optimal search
Forecasts k5;   Forecast k5 values
Origin k6;   Forecasts start on the smoothed value in period k6
Smstore c2;   Smoothed values are stored
Lestore c3;   Level component is stored
Trstore c4;   Trend component is stored
Sestore c5;   Seasonal component is stored
Fostore c6;   Forecast values are stored
Upstore c7;   95 % upper limit values are stored
Lostore c8;   95 % lower limit values are stored
Residuals c9;   Residuals are stored
Noplot;   No plot is requested, default is plot
Table;   Table of data and fitted values
Title 'Winters Multiplicative Exponential Smoothing'.

Winters Additive Exponential Smoothing

%Wintadd c1 k1;   k1 is the length of seasonal pattern such as 4 and 12
Weight K2 K3 K4;   Optional weight values (k2=level, k3=trend, k4=seasonal),
                          default is optimal search
Forecasts k5;   Forecast k5 values
Origin k6;   Forecasts start on the smoothed value in period k6
Smstore c2;   Smoothed values are stored
Lestore c3;   Level component is stored
Trstore c4;   Trend component is stored
Sestore c5;   Seasonal component is stored
Fostore c6;   Forecast values are stored
Upstore c7;   95 % upper limit values are stored
Lostore c8;   95 % lower limit values are stored
Residuals c9;   Residuals are stored
Noplot;   No plot is requested, default is plot
Table;   Table of data and fitted values
Title 'Winters Additive Exponential Smoothing'.

Note that to run these macro files, they must have been installed in the Minitab for Windows Version 9.0.

Exercise Example 13-1: Moving Average Method

Vinnie, owner of Video Village, knows her store profits have seasonal variations. She wants to compute 3-year moving average to use it for forecasting. The following file would plot the time series data and compute 3-year moving average. Run the file and find the answer. File Name: Webst833.inp

Minitab does not have a procedure command for a moving average. But a simple macro file can be written for the 3-month moving average:

$$\hat{y}_t = (y_{t-1} + y_{t-2} + y_{t-3})/3$$

The prediction error is

$$e_t = y_t - \hat{y}_t$$

The RMSE (Root Mean Squared Error) $= [\Sigma(y_t - \hat{y}_t)^2/n]^{1/2}$

```
Note 'Moving Average - 3 month: Webst833.inp'
# Webster, p. 833, Table 16-7 Monthly data: changed data'
Name c1='profit'
# profit 'profit of Vinnie'.
# 1991.1 to 1994.12
Set c1
10   9 11 12 18 23 27 26 18 13 10 10
 9 11 10 12 19 25 28 31 22 15 11 12
10   8 10 12 19 25 29 31 21 16 18 19
10   9 11 12 18 23 27 26 18 13 10 10
End
Note (1) Plotting the series
Tsplot profit;
  Month;
  Year;
  Start 1 1991;
  Title "Vinnie's profit 1989.1 - 1994.12 ".
Note (2) 3-Month Moving Average Predicted Value = c6
Let c2=Lag(c1)
Let c3=Lag(c2)
Let c4=Lag(c3)
Let c5=(c2+c3+c4)/3
Note Predicted Value = c5
Name c5='Predict1' c6='Perror1'
Let  c6=c1-c5
Print c1 c5 c6
Note (3) Root Mean Square Error = k3
Note      Mean Square Error      = k2
Let k1=Count(c5)
Let k2= Sum(((c1-c5)**2)/k1)
Let k3=Sqrt(k2)
Print k2 k3
Tsplot c1 c6;
 Overlay;
 Month 1:11/2;
 Year;
 Start 1 1991;
 Title 'Actual and predicted 1'.
Tsplot c7
Note: TSplot subcommands work for Windows version 9.0.
```

Edited Partial Output:

ROW	profit	Predict1	Perror1
1	10	*	*
2	9	*	*
3	11	*	*
4	12	10.0000	2.0000
5	18	10.6667	7.3333
...			
47	10	19.0000	-9.0000
48	10	13.6667	-3.6667

```
MTB > Note (3) Root Mean Square Error = k3
MTB > Note      Mean Square Error      = k2
MTB > Print k2 k3

K2        49.3239
K3        7.02311
```

Exercise Example 13-2: Trend, Decomposition, and Exponential Smoothing

Vinnie's Video Village manager wants to forecast sales for January 1994 using the simple exponential smoothing method. Run the file and find the answer. File Name: Webst825.inp

```
Note 'Exponential Smoothing-Minitab for Windows: Webst825.inp'
# Webster, p. 825, Table 16-5: Monthly data: changed
Name c1='sales'
# Sales "Vinnie's monthly video sales: 1989.1 -1993.12 "
Set c1
105   110   107   112 117 109   108   115   120   137   142   157
110   125   130   135 140 150   154   160   150   180   170   175
115   130   135   145 156 175   180   170   180   175   168   180
120   125   145   140 130 180   190   185   189   200   210   230
130   135   140   155 170 190   200   210   250   230   220   240
End
Note '(1) Trend'
%Trend c1;
   Growth;
   Forecasts 12;
   Origin 60;
   Table;
   Title 'Trend'.
Note '(2) Decomposition'
%Decomp c1 12;
   Multiplicative;
   Forecasts 12;
   Origin 60;
   Table;
   Title 'Decomposition'.
Note '(3) Single Exponential Smoothing'
%Ses c1;
   Forecasts 12;
   Origin 60;
   Table;
   Title 'Single Exponential Smoothing'.
Note '(4) Double Exponential Smoothing'
%Des c1;
   Forecasts 12;
   Origin 60;
   Table;
   Title 'Double Exponential Smoothing'.
Note '(5) Winters Multiplicative Model'
%Wintmult c1 12;
   Forecasts 12;
   Origin 60;
   Table;
   Title 'Winters Multiplicative Model'.
Note '(6) Winters Additive Model'
%Wintadd c1 12;
   Forecasts 12;
   Origin 60;
   Table;
   Title 'Winters Additive Model'.
```

Exercise Example 13-3: Trend, Decomposition, and Exponential Smoothing

The Northern Natural Gas Company wanted to know the general movement of natural gas sales without seasonal effects. Amir Aczel wanted to forecast for the next 12 quarters. Use the weight value 0.4. Run the file and find the 3-month moving average. File Name: ACZEL569.inp

```
Note 'Exponential Smoothing-Minitab for Windows: ACZEL569.inp'
# Aczel, p. 569, Table 12-3, 1983-1986: Quarterly Data'
Name c1='sales'
# sales 'Quarterly sales of Natural Gas in billions of BTU'
```

```
Set c1
170  148  141  150  161  137  132  158
157  145  128  134  160  139  130  144
End
Note '(1) Trend'
%Trend c1;
   Forecast 4;
   Table;
   Title 'Trend'.
Note '(2) Decomposition'
%Decomp c1 4;
   Forecasts 4;
   Table;
   Title 'Decomposition'.
Note '(3) Single Exponential Smoothing'
Note 'Using the default weight value'
%Ses c1;
   Forecast 4;
   Table;
   Title 'Single Exponential Smoothing 1'.
Note 'Using weight value = 0.4'
%Ses c1;
   Weight 0.4;
   Forecast 4;
   Table;
   Title 'Single Exponential Smoothing 2'.
Note '(4) Double Exponential Smoothing'
%Des c1;
   Forecast 4;
   Table;
   Title 'Double Exponential Smoothing'.
Note '(5) Winters Multiplicative Model'
%Wintmult c1 12;
   Forecast 4;
   Table;
   Title 'Winters Multiplicative Exponential Smoothing'.
Note '(6) Winters Additive Model'
%Wintadd c1 4;
   Forecast 4;
   Table;
   Title 'Winters Additive Exponential Smoothing'.
```

Exercise Example 13-4: Trend, Decomposition, and Exponential Smoothing

The director of development for the Spokane Transit Authority wanted to obtain seasonally adjusted time series data on the new car registration, and make forecast for the next 4 quarters using the exponential smoothing methods. Run the file and find the answer. File Name: Hanke626.inp

```
Note 'Weighted Average: Hanke626.inp'
# Hanke, p. 626, Table 16-8, New passenger car registration'
# 1987 - 93 monthly data
Name c1='cars'
# cars 'monthly car registration'
Set c1
509  546  626  672  708  717  626  627  625  655  678  765
595  569  725  728  773  869  789  773  735  757  701  910
747  782  835  837  886  928  903  852  874  834  816  823
781  790  927  936  912  923  949  926 1105  973  828  849
913  822  848  906  918 1012  934  894 1149  948  719  902
800  671  829  895  830  963  899  903  955  819  718  901
774  810  919  852  874  981  883  901  937  807  764  896
End
Note '(1) Trend'
%Trend c1;
   Forecast 12;
   Table.
   Title 'Trend'.
```

```
Note '(2) Decomposition'
%Decomp c1 12;
   Forecasts 12;
   Table;
   Title 'Decomposition'.
Note '(3) Single Exponential Smoothing'
%Ses c1;
   Forecast 12;
   Table;
   Title 'Single Exponential Smoothing'.
Note '(4) Double Exponential Smoothing'
%Des c1;
   Forecast 12;
   Table;
   Title 'Double Exponential Smoothing'.
Note '(5) Winters Multiplicative Model'
%Wintmult c1 12;
   Forecast 12;
   Table;
   Title 'Winters Multiplicative Model'.
Note '(6) Winters Additive Model'
%Wintadd c1 12;
   Forecast 12;
   Table;
   Title 'Winters Additive Model'.
```

Exercise Example 13-5: Trend, Decomposition, and Exponential Smoothing

Toys International wants to know seasonally adjusted inventory levels and make forecast for the next 4 quarters using exponential smoothing methods. Run the file and find the answer. File Name: Mason702.inp

```
Note 'Exponential Smoothing: Mason702.inp'
# Mason, p. 702, Table 19-8'
# 1988.I - 1993.IV - quarterly data
Name c1='invent'
# invent 'quarterly inventory level'
Set c1
6.7   4.9   10.0   12.7   6.5   4.8    9.8   13.6
6.9   4.3   10.4   13.1   7.0   5.5   10.8   15.0
7.1   4.4   11.1   14.5   8.0   4.2   11.4   14.9
End
Note '(1) Trend'
%Trend c1;
   Forecast 4;
   Table;
   Title 'Trend'.
Note '(2) Decomposition'
%Decomp c1 4;
   Forecasts 4;
   Table;
   Title 'Decomposition'.
Note '(3) Single Exponential Smoothing'
%Ses c1;
   Weight 0.5;
   Forecast 4;
   Table;
   Title 'Single Exponential Smoothing'.
Note '(4) Double Exponential Smoothing'
%Des c1;
   Forecast 4;
   Table;
   Title 'Double Exponential Smoothing'.
Note '(5) Winters Multiplicative Model'
%Wintmult c1 12;
   Forecast 4;
   Table;
```

```
      Title 'Winters Multiplicative Exponential Smoothing'.
Note '(6) Winters Additive Model'
%Wintadd c1 4;
   Forecast 4;
   Table;
   Title 'Winters Additive Exponential Smoothing'.
```

Exercise Example 13-6: Trend, Decomposition, and Exponential Smoothing

Andrew Siegel collected the data on the quarterly revenue of the Washington Water Power Company. He wanted to obtain seasonally adjusted data, and also wanted to make forecast for the next 4 quarters using the exponential smoothing methods. Run the file and find the answer. File Name: Siege595.inp

```
Note 'Weighted average: Siege595.inp'
# Siegel, p. 595, Table 14.2.1, Washington Water Power Company
# 1980 - 86 quarterly data
Name c1='revenue'
# revenue 'revenue in million dollars'
Set c1
91.707    63.048   57.041  78.667    96.794  74.949  56.791  89.127
116.250   71.998   59.620  98.985   106.878  71.800  65.880  94.254
122.915   92.079   80.241 118.075   150.682  96.967  85.492 126.312
129.312  129.762   82.597  74.167   103.340
End
Note '(1) Trend'
%Trend c1;
   Forecast 4;
   Table;
   Title 'Trend'.
Note '(2) Decomposition'
%Decomp c1 4;
   Forecasts 4;
   Desstore c2;
   Table;
   Title 'Decomposition'.
Print c1-c2
Note '(3) Single Exponential Smoothing'
%Ses c1;
   Forecast 4;
   Table;
   Title 'Single Exponential Smoothing'.
Note '(4) Double Exponential Smoothing'
%Des c1;
   Forecast 4;
   Table;
   Title 'Double Exponential Smoothing'.
Note '(5) Winters Multiplicative Model'
%Wintmult c1 12;
   Forecast 4;
   Table;
   Title 'Winters Multiplicative Exponential Smoothing'.
Note '(6) Winters Additive Model'
%Wintadd c1 4;
   Forecast 4;
   Table;
   Title 'Winters Additive Exponential Smoothing'.
```

Exercise Example 13-7: Trend, Decomposition, and Exponential Smoothing

Holton Wilson, an economist wanted to forecast the rate of change in durable goods using moving average and exponential smoothing methods. Run the file and find the answer. File Name: Wils-073.inp

```
Note 'Weighted average: Wils-073.inp'
```

```
# Wilson, p. 73, Table 3-1, 1985 Q1 - 1994 Q2, Quarterly Data
Name c1='price'
# price 'quarterly price change %'
Set c1
4.10   2.70    3.80    5.50    5.30    7.50    7.40   6.60
7.20   7.20    5.50    7.60   11.70    9.10    8.10   8.10
5.40   8.20    6.80    5.70    4.00    4.10    1.90   1.30
2.50   1.40    3.00    3.30    0.40    2.20    0.70   0.80
2.30   0.10   -0.60    1.10    1.50    1.20
End
Note '(1) Trend'
%Trend c1;
   Start 1;
   Forecast 4;
   Table;
   Title 'Trend'.
Note '(2) Decomposition'
%Decomp c1 4;
   Forecasts 4;
   Table;
   Title 'Decomposition'.
Note '(3) Single Exponential Smoothing'
%Ses c1;
   Forecast 4;
   Table;
   Title 'Single Exponential Smoothing'.
Note '(4) Double Exponential Smoothing'
%Des c1;
   Forecast 4;
   Table;
   Title 'Double Exponential Smoothing'.
Note '(5) Winters Multiplicative Model'
%Wintmult c1 12;
   Forecast 4;
   Table;
   Title 'Winters Multiplicative Exponential Smoothing'.
Note '(6) Winters Additive Model'
%Wintadd c1 4;
   Forecast 4;
   Table;
   Title 'Winters Additive Exponential Smoothing'.
```

B. Box-Jenkins ARIMA Models

ARIMA (Autoregressive-Integrated-Moving Average Model) can be expressed by

$$Y_t = a_0 + a_1 Y_{t-1} + a_2 Y_{t-2} + b_1 e_{t-1} + b_2 e_{t-2} + \ldots + e_t$$

$Y_{t-1}, Y_{t-2},$ ....   autoregressive series
$e_t, e_{t-1},$ ....   moving average series (white noise)

MARIMA (Multivariate ARIMA) model may be expressed as

$$Y_t = a_1 Y_{t-1} + b_1 e_{t-1} + c_1 X_t + e_t$$

$$Y_t = a_1 Y_{t-1} + a_2 Y_{t-2} + b_1 e_{t-1} + b_2 e_{t-2} + \ldots + c_1 X_1 + c_2 X_2 + \ldots + e_t$$

$Y_{t-1}, Y_{t-2},$ ....   autoregressive series
$e_t, e_{t-1},$ ....   moving average series (white noise)
$X_1, X_2,$ ....   series of an independent variable

Regression models and ARIMA models look alike in terms of equations. However, regression equations are estimated using the least squares method which uses solved formulas to minimize the sum of squared errors. But ARIMA equations are calculated using a nonlinear least squares method which uses iterative procedures (trial and error process) starting with some numbers.

In using Box-Jenkins ARIMA models, the following 5 steps are suggested:

1. Differencing Process - How Many Times to Difference ?

The first step to build a Box-Jenkins model is to determine whether the raw data should be differenced or not. If the raw data values show a trend, then we have to difference the values once, twice, three times,... until the trend is removed. You could use the Tsplot command to detect any trend in the time plot chart.

First order difference $\Delta = Y_t - Y_{t-1}$
Second order difference $\Delta^2 = \Delta_t - \Delta_{t-1}$

(1) If there is a trend in the raw data, difference it until the trend disappears.
(2) If autocorrelations exhibit a very smooth pattern at high lags, difference it once more.

2. Identification Process - How Many AR and MA terms ?

The second step is to determine the number of AR (autoregressive terms) and MA (moving average) terms. This process is called Identification process. This step computes and plots autocorrelation function (ACF) and partial autocorrelation function (PACF). The plots are called correlograms. Holden, Peel, and Thompson (1990) provide the following guidelines for building ARIMA models:

(1) If ACF falls to zero after a_k, and PACF declines from b_k, then use k number of AR terms:

$$y = a_1 y_{t-1} + a_2 y_{t-2} + ...+ a_k y_{t-k}$$

(2) If ACF declines geometrically after a_k, and PACF falls to zero from b_k, then use k number of MA terms:

$$y = b_1 e_{t-1} + b_2 e_{t-2} + ... b_k e_{t-k}$$

(3) If ACF declines geometrically after a_k, and PACF declines from b_k, then use k AR terms and k MA terms:

$$y = a_1 y_{t-1} + a_2 y_{t-2} + a_k y_{t-k} + b_1 e_{t-1} + b_2 e_{t-2} + .. b_k e_{t-k}$$

3. Estimation Process

Once the ARIMA model is specified, the parameter estimation is easy since it is what Minitab does. In the output, check the Box-Pierce Q statistic (chi-square), which is used for a lack-of-fit test. It is calculated by:

$$Q = n \sum_i^k \rho_i^2$$

The Ljung-Box statistic (Ljung-Box-Pierce statistic, or the modified Box-Pierce statistic) is given by:

$$Q^* = (n - d)(n-d+2) \sum_i^k \rho_i^2 / (n-k)$$

where n = initial total number of observations, the total length of the time series data, d = the degree of differences, k = the number of correlations checked, ρ = the autocorrelation coefficient of the *ith* residual. The degrees of freedom DF = k-p-q.

The Q statistic or Q* statistic is compared with the critical chi-square value for the degrees of freedom DF = k-p-q, at the given α level.

The hypotheses and the decision rules are:

H_0: $\rho = 0$ The autocorrelation of the residuals is zero; The residuals are white noise.
H_A: $\rho \neq 0$ The autocorrelation of the residuals is not equal to zero.

H_0 Accept if computed Q* $\leq$ critical chi-square value
H_A Accept if computed Q* > critical chi-square value

If the autocorrelation is significantly different from zero, the estimated model is inappropriate, and go back to the identification process and specify another model and test it. That is, if the Box-Pierce Q statistic is not significant, it implies that the residuals are white noise (random variable), it implies that the model fits the data well (Ramanathan, 1992, p. 313; Cryer, 1986, p. 153).

4. Forecasting Process

The final step is forecasting. This step is also easy since Minitab will do it. A single-step and extended step forecast may be made. However, the longer the extended period for forecast, the larger is the confidence interval. Since the model can generate unreasonable forecasts, it depends upon the art of the forecaster whether to accept the forecasts or to rebuild the entire model.

5. Plot Process of Actual and Forecast Values

Though this process is not required, the actual and forecast series may be plotted by Minitab to visualize the results.

Exercise Example 13-8: ARIMA Model

Vinnie, owner of Vinnie's Video Village, knows that her store profits have seasonal variations. She wants to use an ARIMA model to predict profits for the next 6 months. Run the file and make forecast. Minitab for Windows must be run in the enhanced mode of Windows. Otherwise, you may get error messages. File Name: Webs833B.inp Note:

```
Note 'ARIMA Model: Webs833B.inp for Windows'
# Webster, p. 833, Table 16-7, 1991-93, Monthly Data
# 1991.1 - 1994.12 Monthly data
Name c1='profit'
# profit 'profit of Vinnie'
Set c1
10   9 11 12 18 23 27 26 18 13 10 10
 9 11 10 12 19 25 28 31 22 15 11 12
10   8 10 12 19 25 29 31 21 16 18 19
10   9 11 12 18 23 27 26 18 13 10 10
End
Note (1) Plotting - To difference or not to difference ?
Tsplot c1
Tsplot c1;
  Month;
  Year;
  Start 1 1991;
  Title 'Profits 1991.1 - 1994.12'.
Note (2) Identification process - ACF, PACF
```

```
ACF in c1
PACF in c1
Note (3) Estimation process and forecast - ARIMA
Name c2='resid' c3='predict'
ARIMA (1 0 1) (0 0 2) 12 c1 resids=c2 predict=c3;
   Constant;
   Forecast origin=45 12 leads.
Tsplot c1 c3;
   Overlay;
   Month 1:11/2;
   Year;
   Title 'Actual and Predicted Profits'.
Tsplot c2
```

Edited Partial Output:

```
(2) Identification process - ACF, PACF
ACF of profit
           -1.0 -0.8 -0.6 -0.4 -0.2  0.0  0.2  0.4  0.6  0.8  1.0
            +----+----+----+----+----+----+----+----+----+----+
    1    0.772                         XXXXXXXXXXXXXXXXXXXX
    2    0.332                         XXXXXXXXX
    3   -0.115                     XXXX
    4   -0.464             XXXXXXXXXXXXX
    5   -0.640       XXXXXXXXXXXXXXXX
    6   -0.652       XXXXXXXXXXXXXXXX
    7   -0.533          XXXXXXXXXXXXX
    8   -0.325              XXXXXXXXX
    9   -0.044                   XX
   10    0.291                      XXXXXXX
   11    0.583                      XXXXXXXXXXXXXXX
   12    0.702                      XXXXXXXXXXXXXXXXXX
   13    0.570                      XXXXXXXXXXXXXXX
   14    0.287                      XXXXXXXX
   15   -0.046                   XX
   16   -0.317              XXXXXXXXX
PACF of profit
           -1.0 -0.8 -0.6 -0.4 -0.2  0.0  0.2  0.4  0.6  0.8  1.0
            +----+----+----+----+----+----+----+----+----+----+
    1    0.772                         XXXXXXXXXXXXXXXXXXXX
    2   -0.654       XXXXXXXXXXXXXXXXX
    3   -0.147                     XXXXX
    4   -0.265              XXXXXXXX
    5   -0.136                     XXXX
    6   -0.269              XXXXXXXX
    7   -0.227               XXXXXXX
    8   -0.246              XXXXXXX
    9   -0.047                   XX
   10    0.150                      XXXXX
   11    0.125                      XXXX
   12    0.010                      X
   13   -0.169                 XXXXX
   14    0.179                      XXXXX
   15   -0.001                      X
   16    0.154                      XXXXX
(3) Estimation process and forecast - ARIMA
Final Estimates of Parameters
Type      Estimate    St. Dev.   t-ratio
AR   1      0.6231      0.1651      3.77
MA   1     -0.4757      0.1847     -2.58
SMA 12     -0.9283      0.2216     -4.19
SMA 24     -0.4848      0.3126     -1.55
Constant    5.752       1.258       4.57
Mean       15.261       3.337
No. of obs.: 48
Residuals: SS = 259.395  (backforecasts excluded) MS = 6.032 DF = 43
Modified Box-Pierce (Ljung-Box) chisquare statistic
Lag                  12            24            36            48
```

```
Chisquare   12.0(DF= 8)    27.9(DF=20)    35.4(DF=32)    * (DF= *)
Forecasts from period 45
                              95 Percent Limits
Period       Forecast        Lower        Upper       Actual
   46         15.5806        10.7656      20.3955     13.0000
   47         19.0229        11.8691      26.1767     10.0000
   48         19.7325        11.8555      27.6094     10.0000
   49         11.9747         3.8343      20.1151
   50         11.6296         3.3891      19.8700
   51         13.0272         4.7482      21.3061
   52         13.2303         4.9365      21.5242
   53         16.5006         8.2010      24.8003
   54         19.1521        10.8502      27.4540
   55         21.6593        13.3566      29.9621
   56         19.7171        11.4140      28.0202
   57         15.5953         7.2921      23.8985
```

Exercise Example 13-9: ARIMA Model

The Northern Natural Gas Company wanted to predict quarterly sales using an ARIMA model. Run the file and find the answer. File Name: Acze569B.inp

```
Note 'ARIMA model: ACZE569B.inp'
# Aczel, p. 569, Table 12-3
# 1991-94 Quarterly Data: Years are changed
Name c1='sales'
# sales 'Sales of Natural Gas in Billions of BTU'
Set c1
170  148  141  150  161  137  132  158
157  145  128  134  160  139  130  144
End
Note (1) Plotting - To difference or not to difference ?
Tsplot c1
Tsplot c1;
   Month;
   Year;
   Start 1 1991;
   Title 'Sales 1991.1 - 1994.4'.
Note (2) Identification process - ACF, PACF
ACF in c1
PACF in c1
Note (3) Estimation process and forecast - ARIMA
Name c2='resid' c3='predict'
ARIMA (1 0 1) (0 0 2) 4 c1 resids=c2 predict=c3;
    Constant;
    Forecast origin=16 4 leads.
Tsplot c1 c3;
   Overlay;
   Quarter;
   Year;
   Title 'Actual and Predicted Profits'.
Tsplot c2
```

Exercise Example 13-10: ARIMA Model

The development director of the Spokane Transit Authority wanted to predict new car registration for the next 4 quarters using an ARIMA model. Run the file and find the answer. File Name: Hank626B.inp

```
Note 'ARIMA Model: Hank626B.inp'
# Hanke, p. 626, Table 16-8, New passenger car registration'
# 1988 - 94 monthly data
Name c1='cars'
# cars 'car registration'
```

```
Set c1
509  546  626  672  708  717  626  627  625  655  678  765
595  569  725  728  773  869  789  773  735  757  701  910
747  782  835  837  886  928  903  852  874  834  816  823
781  790  927  936  912  923  949  926 1105  973  828  849
913  822  848  906  918 1012  934  894 1149  948  719  902
800  671  829  895  830  963  899  903  955  819  718  901
774  810  919  852  874  981  883  901  937  807  764  896
End
Note (1) Plotting - To difference or not to difference ?
Tsplot c1
Tsplot c1;
  Month;
  Year;
  Start 1 1988;
  Title 'Car Registration 1988.1 - 1994.12'.
Note (2) Identification process - ACF, PACF
ACF in c1
PACF in c1
Note (3) Estimation process and forecast - ARIMA
Name c2='resid' c3='predict'
ARIMA (1 1 1) (0 0 2) 12 c1 resids=c2 predict=c3;
    Constant;
    Forecast origin=84 12 leads.
Tsplot c1 c3;
   Overlay;
   Quarter;
   Year;
   Title 'Actual and Predicted Profits'.
Tsplot c2
```

Exercise Example 13-11: ARIMA Model

Toys International wants to use an ARIMA model to predict the next 4 quarterly inventory levels. Run the file and find the answer. File Name: Maso702B.inp

```
Note 'ARIMA Model: Maso702B.inp'
# Mason, p. 702, Table 19-8: years are changed
# 1989.1-1994.4: Quarterly inventory level'
Name c1='invent'
# invent 'quarterly inventory level'
Set c1
6.7   4.9   10.0  12.7  6.5   4.8    9.8   13.6
6.9   4.3   10.4  13.1  7.0   5.5   10.8   15.0
7.1   4.4   11.1  14.5  8.0   4.2   11.4   14.9
End
Note (1) Plotting - To difference or not to difference ?
Tsplot c1
Tsplot c1;
  Quarter;
  Year;
  Start 1 1989;
  Title 'Inventory 1989.1 - 1994.4'.
Note (2) Identification process - ACF, PACF
ACF in c1
PACF in c1
Note (3) Estimation process and forecast - ARIMA
Name c2='resid' c3='predict'
ARIMA (1 1 1) (0 0 2) 4 c1 resids=c2 predict=c3;
    Constant;
    Forecast origin=20 8 leads.
Tsplot c1 c3;
   Overlay;
   Quarter;
   Year;
   Title 'Actual and Predicted Profits'.
Tsplot c2
```

Exercise Example 13-12: ARIMA Model

The Washington Water Power Company wants to predict next 4 quarterly revenues. Run the file and make forecast. File Name: Sieg595B.inp

```
Note 'Seasonal Index: Sieg595B.inp'
# Siegel, p. 595, Table 14.2.1, Washington Water Power Company'
# 1988 - 94 quarterly data
Name c1='revenue'
# revenue 'revenue in million dollars'
Set c1
 91.707   63.048   57.041   78.667    96.794   74.949   56.791   89.127
116.250   71.998   59.620   98.985   106.878   71.800   65.880   94.254
122.915   92.079   80.241  118.075   150.682   96.967   85.492  126.312
129.762   82.597   74.167  103.340
End
Note (1) Plotting - To difference or not to difference ?
Tsplot c1
Tsplot c1;
  Quarter;
  Year;
  Start 1 1988;
  Title 'Washington Power Revenue 1988.1 - 1994.4'.
Note (2) Identification process - ACF, PACF
ACF in c1
PACF in c1
Note (3) Estimation process and forecast - ARIMA
Name c2='resid' c3='predict'
ARIMA (1 1 1) (0 0 2) 4 c1 resids=c2 predict=c3;
    Constant;
    Forecast origin=28 4 leads.
Tsplot c1 c3;
  Overlay;
  Quarter;
  Year;
  Title 'Actual and Predicted Revenues'.
Tsplot c2
```

Exercise Example 13-13: ARIMA and MARIMA Models

An economist at GM wanted to predict car and part sales using ARIMA and MARIMA models. A MARIMA (Multivariate ARIMA) model includes other time series data as additional independent variables. Thus, a MARIMA model is a combination of an ARIMA model and a regression model. Since MARIMA models are not available in Minitab, the following file deals with only an ARIMA model. Run the file and find the answer: File Name: Wils-255.inp

```
Note 'ARIMA Model: Wils-255.inp'
# see Wilson, 1990 ed., p. 255
# Data: Wilson, p. 171, Table 5-1
# 1986.1-1995.4 Quarterly data: Years are changed
Name c1='time' c2='date' c3='income' c4='cars' c5='interest' &
    c6='q1' c7='q2' c8='q3'
# Labels
# date      'year and quarter'
# income    'personal disposable income'
# cars      'motor vehicle and parts sales'
# interest  'prime interest rate, %'
# q1        'quarter 1'
# q2        'quarter 2'
# q3        'quarter 3'
Read c1-c8;
Format (F2.0, A7, F8.0, 2F9.0, 3F3.0).
 1 1986q1   70.20   1983.10   6.83333   1   0   0
 2 1986q2   71.40   1992.80   6.90000   0   1   0
 3 1986q3   73.00   2005.90   7.08667   0   0   1
```

```
 4 1986q4    76.30   2022.20   6.54000   0   0   0
 5 1987q1    84.00   2026.90   6.25000   1   0   0
 6 1987q2    84.40   2049.60   6.47000   0   1   0
 7 1987q3    85.50   2086.90   6.90333   0   0   1
 8 1987q4    87.60   2120.80   7.67333   0   0   0
 9 1998q1    86.30   2128.20   7.97667   1   0   0
10 1988q2    98.10   2167.70   8.30000   0   1   0
11 1988q3    97.20   2176.40   9.14000   0   0   1
12 1988q4    98.70   2202.00   10.8100   0   0   0
13 1989q1    99.00   2216.60   11.7500   1   0   0
14 1989q2    93.70   2206.50   11.7167   0   1   0
15 1989q3    98.90   2213.60   12.1167   0   0   1
16 1989q4    95.90   2213.60   15.0800   0   0   0
17 1990q1    98.30   2225.60   16.3967   1   0   0
18 1990q2    80.10   2185.60   16.3233   0   1   0
19 1990q3    89.60   2207.10   11.6100   0   0   1
20 1990q4    93.20   2238.70   16.7333   0   0   0
21 1991q1   103.20   2242.90   19.2133   1   0   0
22 1991q2    97.10   2235.00   18.9300   0   1   0
23 1991q3   106.50   2262.90   20.3233   0   0   1
24 1991q4    95.40   2253.70   17.0133   0   0   0
25 1992q1   105.70   2245.70   16.2700   1   0   0
26 1992q2   105.70   2260.90   16.5000   0   1   0
27 1992q3   108.30   2263.40   14.7167   0   0   1
28 1992q4   115.70   2271.10   11.9567   0   0   0
29 1993q1   115.00   2288.40   10.8800   1   0   0
30 1993q2   128.50   2311.10   10.5000   0   1   0
31 1993q3   133.70   2335.40   10.9767   0   0   1
32 1993q4   144.40   2392.70   11.0000   0   0   0
33 1994q1   150.40   2446.90   11.0700   1   0   0
34 1994q2   155.80   2460.30   12.3067   0   1   0
35 1994q3   154.40   2481.90   12.9900   0   0   1
36 1994q4   157.60   2493.10   11.8033   0   0   0
37 1995q1   162.30   2495.70   10.5367   1   0   0
38 1995q2   165.30   2550.80   10.1967   0   1   0
39 1995q3   182.80   2524.70   9.50000   0   0   1
40 1995q4   166.40   2540.70   9.50000   0   0   0
End Data.
Note (1) Plotting - To difference or not to difference ?
Tsplot 'cars'
Tsplot cars;
  Quarter;
  Year;
  Start 1 1986;
  Title 'Car Sales 1986.1 - 1995.4'.
Note (2) Identification process - ACF, PACF
ACF  in c4
PACF in c4
Note (3) Cross Correlation Function
CCF  in c4 c3
Note (4) Estimation process and forecast - ARIMA
Name c9='resid' c10='predict'
ARIMA (1 1 1) (0 0 2) 4 'cars' resids=c9 predict=c10;
   Constant;
   Forecast origin=40 4 leads.
Tsplot c4 c10;
   Overlay;
   Quarter;
   Year;
   Title 'Actual and Predicted Values'.
Tsplot c9
```

Exercise Example 13-14: ARIMA Model for Trend and Cycle Data

In the following file, 5 types of time series data are tested: (1) trend data, (2) 12 month perfect cycle data, (3) trend with 12 month cycle data, (4) random number data. Run the file and make observations.

```
Note 'ARIMA Models with Hypothetical Data'
Name c1='trend' c2='cycle12' c3='tcycle12' c4='random48'
# trend     'perfect trend from 1 to 96, increment 2 '
# cycle12   'perfect cycle with 12-month period '
# trend12   'perfect trend with perfect cycle'
# random    '48 random numbers from 1 to 35'
Note (1) Perfect trend with increment =2
Set c1
 1:96/2
End
Note (2) Perfect cycle with 12 month period (4 cycles)
Set c2
4(1:12)
End
Note (3) Trend with prefect cycle (12 month period)
set c3
  1   3   5   7   9  11  13  15  17  19  21  23
  5   7   9  11  13  15  17  19  21  23  25  27
  9  11  13  15  17  19  21  23  25  27  29  31
 13  15  17  19  21  23  25  27  29  31  33  35
End
Note (4) 48 Random numbers
Base k=5
Random 48 observations into c4;
    Integers 1 to 35.
Print c4
print c1-c4
Note (1) Plotting process
Tsplot c1
Tsplot c2
Tsplot c3
Tsplot c4
Note (2) Identification process
ACF in c1
PACF in c1
ACF in c2
PACF in c2
ACF in c3
PACF in c3
ACF in c4
PACF in c4
Note (3) Estimation process: c1= trend - ARIMA
Name c5='resid1' c6='predict1'
ARIMA (1 1 1) c1 resid c5 predict c6;
    Noconstant;
    Forecast 48 12.
Tsplot c2 c6;
    Year;
    Title 'Actual and Predicted Values'.
Tsplot c5
Note (4) Estimation: c2= 12-month cycles - ARIMA
Name c7='resid2' c8='predict2'
ARIMA (0 0 1) (0 0 1) 12 c2 resid c7 predict c8;
    Constant;
    Forecast 48 12.
Tsplot c3 c8;
    Year;
    Title 'Actual and Predicted Values'.
Tsplot c7
Note (5) Estimation c3=trend with cycles - ARIMA
Name c9='resid3' c10='predict3'
ARIMA (0 1 1) (0 0 1) 12  c3 resid c9 predict c10;
    Constant;
    Forecast  48 12.
Tsplot c1 c10;
    Year;
    Title 'Actual and Predicted Values'.
Tsplot c9
Note (6) Estimation c4= random numbers - ARIMA
```

```
Name c11='resid4' c12='predict4'
ARIMA (0 0 1) c4 resid c11 predict c12;
    Constant;
    Forecast 48 12.
Tsplot c4 c12;
    Year;
    Title 'Actual and Predicted Values'.
Tsplot c11
```

Exercise Example 13-15: Spectral Analysis and Periodogram

Economic time series have business cycles. Spectral analysis is used to find periodic patterns of time series data. It analyzes a time series into sine and cosine waves, and produces periodogram which shows the amount of variance accounted for by cycles and frequency. An economist wanted to apply spectral analysis to consumption data. Since spectral analysis is not available in Minitab, an SPSS sample file is shown below. Run the file and find the period of the cycles.

```
* SPSS File:
Title 'Spectral Analysis'.
Data List Free/ year cons income interest.
Variable Labels cons 'consumption'
    /interest 'interest rate (%)'.
Begin Data.
1961  100  120  12
1962  110  130  13
1963  130  150  15
1964  160  190  14
1965  180  200  11
1966  210  240  10
1967  250  290   9
1968  300  360   8
1969  360  450   7
1970  420  500   8
1971  100  120  10
1972  110  130  11
1973  130  150  13
1974  160  190  14
1975  180  200  15
1976  210  240  12
1977  250  290  12
1978  300  360  14
1979  360  450  13
1980  420  500  15
1981  100  120  11
1982  110  130   9
1983  130  150   8
1984  160  190   7
1985  180  200  12
1986  210  240  13
1987  250  290  12
1988  300  360  11
1989  360  450  15
1990  420  500  12
End Data.
Date Year 1961.
Tsplot cons income interest.
Title '(1) ACF, PACF'.
ACF cons.
PACF cons.
Title '(2) Spectra 1'.
Spectra cons
    /Center
    /Plot = P S By Freq.
Title '(3) Spectra 2'.
Spectra cons
    /Window=Tukey(3)
```

```
   /Plot = P S By Freq.
Title '(3) Spectra 2'.
Spectra cons
   /Window=Tukey(3)
   /Plot = P S.
* p .. periodogram.
* S ...smoothed periodogram....spectral density.
Title '(4) Spectra 3'.
Spectra cons
   /Plot = All.
Title '(4) Spectra 4'.
Spectra cons
   /Window=Parzen(11)
   /Plot = P S By Freq.
* spectral density with  Parzen(11) window.
Title '(5) Spectra 5'.
Spectra cons
   /Center
   /Save P(cons) Freq(F).
Title '(6) Cross Spectral Analysis' .
* Cons with income and cons with interest.
* CCF cross correlation functions.
CCF Variables = cons With income interest
CCF cons income
   /LN
   /Diff=1
   /Period=1
   /Mxcross=25.
Spectra cons income interest
   /Cross.
```

C. Making Index Numbers

There are 3 basic methods of computing index numbers: the simple average index method, Laspeyres index method, and the Paasche index method:

Simple index	$= \Sigma \, P_t / \Sigma \, P_0$
Laspeyres index (LI)	$= \Sigma \, P_t \, Q_0 / \Sigma \, P_0 \, Q_0$
Paasche index (PI)	$= \Sigma \, P_t \, Q_t / \Sigma \, P_0 \, Q_t$
Fisher ideal index (FI)	$= [\text{LI} \times \text{PI}]^{1/2}$

where P_t = price in year t, P_0 = base year price, Q_0 = base year quantity, Q_t = quantity in year t. In the Laspeyres index method, $\Sigma P_0 \, Q_0$ = the value (PxQ) in the base year remains constant. $\Sigma P_t \, Q_t$ = the value in the current year changes each year. The base year quantity Q_0 is the weight. In the Paasche index method, the values in the base year and the current year change each year. The current year quantity Q_t is used as the weight. Thus, the values in both years are recalculated. Each method has shortcomings: the simple index and Laspeyres method tend to overestimate inflation (cost of living), and the Paasche index tends to underestimate it. For example, economic theory suggests that when the price of a commodity rises, the demand for the commodity will decrease. And yet, the demand (weight value Q_0) is assumed to stay the same as before the price increase in calculating the Laspeyres index. On the other hand, in the Paasche method, the demand is assumed to have been the same in the preceding year when the price was lower and the demand (weight) was larger before the price increase. Hedonistic price equation is also discussed at the end of the chapter.

Exercise Example 13-16: Laspeyres and Paasche Price Indexes

In the following sample file, there are 3 goods and their prices. Using the data, 3 indexes and their inflation rates are computed: simple index, Laspeyres index, and Paasche index. Run the file and obtain the 3 indexes. File Name: Webst860.inp

```
Name c1='year' c2='p1' c3='p2' c4='p3'  &
     c5='q1' c6='q2' c7='q3'
# p1 'Price of beef'
# p2 'price of pork'
# p3 'price of veal'
# q1 'quantity of beef sold'
# q2 'quantity of pork sold'
# q3 'quantity of veal'
# index1 'price index'
# infla1 'infla using dP/P'
Read c1-c7
1992  3.00  2.00  4.00  250  150   80
1993  3.30  2.20  4.50  320  200   90
1994  4.50  2.10  3.64  350  225   70
End
Name c8='value1' c9='index1' c10='infla1' c11='value2' &
     c12='value3' c13='index2' c14='infla2'
Let 'value1' = 'p1'*250+'p2'*150+'p3'*80
Let 'index1' = 100*'value1'/(3*250+2*150+4*80)
Let 'infla1' = 100*'index1'/Lag('index1') - 100
Let 'value2' = 'p1'*'q1'+'p2'*'q2'+'p3'*'q3'
Let 'value3' = 3*'q1'+2*'q2'+4*'q3'
Let 'index2' = 100*'value2'/(3*'q1'+2*'q2'+4*'q3')
Let 'infla2' = 100*'index2'/Lag('index2') - 100
Note '(1) Year, Value, Laspeyres Index, and Paasche Index'
Print  'year' 'value1' 'value3' 'index1' 'index2'
Note '(2) Year, inflation rate Using Laspeyres and Paasche'
Print  'year' 'infla1' 'infla2'
```

Edited Partial Output:

```
'(1) Year, Value, Laspeyres Index, and Paasche Index'
 ROW    year    value1  value3     index1      index2
  1     1990    1370.0   1370    100.000     100.000
  2     1991    1515.0   1720    110.584     110.523
  3     1992    1731.2   1780    126.365     129.343  .
'(2) Year, inflation rate Using Laspeyres and Paasche'
 ROW    year    infla1     infla2
  1     1990       *          *
  2     1991    10.5839   10.5233
  3     1992    14.2706   17.0276
```

Exercise Example 13-17: Money and Real Income Growth Rates

Money income is expressed in current prices, while real income is expressed in constant base-year prices. Given money and price indexes, you can convert money income in any base year prices. The method of calculating real GDP (Gross Domestic Product) is explained using nominal GDP and CPI (consumer price index, or more appropriately GDP deflator).

Suppose that you want to express income of 1995 in 1980 constant prices:

$$\text{Real GDP in 1995 (in 1980 constant prices)} = \frac{\text{Nominal GDP in 1995}}{\text{CPI (in 1980)}} \times 100$$

If you want to express 1995 income in 1990 constant prices:

$$\text{Real GDP in 1995 (in 1990 constant prices)} = \frac{\text{Nominal GNP in 1995}}{\text{CPI (in 1990)}} \times 100$$

The rate of change in prices (inflation rate) is:

$$dP/P = (P_t - P_{t-1}) / P_{t-1}$$

The growth rate of nominal (money) income is:

$$dY/Y = (Y_t - Y_{t-1}) / Y_{t-1}$$

The growth rate of real income is:

$$dy/y = (y_t - y_{t-1}) / y_{t-1}$$

or $dy/y = dY/Y - dP/P$

where y = real income, Y = money income. The following file computes growth rates of money income, real income, and inflation rate. Run the file and find the answer. File Name: Webst875.inp

```
Note 'Price and GDP: Webst875.inp'
# Webster, p. 875, Table 17-11.
Name c1='year' c2='cpi' c3='income'
# cpi 'consumer price index 1980=100'
# income 'money income'
# infla  'inflation rate(%)'
# growth1 'growth rate of money income(%)'
# growth2 'growth rate of real income(%)'
# realinc 'real income in 1980 prices'.
Read c1-c3
1986   109.6   4140.3
1987   113.6   4526.7
1988   118.3   4864.3
1989   124.3   5116.8
1990   127.2   5463.0
End
Name c4='lagcpi' c5='laginc' c6='infla' c7='growth1' &
     c8='realinc' c9='lagreal' c10='growth2'
Let 'lagcpi' = Lag('cpi')
Let 'laginc' = Lag('income')
Let 'infla'  = 100*'cpi'/'lagcpi' -100
Let 'growth1' = 100*'income'/'laginc' - 100
Let 'realinc' = 100*'income'/'cpi'
Let 'lagreal' = Lag('realinc')
Let 'growth2' = 100*'realinc'/'lagreal' - 100
Print  'year' 'cpi' 'infla' 'income' 'realinc' 'growth1' 'growth2'
```

In the above output, growth1 = growth rate of nominal GNP, and growth2 = the growth rate of real GNP.

Exercise Example 13-18: Stock Price Indexes

There are several stock market price indexes including Dow Jones stock price index, Standard and Poor's stock price index, New York Stock Exchange index, Wilshire Stock index, and American Stock Exchange Stock price index. The Standard and Poor's 500 stock price index is based on the Laspeyres price index method using 500 stocks: 400 industrials, 40 utilities, 20 transportation, and 40 financial. The base period of the current index series is the average value of 1941-43. The index is multiplied by 10. Below is an example of the SP index method. Note that there is a 3-for-1 stock split for stock C on January 9, and a 2-for-1 stock split for stock B on January 10. Run the file and obtain the SP index.

```
Note 'Stock Price Index: Exa13-18.inp'
Name c1='date' c2='p1' c3='p2' c4='p3' c5='q1' c6='q2' c7='q3'
# p1 'stock price of A'
# p2 'stock price of B'
```

```
# p3 'stock price of C'
# q1 'outstanding shares of A'
# q2 'outstanding shares of B'
# q3 'outstanding shares of C'
Read c1-c7;
Format (A7, 2F5.0, 4F4.0).
06Jan92  100  120 130  50  60  40
07Jan92  110  122 132  50  60  40
08Jan92  111  124 124  50  60  40
09Jan92  112  125  42  50  60 120
10Jan92  115   62  45  50 120 120
13Jan92  118   63  45  50 120 120
End
Name c8='base' c9='index1'
Let 'base'  = 10*120+100+60+130*40
Let 'index1'= 10*('p1'*'q1'+'p2'*'q2'+'p3'*'q3')/'base'
Print 'date' 'p1' 'p2' 'p3' 'q1' 'q2' 'q3' 'index1'
```

Exercise Example 13-19: Dow-Jones Stock Price Index Forecasting

A finance student wanted to apply an ARIMA model to forecast the Dow-Jones stock price index and the holding period return (HPR). Run the file and find the answer.

```
Note 'ARIMA model for Dow-Jones Stock holding period return'
Name c1='dow1' c2='yield'
# Dow-Jones Stock Price Index 1955-92 (38 observations)
Set c1
 442.72  493.01  475.71  491.66  632.12  618.04  691.55  639.76
 714.81  834.05  910.88  873.60  879.12  906.00  876.72  753.19
 884.76  950.71  923.88  759.37  802.49  974.92  894.63  820.23
 844.40  891.41  932.92  884.36 1190.34 1178.48 1328.23 1792.76
2275.99 2060.82 2508.91 2678.94 2929.33 3284.29
End
Set c2
4.08  4.09  4.35  3.97  3.23  3.47  2.98  3.37
3.17  3.01  3.00  3.40  3.20  3.07  3.24  3.83
3.14  2.84  3.06  4.47  4.31  3.77  4.62  5.28
5.47  5.26  5.20  5.81  4.40  4.64  4.25  3.49
3.08  3.64  3.45  3.61  3.24  2.99
End
Note 'A. Return on Dow-Jones stocks'
Note return = [P(t) - P(t-1) + D(t)]/P(t-1)
Note P(t) = price (c1), D/P = dividend yield (%) (c2)
Note Since P x D/P = D   c4= c1* c2   c5 = holding period return
Let c3 = Lag(c1)
Let c4= c1*c2/100
Let c5= 100*(c1-c3+c4)/c3
Name c4='dividend' c5='hpr' c6='resi1' c7='pred1'
Note '(1) Identification process for HPR'
Tsplot c5;
  Year;
  Start 1956.
Boxplot c5
ACF in c5
PACF in c5
Note '(2) Estimation process for HPR'
ARIMA (1 0 1) c5 resid c6 pred c7;
   Noconstant;
   Forecast 37 4;
Note '(3) Plot Actual and Predicted HPR'
Tsplot c5 c7;
  Overlay;
  Year;
  Start 1955 1956;
  Tdisplay 11;
Note 'B. Dow-Jones Stock Price Forecasting'
Name c8='resi2' c9='pred2'
```

```
ARIMA (1 0 1) c5 resid c8 pred c9;
   Noconstant;
   Forecast 37 4;
Note '(1) Identification process for Dow-Jones Price'
Tsplot c1;
  Year;
  Start 1955.
Boxplot c1
ACF in c1
PACF in c1
Note '(2) Estimation process Dow-Jones Price'
ARIMA (1 1 1) c1 resid c8 pred c9;
   Noconstant;
   Forecast 37 4;
Note '(3) Plot Actual and Predicted Dow-Jones'
Tsplot c1 c9;
  Overlay;
  Year;
  Start 1955;
  Tdisplay 11.
```

Edited Partial Output:

```
'Dow-Jones Stock Price Index Forecasting'
'(1) Identification process c1'
ACF of dow1
            -1.0 -0.8 -0.6 -0.4 -0.2  0.0  0.2  0.4  0.6  0.8  1.0
            +----+----+----+----+----+----+----+----+----+----+
   1   0.834                          XXXXXXXXXXXXXXXXXXXXXXX
   2   0.695                          XXXXXXXXXXXXXXXXXX
   3   0.568                          XXXXXXXXXXXXXXX
   4   0.434                          XXXXXXXXXXXX
   5   0.335                          XXXXXXXXX
   6   0.197                          XXXXXX
   7   0.101                          XXXX
   8   0.047                          XX
   9   0.007                          X
  10  -0.030                         XX
  11  -0.032                         XX
  12  -0.046                         XX
  13  -0.053                         XX
  14  -0.050                         XX
  15  -0.047                         XX
  16  -0.058                         XX
PACF of dow1
            -1.0 -0.8 -0.6 -0.4 -0.2  0.0  0.2  0.4  0.6  0.8  1.0
            +----+----+----+----+----+----+----+----+----+----+
   1   0.834                          XXXXXXXXXXXXXXXXXXXXXXX
   2  -0.000                          X
   3  -0.037                         XX
   4  -0.097                        XXX
   5   0.018                          X
   6  -0.191                     XXXXXX
   7   0.020                          X
   8   0.057                          XX
   9   0.019                          X
  10  -0.061                        XXX
  11   0.094                          XXX
  12  -0.069                        XXX
  13  -0.023                         XX
  14   0.006                          X
  15   0.030                          XX
  16  -0.099                        XXX
'(2) Estimation process: ARIMA Model (1 1 1)'
Final Estimates of Parameters
Type      Estimate     St. Dev.    t-ratio
AR   1      1.0046       0.1310       7.67
MA   1      0.8139       0.2320       3.51
```

```
Differencing: 1 regular difference
No. of obs.:  Original series 38, after differencing 37
Residuals:    SS =  887700  (backforecasts excluded)
              MS =   25363  DF = 35
Modified Box-Pierce (Ljung-Box) chisquare statistic
Lag               12          24          36              48
Chisquare   8.9(DF=10)  13.4(DF=22)  18.6(DF=34)    * (DF= *)
Forecasts from period 37
                          95 Percent Limits
Period     Forecast      Lower       Upper       Actual
  38       3129.39      2817.19     3441.60      3284.29
  39       3330.38      2844.93     3815.84
  40       3532.31      2882.76     4181.85
  41       3735.16      2920.53     4549.79
  42       3938.96      2954.91     4923.00
```

Exercise Example 13-20: Quality-Adjusted Price (Hedonistic Price)

One difficulty in measuring a price change is when the price change is accompanied with quality change. The true price change should measure only the price change holding the quality of the goods constant. But how can we hold the quality constant, or how can we subtract the quality change from the price change? Under the traditional method called the "matched model", if 2 commodities have identical or similar specifications or characteristics between 2 adjacent time periods, the commodity is included in the computation of price index, and if specification or characteristics are different and cannot be matched to each other, the commodity is excluded from the price index. In the conventional method of constructing price indexes, the current prices are compared with the base year prices such as $\Sigma P_t Q_t / \Sigma P_0 Q_t$ in the Paasche index. In the chained price index, prices in the 2 adjacent years are compared: $\Sigma P_t Q_t / \Sigma P_{t-1} Q_t$.

An alternative method is the hedonistic price method. Under the method, a unit of product is regarded as an aggregate of a number of components (attributes, characteristics). In case of automobiles, for instance, the quality can be specified in terms of the following: engine power, the number of cylinders, the number of doors, safety features (seat belt, air bag), emission control, power steering, power break, power windows, air conditioner, defroster, cruise control, gas mileage, internal space, wheel size, adjustable seat, radio, cassette player, warranty period, maker, model type, raw materials (steel panel, plastic panel), etc. In case of computers (excluding monitor and printer), quality can be expressed in terms of RAM memory size, hard disk memory size, speed (MHz), access time (ms), processor type (286, 386, 486), number and type of the floppy disk drive, expansion slots, math coprocessor, warranty period, size of gas tank, keyboard, etc. In case of television sets, quality can be specified by screen size, stereo, closed captions, picture in picture, programming capability, resolution density, remote control, etc.

When actual price is regressed on "qualitative" variables (variables representing qualities), such equation is called **hedonistic price equation** (quality-adjusted price equation). For a single year cross section data, the hedonistic price equation in semilog may look like

$$\ln p = \beta_0 + \beta_1 x_1 + \beta_2 x_2 + \beta_3 x_3 + \ldots + e$$

where $\ln p$ = price in log, x_i = quality variables, e = error term. The variables can be measured in arithmetic values, semilog or double logarithms. For time series data, the hedonistic price equation usually includes year dummy variables:

$$\ln p_i = \alpha_0 + \alpha_1 D_1 + \alpha_2 D_2 + \ldots + \beta_1 x_1 + \beta_2 x_2 + \beta_3 x_3 + \ldots + e$$

where D_i = year dummy variables. For instance, $D_1 = 1$ for 1993, and $D_1 = 0$ for all other years, $D_2 = 1$ for 1994, and $D_2 = 0$ for all other years. The base year is expressed by dummy variable 0. The inflation rate between 1994 and 1993 is expressed by

$$\ln p_{1994} - \ln p_{1993} = (\alpha_0 + \alpha_{1994}) - (\alpha_0 + \alpha_{1993}) = \alpha_{1994} - \alpha_{1993}$$

If 1993 is the base year, then $\ln p_{1994} - \ln p_{1993} = \alpha_{1994}$. The quality measures x_i are assumed to be equal for all years to measure the pure price change (for detail see Berndt, 1991). In the following sample file, the data are given for a single year. Run the file and obtain the hedonistic price equation.

```
Note 'Hedonistic price regression: File for Windows Version'
Name c1='price' c2='hard' c3='ram' c4='speed' c5='dx486'
# price 'price of computer unit ($)'
# hard  'hard disk memory size' # ram  'ram memory size'
# speed 'speed in MHz' dx486 'DX486'  dx486 1 'Dx486' 0 'SX486'
# Reference model= sx486_25: model 486 SX 25MHz
Read c1-c5
2449  425  8  66  1
1799  210  4  66  1
1909  340  4  66  1
1609  210  4  33  1
1549  130  4  33  1
1390  210  4  25  0
1049  100  2  25  0
End
Name c6='logprice' c7='loghard' c8 ='logram' c9='logspeed'
Let 'logprice' = Loge('price')
Let 'loghard'  = Loge('hard')
Let 'logram'   = Loge('ram')
Let 'logspeed' = Loge('speed')
Note '(1) Multiple OLS'
NAME  c10='fits1' c11='resi1'
Regress c1 on 4 c2-c5;
  Fits 'fits1';
  Residuals 'resi1';
  VIF;
  DW.
Tsplot 'price' 'fits1';
  Overlay;
  Title '(1) Prices of Computers and Fits'.
%Resplots 'fits1'  'resi1'
Note '(2) Stepwise'
Stepwise 'price' 'hard' 'ram' 'speed' 'dx486';
  FEnter 4;
  FRemove 4.0.
Note '(3) Stepwise'
Stepwise 'price' 'hard' 'ram' 'speed' 'dx486';
  FEnter 4;
  FRemove 4.0;
  Best 2.
Note '(4) Double log: log-log except dx486'
Name  c12 ='fits2' c13 = 'resi2'
Regress 'logprice' 4 'loghard' 'logram' 'logspeed' 'dx486';
  Fits 'fits2';
  Residuals 'resi2';
  VIF;
  DW.
Tsplot 'logprice' 'fits2';
  Overlay;
  Title '(2) Prices of Computers and Fits'.
%Resplots 'resi2' 'fits2'
Note '(5) Semilog: Logprice'
Name c13 = 'fits3' c14 ='resi3'
Regress 'logprice' 4 'hard' 'ram' 'speed' 'dx486';
  Fits 'fits3';
  Residuals 'resi3';
  VIF;
```

```
   DW.
Tsplot 'logprice' 'fits3';
   Overlay;
   Title '(3) Prices of Computers and Fits'.
%Resplots 'resi3' 'fits3'

Note 'Hedonistic price regression: File for DOS Version'
# Sample File for Minitab for DOS
Name c1='price' c2='hard' c3='ram' c4='speed' c5='dx486'
# price 'price of computer unit ($)'
# hard  'hard disk memory size'
# ram   'ram memory size'  speed 'speed in MHz'
# dx486 'DX486'  dx486 1 'Dx486' 0 'SX486'
# Reference model= sx486_25: model 486 SX 25MHz
Read c1-c5
2449   425   8   66   1
1799   210   4   66   1
1909   340   4   66   1
1609   210   4   33   1
1549   130   4   33   1
1390   210   4   25   0
1049   100   2   25   0
End
Name c6='logprice' c7='loghard' c8 ='logram' c9='logspeed'
Let 'logprice' = Loge('price')
Let 'loghard'  = Loge('hard')
Let 'logram'   = Loge('ram')
Let 'logspeed' = Loge('speed')
Note '(1) Multiple OLS'
Regress c1 on 4 c2-c5  stddev c10  fits c11;
   Residuals c12;
   VIF;
   DW.
Mtsplot 'price' c11
Note '(2) Stepwise'
Stepwise 'price' 'hard' 'ram' 'speed' 'dx486';
   FEnter 4;
   FRemove 4.0.
Note '(3) Stepwise'
Stepwise 'price' 'hard' 'ram' 'speed' 'dx486';
   FEnter 4;
   FRemove 4.0;
   Best 2.
Note '(4) Double log: log-log except dx486'
Regress 'logprice' 4 'loghard' 'logram' 'logspeed' 'dx486' &
      stdresid c13 fits c14;
   Residuals c15;
   VIF;
   DW.
Mtsplot 'logprice' c14
Note '(5) Semilog: Logprice'
Regress 'logprice' 4 'hard' 'ram' 'speed' 'dx486' &
      stdresid c16 Fits c17;
   Residuals c18;
   VIF;
   DW.
Mtsplot 'logprice' c17
```

Chapter 14. Multivariate Analysis
and Other Miscellaneous Models

The concepts of univariate analysis and multivariate analysis are used in different ways. (1) Univariate analysis deals with only one variable at a time to obtain information from the data. Bivariate analysis deals with 2 variables simultaneously. Multivariate analysis deals with 3 or more variables simultaneously. (2) Multivariate analysis, however, often refers to the cases when 2 or more dependent variables (equations) are analyzed simultaneously, or when 2 or more variables are analyzed without specifying dependent and independent variables. In this sense, conventional multivariate analysis includes MANOVA (multivariate ANOVA), discriminant analysis, multivariate logit probit models, factor analysis and principal component analysis. Some of these models are discussed in this chapter. MANOVA (multivariate ANOVA is discussed in chapter 6 together with ANOVA and ANCOVA.

A. Discriminant, Logit, and Probit Models

When dependent variable is a categorical (nominal) variable, OLS estimation produces inefficient estimates. That is, the estimated variances are not minimum variances. The reason is that the OLS method is based on the assumption that the dependent variable is normally distributed. If the dependent variable is categorical, such assumption does not hold.

Discriminant, probit, and logit models can be used when the dependent variable is a binary or categorical variable. The above 3 models can be expressed in the following equation:

$$Y = b_0 + b_1 X_1 + b_2 X_2 + b_3 X_3 + ... + e$$

where Y = categorical variable, 0 or 1; X_i = independent variables, b_i = parameters to be estimated, and e = the error term.

In the discriminant model, the parameters are estimated such that two groups of the dependent variable are most well separated (largest distance). However, discriminant method assumes that the independent variables are normally distributed for optimal prediction. Thus, if independent variables include categorical variables, such assumption will be violated.

In the logit and probit models, such assumption is not required. In the logit model, the categorical dependent variable is transformed to a logit which is a log of the odds ratio:

$$\ln [p/(1-p)] = b_o + b_i X_i$$

In the probit model, the dependent variable is transformed to a normit (normal deviate) which is an inverse of the cumulative normal probability function:

$$F^{-1}(P) = b_o + b_i X_i$$

where $F^{-1}(P)$ = the inverse of cumulative normal probability function. In both models, the parameters are estimated by the maximum likelihood method. Logit and probit models can be interchangeably used since cumulative logit and probit distributions are very similar. Independent variables can be binary. However, linear discriminant function is not appropriate if independent variables are all binary variables (1, 0), or a mixture of continuous and discrete variables.

Exercise Example 14-1: Discriminant Analysis

To give a loan or not is an important decision to make for a bank. The loan manager wanted to predict possible bad loans. He collected the data on income, debt, family size, number of years with present employer, and pay-default status for 32 past cases. Since the dependent variable is a binary variable, default (0), completed payment (1), discriminant analysis, logit analysis, and probit analysis may be used. In Minitab, discriminant analysis, principal component analysis, and factor analysis are available. Probit and logit models are not available in Minitab. They are available in SAS, SPSS, Shazam, Soritec, Limdep, Statgraphics, and Systat. Run the file and find significant variables in the discriminant function. File Name: ACZEL791.inp

```
Note 'Discriminant Analysis: ACZEL791.inp'
# Aczel, p. 791, Table 16-4, Example (c)
Name c1='assets' c2='income' c3='debt' c4='famsize' &
     c5='years' c6='pay'
# assets 'family assets in $1,000'
# income 'family income in $1,000'
# famsize 'family size'
# years    'years with present employment'
# pay       'pay or default'
# pay 1 'paid' 0 'default'
Read c1-c6
98   35   12    4    4    1
65   44    5    3    1    1
22   50    0    2    7    1
78   60   34    5    5    1
50   31    4    2    2    1
21   30    5    3    7    1
42   32   21    4   11    1
20   41   10    2    3    1
33   25    0    3    6    1
57   32    8    2    5    1
 8   23   12    2    1    0
 0   15   10    4    2    0
12   18    7    3    4    0
 7   21   19    4    2    0
15   14   28    2    1    0
30   27   50    4    4    0
29   18   30    3    6    0
 9   22   10    4    5    0
12   25   39    5    3    0
23   30   65    3    1    0
34   45   21    2    5    0
21   12   28    3    2    1
10   17    0    2    3    1
57   39   13    5    8    0
60   40   10    3    2    1
78   60    8    3    5    1
45   33    9    4    7    0
 9   18    9    3    5    1
12  ·23   10    4    4    1
55   36   12    2    5    1
67   33   35    2    4    1
42   45   12    3    8    0
End
Note (1) Linear Discriminant Model
Discriminant groups in 'pay' predictors 'assets'  &
     'income' 'debt' 'years' 'famsize';
     LDF c7 c8;
     Fits c9;
     Xval;
     Predict 50 45 5 6 3;
     Brief 4.
Let c10='pay' - c9
Name c10 = 'Error1'
Print c1 c9 c10
```

```
Note (2) Quadratic Discriminant Model
Discriminant 'pay' 'assets' 'income' 'debt' 'years' 'famsize';
     Quadratic;
     Fits c11;
     Xval;
     Predict 50 45 5 6 3;
     Brief 4.
Let c12='pay' - c11
Name c12 = 'Error2'
Print c1 c11 c12
```

Note: LDF c7 c8 .. stores the 2 linear discriminant functions in the 2 columns.

Edited Partial Output:

```
(1) Linear Discriminant Model
Linear Discriminant Analysis for pay
Group          0         1
Count         14        18
Summary of Classification
Put into       ....True Group....
Group              0         1
0                 10         5
1                  4        13
Total N           14        18
N Correct         10        13
Proport.       0.714     0.722
N =   32     N Correct =   23     Prop. Correct = 0.719
Summary of Classification with Cross-validation
Put into       ....True Group....
Group              0         1
0                  9         6
1                  5        12
Total N           14        18
N Correct          9        12
Proport.       0.64      0.67
N =   32     N Correct =   21     Prop. Correct = 0.656
Squared Distance Between Groups
                   0         1
0          0.00000   2.26482
1          2.26482   0.00000
          Linear Discriminant Function for Group
                   0         1
Constant     -9.7347   -7.9211
assets       -0.0839   -0.0282
income        0.2338    0.2266
debt          0.1010    0.0354
years         0.2193    0.2065
famsize       3.4722    2.7538

Variable    Pooled    Means for Group
            Mean          0         1
assets      35.031    23.071    44.333
income      31.063    26.786    34.389
debt        16.750    23.214    11.722
years       4.3125    4.0714    4.5000
famsize     3.1250    3.4286    2.8889
Variable    Pooled    Stdev for Group
            Stdev         0         1
assets      23.20     16.91     27.04
income      12.18     10.35     13.42
debt        14.11     17.48     10.83
years       2.432     2.526     2.358
famsize     0.9523    1.0163    0.9003
Prediction for Test Observations
 Observation Pred. Group  From Group Sqrd Distnc Probability
      1           1
                            0          4.637       0.153
```

```
                              1          1.211        0.847
(2) Quadratic Discriminant Model
Quadratic Discriminant Analysis for pay
Group          0       1
Count         14      18
Summary of Classification
Put into       ....True Group....
Group          0       1
0             12       4
1              2      14
Total N       14      18
N Correct     12      14
Proport.    0.857   0.778
N =   32      N Correct =   26      Prop. Correct = 0.812
Summary of Classification with Cross-validation
Put into       ....True Group....
Group          0       1
0              9       6
1              5      12
Total N       14      18
N Correct      9      12
Proport.     0.64    0.67
N =   32      N Correct =   21      Prop. Correct = 0.656
From    Generalized Squared Distance to Group
Group          0       1
0            15.22   20.17
1            23.10   17.10
```

Exercise Example 14-2: Discriminant Analysis

Edward Altman applied discriminant analysis to predict bankruptcy of firms. He collected the data for two groups of firms. One that went bankrupt, and the other that did not. Then dummy variable 0 is assigned to the bankrupt firms, and 1 is assigned to non-bankrupt firms. A finance manager of a firm applied a similar model to 18 firms. Run the file and find significant variables in the discriminant function.

```
Note 'Discriminant Analysis'
# Predicting Bankruptcies
Name c1='company' c2='debt' c3='return'  &
     c4='current' c5='sales' c6='bankrupt'
# debt 'Debt/Asst (%)'
# return  'EAT/TA (%)'
# current 'CA/CL (%)'
# sales   'Sales/TA (%)';
# bankrupt 'yes' "0" 'no' "1"
Read c1-c6;
Format (A10, F3.0, F4.0, F6.0, F5.0, F4.0).
Adam Co.   20   15    2.0   12   1
Barny Co.  35   20    3.0   15   1
Carol Co.  65   15    4.0   20   1
David Co.  50   18    5.5   30   1
Ellen Co.  30   25    6.0   25   1
Franco Co. 25   20    5.0   30   1
Ginny Co.  60   40    8.0   40   1
Henry Co.  70   30   10.0   25   1
Hyonju Co. 20   15    9.0   12   1
Sonyo Co.  85    9    0.5    8   0
Takson Co. 70    5    1.0    7   0
Young Co.  90    7    4.0    2   0
Martin Co. 85    8    2.0    5   0
Nancy Co.  95    6    1.5    3   0
Owen Co.   65    4    3.0    4   0
Pat Co.    70   10    4.0    8   0
Quincy Co. 80    9    7.0   10   0
Rose Co.   70    3    0.5    8   0
```

```
End
Note (1) Linear Discriminant Model
Discriminant groups in 'bankrupt' 'debt' &
            'return' 'current' 'sales';
     LDF c7 c8;
     Fits c9;
     Xval;
     Predict  56  8  2.5  6;
     Brief 4.
Let c10=c6 - c9
Name c10 = 'Error1'
Print c1 c9 c10
Note (2) Quadratic Discriminant Model
Discriminant  c6 c2-c5;
     Quadratic;
     Fits c11;
     Xval;
     Predict 56 8 2.5  6;
     Brief 4.
Let c12=c6 - c11
Name c12 = 'Error2'
Print c1 c11 c12
```

Exercise Example 14-3: Discriminant Analysis

A political economist wanted to predict party affiliation of voters in terms of income, consumption, age, and sex. Run the file and find significant variables in the discriminant function.

```
Note 'Multinomial Discriminant Model'
# 3-Level Discriminant Function
Name c1='person' c2='cons' c3='income' c4='age'  &
     c5='sex' c6='party'
#  cons     'expenditures'
#  income 'disposable income'
#  sex 0  'female' 1  'male'
# party 1 'democrat' 2 'republican' 3 'independent'
# age 1='young' 2='middle'  3='old'
Read c1-c6
  1  51  40  15  1  1
  2  20  25  20  0  2
  3  32  27  40  0  3
  4  45  32  30  1  1
  5  51  45  20  1  2
  6  31  29  50  0  3
  7  50  42  40  1  1
  8  47  38  60  1  2
  9  45  30  25  0  3
 10  39  29  56  1  1
 11  50  30  20  0  2
 12  80  70  45  1  3
 13  20  50  15  0  1
 14  30  40  19  1  2
 15  40  60  59  0  3
End
Code (0:39)1 (40:49)2 (50:100)3 in c4 put in c7
# Age is recoded into 3 groups
Note (1) Linear Discriminant Model
Discriminant groups in c6 predictors c2 c3 c5 c7;
     LDF c8 c9 c10;
     Fits c11;
     Xval;
     Predict 50 45 1 3;
     Brief 4.
Let c12 = c6 - c11
Name c12 = 'Error1'
Print c6 c11 c12
Print c8-c10
```

```
Note (2) Quadratic Discriminant Model
Discriminant groups in c6 predictors c2;
     Fits c13;
     Xval;
     Predict 50;
     Brief 4.
Let c14 = c6 - c13
Name c14 = 'Error2'
Print c6 c13 c14
# LDF stores 3 discriminant functions in 3 columns
```

B. Cluster Analysis and Factor Analysis

Assume there are, for instance, 10 variables. Which variables are closer or similar to each other? A factor analysis classifies the 10 variables into 2 or more groups of similar variables. A factor analysis computes the following equation for each variable:

$$v_1 = a_{11} F_1 + a_{12} F_2 + ... a_{1n} F_n \qquad \text{income}$$
$$v_2 = a_{21} F_1 + a_{22} F_2 + ... a_{2n} F_n \qquad \text{consumption}$$
$$....$$
$$v_i = a_{i1} F_1 + a_{i2} F_2 + ... a_{in} F_n \qquad \text{interest}$$

where v_i = variable, F_i = factor, a = factor loading (correlation coefficient of a variable with a factor). Σa^2_i = communality of a variable. Given the computer output, a researcher will determine a particular factor for the variable based on the factor loading. For instance, income and consumption may be grouped into the same group (factor), while interest rate and inflation may be grouped into another group (factor).

In the cluster analysis, instead of the variables, each observation is classified to 2 or more groups (clusters). The cluster analysis will compute the following cluster equations.

$$z_1 = b_{11} C_1 + b_{12} C_2 + ... b_{1n} C_n \qquad \text{Adam Smith}$$
$$z_2 = b_{21} C_1 + b_{22} C_2 + ... b_{2n} C_n \qquad \text{David Ricardo}$$
$$....$$
$$z_i = b_{i1} C_1 + b_{i2} C_2 + ... b_{in} C_n \qquad \text{John Keynes}$$

where z = case (observations), C = cluster, b = distance coefficient of each case to a cluster. For example, the Euclidean distance is given by $\sqrt{\Sigma(x_i - y_i)^2}$, and the squared Euclidean distance is $\Sigma(x_i - y_i)^2$, where $x_i - y_i$ is the distance between case x_i and y_i. Cluster analysis will compute the distance coefficient to each cluster and each case will be assigned to the cluster that is closest (membership). For instance, cluster analysis answers the question of whether or not Adam Smith and David Ricardo belong to the same group (cluster).

Exercise Example 14-4: Cluster Analysis

A sociology student wanted to know which cities are similar in terms of crime rates. She gathered the data on 7 crime rates for 14 cities. Since Minitab does not have the procedure, an SPSS sample file is given below. Run the file and find the clusters.

* SPSS File:
```
Title 'Cluster Analysis'.
* Set Length=65 /Width=132.
Data List Fixed /city 1-16 (A) murder 19-22 rape 25-27
    robbery 30-33 assault 35-38 burglary 41-44
    theft 47-50 motor 53-56 region 60.
Variable Labels motor 'motor vehicle theft'.
```

```
* Cluster analysis groups observations (cities) of similarities.
Begin Data.
Baltimore         27.6    77    898 1008   1799   3985    781   1
Chicago           22.2    60    897  970   1756   4044   1497   2
Dallas            30.2   115    607  688   3154   7359   1030   3
Detroit           58.2   144   1538  635   3703   4219   3452   2
Indianapolis      12.5    73    381  514   1740   2953    613   2
Los Angeles       24.4    73    877  684   2007   3953   1621   4
Memphis           18.6   138    766  565   2427   3452   1794   3
New York          19.3    54   1107  701   1738   3648   1105   1
Philadelphia      16.6    62    572  337   1159   2184    770   1
Phoenix           10.0    71    272  491   2621   5248    552   3
San Antonio       20.9    95    311  198   2843   5350    870   3
San Diego          9.7    34    310  279   1656   3564   1018   4
San Francisco     11.6    70    697  517   1603   4281    809   4
Washington, D.C.  23.5    54    835  712   1598   3973    803   1
End Data.
Title '(1) Cluster analysis'.
Cluster murder rape robbery assault burglary theft motor
   /Print= Clusters(2,3) Distance
   /Measure = Euclid
   /Method= Baverage(Clusmem)
   /Plot= Hicicle Vicicle Dendrogram
   /Print =Clusters(2,3) Schedule
   /Save= Clusters(2,3)
Title '(2) Table Presentation'.
* Note: above results are presented in tables.
Tables Observation = murder rape robbery assault burglary
      theft motor
   /Ftotal=Total
   /Format =Cwidth(10,9)
   /Table=Clusmem3 + Total
    By murder+rape+robbery+assault+burglary+theft+motor
   /Statistics= Mean Stddev.
Title '(3) Cluster-Discriminant Connection'.
Dscriminant Groups = Clusmem3(1,3)
   /Variables = murder rape robbery assault burglary
               theft motor
   /Method=Wilks
   /Statistics=All.
Title '(4) Cluster-Probit Connection'.
Compute case=1.
Compute cluster1=0.
Compute cluster2=0.
Compute cluster3=0.
If (clusmem3=1) cluster1=1.
If (clusmem3=2) cluster2=1.
If (clusmem3=3) cluster3=1.
Probit cluster1 of case With murder rape robbery assault burglary
               theft motor
   /Model=probit
   /Print=All.
Probit cluster2 of case With murder rape robbery assault burglary
               theft motor
   /Model=probit
   /Print=All.
Probit cluster3 of case With murder rape robbery assault burglary
               theft motor
   /Model=probit
   /Print=All.
```

Exercise Example 14-5: Quick Cluster Analysis

A student of economic development wanted to know which countries are similar in terms of economic variables. He gathered the data on economic variables for 8 countries. Since Minitab does not have a procedure for cluster analysis, an SPSS sample file is given. Run the file and find the clusters.

* SPSS File:
```
Title 'Cluster Analysis'.
Data List Free / country (A) gnp invest unemp infla interest.
Variable Labels gnp 'GNP growth rate(%)'
   /invest 'investment ratio to gnp(%)'
   /unemp  'unemployment rate(%)'
   /infla  'inflation (%)'
   /interest 'interest rate(%)'.
* cluster analysis produces groups of
  observations (countries) with similarities.
Begin Data.
Korea        12.0     34.1      3.1     3.0    12.0
USA           2.9     13.3      6.2     3.6     8.21
UK            3.6     16.3     10.6     4.2     9.25
Germany       1.7     25.1      8.9     0.2     2.5
France        2.1     20.2     10.4     2.5     9.5
Japan         4.4     42.4      2.8     0.1     5.09
Taiwan       11.0     40.4      2.0     0.5     4.50
Singap.       1.9     40.4      6.5     0.5     6.8
End Data.
Title '(1) Cluster analysis'.
Cluster gnp invest unemp infla interest
   /Print= Clusters(2,3) Distance
   /Measure = Euclid
   /Method= Baverage(Clusmem)
   /Plot= Hicicle Vicicle Dendrogram
   /Print =Clusters(2,3) Schedule
   /Save= Clusters(2,3).
Title '(2) Table Presentation'.
* Note: above results are presented in tables.
Tables Observation = gnp invest unemp infla interest
   /Ftotal=Total
   /Format =Cwidth(10,9)
   /Table=Clusmem3 + Total
   By gnp+invest+unemp+infla+interest
   /Statistics= Mean Stddev.
Title '(4) Cluster-Discriminant Connection'.
Dscriminant Groups = Clusmem3(1,3)
   /Variables = gnp invest unemp infla interest
   /Method=Wilks
   /Statistics=All.
Title '(4) Cluster-Probit Connection'.
Compute case=1.
Compute cluster1=0.
Compute cluster2=0.
Compute cluster3=0.
If (clusmem3=1) cluster1=1.
If (clusmem3=2) cluster2=1.
If (clusmem3=3) cluster3=1.
Probit cluster1 of case With gnp invest unemp infla interest
    /Model=probit
    /Print=All.
Probit cluster2 of case With gnp invest unemp infla interest
    /Model=probit
    /Print=All.
Probit cluster3 of case With gnp invest unemp infla interest
    /Model=probit
    /Print=All.
```

* Cluster methods include: Baverage, Waverage, Single, Complete, Centroid, Median, Ward. Baverage is the default.

Exercise Example 14-6: Quick Cluster Analysis

Cluster analysis is used to divide cases (observations rather than variables) into a specified number of groups of similarities. When the data size is large, the Quick Cluster procedure may be used. The same data for the Cluster procedure in Exercise Example 14-4 are used again to show the Quick Cluster procedure. Run the file and compare the results for the 2 procedures.

* SPSS File:

```
Title 'Quick Cluster Analysis '.
Data List Fixed /city 1-16 (A) murder 19-22 rape 25-27
    robbery 30-33 assault 35-38 burglary 41-44
    theft 47-50 motor 53-56 region 60.
Variable Labels motor 'motor vehicle theft'.
Begin Data.
Baltimore         27.6   77    898 1008  1799 3985   781  1
Chicago           22.2   60    897  970  1756 4044  1497  2
Dallas            30.2  115    607  688  3154 7359  1030  3
Detroit           58.2  144   1538  635  3703 4219  3452  2
Indianapolis      12.5   73    381  514  1740 2953   613  2
Los Angeles       24.4   73    877  684  2007 3953  1621  4
Memphis           18.6  138    766  565  2427 3452  1794  3
New York          19.3   54   1107  701  1738 3648  1105  1
Philadelphia      16.6   62    572  337  1159 2184   770  1
Phoenix           10.0   71    272  491  2621 5248   552  3
San Antonio       20.9   95    311  198  2843 5350   870  3
San Diego          9.7   34    310  279  1656 3564  1018  4
San Francisco     11.6   70    697  517  1603 4281   809  4
Washington, D.C.  23.5   54    835  712  1598 3973   803  1
End Data.
Title 'Quick Cluster Analysis'.
Quick Cluster murder rape robbery assault
     burgla theft Zmotor
   /Criteria= Cluster(3)
   /Print = ID(city) Cluster Distance Anova.
```

Exercise Example 14-7: Quick Cluster Analysis

The data used for the Cluster procedure in Exercise Example 14-5 are used again to show the Quick Cluster procedure which is used when the sample size is very large. Run the file and compare the 2 results.

* SPSS File:

```
Title 'Quick Cluster Analysis'.
Data List Free / country (A) gnp invest unemp infla interest region.
Variable Labels gnp 'GNP growth rate(%)'
   /invest 'investment ratio to gnp(%)'
   /unemp  'unemployment rate(%)'
   /infla  'inflation (%)'
   /interest 'interest rate(%)'.
Value Labels
     region 1 'Asia' 2 'Europe' 3 'America'.
Begin Data.
Korea      12.0   34.1    3.1   3.0  12.0    1
USA         2.9   13.3    6.2   3.6   8.21   3
U.K.        3.6   16.3   10.6   4.2   9.25   2
Germany     1.7   25.1    8.9   0.2   2.5    2
France      2.1   20.2   10.4   2.5   9.5    2
Japan       4.4   42.4    2.8   0.1   5.09   1
Taiwan     11.0   40.4    2.0   0.5   4.50   1
Singap.     1.9   40.4    6.5   0.5   6.8    1
End Data.
Title 'Quick Cluster Analysis'.
Quick Cluster gnp invest unemp infla inter
   /Criteria= Cluster(3)
```

```
/Print = ID(country) Cluster Distance Anova.
```

Exercise Example 14-8: Factor Analysis

A student who is doing a research on economics of crime gathered the data on 7 crime rates for 14 cities. She wanted to know which crime rates are similar or closely correlated to each other. Run the file and find the factors.

```
Note 'Factor Analysis and PCA'.
Name c1='city' c2='murder' c3='rape' c4='robbery'  &
    c5='assault' c6='burglary' c7='theft' c8='motor' c9='region'
#  motor= 'motor vehicle theft'
Read c1-c9;
Format (A18, F4.0, F5.0, F6.0, F5.0, 3F6.0, F4.0).
Baltimore          27.6   77   898 1008  1799  3985   781  1
Chicago            22.2   60   897  970  1756  4044  1497  2
Dallas             30.2  115   607  688  3154  7359  1030  3
Detroit            58.2  144  1538  635  3703  4219  3452  2
Indianapolis       12.5   73   381  514  1740  2953   613  2
Los Angeles        24.4   73   877  684  2007  3953  1621  4
Memphis            18.6  138   766  565  2427  3452  1794  3
New York           19.3   54  1107  701  1738  3648  1105  1
Philadelphia       16.6   62   572  337  1159  2184   770  1
Phoenix            10.0   71   272  491  2621  5248   552  3
San Antonio        20.9   95   311  198  2843  5350   870  3
San Diego           9.7   34   310  279  1656  3564  1018  4
San Francisco      11.6   70   697  517  1603  4281   809  4
Washington, D.C.   23.5   54   835  712  1598  3973   803  1
End
Note (1) Factor analysis- Vmax
Factor c2-c8;
  Vmax;
  Sort;
  Brief 3.
Note (2) Factor analysis- ML-Vmax
Factor c2-c8;
  NFAC = 3;
  ML;
  Vmax;
  Sort;
  Brief 3.
Note (3) Correlation and Covariance Matrices
Correlation c2-c8 put in M1
Covariance c2-c8 put in M2
Print M1
Print M2
```

Note: Minitab has the following extraction options: PCA (default) and ML. The rotation options are: Vmax, Qmax, Emax, and Omax

Edited Partial Output:

```
Maximum Likelihood Factor Analysis of the Correlation Matrix
Unrotated Factor Loadings and Communalities
Variable    Factor1    Factor2    Factor3   Commnlty
murder        0.923     -0.069      0.041     0.859
rape          0.672     -0.481      0.201     0.723
robbery       0.887      0.462      0.000     1.000
assault       0.438      0.453     -0.457     0.605
burglary      0.664     -0.747      0.000     1.000
theft         0.223     -0.692     -0.662     0.968
motor         0.873     -0.021      0.348     0.884
Variance     3.5363     1.6929     0.8103     6.0395
% Var         0.505      0.242      0.116      0.863

Rotated Factor Loadings and Communalities
```

```
Varimax Rotation
Variable    Factor1     Factor2     Factor3     Commnlty
murder       0.798      -0.452       0.133       0.859
rape         0.805       0.036       0.273       0.723
robbery      0.571      -0.794      -0.209       1.000
assault     -0.006      -0.775       0.067       0.605
burglary     0.794       0.107       0.598       1.000
theft        0.105      -0.028       0.978       0.968
motor        0.884      -0.294      -0.125       0.884

Variance     3.0344      1.5353      1.4698      6.0395
% Var        0.433       0.219       0.210       0.863

Sorted Rotated Factor Loadings and Communalities

Variable    Factor1     Factor2     Factor3     Commnlty
motor        0.884      -0.294      -0.125       0.884
rape         0.805       0.036       0.273       0.723
murder       0.798      -0.452       0.133       0.859
burglary     0.794       0.107       0.598       1.000
robbery      0.571      -0.794      -0.209       1.000
assault     -0.006      -0.775       0.067       0.605
theft        0.105      -0.028       0.978       0.968

Variance     3.0344      1.5353      1.4698      6.0395
% Var        0.433       0.219       0.210       0.863

Factor Score Coefficients
Variable    Factor1     Factor2     Factor3
murder       0.008       0.010      -0.013
rape         0.021       0.023      -0.032
robbery      0.179      -1.122      -0.037
assault     -0.033      -0.037       0.051
burglary     1.064       0.732       0.129
theft       -0.586      -0.657       0.894
motor        0.088       0.099      -0.134
```

Exercise Example 14-9: Factor Analysis

Economic variables are closely related to each other. An economics student gathered the data on GDP (gross domestic product), the investment ratio, unemployment rate, inflation rate, and the interest rate. He wanted to classify these economic variables into groups of similar variables. Run the file and find the factors.

```
Note 'Factor Analysis'
Name c1='country' c2='gnp' c3='invest' c4='unemp' &
    c5='infla' c6='interest'
# gnp 'GDP growth rate(%)'
# invest 'investment ratio to gnp(%)'
# unemp  'unemployment rate(%)'
# infla  'inflation (%)'
# interest 'interest rate(%)'
# region 1 'Asia' 2 'Europe' 3 'America'
Read c1-c6;
Format (A11, F4.0, 2F8.0, F6.0, F7.0).
Korea      12.0    34.1     3.1    3.0   12.00
USA         2.9    13.3     6.2    3.6    8.21
U.K.        3.6    16.3    10.6    4.2    9.25
Germany     1.7    25.1     8.9    0.2    2.50
France      2.1    20.2    10.4    2.5    9.50
Japan       4.4    42.4     2.8    0.1    5.09
Taiwan     11.0    40.4     2.0    0.5    4.50
Singapore   1.9    40.4     6.5    0.5    6.80
End
Note (1) Factor analysis- Vmax
```

```
Factor c2-c5;
  Vmax;
  Sort;
  Brief 3.
Note (2) Factor analysis- ML-Vmax
Factor c2-c5;
  NFAC = 2;
  ML;
  Vmax;
  Sort;
  Brief 3.
Note (3) Correlation and Covariance Matrices
Correlation c2-c6 put in M3
Correlation c2-c6 put in M4
Print M3
Print M4
```

Exercise Example 14-10: Principal Component Analysis

Principal component analysis (PCA) is a variation of factor analysis. It is used to extract factors (components). If there are 10 variables, 10 components will be extracted. In PCA, a component is a weighted combination of the input variables. On the other hand, in factor analysis, a variable is a weighted combination of factors. In PCA, the first extracted factor explains the largest part of the total variance, and the succeeding components account for less and less of the total variance. Run the file and find principal components.

```
Note 'Principal Component Analysis'
Name c1='country' c2='GDP' c3='invest' c4='unemp' &
     c5='infla' c6='interest'
# gnp 'GDP growth rate(%)'
# invest 'investment ratio to gnp(%)'
# unemp  'unemployment rate(%)'
# infla  'inflation (%)'
# interest 'interest rate(%)'
# region 1 'Asia' 2 'Europe' 3 'America'
Read c1-c6;
Format (A11, F4.0, 2F8.0, F6.0, F7.0).
Korea       12.0    34.1     3.1   3.0   12.00
USA          2.9    13.3     6.2   3.6    8.21
U.K.         3.6    16.3    10.6   4.2    9.25
Germany      1.7    25.1     8.9   0.2    2.50
France       2.1    20.2    10.4   2.5    9.50
Japan        4.4    42.4     2.8   0.1    5.09
Taiwan      11.0    40.4     2.0   0.5    4.50
Singapore    1.9    40.4     6.5   0.5    6.80
End
Note '(1) PCA'
PCA  for c2-c6;
     Scores putin c7-c11.
Print c7-c11
Note '(2) Factor Analysis - Qmax'
Factor c2-c5;
  Qmax;
  Sort;
  Brief 3.
Note '(3) Factor Analysis - ML-Emax'
Factor c2-c5;
  NFAC = 2;
  ML;
  Emax;
  Sort;
  Brief 3.
```

Note: An eigenvalue is the variance explained by a factor.

Exercise Example 14-11: Unit Root Test and Cointegration Test [*]

Unit Root Test:

Unit root test is used to test if a time series is a random walk. A time series is a random walk

if $y_t = y_{t-1} + e_t$ (1)

or $y_t = a\,t + y_{t-1} + e_t$ (2)

where t = time and e = the error term. The coefficient of y_{t-1} is equal to 1.0. If ρ is not equal to 1.0, we would reject the null hypothesis (random walk hypothesis). Equation (2) represents a random walk with time drift. Neither the conventional DW statistic nor the conventional F test can be used when $\rho = 1$. In such a case, the Dickey-Fuller F test can be used.

The unit root test requires the following 4 steps:

Step 1: Calculate a regression equation for the unrestricted model:

$$\Delta y_t = a + b\,t + (\rho - 1)\,y_{t-1} + \sum_{i=1}^{p} c_i\,\Delta y_{t-i} + e_t \qquad (\text{UR})$$

where p = the order of lags selected by a researcher.

From the above regression results, find ESSur (Error Sum of Squares) $\sum (y_t - \hat{y})^2$ for the unrestricted case.

Step 2: Calculate a regression equation for the restricted model:

$$\Delta y_t = a + \sum_{i=1}^{p} c_i\,\Delta y_{t-i} + e_t \qquad (\text{R})$$

From the above regression results, find ESS (Error Sum of Squares) $\sum (y_t - \hat{y})^2$ for the restricted model.

Step 3: Compute the F ratio by substituting the values of ESS in the following formula:

$$F = \frac{(ESSr - ESSur)/Q}{ESSur / (N-k)}$$

where   ESSr = Error Sum of Squares (Squared Sum of Residuals) for restricted equation
ESSur = Error Sum of Squares, Squared Sum of Residuals for unrestricted equation
N = Number of observations in unrestricted equations
k = Number of parameters estimated in the unrestricted equation
Q = Number of parameters estimated in the restricted equation

---

[*] For detailed explanations and examples, see: Ramanathan, R., *Introductory Econometrics with Applications*, 2nd ed., 1992, pp. 501-505, 438-440, and Pindyck and Rubinfeld, *Econometric Models and Economic Forecasts*, pp. 110-111, 461-465.

Step 4: Compare the computed F ratio with the critical Dickey-Fuller F ratio:

If computed F ≤ Critical F, accept the null hypothesis (random walk)
If computed F > Critical F, reject the null hypothesis (random walk)

The critical F ratios are given below:

Critical Values of Dickey-Fuller F Ratio (5% and 10% Levels)

N	25	50	100	250	500	∞
5 %	7.24	6.73	6.49	6.34	6.30	6.25
10 %	5.91	5.61	5.47	5.39	5.36	5.34

Source: Dickey, D.A., and Fuller, W.A., "Likelihood Ratio Statistics for Autoregressive Time Series with a Unit Root", *Econometrica*, July 1981, pp.1057-1072.

Example: If N = 25, and if the computed F-ratio is less than 7.24, accept the random walk hypothesis at the 5% level. If the computed F-ratio is greater than 7.24, reject the random walk hypothesis.

Cointegration Test:

Cointegration test is used to see if two time series variables do not depart away over the long run. That is, if two time series x and y are random walks (nonstationary), OLS regression in levels can cause a spurious correlation (a false correlation caused by chance or by statistical manipulation), and inconsistent estimation. (1) In such a case, differenced variables may be used for regression if the differenced variables are no longer random walks. (2) However, if x and y hold the property of "cointegration", OLS estimation in level variables without differencing can be used to estimate a long-run relationship between the variables. Cointegrated time series imply that the two series will not depart away as time passes, and will stay close to each other.

Two variables x and y are said to be "co-integrated" variables if a linear combination of x and y such as $z = x - \lambda y$ is stationary, where λ is a cointegrating constant. A time series is stationary if the series has a constant mean and variance. A nonstationary time series has an increasing or decreasing mean and variance.

Then, the question is how can we tell if the variables are cointegrated? There are 2 test methods:

(1) Method 1 - Cointegrating regression test (Augmented DW statistic test):

Apply the OLS to obtain the following regression equation (cointegration regression):

$$y_t = a + b x_t + e_t$$

Then, obtain the DW statistic for the above equation. The computed DW statistic should be compared with the critical values of the Dickey-Fuller augmented DW statistic, not the regular DW statistic.

If computed DW ≤ critical F, accept the null hypothesis of no-cointegration.
If computed DW > critical F, reject the null hypothesis of no-cointegration.

The critical augmented Dickey-Fuller DW values are given on the next page.

If the computed DW statistic is less than the critical value of Cointegration (Engle-Granger) DW statistic (for instance, 0.386 at 5% level, N = 100), accept the null hypothesis of "no-cointegration". Otherwise, accept the co-integration hypothesis" (see the table below).

(2) Method 2 - Dickey-Fuller t test (augmented t statistic):

First, apply the OLS for the following regression (cointegration regression):

$$y_t = a + b\,x_t + e_t$$

And obtain the error terms:

$$e_t = y_t - a - b\,x_t$$

Using the error term e_t, run the following Dickey-Fuller regression:

$$\Delta e_t = -\alpha\, e_{t-1} + \sum_{i=1}^{p} \beta_i\, \Delta e_{t-i} + v_t$$

where p = the order of lags selected by a researcher, v_t = the error term of the Dickey-Fuller regression.

If computed t value for the coefficient α of the lagged error term e_{t-1} is less than the Augmented Dickey-Fuller (Engle-Granger) t-statistic (for instance, 3.17 at 5% level, N = 100), accept the null hypothesis of no-cointegration. Otherwise, we accept cointegration hypothesis.

Critical Values of Cointegration Tests (N = 100)

	1 %	5 %	10 %
Cointegration DW statistic	0.511	0.386	0.322
Augmented DF t-statistic	3.77	3.17	2.84

DF = Dickey-Fuller, DW = Durbin-Watson Source: Engle, R.F., and Granger, C.W.J., "Co-integration and Error Correction: Representation, Estimation, and Testing", *Econometrica*, March 1987, pp. 251-276.

The following file tests if the US and UK stock prices are random walks, the sample file in Example 17-5 tests if they are cointegrated.

```
Note 'Unit Root Test of Random Walk Hypothesis'
Name c1 = 'year' c2='Korea' c3='USA' c4='UK' c5='Germany'
Name c6 = 'France' c7 = 'Japan'
# stock price indexes in each country
# USA .. New York Stock Exchange
Read c1-c7
1971     *       54.23   163.94    675.20    97.50   179.72
1972     *       60.34   214.81    737.40   120.30   282.42
1973     *       57.42   184.67    670.80   103.50   362.46
1974     *       43.84   106.74    564.20    85.30   307.21
1975     *       45.74   133.16    688.40   125.50   312.06
1976    97.90    54.48   153.04    753.80    93.30   347.51
1977   113.40    53.69   191.83    762.90    90.70   376.78
1978   143.70    53.70   217.66    812.60   134.20   415.41
1979   120.60    58.32   245.50    761.70   109.80   449.88
1980   180.80    68.10   271.43    712.60   102.10   474.00
1981   126.30    74.02   307.73    701.40    83.70   552.29
1982   122.03    68.92   342.61    699.00   101.40   548.28
1983   127.70    92.67   434.99    920.20   128.50   647.41
1984   131.88    92.47   516.25   1030.80   174.60   815.47
```

```
1985    138.93    108.07    631.30   1411.00    208.80    997.72
1986    227.78    136.03    785.17   2013.20    362.20   1324.26
1987    417.55    161.78   1026.21   1757.10    379.60   1963.29
1988    693.14    149.96    932.21   1452.10    330.50   2134.24
1989    918.60    180.14   1110.37   1823.30    482.10   2569.27
1990    747.00    183.48   1092.63   2108.30    471.70   2177.96
1991    657.13    206.34   1187.68   1875.20    470.40   1827.54
End
Set c9
1:21/1
End
# -----------------------------------------------------
# A. Unit Root Test for USA stocks
Name c9='time' c10 = 'ChangeP' c11 = 'LagP' c12='loglagP'
Let c10 = c3 - Lag(c3)
Let c11 = Lag(c10)
Let c12 = Lag(c3)
# (1) Restricted regression
Regress c10 on 1 c11;
   Resid in c13;
   DW.
Let c14 = c13*c13
Let k1 = Sum(c14)
# (2) Unrestricted regression
Regress c10 on 3 c9 c12 c11;
   Resid in c15;
   DW.
Let c16=c15*c15
Let k2 = sum(c16)
# (3) Dickey-Fuller F ratio
# F = (N-K)(ESSr - ESSur)/[Q(ESSur)]
Let k3 = (21-4)*(k1-k2)/(2*k2)
print c1, c3, c9-c16
# k1 = ESSr, k2 = ESSur, k3 = F-ratio
# ESS = Error Sum of Squares, Sum of Squared Residuals : r =
restricted,
#  ur = unrestricted
print k1,k2,k3
# -------------------------------------------
# B. Unit Root Test for UK stocks
Let c20 = c4 - Lag(c4)
Let c21 = Lag(c20)
Let c22 = Lag(c4)
# (1) Restricted regression
Regress c20 on 1 c21;
   Resid in c23;
   DW.
Let c24 = c23*c23
Let k11 = Sum(c24)
# (2) Unrestricted regression
Regress c20 on 3 c9 c22 c21;
   Resid in c25;
   DW.
Let c26=c25*c25
Let k12 = sum(c26)
# (3) Dickey-Fuller F ratio
# F = (N-K)(ESSr - ESSur)/[Q(ESSur)]
Let k13 = (21-4)*(k11-k12)/(2*k12)
print c1, c4, c9-c26
# k11 = ESSr, k12 = ESSur, k13 = F-ratio
# ESS = Error Sum of Squares, Sum of Squared Residuals
# : r = restricted,
#  ur = unrestricted
print k11,k12,k13
```

Edited Partial Output:

```
MTB > # A. Unit Root Test for USA stocks
```

```
MTB > Name c9='time' c10 ='ChangeP' c11 ='DLagP' c12='LagP'
MTB > Let c10 = c3 - Lag(c3)
MTB > Let c11 = Lag(c10)
MTB > Let c12 = Lag(c3)
MTB > # (1) Restricted regression
MTB > Regress c10 on 1 c11;
SUBC>    Resid in c13;
SUBC>    DW.
```

The regression equation is
ChangeP = 8.55 - 0.127 DLagP
19 cases used 2 cases contain missing values

Predictor	Coef	Stdev	t-ratio	p
Constant	8.548	3.544	2.41	0.027
LagP	-0.1270	0.2505	-0.51	0.619

s = 13.55   R-sq = 1.5%   R-sq(adj) = 0.0%
Analysis of Variance

SOURCE	DF	SS	MS	F	p
Regression	1	47.2	47.2	0.26	0.619
Error	17	3119.1	183.5		
Total	18	3166.3			

Durbin-Watson statistic = 1.85
```
MTB > Let c14 = c13*c13
MTB > Let k1 = Sum(c14)
MTB > # (2) Unrestricted regression
MTB > Regress c10 on 3 c9 c12 c11;
SUBC>    Resid in c15;
SUBC>    DW.
```
The regression equation is
ChangeP = - 9.54 + 2.89 time - 0.160 loglagP - 0.404 LagP
19 cases used 2 cases contain missing values

Predictor	Coef	Stdev	t-ratio	p
Constant	-9.537	5.784	-1.65	0.120
time	2.888	1.022	2.83	0.013
loglagP	-0.1601	0.1256	-1.28	0.222
LagP	-0.4036	0.2186	-1.85	0.085

s = 10.24   R-sq = 50.3%   R-sq(adj) = 40.4%
Analysis of Variance

SOURCE	DF	SS	MS	F	p
Regression	3	1592.4	530.8	5.06	0.013
Error	15	1573.8	104.9		
Total	18	3166.3			

SOURCE	DF	SEQ SS
time	1	902.6
loglagP	1	332.2
LagP	1	357.6

Durbin-Watson statistic = 2.36
```
MTB > Let c16=c15*c15
MTB > Let k2 = sum(c16)
MTB > # (3) Dickey-Fuller F ratio
MTB > # F = (N-K)(ESSr - ESSur)/[Q(ESSur)]
MTB > Let k3 = (21-4)*(k1-k2)/(2*k2)
MTB > print c1, c3, c9-c16
MTB > print k1,k2,k3
K1       3119.12
K2       1573.85
K3       8.34567
MTB > # ------------------------------------------
MTB > # B. Unit Root Test for UK stocks
MTB > Let c20 = c4 - Lag(c4)
MTB > Let c21 = Lag(c20)
MTB > Let c22 = Lag(c4)
MTB > # (1) Restricted regression
MTB > Regress c20 on 1 c21;
SUBC>    Resid in c23;
SUBC>    DW.
```
The regression equation is

```
C20 = 56.1 - 0.100 C21
19 cases used 2 cases contain missing values
Predictor        Coef       Stdev      t-ratio         p
Constant        56.09       22.87        2.45       0.025
C21            -0.0999      0.2433      -0.41       0.687
s = 85.15      R-sq = 1.0%     R-sq(adj) = 0.0%
Analysis of Variance
SOURCE        DF          SS         MS        F        p
Regression    1         1222       1222      0.17    0.687
Error        17       123268       7251
Total        18       124490
Durbin-Watson statistic = 1.86
MTB > Let c24 = c23*c23
MTB > Let k11 = Sum(c24)
MTB > # (2) Unrestricted regression
MTB > Regress c20 on 3 c9 c22 c21;
SUBC>    Resid in c25;
SUBC>    DW.
The regression equation is
C20 = - 89.3 + 21.8 time - 0.229 C22 - 0.290 C21
19 cases used 2 cases contain missing values
Predictor        Coef       Stdev      t-ratio         p
Constant       -89.33       44.74       -2.00       0.064
time           21.822       7.158        3.05       0.008
C22           -0.2288      0.1165       -1.96       0.068
C21           -0.2898      0.2133       -1.36       0.194
s = 66.78      R-sq = 46.3%    R-sq(adj) = 35.5%
Analysis of Variance
SOURCE        DF          SS         MS        F        p
Regression    3        57590      19197     4.30    0.022
Error        15        66900       4460
Total        18       124490
SOURCE        DF       SEQ SS
time          1        27219
C22           1        22142
C21           1         8229
Durbin-Watson statistic = 2.03
MTB > Let c26=c25*c25
MTB > Let k12 = sum(c26)
MTB > # (3) Dickey-Fuller F ratio
MTB > # F = (N-K)(ESSr - ESSur)/[Q(ESSur)]
MTB > Let k13 = (21-4)*(k11-k12)/(2*k12)
MTB > print c1, c4, c9-c26
MTB > # k11 = ESSr, k12 = ESSur, k13 = F-ratio
MTB > # ESS = Error Sum of Squares, Sum of Squared Residuals
MTB > # : r = restricted,
MTB > #  ur = unrestricted
MTB > print k11,k12,k13
K11       123268
K12       66900.2
K13        7.16187
```

The computed F value for US stocks is:

$$F = \frac{(ESSr - ESSur)/Q}{ESSur / (N-k)} = \frac{(3119.12-1573.85)/2}{1573.85/(21-4)} = 8.3457 = k3$$

The computed F value for UK stocks is:

$$F = \frac{(ESSr - ESSur)/Q}{ESSur / (N-k)} = \frac{(123268-66900)/2}{66900/(21-4)} = 7.1619 = k13$$

The critical F value is 7.24 at $\alpha = 0.05$, N = 25.

For US stock, 8.3457 > 7.24, so we reject the null hypothesis (random walk, unit root). For UK stock 7.1619 < 7.24, so we cannot reject the null hypothesis.

Cointegration Test:

```
Note 'Cointegration Test for USA and UK stocks'
Name c1 = 'year' c2='Korea' c3='USA' c4='UK' c5='Germany'
Name c6 = 'France' c7 = 'Japan'
# stock price indexes in each country
# USA .. New York Stock Exchange
Read c1-c7
1971      *        54.23    163.94    675.20     97.50    179.72
1972      *        60.34    214.81    737.40    120.30    282.42
1973      *        57.42    184.67    670.80    103.50    362.46
1974      *        43.84    106.74    564.20     85.30    307.21
1975      *        45.74    133.16    688.40    125.50    312.06
1976     97.90     54.48    153.04    753.80     93.30    347.51
1977    113.40     53.69    191.83    762.90     90.70    376.78
1978    143.70     53.70    217.66    812.60    134.20    415.41
1979    120.60     58.32    245.50    761.70    109.80    449.88
1980    180.80     68.10    271.43    712.60    102.10    474.00
1981    126.30     74.02    307.73    701.40     83.70    552.29
1982    122.03     68.92    342.61    699.00    101.40    548.28
1983    127.70     92.67    434.99    920.20    128.50    647.41
1984    131.88     92.47    516.25   1030.80    174.60    815.47
1985    138.93    108.07    631.30   1411.00    208.80    997.72
1986    227.78    136.03    785.17   2013.20    362.20   1324.26
1987    417.55    161.78   1026.21   1757.10    379.60   1963.29
1988    693.14    149.96    932.21   1452.10    330.50   2134.24
1989    918.60    180.14   1110.37   1823.30    482.10   2569.27
1990    747.00    183.48   1092.63   2108.30    471.70   2177.96
1991    657.13    206.34   1187.68   1875.20    470.40   1827.54
end
Set c9
1:21/1
End
# (1) DW test for Cointegration
Regress c3 on 1 c4;
   Resid in c9;
   DW.
# If the computed DW statistic is less than the critical value of
# Cointegration (Engle-Granger) DW statistic (0.386 at 5 % level,
N = 100),
# accept the null hypothesis of "no-cointegration".
# Otherwise, accept co-integration hypothesis".
# (2) Dickey-Fuller test for Cointegration
Let c10 = Lag(c9)
Let c11 = c9 - c10
Let c12 = Lag(c11)
Let c13 = Lag(c12)
# 2nd order lag process is assumed:
Regress c11 on 3 c10 c12 c13;
   Noconstant;
   DW.
```

Edited Output:

```
MTB > # (1) DW test for Cointegration
MTB > Regress c3 on 1 c4;
SUBC>    Resid in c9;
SUBC>    DW.
The regression equation is
usa = 28.0 + 0.138 uk
Predictor       Coef      Stdev     t-ratio        p
Constant      27.987      2.065      13.55      0.000
UK          0.138149   0.003385      40.82      0.000
```

```
s = 5.681        R-sq = 98.9%      R-sq(adj) = 98.8%
Analysis of Variance
SOURCE       DF        SS          MS        F         p
Regression    1       53767       53767    1665.87    0.000
Error        19         613          32
Total        20       54380
Durbin-Watson statistic = 1.23


MTB > # (2) Dickey-Fuller test for Cointegration
MTB > Let c10 = Lag(c9)
MTB > Let c11 = c9 - c10
MTB > Let c12 = Lag(c11)
MTB > Let c13 = Lag(c12)
MTB > # 2nd order lag process is assumed:
MTB > Regress c11 on 3 c10 c12 c13;
SUBC>    Noconstant;
SUBC>    DW.
The regression equation is
C11 = - 0.746 C10 + 0.031 C12 - 0.023 C13
Predictor      Coef       Stdev     t-ratio       p
Noconstant
C10          -0.7460      0.4743     -1.57      0.137
C12           0.0314      0.4059      0.08      0.939
C13          -0.0227      0.3123     -0.07      0.943
s = 6.034
Analysis of Variance
SOURCE       DF         SS          MS        F         p
Regression    3       203.20       67.73     1.86      0.180
Error        15       546.22       36.41
Total        18       749.42
SOURCE       DF       SEQ SS
C10           1       202.08
C12           1         0.92
C13           1         0.19
Durbin-Watson statistic = 1.68
```

Cointegration Test Results:

(1) The computed DW statistic for the cointegration regression equation is 1.23. The critical value of DW statistic is 0.386 at the 5% level for N = 100. Since the computed DW (1.23) > critical DW (0.386), we reject the null hypothesis of no-cointegration. That is, US and UK stocks are co-integrated.

(2) The computed t ratio for the lagged error term (e_{t-1}) is -1.57. The critical value of augmented Dickey-Fuller t-statistic is 3.17 at the 5% level for N = 100. Since the computed DW (1.57) < critical t (3.17), we accept the null hypothesis of no-cointegration.

The two test results are conflicting, but it should be noted that the critical values were obtained from simulations on sample size N = 100. The critical values are not available for other sample sizes.

Chapter 15.
Techniques of Quality Control

Quality control or process control is a statistical method of evaluating a series or process of events and objects. A process or series of events and objects may include production of goods and sales. It examines sample items to see if they are within an acceptable confidence interval. If the sample items are out of a given confidence interval, the process is regarded as out of control. The categories of industrial quality control include the size and weight of products, the life of bulbs, tires and batteries, print quality, softness or hardness of goods, defective video-phone, etc.

Quality Control Charts

Minitab quality control charts include the following 17 charts:

A: Variable Control Charts

(1) X-bar chart	Mean or median chart
(2) R chart	R chart for subgroup ranges
(3) S chart	S chart for standard deviations in subgroups
(4) X-R chart	Mean and R charts for subgroup averages and ranges
(5) X-S chart	Mean and S charts for subgroup averages and standard deviations
(6) I chart	Individual moving range chart (IR chart)
(7) MR chart	Median and range charts
(8) I-MR chart	Mean chart for subgroup averages with an optional time trend plot
(9) EWMA-chart	Exponentially weighted moving average chart
(10) MA-chart	Moving average chart
(11) CUSUM	Cumulative sum chart

B. Attributes Control Charts

(12) NP chart	NP chart for number of defective items in subgroups
(13) P chart	P chart for proportions of defective items in subgroups
(14) U chart	U cart for number of defects per unit
(15) C chart	C chart for the number of defects per unit

C. Quality Control Planning Charts

(16) Pareto	Pareto chart (%Pareto)
(17) Fishbone	Fishbone chart (%Fishbone)

Some of the formulas for the control charts are:

X-bar chart: (Normal distribution)
    Center line μ
    LCL $\mu - k\ \sigma/\sqrt{n}$
    UCL $\mu + k\ \sigma/\sqrt{n}$

R-chart: (Normal distribution)
    Center line $d_2\ (n)\ \sigma$
    LCL $\max\ \{d_2\ (n)\ \sigma - k\ d_3\ (n)\ \sigma, 0\}$

P-chart: (Binomial distribution)
    Center line   p
    LCL $\max\{p - k\sqrt{p(1-p)/n}, 0\}$
    UCL $\min\{p + k\sqrt{p(1-p)/n}, 1\}$

C-chart: (Poisson distribution)
    Center line   c
    LCL $\max\{c - k\sqrt{c}, 0\}$
    UCL $c + k\sqrt{\mu}$

Note: For the full set of formulas, see Minitab QC Manual, Release 9 for Windows, 1993.

Exercise Example 15-1: X-Bar Chart

ATT produces frames for desktop computers. Janet Lugg, director of quality control, collected 10 different samples of size 12 and measured the width of each frame. She wanted to know if the process machine is in control. Run the file and determine if the process is in control. File Name: Webst891.inp

```
Note 'X-bar chart: Webst891.inp'
# Webster, p. 891, Table 18-1 computer frame
Name c1='frame'
# frame ='computer frame'
Set c1
16.2  17.1  15.9  15.8  17.2  16.9  16.8  17.1
17.2  16.5  16.4  16.3
17.3  16.5  15.1  15.9  16.2  16.2  16.8  17.5
17.1  16.2  16.3  16.4
17.1  16.5  16.5  15.8  15.7  15.7  15.8  16.2
17.2  15.3  16.1  16.4
17.3  16.2  17.1  17.1  15.8  15.9  15.9  16.2
17.1  17.0  17.1  15.2
16.2  15.1  15.3  16.1  17.3  17.1  17.0  16.0
15.3  15.1  16.1  17.1
17.1  17.0  16.0  15.3  17.5  17.3  17.1  17.2
17.2  16.9  16.1  16.5
17.0  17.1  16.2  16.2  16.3  15.8  17.1  16.0
15.3  16.9  16.5  17.3
17.5  15.2  17.3  16.3  16.3  15.1  15.9  15.8
17.1  17.1  16.9  16.3
17.3  17.2  16.3  16.1  16.5  15.6  15.7  15.7
15.8  16.1  17.1  17.1
17.1  15.2  15.3  15.3  15.5  16.1  17.1  17.3
17.1  17.2  17.2  17.2
End
Note '(1) X-Bar chart'
Xbarchart c1 12
Note '(2) X-bar chart'
Xbarchart c1 12;
  Slimits 1 2 3;
  Test 1:8.
%Capa c1 12;
  USpec 18;
  Lspec 15.
%Sixpack c1 12;
  Uspec 18;
  Lspec 15.
```

Note: %Capa and %Sixpack are macro files that show normality fit, histograms, Xbar and R chart, etc. Uspec 18 and Lspec 15 are approximate upper and lower limits of the values in the data set. These macro files are available in Minitab for Windows version 9.0.

Edited Output:

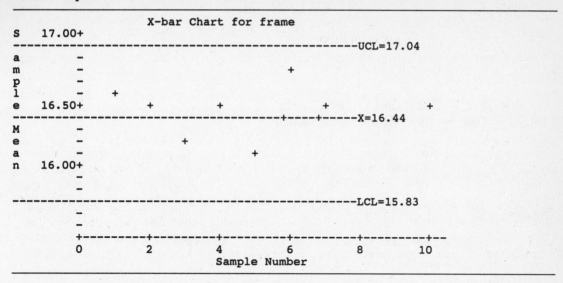

```
                        X-bar Chart for frame
S    17.00+
     ---------------------------------------------------UCL=17.04
a          -
m          -                               +
p          -
l          -      +
e    16.50+       +          +              +              +
     ----------------------------------+----+-----X=16.44
M          -
e          -          +
a          -                  +
n    16.00+
           -
           -
     ---------------------------------------------------LCL=15.83
           -
           -
           +---------+---------+---------+---------+---------+--
           0         2         4         6         8         10
                              Sample Number
```

Exercise Example 15-2: R-Chart and Other Charts

In the previous example, the control levels were set in terms of standard deviations of the means. In the R-chart, the control levels are set in terms of the standard deviation of the sample ranges. Janet Lugg wanted to draw the R-chart and all other available charts using the same data. Run the file and find if the process is in control. File Name: Webs891B.inp

```
Note 'R-Chart and Other Charts: Webs891B.inp'
# Webster, p. 891, Table 18-1 computer frame
Name c1='frame'
# frame ='computer frame'
Set c1
16.2   17.1   15.9   15.8   17.2   16.9   16.8   17.1
17.2   16.5   16.4   16.3
17.3   16.5   15.1   15.9   16.2   16.2   16.8   17.5
17.1   16.2   16.3   16.4
17.1   16.5   16.5   15.8   15.7   15.7   15.8   16.2
17.2   15.3   16.1   16.4
17.3   16.2   17.1   17.1   15.8   15.9   15.9   16.2
17.1   17.0   17.1   15.2
16.2   15.1   15.3   16.1   17.3   17.1   17.0   16.0
15.3   15.1   16.1   17.1
17.1   17.0   16.0   15.3   17.5   17.3   17.1   17.2
17.2   16.9   16.1   16.5
17.0   17.1   16.2   16.2   16.3   15.8   17.1   16.0
15.3   16.9   16.5   17.3
17.5   15.2   17.3   16.3   16.3   15.1   15.9   15.8
17.1   17.1   16.9   16.3
17.3   17.2   16.3   16.1   16.5   15.6   15.7   15.7
15.8   16.1   17.1   17.1
17.1   15.2   15.3   15.3   15.5   16.1   17.1   17.3
17.1   17.2   17.2   17.2
End
# Variable Control Charts (total 11 charts)
Rchart      c1 12
Xbarchart c1 12
Schart      c1 12
%XRchart c1 12
%XSchart c1 12
Ichart      c1
MRchart    c1
```

```
%IMRchart c1
EWMAchart c1 12
MAchart    c1 12
%Cusum     c1 12
```

Note: XRchart, XSchart, %IMRchart, and %Cumsum are available In Minitab for Windows version 9.0.

Example 15-3: P-Chart and Other Charts
- Percent of Defective Units: Binomial Distribution

Opus, Inc. makes electric guitars. The quality control manager selected 15 different samples (k=15) of size 40 (n=40), and recorded the number of defective guitars in each sample as shown in the data set. That is, he inspected 15x40 = 600 guitars and 211 guitars were defective. He wanted to know if the process is in control. Run the file and find if the process is in control. File Name: Webst898.inp

```
Note 'P-Chart: Proportion of defective Units - Webst898.inp'
# P-chart: percent (proportion) of defective units: Binomial Distribution
# Attribute control charts
# Webster, p. 898, Table 18-2
Name c1='sample' c2='defect' c3='size'
# sample='sample no.'
# defect='No. of  defects'
# size = 'sample size'
Read c1-c3
1   10    40
2   12    40
3    9    40
4   15    40
5   27    40
6    8    40
7   11    40
8   11    40
9   13    40
10  15    40
11  17    40
12   3    40
13  25    40
14  18    40
15  17    40
End
Pchart  c2 c3
NPchart c2 c3
Cchart  c2
Uchart  c2 c3
```

Edited Partial Output:

```
MTB > Pchart   c2 c3
                         P Chart for defect
      0.750+
          -
          -              +
P         - -------------------------------------------+-------UCL=0.5782
r         -
o     0.500+
p         -                                         +
o         -                               +       +
r         - -----------+-------------------------+----------------P=0.3517
t         -         +                     +
i     0.250+  +                  +  +
o         -          +         +
n         - -----------------------------------------------------LCL=0.1252
```

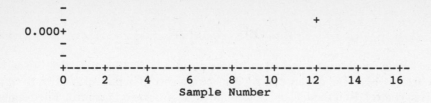

```
           -
           -
   0.000+                                              +
           -
           -
          +-----+-----+-----+-----+-----+-----+-----+-----+-
          0     2     4     6     8    10    12    14    16
                         Sample Number
```

Exercise Example 15-4: C-Chart
- Number of Defects per Unit: Poisson Distribution

International Paper selected 20 sheets (samples) of gift wrap paper for defects. The number of defects on each sheet is recorded as shown in the data set. The quality control manager wants to know if the paper production process is in control. A c-chart can be used for the number of defects per unit which may be a computer unit, 100 computer units, 10-printed pages, 100-square-yard piece of carpet. In the following file, 2 types of units are used as examples: defects per unit and defects per 20 units. Run the file and find if the process is in control. File Name: Webst901.inp

```
Note 'C-Chart Quality Control: Webst901.inp'
# imperfect part per unit: Poisson distribution
# Webster, p. 901, Table 18-3
Name c1='sample' c2='defect'
# sample ='sample number'
# defect ='no. of defects'
Set c1
1:20
End
Set c2
5    4    3  5  16  1   8   9  9   4
3   15   10  8   4  2  10  12  7  17
End
Cchart   c2
Uchart   c2 1
```

Exercise Example 15-5: IR Chart
- Individual Observations

Nashua Corporation makes thermally responsive papers which is used in printers and recording instruments. The paper is coated with a chemical mixture, and the amount of material coated on the paper (weight coat) must be in control. In each shift, 12 rolls of paper are coated. For 2 shifts, 24 values of weight coat, in pounds per 3,000 square feet, were measured as given in the data set. Run the file and find if the process is in control. File Name: ACZEL622.inp

```
Note 'Box Chart and IR Chart: Aczel622.inp'
# Aczel, p. 622
Name c1='weight'
set c1
3.46    3.56    3.58    3.49    3.45    3.51
3.54    3.48    3.54    3.49    3.55    3.60
3.62    3.60    3.53    3.60    3.51    3.54
3.60    3.61    3.49    3.60    3.60    3.49
End
Ichart      c1
MRchart     c1
%IMRchart   c1
%Capa c1 2;
  USpec 3.6;
  LSpec 3.45.
%Sixpack c1 2;
  USpec 3.6;
```

```
    LSpec 3.45.
```

Exercise Example 15-6: Range Chart and Other Charts

At Cool-Cola plant bottle weights are checked at 4 time periods, 8, 9, 10 and 11 a.m. At each time period, 5 bottles are weighed. The quality-control inspector wants to obtain an R-chart to find if the bottle machine is in control. Run the file and determine if the process is in control. File Name: Mason755.inp

```
Note 'R-Chart for Quality Control: Mason755.inp'
# Mason, p. 755, Example
Name c1='weight'
# weight='bottle weight'
Set c1
41   43   42   41   43
39   40   40   39   42
41   44   43   46   41
38   39   40   39   39
End
Xbarchart    c1 5
Rchart       c1 5
Schart       c1 5
%XRchart     c1 5
%XSchart     c1 5
Ichart       c1
MRchart      c1
%IMRchart    c1
EWMAchart    c1 5
MAchart      c1 5
%Cusum       c1 5
```

Exercise Example 15-7: X-Bar Chart and R chart

The quality control manager of Slippery Soap, Inc. selected at random 5 boxes from each batch of 150 boxes of dishwater detergent and weighed the contents. Since there were 25 batches, 75 detergent boxes were selected and weighed. She wanted to know if the packaging equipment is in control. Run the file and find if the process is in control. File Name: Siege739.inp

```
Note 'Quality Control Charts: Siege739.inp'
# Siegel, p. 739, Table 18.3.4 - net weights of boxes
# weight ='soap weight in ounces';
Name c1='weight'
set c1
16.12   16.03   16.25   16.19   16.24
16.11   16.10   16.28   16.18   16.16
16.16   16.21   16.10   16.09   16.04
15.97   15.99   16.34   16.18   16.02
16.21   16.00   16.14   16.12   16.10
15.77   16.11   16.01   16.02   16.17
16.02   16.29   16.08   15.96   16.11
15.83   16.08   16.25   16.14   16.15
16.16   15.90   16.08   15.98   16.09
16.08   16.10   16.13   16.03   16.03
15.90   16.16   16.15   15.99   16.07
16.09   16.05   16.07   15.98   15.95
15.98   16.18   16.08   16.08   16.07
16.23   16.05   16.10   16.07   16.16
15.96   16.20   16.35   16.11   16.08
16.00   16.04   16.02   16.03   16.09
16.12   16.12   15.95   15.98   16.10
16.30   16.05   16.10   16.09   16.07
16.11   16.15   16.25   16.03   16.05
15.85   16.06   15.96   16.20   16.25
```

```
15.94   15.88   16.02   16.06   16.10
16.15   16.15   16.21   15.95   16.13
16.10   16.17   16.24   16.00   15.87
16.22   16.34   16.40   16.07   16.12
16.32   15.97   15.88   16.03   16.27
End
Xbarchart  c1 5
Rchart     c1 5
Schart     c1 5
%XRchart   c1 5
%XSchart   c1 5
Ichart     c1
MRchart    c1
%IMRchart  c1
EWMAchart  c1 5
MAchart    c1 5
%Cusum     c1 5
```

Exercise Example 15-8: P-Chart and Other Charts

The quality control manager selected 12 samples (k = 12) of sample size 500 (n = 500). The number of defective items was recorded for each sample. Run the file and find if the process is in control. File Name: Siege742.inp

```
Note 'P-Chart: Attribute control charts: Siege742.inp'
# Siegel, p. 742
Name c1='sample' c2='defect' c3='size'
# sample='No.'
# defect='defects'
# size = 'sample size'
Read c1-c3
1   10    500
2   11    500
3   10    500
4   12    500
5    7    500
6   14    500
7   13    500
8   11    500
9    6    500
10  12    500
11  11    500
12  13    500
End
Pchart    c2 c3
NPchart   c2 c3
Cchart    c2
Uchart    c2 c3
```

Exercise Example 15-9: P-Chart and Other Charts

In data entry operation, 200 data entries were inspected for 24 consecutive days. The number of defective entries was recorded. The quality control manager wanted to know if the data entry operation is in control. Run the file and find the answer. File Name: Gitlo168.inp

```
Note 'P chart: Attribute control charts: Gitlo168.inp'
# Gitlow, p. 168, Figure 8.5
Name c1=defect' c2='size'
# sample defect size;
# defect='number of defective entries'
# 200  ='sample size'
Set c1
6  6  6  5  0  0  6  14  4   0  1  8
2  4  7  1  3  1  4   0  4  15  4  1
End
```

```
Set c2
Pchart   c1 200
NPchart  c1 200
Cchart   c1
Uchart   c1 200
```

Exercise Example 15-10: P-Chart and Other Charts

The quality control manager of an orange juice firm selected 50 cans (n = 50) from each production run of 30 (k = 30). The number of defective cans was recorded. She wanted to know if the orange juice can process is in control. Run the file and find the answer. File Name: Gitlo177.inp

```
Note 'P-Chart: Attribute control charts: Gitlo177.inp'
# Gitlow, p. 177, Figure 8.10
Name c1='defect'
# defect='number of defectives'
# 50 ='sample size';
Set c1
12   15   8 10   4   7 16   9 14 10   5   6   17   12   22
 8   10   5 13  11  20 18 24 15   9 12   7   13    9    6
End
Pchart   c1 50
NPchart  c1 50
Cchart   c1
Uchart   c1 50
```

Exercise Example 15-11: R-Chart and Other Charts

Liquid medication is filled to a specification of 52 grams in a vial at a pharmaceutical firm. The firm selected 6 vials every 5 minutes during a 105 minute period. The firm wanted to know if the vial weights are in control. Run the file and find the answer in the Range chart. File Name: Gitlo180.inp

```
Note 'R charts and other charts: Gitlo180.inp'
# Gitlow, p. 180, Figure 8.12
Data gitlo180;
Name c1='weight'
# weight ='vial weight'
Set c1
   52.22   52.85   52.41   52.55   53.10   52.47
   52.25   52.14   51.79   52.18   52.26   51.94
   52.37   52.69   52.26   52.53   52.34   52.81
   52.46   52.32   52.34   52.08   52.07   52.07
   52.06   52.35   51.85   52.02   52.30   52.20
   52.59   51.79   52.20   51.90   51.88   52.83
   51.82   52.12   52.47   51.82   52.49   52.60
   52.51   52.80   52.00   52.47   51.91   51.74
   52.13   52.26   52.00   51.89   52.11   52.27
   51.18   52.31   51.24   51.59   51.46   51.47
   51.74   52.23   52.23   51.70   52.12   52.12
   52.38   52.20   52.06   52.08   52.10   52.01
   51.68   52.06   51.90   51.78   51.85   51.40
   51.84   52.15   52.18   52.07   52.22   51.78
   51.98   52.31   51.71   51.97   52.11   52.10
   52.32   52.43   53.00   52.26   52.15   52.36
   51.92   52.67   52.80   52.89   52.56   52.23
   51.94   51.96   52.73   52.72   51.94   52.99
   51.39   51.59   52.44   51.94   51.39   51.67
   51.55   51.77   52.41   52.32   51.22   52.04
   51.97   51.52   51.48   52.35   51.45   52.19
   52.15   51.67   51.67   52.16   52.07   51.81
End
Xbarchart c1 6
Rchart    c1 6
Schart    c1 6
%XRchart  c1 6
```

```
%XRchart   c1 6
%XSchart   c1 6
Ichart     c1
MRchart    c1
%IMRchart  c1
EWMAchart  c1 6
MAchart    c1 6
%Cusum     c1 6
```

Exercise Example 15-12: P-Chart and Other Charts

A firm imports decorative ceramic tiles. Some tiles are cracked or broken before or during transit. The firm draws a sample of 100 tiles from all tiles received from each tile vendor. The number of defective tiles are recorded for 30 shipments received. The firm wants to know if the tiles are in control. Run the file and find the answer. File Name: Gitlo225.inp

```
Note 'P chart and others: Gitlo225.inp'
# Gitlow, p. 225, Figure 9.3
Name c1='defects'
# defects='number of defectives'
# 100    ='sample size'
Set c1
14  2  1  4  9  7  4  6  3  2
 3  8  4 15  5  3  8  4  2  5
 5  7  9  1  3 12  9  3  6  9
End
Pchart   c1 100
NPchart  c1 100
Cchart   c1
Uchart   c1 100
```

Exercise Example 15-13: P-Chart and Other Charts

A firm makes low tension electric insulators, and the quality control manager inspects the products each day during a one-month period. The number inspected is not fixed each day and varies somewhat. The number of defective units was recorded. The manager wants to know if the manufacturing process is in control. Run the file and find the answer. File Name: Gitlo236.inp

```
Note 'P, NP, C, U Charts: Gitlo236.inp'
# Gitlow, p. 236, Figure 9.8 - Electric Insulators Example
Name c1='day' c2='defect' c3='size'
# day='sample day'
# defect='number of defectives'
# size='sample size';
Read c1-c3;
Format (A10, F2.0, F5.0).
01Sep93    22   350
03Sep93    27   420
04Sep93    20   405
05Sep93    12   390
06Sep93    23   410
09Sep93    23   384
10Sep93    25   392
11Sep93    26   415
12Sep93    24   364
13Sep93    29   377
16Sep93    12   409
17Sep93    36   376
18Sep93    23   399
19Sep93    21   355
20Sep93    26   410
23Sep93    21   414
24Sep93    24   366
25Sep93    22   377
```

```
26Sep93    24   404
27Sep93    26   387
30Sep93    27   402
01Oct93    30   358
02Oct93    28   411
03Oct93    17   404
04Oct93    26   390
End
Pchart   c2 c3
NPchart  c2 c3
Cchart   c2
Uchart   c2 c3
```

Exercise Example 15-14: C-Chart
- Defects per Unit

The paper product is rolled onto a spool called a reel. Every reel is examined for blemishes, which are imperfections. The quality control manager selected 25 rolls, and recorded the number of blemishes for each roll. The manager wanted to know if the paper production process is in control. Run the file and find the answer. File Name: Gitlo254.inp

```
Note 'C, U Charts: gitlo254.inp'
# Gitlow, p. 254, Figure 9.19
# blemish='number of blemishes per reel'
Name c1='blemish'
Set c1
  4   5   5  10   6   4   5   6   3   6   6   7  11
  9   1   1   6  10   3   7   4   8   7   9   7
End
Cchart      c1
Uchart      c1 1
Ichart      c1
MRchart     c1
%IMRchart   c1
```

Exercise Example 15-15: C-Chart and U-Chart

An employees union in a mill is concerned with the safe work environment. It gathered the data on accidents per month for the past 26 months as shown in the data set. The union wanted to know if the work environment has become safer or accidents continue to take place at the same rate. Run the file and find the answer. File Name: Gitlo265.inp

```
Note 'U-Chart and C-Chart: Gitlo265.inp'
# Gitlow, p. 265, Figure 9.30
# number of accidents per month
Name c1='accident'
Set c1
3   2   0   2   1  12   1   0   0   1   1   3   0
2   0   0   3   2   0   1   0   1   0   0   1   1
End
Cchart   c1
Ichart   c1
```

Exercise Example 15-16: C-Chart and U-Chart

A manufacturing firm produces plastic in rolls. Samples are taken 5 times daily, and because of the nature of the process, the square footage of each sample varies with inspection lot. Run the file and find if the process is in control. File Name: Gitlo268.inp

```
Note 'U-Chart and C-Chart:Gitlo268.inp'
# Gitlow, p. 268, Figure 9.30 - Defects in Rolls of Plastic;
Data gitlo268;
```

```
Name c1='sample' c2='area' c3='defect'
# sample = 'inspection lot'
# area   = 'square feet'
# defect = 'number of blemish'
Read c1-c3
1   200   2.0
2   250   2.5
3   100   1.0
4    90   0.9
5   120   1.2
6    80   0.8
7   200   2.0
8   220   2.2
9   140   1.4
10   80   0.8
11  170   1.7
12   90   0.9
13  200   2.0
14  250   2.5
15  230   2.3
16  180   1.8
17   80   0.8
18  100   1.0
19  140   1.4
20  120   1.2
21  250   2.5
22  130   1.3
23  220   2.2
24  200   2.0
25  100   1.0
26  160   1.6
27  250   2.5
28   80   0.8
29  150   1.5
30  210   2.1
End
Pchart   c2 c3
NPchart  c2 c3
Cchart   c2
Uchart   c2 c3
```

Exercise Example 15-17: C-Chart and U-Chart

An automatic welding machine is used to produce chemical process equipment. The welds are x-rayed and the x-rays are examined for imperfections in the welds. The lengths of the welds are measured in inches and vary with the particular unit or portion of the unit being assembled. The quality control manager selected 25 units and the number of imperfections were recorded for each unit. Run the file and find if the process is in control. File Name: Gitlo275.inp

```
Note 'C-Chart and U-Chart: Gitlo275.inp'
# Gitlow, p. 275, Figure 9.34 - Imperfections in Welds
Name c1='unit' c2='length' c3='defect'
# unit='sample unit number'
# length='weld length in inches'
# defect='imperfections in each unit';
Read c1-c3
 1 187   2
 2 302   1
 3 302   0
 4 172   2
 5 240   5
 6 144   1
 7 120   1
 8 320   2
 9 264   2
10 180   1
```

```
11 208    1
12 234    5
13 180    1
14 288    3
15 108    1
16 254    7
17 144    6
18 180    2
19 288    2
20 360    3
21 220    5
22 156    0
23 348    1
24 288    2
25 144    1
End
Pchart   c2 c3
NPchart  c2 c3
Cchart   c2
Uchart   c2 c3
```

Exercise Example 15-18: Fishbone Chart
- Control Planning

Fishbone chart (Ishikawa chart, tree chart, cause-and-effect chart, river chart, branch-and-stem chart) is used to list possible areas of problems or quality control characteristics in a graph for the purpose of systematic quality control planning. In the Minitab Fishbone chart, there are 6 main areas of problems: Men, Machine, Materials, Methods, Measure, and Environment. The 6 areas are brahcnes, and each branch has many stems of quality control characteristics. In the following sample, airline ticket errors are used to illustrate the fishbone chart. Run the file and obtain the fishbone chart. File Name: Gitlo384.inp

```
Note 'Fishbone Chart: Gitlo384.inp'
# Fishbone chart, Ishikawa chart, River chart, Tree chart
# Cause-and-effect chart, Tree-and-branch chart
Name c1='Men' c2='Machine' c3='Material' c4='Method'  &
     c5='Measure' c6='Environ'
Read c1-c6;
Format(A13, A16, A16, A8, A2, A2).
Ability         Maint_frequency  Age            Quality * *
Ab_attention    M_adjustment     Carbon_density Speed
Training        M_print quality  Paper
Supervision     Age
                Type
End
%Fishbone;
Men       c1;
Machine   c2;
Materials c3;
Methods   c4;
Measures  c5;
Environ   c6;
Effect    'Airline Ticket Errors';
Title     'Gitlow, p. 384'.
%Fishbone;
   Title  'Minitab QC Manual, Release 9, 1993, p.3.8'.
```

Exercise Example 15-19: Fishbone Chart
- Control Planning

Quality control manager of Tasty Food Company wanted to identify possible areas of problems in the food processing plant. Run the file and obtain the fishbone chart.

```
Note 'Fishbone Chart'
# Fishbone chart, Ishikawa chart, River chart, Tree chart
# Cause-and-effect chart, Tree-and-branch chart
Name c1='Men' c2='Machine' c3='Material' c4='Method'  &
     c5='Measure' c6='Environ'
Read c1-c6;
Format(A12, A8, A8, A8, A10, A7).
plant mana    computer    fish     labor    moisture   rain
supervisor    truck       meat     machine  salt       clear
office mana    cars        chicken           sweet      hot
receptionist  dryer       corn              hardness   cold
typist        compressor  rice                         snow
workers                   wheat                         storm
                          salt
                          sugar

End
%Fishbone;
Men        c1;
Machine    c2;
Materials  c3;
Methods    c4;
Measures   c5;
Environ    c6;
Effect     'Food Processing Plant Problems';
Title      'Minitab QC Manual, Release 9, 1993, p.3.8'.
%Fishbone;
   Title 'Fishbone chart without specifications'.
```

Exercise Example 15-20: Pareto Chart
- Control Planning

In the following sample file, computer data entry errors are used to illustrate a Pareto chart. There are 7 causes of errors, and the data were gathered for 4 months. Run the file and obtain the Pareto chart. File Name: Gitlo391.inp

```
Note  'Pareto Chart: Gitlo391.inp'
# Gitlow, p. 391
# For Grouped observations
Name c1='cause' c2='date1' c3='date2' c4='date3' c5='date4'
Read c1-c5;
Format(A18, F2.0, F4.0, F3.0, F3.0).
Transposed numbers 7 10  6  5
Off-punched card   1   0  2  0
Wrong character    6   8  5  9
Too light print    0   1  1  0
Warped card        1   1  0  2
Torn card          0   0  1  1
Illegible source   0   0  1  0
End
Describe c2-c5
Let c6=c2+c3+c4+c5
%Pareto c1;
  Counts c6.
```

Exercise Example 15-21: Pareto Chart
- Control Planning

A Pareto chart is used to determine the frequencies of the problems. The micro-manager of a publishing company wanted to record the problems occurring with the micro computers of the firm. He recorded the problems in order of occurrence. Run the file and discuss the results.

```
Note 'Pareto chart'
# Pareto chart works for the Windows Version 9.0
# Computer problems
```

```
Name c1='problem'
# monitor = trouble with monitor
# hard    = hard disk crash
# drive   = trouble with drive
# printer = problem with the printer
Read c1;
 Format (A15).
hard
printer
driver
monitor
hard
hard
monitor
hard
driver
hard
monitor
drive
hard
End
%Pareto c1
```

Exercise Example 15-22: Pareto Chart
- Control Planning

In the previous example, the problems of the microcomputers were recorded in the order of occurrence. In this example, the frequencies of the problems are already computed by the type of problems. The objective is to show the frequencies in terms of histograms and cumulative frequencies. Run the file and obtain Pareto chart.

```
Note 'Pareto chart'
# Pareto chart works for the Windows Version 9.0
Name c1='problem' c2='count'
# monitor = trouble with monitor
# hard    = hard disk crash
# drive   = trouble with drive
# printer = problem with the printer
# count   = number of problems per month
Read c1-c2;
Format (A10, F3.0).
Monitor     4
Hard       15
Driver      7
Printer     3
End
%Pareto c1;
  Counts c2.
```

Exercise Example 15-23: Pareto Chart
- Control Planning

An economist at the Federal Reserve gathered the data on the number of bankrupt banks in 6 districts of Federal Reserve Banks for the past 3 years. He wanted to draw a pareto chart with the data. Run the file and obtain the Pareto chart.

```
Note  'Pareto Chart'
# No. of banks bankrupt in the FRB districts
# For Grouped observations
Name c1='city' c2='year1' c3='year2' c4='year3'
# city ='Federal Reserve City'
# year1='bankrupt in year 1'
# year2='bankrupt in year 2'
# year3='bankrupt in year 3'
```

```
Read c1-c4;
Format(A16, F2.0, F4.0,F5.0).
New York          10   15   20
San Francisco     12   18   25
Chicago           13   14   16
Boston            15   11   10
Atlanta           15   16   11
Philadelphia       8    9   10
End
Let c5=c2+c3+c4
%Pareto c1;
   Counts c5.
```

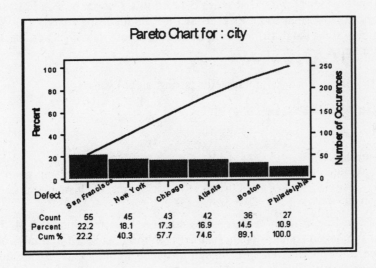

Pareto Chart for : city

Defect	San Francisco	New York	Chicago	Atlanta	Boston	Philadelphia
Count	55	45	43	42	36	27
Percent	22.2	18.1	17.3	16.9	14.5	10.9
Cum %	22.2	40.3	57.7	74.6	89.1	100.0

Chapter 16.
Data Format and Generating New Variables

Data Format

There are essentially 2 methods of data entry: read format and set format. Read c1-c2, for instance, signifies that the data are entered in columns by order of observations (Read Format). Set c1 signifies that all observations for a variable are entered in a row or rows. A Fortran forma can be used with both the Read format and the Set format for the following 2 cases: (1) When the data values are string values (alpha data). (2) When there are 2 or more data lines per observation in the Read format of data entry.

1. Fixed Format: Fortran Format for character (string, alpha) values

```
Name c1='name' c2='income' c3='cons'
Read c1-c3;
Format(A14, F6.0, F8.0).
Adam Smith     250.15  146.25
Barbara Candy 320.00   *
Linda Martin   400.53  350.46
End
Print c1-c3
```

Note: In the above Fortran format, A14 signifies string values in columns 1-14. F6.0 signifies numerical values in the next 6 columns (right justified). In the data set, if a numerical value has a decimal point, it overrides the Fortran specification of decimal point. Thus, for instance, 250.15 is read as it is. A missing data value is indicated by an asterisk *.

2. Fixed Format: Fortran Format for decimal places

```
Name c1='name' c2='income' c3='cons'
Read c1-c3;
Format (A14, F5.2, F5.3).
Begin Data.    1234567890
Adam Smith     2501514625
Barbara Candy 3200029032
Linda Martin   4005335046
End
Print c1-c3
```

Note: In the above file, 2 decimal points are indicated by the Fortran format F5.2. Thus, 12345 will be read as 123.45, and 67890 will be read as 67.890.

3. Fixed Format: Fortran Format for character values in a separate data file

```
Name c1='name' c2='income' c3='cons'
Read c1-c3;
File 'A:income.dat';
Format(A14, F6.0, F8.0).
Print c1-c3
```

Data File Name: income.dat

```
Adam Smith     250.15  146.25
```

```
Barbara Candy 320.00   290.32
Linda Martin  400.53   350.46
```

4. Free Format: For Numeric Data Values :

```
Name c1='income' c2='cons' c3='interest'
Read c1-c3;
250.15   146.25   10
320.00   290.32    *
400.53   350.46    8
End Data.
Print c1-c3
```

A missing value is indicated by an asterisk *.

5. Free Format: For Numeric Data Values in a Separate Data File

Command File: income.cmd

```
Name c1='name' c2='income' c3='cons'
Read 'A:income.dat' c1-c3
Print c1-c3
```

Data File: income.dat on disk A

```
250.15   146.25   10
320.00   290.32    *
400.53   350.46    8
```

A missing value is indicated by an asterisk *.

6. Free Format: Set Command for Data Entry by Variables

```
Name c1='income' c2='cons' c3='year'
Set c1
250.15   320     400.53   620.12   726.27   800.25   915
End
Set c2
146.25   290.32   350.46 540.15   600.26   700.12   800
End
Set c3
1988:1994/1
End
```

7. Mixed Format: Read Format, Set Format, and Fortran Format Mixed

```
Name c1='income' c2='cons' c3='interest' c4='age'
Read c1-c3;
250.15   146.25   10
320.00   290.32    *
400.53   350.46    8
End Data.
Set c4
20 25 35 65 37 48 57
End
Set c5;
Format (A17).
New York
New Jersey
New Mexico
New Orleans
End
Print c1-c5
```

8. Matrix Data

```
Read 4 by 5 matrix M1
  1  2  3  4  5
  6  7  8  9 10
 11 12 13 14 15
End
Print M1
```

9. Missing Values

A missing data value is indicated by an asterisk (*) in numeric columns and a blank in character columns in the fixed format.

```
Name c1='income' c2='cons' c3='interest'
Read c1-c3;
250.15   146.25   10
320.00   290.32    *
  *      350.46    8
End Data.
Print c1-c3

Name c1='name' c2='income' c3='cons'
Read c1-c3;
Format(A14, F6.0, F8.0).
Adam Smith     250.15  146.25
               320.00  *
Linda Martin   400.53  350.46
End
Print c1-c3
```

10. Continuation to the Next Line

If the data line is continued to a next line, a Fortran format is used. If the command line is continued to the next line place an '&' symbol at the end of the line to be continued:

```
Name c1='year'  c2='cons'  c3='income' c4='interest' &
     c5='unemp' c6='infla'
Read c1-c6;
Format (F4.0, F5.0, F5.0, F4.0/4X, F5.0, F5.0).
1992   300   400   12
       5.0   4.0
1993   400   450   13
       6.0   5.1
1994   500   560   11
       8.5   5.2
1995   600   590    8
       7.0   4.3
End
Regress c2 on 2 c3 c4  &
     Std.resid in c5 Fits in c6;
     VIF;
     Residuals in c7;
     DW.
```

11. Conversion between Character and Numeric Data

In the following sample file, the character (alpha, string) values, 'male' and 'female' are converted to the numeric values '1' and '0' using the Convert procedure. For the data values c5-c6, the numeric data values must be typed first.

```
Note 'Conversion between Character-Numeric Data Values'
```

```
Name c1='name' c2='income' c3='cons' c4='sex' c5='educa'
# educa =educational level, 1=elementary, 2=secondary, 3=college
Read c1-c5;
Format (A15, F6.0, F8.0, 2X, A6, 2X, F2.0).
Adam  Smith      500.20  300.56  male     1
Nancy Smith      400.30  350.12  female   2
David Ricardo    600.50  530.23  male     3
Debbie Ricardo 800.32  720.35  female   1
Alice Marshall 900.60  800.00  female   2
End
Print c1-c4
Read c5-c6;
Format (F1.0, 2X, A6).
0   female
1   male
End
Note (1) Converts Alpha (string, character data to numeric data)
Convert using c6 - c5 in c4 put in c7
# Note the order c6-c5.
Print c1-c7
Regress c3 on 2 c2 c7;
   DW.
Note (2) Converts Numeric data to Alpha (string, character data)
Read c8-c9;
Format (F1.0, 2X, A7).
1   element
2   second
3   college
End
Convert using c8-c9 in c5 put in c10
# c6 will be converted to alpha data.
```

Edited Partial Output:

ROW	name	income	cons	sex	educa	C6	C7
1	Adam Smith	500.20	300.56	male	1	0	female
2	Nancy Smith	400.30	350.12	female	2	1	male
3	David Ricardo	600.50	530.23	male	3		
4	Debbie Ricardo	800.32	720.35	female	1		
5	Alice Marshall	900.60	800.00	female	2		

ROW	c8	C9	C10
1	1	1	element
2	0	2	second
3	1	3	college
4	0		element
5	0		second

12. Fortran Format to Read 2 or More Data Lines per Observation

When there are two or more lines per observation, the Format subcommand must be used.

```
Name c1='year'  c2='cons'  c3='income' c4='interest' &
     c5='unemp' c6='infla'
Read c1-c6;
Format (F4.0, F5.0, F5.0, F4.0/4X, F5.0, F5.0).
1992  300  400  12
      5.0  4.0
1993  400  450  13
      6.0  5.1
1994  500  560  11
      8.5  5.2
```

Note: When you are using a Fortran format, you have to count from the first column on the left including the blanks, and the format must be right-justified. If you are using an external text editor, to start with the first column on the left, the margin may be set as left-justified.

NOBS=K: to Read the First K Observations

If you want to use the first K observations of the data set, use NOBS=K statement:

```
Name c1='year' c2='cons' c3='income' c4='interest'
Read c1-c4;
Format (F4.0, F5.0, F5.0, F4.0);
NOBS= 4.
1989  300  400  12
1990  400  450  13
1991  500  560  11
1992  530  600  15
1993  600  800   9
1994  450  520   8
```

Skip=K: to Skip the First K Observations

If you want to skip the first K lines of the data set, use Skip=K statement:

```
Name c1='year' c2='cons' c3='income' c4='interest'
Read c1-c4;
Format (F4.0, F5.0, F5.0, F4.0);
Skip= 4.
1989  300  400  12
1990  400  450  13
1991  500  560  11
1992  530  600  15
1993  600  800   9
1994  450  520   8
```

The above format will skip the first 4 lines (1989-92).

13. To Generate a Series of Numbers - Patterned Data

If the data value changes by a constant number, then use the following:

```
Set c1
1990:1994
End
```
.... will generate 1990 1991 1992 1993 1994

```
Set c1
1994:1990
End
```
.... will generate   1994 1993 1992 1991 1990

```
Set c1              Or   Set c1
1986:1991/step 2         1986:1991/2
End                      End
```

..... will generate 1986 1988 1990 1992 1994

```
Set c1
-1:2/0.5
End
```
.... will generate -1 -0.5 0.0 0.5 1.0 1.5 2.0

```
Set c1
5(1)
End
```
...... will generate 1, 1, 1, 1, 1

```
Set c1      or      Set c1
```

```
3(1:4)              3(1  2  3  4)
End                 End
```

...... will generate 1 2 3 4 1 2 3 4 1 2 3 4

```
Set c1
(1:4)3
End
```
..... will generate 1 1 1 2 2 2 3 3 3 4 4 4

```
Set c1
3(1:4)2
End
```
...... will generate 1 1 2 2 3 3 4 4 1 1 2 2 3 3 4 4 1 1 2 2 3 3 4 4

14. Set Command with Fortran Format

```
Set c1;
Format (5F3.0).
123123123123123
End
```
...... will read as 123 123 123 123 123

15. Fortran Format for Print Command

The Fortran format may be used with the Print command. If there is only one column, the data values will be printed in rows. If there are 2 or more columns, the data values will be printed in columns:

```
Print c1-c4;
   Format (F4.0, F5.0, F5.0, F4.0).
```

will print c1-c4 in the following format:

```
1985   300   400   12
1986   400   450   13
1987   500   560   11
1988   530   600   15
1989   600   800   09
1990   450   520   08
```

16. Write and Read - To save and retrieve an ASCII data file

If a Minitab file is saved using 'Write' command, the data file will be saved in the ASCII format (that is, files with extension DAT, MTB or MTJ), and you can retrieve the file in any computer system that runs Minitab. Use the 'Read' command to retrieve it.

```
MTB > Write 'b:abc.dat' c1-c3

MTB > Read 'b:abc.dat' c1-c3

MTB > Write 'b:abc.dat' c1-c3;
Subc> Format (F5.2, F4.2).

MTB > Read 'b:abc.dat' c1-c3;
Subc> Format (F5.2, F4.2).
```

If a Minitab file is saved using 'Save' command, the data file will be saved in the Minitab system format (with the extension MTW), and you can 'Retrieve' the file into Minitab only on the same type of computer, but you cannot retrieved it on different types of computers.

```
MTB > Save 'b:abc:dat c1-c3

MTB > Retrieve 'b:abc.dat' c1-c3
```

If you are going to use a system file on a different type of computer, use the 'Portable'
subcommand when you save:

```
MTB > Save 'b:abc.mtw';
SUBC>  Portable.

MTB > Retrieve 'b:abc.mtw';
SUBC>  Portable.
```

17. Store and Execute

```
MTB > Store 'b:abc.mtb'
MTB > Read c1-c2
DATA> 10   20
DATA> 30   40
DATA> End
MTB > Execute 'b:abc.mtb'
```

18. Journal and Nojournal - To save keyboard input (data and commands)

```
MTB > Journal 'abc.mtj'
```

Everything you type from the keyboard is saved including commands, data, and typing errors in the
ASCII format. Output is not saved in this journal. To save the output, use the Outfile command. At
the end of the session, the Nojournal command is required as shown below.

```
MTB > Nojournal 'abc.mtj'
```

The Journal command is closed. It stops saving further inputs.

19. Execute

```
MTB > Execute 'a:abc.mtj'
```

The file 'abc.mtj' on disk A will be retrieved and executed.

20. Outfile and Nooutfile

```
MTB > Outfile 'a:abc.out'
```

The output will be saved in the ASCII file 'abc.out' on disk A. If you do not specify the extension,
the output will be saved with the extension LIS. So, ABC.LIS will be created. This file can be edited
and printed using a text editor or wordprocessor.

```
MTB > Nooutfile
```

It will close the Outfile command. It stops saving the output.

21. Print and Write Format

The Format subcommand may be used for printing and writing. The following sample file uses the
Format subcommand for the following 4 cases:

(1) Read the alpha data

(2) Read the data values in fixed columns
(3) Print the output in the desired format
(4) Write the output in an ASCII file in the desired format

```
Note 'Print and Write Format - File Name: Format-1.dat'
Name c1='name' c2='income' c3='cons' c4='number'
Read c1-c4;
Format (A17, F7.0, 2X, F7.0, 1X, F4.2).
Adam Smith         1000.00    800.13 1234
David Ricardo      1250.00   1200.56 1234
John  Mill         1800.50   1650.26 1234
Alfred Marshall    1600.20   1320.13 1234
John Hicks         1530.12   1245.25 1234
Joan Robinson      1750.56   1540.32 1234
End
Let c5=Loge(c2)
Let c6=Loge(c3)
Let c7=Lag(c5)
Let c8=Lag(c6)
Print   c1-c4
Print   c1-c4;
Format(A17, F7.2, 2X, F7.2, 3X, F5.2).
Write   c1-c4;
Format(A17, F7.2, 2X, F7.2, 3X, F5.2).
Write 'a:file-2.out' c1-c4;
Format(A17, F7.2, 2X, F7.2, 3X, F5.2).
```

In the above sample file, there are two Print commands and two Write commands. The first Print command prints the output in the Minitab defined format. It produces the variable names and the row numbers. In the second Print command with the Format subcommand produces output but removes the variable names and the row numbers. In the Print command the file name is not used. If you want to use a file name for the output, use the Write command. In the first Write command with the Format subcommand produces the same output as the Print-Format command. In the second Write command with the Format subcommand, the file name is added. The output is directed to the disk file, and the output will not show up on the screen. If you do not want the variable names and column numbers, you can use the Print-Format and Write Format commands.

22. To Set a Page Size of the Output File

```
MTB > Outfile 'b:abc.out'
MTB >   OW = k
MTB >   OH = k
MTB >   Noterm
```

OW = width of the file, k= 30 to 132
OH = length, lines of the file k = 0 to ...

Default length is 24 lines.
Noterm = sends the output only to a disk file, and the output does not show up on the screen.
Only error messages will show up on the screen.

23. Sending the Output to a Printer

If you want to send the output directly to a printer, before you submit the file to Minitab, turn on the printer and type

```
MTB > Paper
```

To stop printing on the paper, type

```
MTB > Nopaper

MTB > Paper
MTB > OW = k      default  78  (maximum 132)
MTB > OH = k
```

OW = width of the file per page
OH = length of the file per page
k such as k1, k2, k3,..... represents a constant.
c such as c1, c2, c3, ... represents a column variable.
E such as E1, E2, E3...... either k or c

Height of plots: 17
Width of plots: 57

```
MTB > Paper
MTB > Newpage

MTB > UC
MTB > LC
```

UC = upper cases only
LC = Lower cases only

24. To Sort the Column Data

To sort a column data and store the results, type

```
MTB > sort c1 and save in c10
```

   The sorted data of C1 is saved in c10. The original column c1 remains intact. If you want to remove the initial series and keep the sorted series only, type

```
MTB > Sort c1 c1
```

C1 is sorted, and stored in c1. The original c1 disappears.

Generating New Variables

25. Mathematical Equations

Column Mathematics

```
Let k1=Count(c1)
Let k2=N(c1)       .... count the nonmissing values
Let k3=Nmiss(c1) .... count the missing values
Let k4=Sum(c1)
Let k5=Mean(c1)
Let k6=Stdev(c1)
Let k7=Median(c1)
Let k8=Minimum(c1)
Let k9=Maximum(c1)
Range in c1 k10
Let k11=SSQ(c1)..... sum of squares
print k1-k11
```

Mathematics for Constants and Columns

```
Let k3 = 100 + 20        Let c3 = c1 + c2
```

```
Let  k4 = 100 - 20          Let c4 = c1 - c2
Let  k5 = 100 / 20          Let c5 = c1 / c2
Let  k6 = 100*20            Let c6 = c1*c2
Let  k1=5**2                Let c11=c10**2

Let  k2=Round(5.24)         Let c12=Round(c10)
Let  k3=Sin(2.35)           Let c13=Sin(c10)
Let  k4=Cos(2.35)           Let c14=Cos(c10)
Let  k5=Tan(2.35)           Let c15=Tan(c10)
Let  k6=Asin(0.15)          Let c16=Asin(c10)
Let  k7=Acos(0.15)          Let c17=Acos(c10)
Let  k8=Atan(0.15)          Let c18=Atan(c10)
Let  k9=Signs(0.15)         Let c19=Signs(c10)

let  c4=Parsums(c1)      .... cumulative sum of values in column c1
Let  c5=Parproducts(c1)  .... cumulative product of values in column c1

Let  k1 = Absolute(-100)    Let c1=Absolute(c10)
Let  k2 = Sqrt(100)         Let c2=Sqrt(c10)
Let  k3 = Loge(100)         Let c3=Loge(c10)
Let  k4 = Logten(100)       Let c4=Logten(c10)
Let  k5 = 100**2            Let c5=c1**2
Let  k6 = Antilog(0.15)     Let c6=Antilog(c1)
```

Row Mathematics

```
Rcount c1-c3 c5   .... count the number of rows
Rn c1-c3   c6     .... count the nonmissing values
Rnmiss c1-c3   c7 .... count the missing values
Rsum in c1-c3 c7
Rmean in c1-c3 c8
Rstdev in c1-c3 c9
Rmedian c1-c3 c10
Rmaximum c1-c3 c11
Rminimum c1-c3 c12
Rrange c1-c3 c13
Rssq c1-c3 c14 ...... sum of squares
Print c5-c14

Difference in c1 putin c2

Let c2=Lag(c1)
Let c3= c1 - Lag(c1)

Sort c1 carry c2-c3 put in c17-19

Sort c1;
  by c2 c3 put in c1-c3.

Sort c1 ;
  by c2 c3;
  Descending.
Rank c1 put in c2
```

The following last 3 constants are Minitab-defined:

```
k98  = *             .............. for missing value
k99  = 2.718         ........ e ( 2.7182818 the base of  natural logarithm)
k100 = 3.141         ....... π (3.1415927)
```

26. Coding the Data Values (Recoding)

Example 1: Coding Data Values

Suppose you have the following data set:

```
  year cons   income interest
```

```
1987   400   500    10.0
1988   500   600    12.0
1989   550   700     8.0
1990   600   800     7.0
```

Suppose you want to divide the income values into 3 income groups: low income '1', middle income '2', and high income '3' such that

```
If    0   ≤ c3 <= 500   c3 = 1
If   500 < c3 <= 700    c3 = 2
If   700 < c3           c3 = 3
```

In Minitab, the above coding is set as follows:

```
Code (0:500) 1  (500:700) 2 (700:1000) 3  in c3 put in c5
```

There are duplicated numbers in 500 and 700. In such a case, the first number is inclusive, and the second number is exclusive. If there is no overlapping numbers, starting and ending values will be inclusive. The above coding will generate a new variable c5 as shown below:

```
year  cons   income interest   c5

1986   200   300     8.0        1
1987   400   500    10.0        1
1988   500   600    12.0        2
1989   550   700     8.0        2
1990   600   800     7.0        3
```

Suppose you want to code income 200-400 and 500 as group 1, and income 600-700 and 800 as group 2:

```
Code (200:400, 500) 1  (600-700, 800) 2 in c3 put in c5
```

In the above code, income 401-499, and 701-799 are dropped.

Suppose you want to code each specific number in the income data.

```
Code (300, 500) 1 (600, 700, 800) 2 in 'income' put in c6
```

or

```
Code (300) 1 (500) 1 (600:800) 2 in 'income' put in c6
```

The recoded numbers in c6 will be: 1 1 2 2 2

Example 2: Coding Data Values

Suppose you have the following data set:

```
Name  cons   income int   age   sex
c1    c2     c3     c4    c5    c6
Adam  200    300    8.0   30    1
Bob   400    500   10.0   45    1
Carol 500    600   12.0   55    0
David 550    700    8.0   67    1
Ellen 600    800    7.0   25    0
```

You want to recode income, cons, and age

```
Code (200:350) 1 (350:500) 2 (500:650) 3 in c2 put in c7
Code (200:400) 1 (400:600) 2 (600:800) 3 in c3 put in c8
```

```
Code (20:35)   1 (35:50)   2 (50:70)   3 in c5 put in c9
```

In the above code, the limiting values are inclusive. So, consumptions of 200-350 will be coded as 1. The coded data output is:

```
Name  cons  income int   age   sex
c1    c2    c3     c4    c5    c6    c7    c8    c9
Adam  200   300    8.0   30    1     1     1     1
Bob   400   500    10.0  45    1     2     2     2
Carol 500   600    12.0  55    0     3     2     3
David 550   700    8.0   67    1     3     3     3
Ellen 600   800    7.0   25    0     3     3     1
```

Example 3: Coding Data Values in Multiple Columns

In the above data set, coding for multiple columns can be set as follows:

```
Name  cons  income int   age   sex
c1    c2    c3     c4    c5    c6
Adam  200   300    8.0   30    1
Bob   400   500    10.0  45    1
Carol 500   600    12.0  55    0
David 550   700    8.0   67    1
Ellen 600   800    7.0   25    0
```

```
Code (200:350) 1 (350:500) 2 (500:800) 3 in c2-c5 put in c7-c9
```

The coded data output will be:

```
Name  cons  income int   age   sex
c1    c2    c3     c4    c5    c6    c7    c8    c9
Adam  200   300    8.0   30    1     1     1     1
Bob   400   500    10.0  45    1     2     2     2
Carol 500   600    12.0  55    0     2     2     2
David 550   700    8.0   67    1     3     3     3
Ellen 600   800    7.0   25    0     3     3     3
```

Example 4. Coding Data Values to 0 and 1

The data values can be coded to either 0 or 1.

```
Read c1-c3
c1      c2   c3
1986   100   50
1987   200   80
1988   400   60
1989   500   40
1991   300   20
Let c4 = (c1 > 1988)
Let c5 = (c1 < 1988)
Print c1-c5
```

The above file will create new columns c4-c5 with the following dummy variables.

```
c1      c2   c3   c4    c5
1986   100   50   0     1
1987   200   80   0     1
1988   400   60   0     0
1989   500   40   1     0
1991   300   20   1     0
```

Example 5: Missing Values using Code

In Minitab, missing values are denoted by an asterisk *. Also, the code command can be used to specify missing values:

```
year cons  income interest
  1986  200   300     8.0
  1987    0   500      *
  1988  500   -99    12.0
  1989    0     0      *
  1990  600   -99     7.0
```

In the above data set, we want to specify the values 0 consumption and -99 for income as the missing values. We can use the Code command. The asterisk * in the interest column is automatically taken as a missing value by Minitab without further specification.

```
Code (0)    ' * '    in c2 put in c2
code (-99)  ' * '    in c3 put in c3
```

By the above two Code commands, 0 in consumption will be replaced by *, and for income -99 will be replaced by *, but the 0 will remain intact.

27. Matrix Operation

```
Note 'Matrix Operation in Minitab'
Read 3 by 3 matrix data in M1
  1   2   3
  4   5   6
  7   8   9
Read 3 by 3 matrix in M2
  7   8   9
 10  11  12
 13  14  15
Add M1 and M2 put in M3
Subtract M1 from M2 putin M4
Multiply M1 and M2 put in M5
Transpose M1 and put in M6
Print m1-m6
Read 3 by 3 matrix M7
4   1   2
0   5   3
4   2   3
Invert M7 and put in M8
Transpose M1 put in M9
Print m7-m9
Diagonal of m1 put in c1
Print c1
Set c2
1 2 3
End
Diagonal is in c2 put in M8
Eigen values in m8 put in c3
Print c3
Read 3 by 3 matrix put in M10
1   2   3
2   5  10
3  10   7
Eigen analysis of M10 put in c4
Print M10 c4
```

28. Comment Lines: Note and

Note 'This is a comment' The keyword note is not printed. The rest is printed.

The pound sign is used to indicate a comment line. The entire line is ignored and not printed.

29. Restart

To clear the current data and start a new data.

30. System and Exit

To exit Minitab temporarily to DOS prompt. To return to Minitab, type Exit.

31. Stop

To quit Minitab session.

Bibliography

A. Minitab Publications

Minitab Reference Manual for Windows, Release 9, 1993
Minitab Graphics Manual for Windows, Release 9, 1993
Minitab QC Manual for Windows, Release 9, 1993
Ryan, B. F., Joiner, B. L., and Ryan, T. A.,Jr., Minitab Handbook, 2nd ed., 1985

B. Statistics and Econometrics Books

Aczel, A. D., Complete Business Statistics, 2nd ed., 1993
Berndt, E. R., The Practice of Econometrics: Classic and Contemporary, 1991.
Dougherty, C., Introduction to Econometrics, 1992
Draper, N. R., and Smith, H., Applied Regression Analysis, 1981
Emory, C. W., and Cooper, D. R., Business Research Methods, 4th ed., 1991
Gitlow, H., Gitlow, S., Oppenheim, A., and Oppenheim, R., Tools and Methods for the Improvement of Quality, 1989
Granger, C. W. J., Forecasting in Business and Economics, 1980, pp. 41-77.
Granger, C. W. J., and Newbold, P., Forecasting Economic Time Series, 2nd ed., 1986
Greene, W. H., Econometric Analysis, 1990
Gujarati, D. N., Basic Econometrics, 2nd ed., 1988
Hanke, J. E., and Reitsch, A. G., Understanding Business Statistics, 1991
Harnett, D. L., and Murphy, J. L., Statistical Analysis for Business and Economics, 3rd ed., 1985
Holden, K., Peel, D. A., and Thompson, J. L, Economic Forecasting: An Introduction, 1990.
Johnson, R. A., and Wichern, D. W., Applied Multivariate Statistical Analysis, 2nd ed., 1988, 3rd ed., 1993
Judge, G. G., Griffiths, W. E., Hill, R. C., Lutkepohl, H., Lee, T., The Theory and Practice of Econometrics, 2nd ed., 1985
Kachigan, S. K., Multivariate Statistical Analysis, 1982
Kachigan, S. K., Statistical Analysis, 1982, 1986
Keller, G., Warrack, B., and Bartel, H., Statistics for Management and Economics, 2nd ed., 1990
Koutsoyiannis, A., Theory of Econometrics, 2nd ed., 1977
Maddala, G. S., Limited-Dependent and Qualitative Variables in Econometrics, 1983
Makridakis, S., and Wheelwright, S. E., Forecasting Methods and Applications, 1978, pp. 252-325
Mason, R. D., and Lind, D. A., Statistical Techniques in Business and Economics, 8th ed., 1993.
Morrison, D. F., Multivariate Statistical Methods, 3rd ed., 1990
Myers, J. L., Fundamentals of Experimental Design, 1979.
Neter, J., Wasserman, W., and Kutner, M. H., Applied Linear Statistical Models, 3rd ed., 1990
Neter, J., Wasserman, W., and Kutner, M. H., Applied Linear Regression Models, 2nd ed., 1989
Newbold, P., and Bos, T., Introductory Business and Economic Forecasting, 2nd ed., 1994
Pedhazur, E. J., Multiple Regression in Behavioral Research, 2nd ed., 1982
Pindyck, R. S., and Rubinfeld, D. L., Econometric Models and Economic Forecasts, 3rd ed., 1991
Ramanathan, R., Introductory Econometrics with Applications, 2nd ed, 1992
Romesburg, H. C., Cluster Analysis for Researchers, 1990
Siegel, A. F, Practical Business Statistics with Statpad, 1990
Siegel, S., and Castellan, N. J., Jr., Nonparametric Statistics for the Behavioral Sciences, 2nd ed., 1988
Summers, G., Peters, W. S., Armstrong, C. P., Basic Statistics in Business and Economics, 4th ed., 1985.

Webster, A., Applied Statistics for Business and Economics, 1992

Weiers, R. M., Introduction to Business Statistics, 1991

Wilson, J. H., and Keating, B., Business Forecasting, 1990, 2nd ed., 1994

Winer, B. J., Statistical Principles in Experimental Design, 2nd ed., 1971

Winer, B. J., Brown, D. R., Michels, K. M., Statistical Principles in Experimental Design, 3rd ed., 1991

Minitab Software Publisher's Address:

Minitab Inc.
3081 Enterprise Drive
State College, PA 16801-3008

Tech support: (301) 231-2682
Sales: (800) 448-3555
Fax: (312) 329-3668

Table 1: Durbin-Watson Test Statistic
Lower and Upper Limits at 5 % Level

N	k'= 1 dL	k'= 1 dU	k'= 2 dL	k'= 2 dU	k'= 3 dL	k'= 3 dU	k'= 4 dL	k'= 4 dU
6	0.610	1.400	–	–	–	–	–	–
7	0.700	1.356	0.467	1.896	–	–	–	–
8	0.763	1.332	0.559	1.777	0.368	2.287	–	–
9	0.824	1.320	0.629	1.699	0.455	2.128	0.296	2.588
10	0.879	1.320	0.697	1.641	0.523	2.016	0.376	2.414
11	0.927	1.324	0.758	1.604	0.595	1.928	0.444	2.283
12	0.971	1.331	0.812	1.579	0.658	1.864	0.512	2.177
13	1.010	1.340	0.861	1.562	0.715	1.816	0.574	2.094
14	1.045	1.350	0.905	1.551	0.767	1.779	0.632	2.030
15	1.077	1.361	0.946	1.543	0.814	1.750	0.685	1.977
16	1.106	1.371	0.982	1.539	0.857	1.728	0.734	1.935
17	1.133	1.381	1.015	1.536	0.897	1.710	0.779	1.900
18	1.158	1.391	1.046	1.535	0.933	1.696	0.820	1.872
19	1.180	1.401	1.074	1.536	0.967	1.685	0.859	1.848
20	1.201	1.411	1.100	1.537	0.998	1.676	0.894	1.828
21	1.221	1.420	1.125	1.538	1.026	1.669	0.927	1.812
22	1.239	1.429	1.147	1.541	1.053	1.664	0.958	1.797
23	1.257	1.437	1.168	1.543	1.078	1.660	0.986	1.785
24	1.273	1.446	1.188	1.546	1.101	1.656	1.013	1.775
25	1.288	1.454	1.206	1.550	1.123	1.654	1.038	1.767
26	1.302	1.461	1.224	1.553	1.143	1.652	1.062	1.759
27	1.316	1.469	1.240	1.556	1.162	1.651	1.084	1.753
28	1.328	1.476	1.255	1.560	1.181	1.650	1.104	1.747
29	1.341	1.483	1.270	1.563	1.198	1.650	1.124	1.743
30	1.352	1.489	1.284	1.567	1.214	1.650	1.143	1.739
31	1.363	1.496	1.297	1.570	1.229	1.650	1.160	1.735
32	1.373	1.502	1.309	1.574	1.244	1.650	1.177	1.732
33	1.383	1.508	1.321	1.577	1.258	1.651	1.193	1.730
34	1.393	1.514	1.333	1.580	1.271	1.652	1.208	1.728
35	1.402	1.519	1.343	1.584	1.283	1.653	1.222	1.726
36	1.411	1.525	1.354	1.587	1.295	1.654	1.236	1.724
37	1.419	1.530	1.364	1.590	1.307	1.655	1.249	1.723
38	1.427	1.535	1.373	1.594	1.318	1.656	1.261	1.722
39	1.435	1.540	1.382	1.597	1.328	1.658	1.273	1.722
40	1.442	1.544	1.391	1.600	1.338	1.659	1.285	1.721
45	1.475	1.566	1.430	1.615	1.383	1.666	1.336	1.720
50	1.503	1.585	1.462	1.628	1.421	1.674	1.378	1.721
55	1.528	1.601	1.490	1.641	1.452	1.681	1.414	1.724
60	1.549	1.616	1.514	1.652	1.480	1.689	1.444	1.727
65	1.567	1.629	1.536	1.662	1.503	1.696	1.471	1.731
70	1.583	1.641	1.554	1.672	1.525	1.703	1.494	1.735
75	1.598	1.652	1.571	1.680	1.543	1.709	1.515	1.739
80	1.611	1.662	1.586	1.688	1.560	1.715	1.534	1.743
85	1.624	1.671	1.600	1.696	1.575	1.721	1.550	1.747
90	1.635	1.679	1.612	1.703	1.589	1.726	1.556	1.751
95	1.645	1.687	1.623	1.709	1.602	1.732	1.579	1.755
100	1.654	1.694	1.634	1.715	1.613	1.736	1.592	1.758
150	1.720	1.746	1.706	1.760	1.693	1.774	1.679	1.788
200	1.758	1.778	1.748	1.789	1.738	1.799	1.728	1.810

N = number of observations, k' = number of independent variables (excluding intercept constant), dL = lower limit, dU = upper limit.

Durbin-Watson Statistic: Upper and Lower Limits at 5 % Level

N	k′= 5 dL	k′= 5 dU	k′= 6 dL	k′= 6 dU	k′= 7 dL	k′= 7 dU	k′= 8 dL	k′= 8 dU
6	–	–	–	–	–	–	–	–
7	–	–	–	–	–	–	–	–
8	–	–	–	–	–	–	–	–
9	–	–	–	–	–	–	–	–
10	0.243	2.822	–	–	–	–	–	–
11	0.316	2.645	0.203	3.005	–	–	–	–
12	0.379	2.506	0.268	2.832	0.171	3.149	–	–
13	0.445	2.390	0.328	2.692	0.230	2.985	0.147	3.266
14	0.505	2.296	0.389	2.572	0.286	2.848	0.200	3.111
15	0.562	2.220	0.447	2.472	0.343	2.727	0.251	2.979
16	0.615	2.157	0.502	2.388	0.398	2.624	0.304	2.860
17	0.664	2.104	0.554	2.318	0.451	2.537	0.356	2.757
18	0.710	2.060	0.603	2.257	0.502	2.461	0.407	2.667
19	0.752	2.023	0.649	2.206	0.549	2.396	0.456	2.589
20	0.792	1.991	0.692	2.162	0.595	2.339	0.502	2.521
21	0.829	1.964	0.732	2.124	0.637	2.290	0.547	2.460
22	0.863	1.940	0.769	2.090	0.677	2.246	0.588	2.407
23	0.895	1.920	0.804	2.061	0.715	2.208	0.628	2.360
24	0.925	1.902	0.837	2.035	0.751	2.174	0.666	2.318
25	0.953	1.886	0.868	2.012	0.784	2.144	0.702	2.280
26	0.979	1.873	0.897	1.992	0.816	2.117	0.735	2.246
27	1.004	1.861	0.925	1.974	0.845	2.093	0.767	2.216
28	1.028	1.850	0.951	1.958	0.874	2.071	0.798	2.188
29	1.050	1.841	0.975	1.944	0.900	2.052	0.826	2.164
30	1.071	1.833	0.998	1.931	0.926	2.034	0.854	2.141
31	1.090	1.825	1.020	1.920	0.950	2.018	0.879	2.120
32	1.109	1.819	1.041	1.909	0.972	2.004	0.904	2.102
33	1.127	1.813	1.061	1.900	0.994	1.991	0.927	2.085
34	1.144	1.808	1.080	1.891	1.015	1.979	0.950	2.069
35	1.160	1.803	1.097	1.884	1.034	1.967	0.971	2.054
36	1.175	1.799	1.114	1.887	1.053	1.957	0.991	2.041
37	1.190	1.795	1.131	1.870	1.071	1.948	1.011	2.029
38	1.204	1.792	1.146	1.864	1.088	1.939	1.029	2.017
39	1.218	1.789	1.161	1.859	1.104	1.932	1.047	2.007
40	1.230	1.786	1.175	1.854	1.120	1.924	1.064	1.997
45	1.287	1.776	1.238	1.835	1.189	1.895	1.139	1.958
50	1.335	1.771	1.291	1.822	1.246	1.875	1.201	1.930
55	1.374	1.768	1.334	1.814	1.294	1.861	1.253	1.909
60	1.408	1.767	1.372	1.808	1.335	1.850	1.298	1.894
65	1.438	1.767	1.404	1.805	1.370	1.843	1.336	1.882
70	1.464	1.768	1.433	1.802	1.401	1.837	1.369	1.873
75	1.487	1.770	1.458	1.801	1.428	1.834	1.399	1.867
80	1.507	1.772	1.480	1.801	1.453	1.831	1.425	1.861
85	1.525	1.774	1.500	1.801	1.474	1.829	1.448	1.857
90	1.542	1.776	1.518	1.801	1.494	1.827	1.469	1.854
95	1.557	1.778	1.535	1.802	1.512	1.827	1.489	1.852
100	1.571	1.780	1.550	1.803	1.528	1.826	1.506	1.850
150	1.665	1.802	1.651	1.817	1.637	1.832	1.622	1.847
200	1.718	1.820	1.707	1.831	1.697	1.841	1.686	1.852

Durbin-Watson Statistic: Upper and Lower Limits at 5 % Level

N	k'= 9 dL	dU	k'= 10 dL	dU	k'= 11 dL	dU	k'= 12 dL	dU
6	–	–	–	–	–	–	–	–
7	–	–	–	–	–	–	–	–
8	–	–	–	–	–	–	–	–
9	–	–	–	–	–	–	–	–
10	–	–	–	–	–	–	–	–
11	–	–	–	–	–	–	–	–
12	–	–	–	–	–	–	–	–
13	–	–	–	–	–	–	–	–
14	0.127	3.360	–	–	–	–	–	–
15	0.175	3.216	0.111	3.438	–	–	–	–
16	0.222	3.090	0.155	3.304	0.098	3.503	–	–
17	0.272	2.975	0.198	3.184	0.138	3.378	0.087	3.557
18	0.321	2.873	0.244	3.073	0.177	3.265	0.123	3.441
19	0.369	2.783	0.290	2.974	0.220	3.159	0.160	3.335
20	0.416	2.704	0.336	2.885	0.263	3.063	0.200	3.234
21	0.461	2.633	0.380	2.806	0.307	2.976	0.240	3.141
22	0.504	2.571	0.424	2.734	0.349	2.897	0.281	3.057
23	0.545	2.514	0.465	2.670	0.391	2.826	0.322	2.979
24	0.584	2.464	0.506	2.613	0.431	2.761	0.362	2.908
25	0.621	2.419	0.544	2.560	0.470	2.702	0.400	2.844
26	0.657	2.379	0.581	2.513	0.508	2.649	0.438	2.784
27	0.691	2.342	0.616	2.470	0.544	2.600	0.475	2.730
28	0.723	2.309	0.650	2.431	0.578	2.555	0.510	2.680
29	0.753	2.278	0.682	2.396	0.612	2.515	0.544	2.634
30	0.782	2.251	0.712	2.363	0.643	2.477	0.577	2.592
31	0.810	2.226	0.741	2.333	0.674	2.443	0.608	2.553
32	0.836	2.203	0.769	2.306	0.703	2.411	0.638	2.517
33	0.861	2.181	0.795	2.281	0.731	2.382	0.668	2.484
34	0.885	2.162	0.821	2.257	0.758	2.355	0.695	2.454
35	0.908	2.144	0.845	2.236	0.783	2.330	0.722	2.425
36	0.930	2.127	0.868	2.216	0.808	2.306	0.748	2.398
37	0.951	2.112	0.891	2.198	0.831	2.285	0.772	2.374
38	0.970	2.098	0.912	2.180	0.854	2.265	0.796	2.351
39	0.990	2.085	0.932	2.164	0.875	2.246	0.819	2.329
40	1.008	2.072	0.945	2.149	0.896	2.228	0.840	2.309
45	1.089	2.022	1.038	2.088	0.988	2.156	0.938	2.225
50	1.156	1.986	1.110	2.044	1.064	2.103	1.014	2.163
55	1.212	1.959	1.170	2.010	1.129	2.062	1.087	2.116
60	1.260	1.939	1.222	1.984	1.184	2.031	1.145	2.079
65	1.301	1.923	1.266	1.964	1.231	2.006	1.195	2.049
70	1.337	1.910	1.305	1.948	1.272	1.986	1.239	2.026
75	1.369	1.901	1.339	1.935	1.308	1.970	1.277	2.006
80	1.397	1.893	1.369	1.925	1.340	1.957	1.311	1.991
85	1.422	1.886	1.396	1.916	1.369	1.946	1.342	1.977
90	1.445	1.881	1.420	1.909	1.395	1.937	1.369	1.966
95	1.465	1.877	1.442	1.903	1.418	1.929	1.394	1.956
100	1.484	1.874	1.462	1.898	1.439	1.923	1.416	1.948
150	1.608	1.862	1.594	1.877	1.579	1.892	1.564	1.908
200	1.675	1.863	1.665	1.874	1.654	1.885	1.643	1.896

Durbin-Watson Statistic: Upper and Lower Limits at 5 % Level

N	k'= 13 dL	dU	k'= 14 dL	dU	k'= 15 dL	dU	k'= 16 dL	dU
6	-	-	-	-	-	-	-	-
7	-	-	-	-	-	-	-	-
8	-	-	-	-	-	-	-	-
9	-	-	-	-	-	-	-	-
10	-	-	-	-	-	-	-	-
11	-	-	-	-	-	-	-	-
12	-	-	-	-	-	-	-	-
13	-	-	-	-	-	-	-	-
14	-	-	-	-	-	-	-	-
15	-	-	-	-	-	-	-	-
16	-	-	-	-	-	-	-	-
17	-	-	-	-	-	-	-	-
18	0.078	3.603	-	-	-	-	-	-
19	0.111	3.496	0.070	3.642	-	-	-	-
20	0.145	3.395	0.100	3.542	0.063	3.676	-	-
21	0.182	3.300	0.132	3.448	0.091	3.583	0.058	3.705
22	0.220	3.211	0.166	3.358	0.120	3.495	0.083	3.619
23	0.259	3.128	0.202	3.272	0.153	3.409	0.110	3.535
24	0.297	3.053	0.239	3.193	0.186	3.327	0.141	3.454
25	0.335	2.983	0.275	3.119	0.221	3.251	0.172	3.376
26	0.373	2.919	0.312	3.051	0.256	3.179	0.205	3.303
27	0.409	2.859	0.348	2.987	0.291	3.112	0.238	3.233
28	0.445	2.805	0.383	2.928	0.325	3.050	0.271	3.168
29	0.479	2.755	0.418	2.874	0.359	2.992	0.305	3.107
30	0.512	2.708	0.451	2.823	0.392	2.937	0.337	3.050
31	0.545	2.665	0.484	2.776	0.425	2.887	0.370	2.996
32	0.576	2.625	0.515	2.773	0.457	2.840	0.401	2.946
33	0.606	2.588	0.546	2.692	0.488	2.796	0.432	2.899
34	0.634	2.554	0.575	2.654	0.518	2.754	0.462	2.854
35	0.662	2.521	0.604	2.619	0.547	2.716	0.492	2.813
36	0.689	2.492	0.631	2.586	0.575	2.680	0.520	2.774
37	0.714	2.464	0.657	2.555	0.602	2.646	0.548	2.738
38	0.739	2.438	0.683	2.526	0.628	2.614	0.575	2.703
39	0.763	2.413	0.707	2.499	0.653	2.585	0.600	2.671
40	0.785	2.391	0.731	2.473	0.678	2.557	0.626	2.641
45	0.887	2.296	0.838	2.367	0.788	2.439	0.740	2.512
50	0.973	2.225	0.927	2.287	0.882	2.350	0.836	2.414
55	1.045	2.170	1.003	2.225	0.961	2.281	0.919	2.338
60	1.106	2.127	1.068	2.177	1.029	2.227	0.990	2.278
65	1.160	2.093	1.124	2.138	1.088	2.183	1.052	2.229
70	1.206	2.066	1.172	2.106	1.139	2.148	1.105	2.189
75	1.247	2.043	1.215	2.080	1.184	2.118	1.153	2.156
80	1.283	2.024	1.253	2.059	1.224	2.093	1.195	2.129
85	1.315	2.009	1.287	2.040	1.260	2.073	1.232	2.105
90	1.344	1.995	1.318	2.025	1.292	2.055	1.266	2.085
95	1.370	1.984	1.345	2.012	1.321	2.040	1.296	2.068
100	1.393	1.974	1.371	2.000	1.347	2.026	1.324	2.053
150	1.550	1.924	1.535	1.940	1.519	1.956	1.504	1.972
200	1.632	1.908	1.621	1.919	1.610	1.931	1.599	1.943

Durbin-Watson Statistic: Upper and Lower Limits at 5 % Level

N	k'= 17 dL	dU	k'= 18 dL	dU	k'= 19 dL	dU	k'= 20 dL	dU
6	-	-	-	-	-	-	-	-
7	-	-	-	-	-	-	-	-
8	-	-	-	-	-	-	-	-
9	-	-	-	-	-	-	-	-
10	-	-	-	-	-	-	-	-
11	-	-	-	-	-	-	-	-
12	-	-	-	-	-	-	-	-
13	-	-	-	-	-	-	-	-
14	-	-	-	-	-	-	-	-
15	-	-	-	-	-	-	-	-
16	-	-	-	-	-	-	-	-
17	-	-	-	-	-	-	-	-
18	-	-	-	-	-	-	-	-
19	-	-	-	-	-	-	-	-
20	-	-	-	-	-	-	-	-
21	-	-	-	-	-	-	-	-
22	0.052	3.731	-	-	-	-	-	-
23	0.076	3.650	0.048	3.753	-	-	-	-
24	0.101	3.572	0.070	3.678	0.044	3.773	-	-
25	0.130	3.494	0.094	3.604	0.065	3.702	0.041	3.790
26	0.160	3.420	0.120	3.531	0.087	3.632	0.060	3.724
27	0.191	3.349	0.149	3.460	0.112	3.563	0.081	3.658
28	0.222	3.283	0.178	3.392	0.138	3.495	0.104	3.592
29	0.254	3.219	0.208	3.327	0.166	3.431	0.129	3.528
30	0.286	3.160	0.238	3.266	0.195	3.368	0.156	3.465
31	0.317	3.103	0.269	3.208	0.224	3.309	0.183	3.406
32	0.349	3.050	0.299	3.153	0.253	3.252	0.211	3.348
33	0.379	3.000	0.329	3.100	0.283	3.198	0.239	3.293
34	0.409	2.954	0.359	3.051	0.312	3.147	0.267	3.240
35	0.439	2.910	0.388	3.005	0.340	3.099	0.295	3.190
36	0.467	2.868	0.417	2.961	0.369	3.053	0.323	3.142
37	0.495	2.829	0.445	2.920	0.397	3.009	0.351	3.097
38	0.522	2.792	0.472	2.880	0.424	2.968	0.378	3.054
39	0.549	2.757	0.499	2.843	0.451	2.929	0.404	3.013
40	0.575	2.724	0.525	2.808	0.477	2.892	0.430	2.974
45	0.692	2.586	0.644	2.659	0.598	2.733	0.553	2.807
50	0.792	2.479	0.747	2.544	0.703	2.610	0.660	2.675
55	0.877	2.396	0.836	2.454	0.795	2.512	0.754	2.571
60	0.951	2.330	0.913	2.382	0.874	2.434	0.836	2.487
65	1.016	2.276	0.980	2.323	0.944	2.371	0.908	2.419
70	1.072	2.232	1.038	2.275	1.005	2.318	0.971	2.362
75	1.121	2.195	1.090	2.235	1.058	2.275	1.027	2.315
80	1.165	2.165	1.136	2.201	1.106	2.238	1.076	2.275
85	1.205	2.139	1.177	2.172	1.149	2.206	1.121	2.241
90	1.240	2.116	1.213	2.148	1.187	2.179	1.160	2.211
95	1.271	2.097	1.247	2.126	1.222	2.156	1.197	2.186
100	1.301	2.080	1.277	2.108	1.253	2.135	1.229	2.164
150	1.489	1.989	1.474	2.006	1.458	2.023	1.443	2.040
200	1.588	1.955	1.576	1.967	1.565	1.979	1.554	1.991

Source: The original table of Durbin-Watson d statistic (J. Durbin and G.S. Watson, "Testing for Serial Correlation in Least Squares Regression", *Biometrika*, Vol. 38, 1951, pp. 159-177) was expanded by N.E. Savin and K.J. White, "The Durbin-Watson Test for Serial Correlation with Small Samples or Many Regressors", *Econometrica*, Vol. 45, Nov. 1977, pp. 1989-96, and corrected by R. W. Farebrother, "The Durbin-Watson Test for Serial Correlation When There is No Intercept in the Regression", *Econometrica*, vol. 48, Sept. 1980, p. 1953-55.

Reprinted by permission of Econometric Society.

Table 2: Chi-Square (χ^2) Values (Upper Level)

DF	$\alpha = 0.10$	0.05	0.025	0.010	0.005
1	2.7055	3.84146	5.02389	6.63490	7.87950
2	4.6052	5.9915	7.3778	9.2103	10.5966
3	6.2514	7.8147	9.3484	11.3449	12.8382
4	7.7794	9.4877	11.1433	13.2767	14.8603
5	9.2364	11.0705	12.8325	15.0863	16.7496
6	10.6446	12.5916	14.4494	16.8119	18.5476
7	12.0170	14.0671	16.0128	18.4753	20.2778
8	13.3616	15.5073	17.5346	20.0902	21.9550
9	14.6837	16.9190	19.0228	21.6660	23.5893
10	15.9872	18.3070	20.4832	23.2093	25.1882
11	17.2750	19.6751	21.9201	24.7250	26.7569
12	18.5493	21.0261	23.3367	26.2170	28.2996
13	19.8119	22.3620	24.7356	27.6882	29.8194
14	21.0641	23.6848	26.1190	29.1413	31.3194
15	22.3071	24.9958	27.4884	30.5779	32.8013
16	23.5418	26.2963	28.8454	32.0001	34.2674
17	24.7690	27.5871	30.1910	33.4085	35.7182
18	25.9894	28.8693	31.5264	34.8053	37.1564
19	27.2036	30.1435	32.8523	36.1907	38.5820
20	28.4120	31.4104	34.1696	37.5662	39.9968
21	29.6151	32.6706	35.4789	38.9322	41.4011
22	30.8133	33.9245	36.7808	40.2895	42.7960
23	32.0069	35.1724	38.0755	41.6382	44.1808
24	33.1962	36.4150	39.3641	42.9798	45.5586
25	34.3816	37.6525	40.6466	44.3144	46.9285
26	35.5632	38.8852	41.9233	45.6419	48.2903
27	36.7412	40.1133	43.1946	46.9631	49.6452
28	37.9159	41.3372	44.4608	48.2783	50.9936
29	39.0875	42.5570	45.7224	49.5881	52.3360
30	40.2560	43.7730	46.9793	50.8922	53.6720
31	41.4218	44.9854	48.2320	52.1915	55.0030
32	42.5847	46.1942	49.4804	53.4856	56.3278
33	43.7451	47.3998	50.7250	54.7753	57.6479
34	44.9031	48.6023	51.9659	56.0608	58.9636
35	46.0588	49.8019	53.2035	57.3424	60.2755
36	47.2122	50.9985	54.4373	58.6193	61.5813
37	48.3635	52.1925	55.5683	59.8932	62.8847
38	49.5127	53.3837	56.8958	61.1628	64.1827
39	50.6598	54.5724	58.1203	62.4287	65.4767
40	51.8051	55.7586	59.3420	63.6914	66.7673
41	52.9485	56.9424	60.5606	64.9501	68.0528
42	54.0902	58.1241	61.7769	66.2065	69.3365
43	55.2301	59.3034	62.9902	67.4589	70.6151
44	56.3685	60.4808	64.2014	68.7093	71.8921
45	57.5053	61.6563	65.4102	69.9570	73.1663
46	58.6405	62.8295	66.6162	71.2007	74.4353
47	59.7742	64.0010	67.8204	72.4428	75.7031
48	60.9065	65.1706	69.0223	73.6820	76.9675
49	62.0375	66.3386	70.2224	74.9195	78.2307
50	63.1671	67.5048	71.4201	76.1537	79.4896

DF = degrees of freedom.

Chi-Square (χ^2) Values (Upper Level)

DF	$\alpha = 0.10$	0.05	0.025	0.010	0.005
51	64.2954	68.6693	72.6160	77.3860	80.7468
52	65.4224	69.8321	73.8098	78.6156	82.0005
53	66.5482	70.9934	75.0018	79.8432	83.2522
54	67.6729	72.1534	76.1924	81.0697	84.5036
55	68.7962	73.3115	77.3805	82.2923	85.7493
56	69.9187	74.4686	78.5677	83.5146	86.9960
57	71.0397	75.6238	79.7523	84.7330	88.2368
58	72.1596	76.7774	80.9349	85.9486	89.4738
59	73.2791	77.9309	82.1181	87.1674	90.7185
60	74.3972	79.0823	83.2984	88.3810	91.9547
61	75.5139	80.2318	84.4758	89.5898	93.1833
62	76.6300	81.3807	85.6531	90.8001	94.4159
63	77.7456	82.5291	86.8302	92.0115	95.6520
64	78.8597	83.6753	88.0042	93.2172	96.8787
65	79.9728	84.8203	89.1764	94.4204	98.1019
66	81.0856	85.9650	90.3492	95.6263	99.3315
67	82.197	87.109	91.520	96.830	100.558
68	83.308	88.250	92.688	98.028	101.775
69	84.418	89.391	93.857	99.228	102.998
70	85.527	90.531	95.023	100.424	104.213
71	86.635	91.670	96.188	101.620	105.429
72	87.743	92.808	97.353	102.817	106.649
73	88.850	93.945	98.516	104.009	107.860
74	89.956	95.082	99.679	105.203	109.076
75	91.061	96.217	100.839	106.392	110.285
76	92.166	97.351	101.999	107.582	111.495
77	93.270	98.485	103.159	108.772	112.706
78	94.374	99.617	104.316	109.959	113.913
79	95.476	100.749	105.473	111.145	115.118
80	96.578	101.879	106.628	112.328	116.320
81	97.680	103.010	107.784	113.513	117.525
82	98.780	104.139	108.938	114.695	118.727
83	99.880	105.267	110.090	115.877	119.927
84	100.980	106.395	111.242	117.056	121.125
85	102.079	107.522	112.393	118.236	122.324
86	103.177	108.648	113.544	119.414	123.521
87	104.275	109.773	114.693	120.591	124.717
88	105.372	110.898	115.841	121.767	125.912
89	106.469	112.022	116.988	122.941	127.103
90	107.565	113.145	118.135	124.115	128.296
91	108.661	114.268	119.282	125.291	129.493
92	109.755	115.390	120.427	126.461	130.679
93	110.850	116.511	121.572	127.633	131.871
94	111.944	117.632	122.715	128.804	133.060
95	113.037	118.751	123.857	129.970	134.241
96	114.130	119.870	124.999	131.139	135.429
97	115.223	120.989	126.141	132.308	136.617
98	116.315	122.107	127.281	133.473	137.798
99	117.407	123.225	128.421	134.639	138.982
100	118.499	124.343	129.563	135.811	140.177

Note: Generated by a computer program.

Table 3: Critical t - Values (Upper One-Tail Level)

DF	$\alpha=0.10$	0.05	0.025	0.01	0.005
1	3.07770	6.31380	12.70620	31.8206	63.6570
2	1.88562	2.91999	4.30265	6.96456	9.92485
3	1.63774	2.35336	3.18245	4.54070	5.84091
4	1.53321	2.13187	2.77645	3.74696	4.60410
5	1.47592	2.01505	2.57058	3.36493	4.03215
6	1.43976	1.94318	2.44691	3.14267	3.70745
7	1.41492	1.89459	2.36463	2.99795	3.49948
8	1.39682	1.85955	2.30601	2.89646	3.35539
9	1.38304	1.83311	2.26216	2.82144	3.24986
10	1.37220	1.81246	2.22814	2.76378	3.16928
11	1.36343	1.79589	2.20099	2.71808	3.10582
12	1.35622	1.78229	2.17882	2.68100	3.05456
13	1.35017	1.77093	2.16037	2.65031	3.01228
14	1.34503	1.76131	2.14480	2.62450	2.97686
15	1.34061	1.75305	2.13145	2.60248	2.94672
16	1.33679	1.74589	2.11991	2.58349	2.92078
17	1.33340	1.73961	2.10982	2.56694	2.89824
18	1.33040	1.73407	2.10093	2.55238	2.87844
19	1.32773	1.72914	2.09303	2.53948	2.86095
20	1.32534	1.72473	2.08598	2.52798	2.84534
21	1.32320	1.72075	2.07963	2.51765	2.83137
22	1.32124	1.71715	2.07390	2.50832	2.81878
23	1.31946	1.71388	2.06866	2.49987	2.80734
24	1.31784	1.71089	2.06390	2.49217	2.79694
25	1.31635	1.70814	2.05954	2.48511	2.78744
26	1.31499	1.70562	2.05553	2.47863	2.77871
27	1.31370	1.70331	2.05183	2.47266	2.77068
28	1.31253	1.70113	2.04841	2.46714	2.76326
29	1.31143	1.69914	2.04523	2.46202	2.75639
30	1.31042	1.69726	2.04227	2.45726	2.75000

Note: DF = Degrees of freedom. Generated by a computer program.

Table 4: Critical F Values (One-Tail Test: Upper 5% Level)

DF2	DF1 1	2	3	4	5
1	161.448	199.500	215.707	224.583	230.161
2	18.5128	19.0000	19.1643	19.2468	19.2963
3	10.1280	9.55211	9.27663	9.11721	9.01348
4	7.70865	6.94427	6.59138	6.38823	6.25606
5	6.60789	5.78613	5.40945	5.19217	5.05033
6	5.98738	5.14328	4.75707	4.53369	4.38739
7	5.59149	4.73749	4.34685	4.12031	3.97156
8	5.31766	4.45899	4.06618	3.83787	3.68750
9	5.11736	4.25649	3.86255	3.63309	3.48167
10	4.96461	4.10288	3.70826	3.47806	3.32584
11	4.84434	3.98230	3.58743	3.35670	3.20388
12	4.74724	3.88531	3.49030	3.25917	3.10589
13	4.66719	3.80560	3.41054	3.17913	3.02545
14	4.60015	3.73894	3.34390	3.11225	2.95825
15	4.54308	3.68237	3.28740	3.05557	2.90131
16	4.49400	3.63376	3.23891	3.00692	2.85241
17	4.45134	3.59155	3.19672	2.96472	2.81000
18	4.41390	3.55456	3.15991	2.92776	2.77286
19	4.38079	3.52192	3.12735	2.89513	2.74006
20	4.35130	3.49283	3.09839	2.86611	2.71089
21	4.32487	3.46683	3.07247	2.84014	2.68478
22	4.30104	3.44336	3.04912	2.81671	2.66127
23	4.27935	3.42214	3.02802	2.79554	2.64000
24	4.25968	3.40283	3.00879	2.77629	2.62066
25	4.24170	3.38519	2.99125	2.75871	2.60299
26	4.22520	3.36902	2.97515	2.74259	2.58682
27	4.21001	3.35418	2.96040	2.72777	2.57189
28	4.19597	3.34039	2.94669	2.71410	2.55813
29	4.18296	3.32766	2.93403	2.70140	2.54539
30	4.17088	3.31584	2.92228	2.68965	2.53355
31	4.15961	3.30483	2.91133	2.67867	2.52254
32	4.14910	3.29455	2.90112	2.66846	2.51226
33	4.13932	3.28494	2.89157	2.65887	2.50266
34	4.13005	3.27592	2.88263	2.64990	2.49362
35	4.12135	3.26744	2.87423	2.64148	2.48515
36	4.11317	3.25946	2.86627	2.63353	2.47717
37	4.10548	3.25194	2.85880	2.62606	2.46967
38	4.09817	3.24483	2.85174	2.61900	2.46255
39	4.09128	3.23810	2.84507	2.61233	2.45583
40	4.08476	3.23173	2.83874	2.60597	2.44947
41	4.07864	3.22568	2.83275	2.59997	2.44343
42	4.07265	3.21995	2.82705	2.59426	2.43770
43	4.06705	3.21453	2.82163	2.58884	2.43225
44	4.06171	3.20928	2.81647	2.58367	2.42704
45	4.05661	3.20432	2.81154	2.57874	2.42208
46	4.05175	3.19958	2.80685	2.57404	2.41736
47	4.04712	3.19506	2.80236	2.56954	2.41284
48	4.04265	3.19073	2.79806	2.56524	2.40851
49	4.03839	3.18658	2.79395	2.56112	2.40438
50	4.03431	3.18261	2.79001	2.55718	2.40041
60	4.00118	3.15041	2.75808	2.52521	2.36827
70	3.97778	3.12768	2.73554	2.50266	2.34559
80	3.96036	3.11077	2.71882	2.48588	2.32872
90	3.94689	3.09770	2.70586	2.47293	2.31569
100	3.93613	3.08729	2.69553	2.46261	2.30532
110	3.92739	3.07881	2.68718	2.45423	2.29687
120	3.92017	3.07178	2.68017	2.44724	2.28986
130	3.91399	3.06584	2.67429	2.44135	2.28394
140	3.90873	3.06076	2.66927	2.43631	2.27887
150	3.90423	3.05638	2.66495	2.43197	2.27450
160	3.90031	3.05253	2.66113	2.42815	2.27066
170	3.89676	3.04916	2.65777	2.42482	2.26730
180	3.89366	3.04616	2.65480	2.42185	2.26431
190	3.89092	3.04349	2.65214	2.41919	2.26164
200	3.88838	3.04105	2.64973	2.41679	2.25924
250	3.87891	3.03191	2.64072	2.40774	2.25013
1000	3.85063	3.00471	2.61369	2.38079	2.22294

Critical F Values (Upper 5% Level)

DF2	DF1 6	7	8	9	10
1	233.985	236.768	238.882	240.543	241.881
2	19.3292	19.3525	19.3710	19.3848	19.3959
3	8.94065	8.88674	8.84525	8.81238	8.78572
4	6.16313	6.09439	6.04105	5.99878	5.96437
5	4.95029	4.87587	4.81832	4.77247	4.73506
6	4.28387	4.20656	4.14680	4.09902	4.05998
7	3.86603	3.78707	3.72573	3.67667	3.63652
8	3.58064	3.50046	3.43810	3.38817	3.34717
9	3.37375	3.29275	3.22958	3.17889	3.13728
10	3.21719	3.13549	3.07166	3.02038	2.97824
11	3.09461	3.01236	2.94800	2.89622	2.85363
12	2.99613	2.91336	2.84857	2.79638	2.75342
13	2.91529	2.83211	2.76692	2.71436	2.67102
14	2.84776	2.76423	2.69869	2.64579	2.60216
15	2.79048	2.70659	2.64083	2.58764	2.54372
16	2.74131	2.65720	2.59110	2.53770	2.49353
17	2.69867	2.61432	2.54796	2.49429	2.44994
18	2.66131	2.57673	2.51016	2.45628	2.41170
19	2.62832	2.54354	2.47679	2.42270	2.37793
20	2.59898	2.51401	2.44707	2.39281	2.34788
21	2.57271	2.48758	2.42046	2.36606	2.32095
22	2.54906	2.46378	2.39651	2.34194	2.29670
23	2.52769	2.44223	2.37481	2.32011	2.27474
24	2.50819	2.42266	2.35508	2.30027	2.25474
25	2.49041	2.40473	2.33706	2.28210	2.23647
26	2.47411	2.38832	2.32053	2.26545	2.21972
27	2.45911	2.37322	2.30532	2.25013	2.20429
28	2.44526	2.35929	2.29128	2.23599	2.19005
29	2.43243	2.34634	2.27825	2.22289	2.17685
30	2.42052	2.33434	2.26616	2.21070	2.16459
31	2.40946	2.32314	2.25491	2.19936	2.15313
32	2.39908	2.31276	2.24440	2.18877	2.14249
33	2.38939	2.30299	2.23456	2.17886	2.13250
34	2.38031	2.29383	2.22534	2.16956	2.12314
35	2.37178	2.28524	2.21667	2.16083	2.11434
36	2.36375	2.27714	2.20852	2.15261	2.10605
37	2.35618	2.26951	2.20082	2.14485	2.09824
38	2.34904	2.26230	2.19357	2.13753	2.09085
39	2.34226	2.25548	2.18668	2.13060	2.08387
40	2.33585	2.24902	2.18018	2.12403	2.07725
41	2.32977	2.24289	2.17399	2.11780	2.07096
42	2.32399	2.23709	2.16812	2.11190	2.06499
43	2.31850	2.23153	2.16253	2.10624	2.05931
44	2.31327	2.22627	2.15721	2.10087	2.05390
45	2.30827	2.22122	2.15213	2.09576	2.04874
46	2.30351	2.21643	2.14729	2.09087	2.04381
47	2.29897	2.21183	2.14267	2.08620	2.03911
48	2.29463	2.20744	2.13823	2.08173	2.03460
49	2.29043	2.20323	2.13399	2.07745	2.03028
50	2.28644	2.19920	2.12992	2.07335	2.02614
60	2.25405	2.16654	2.09697	2.04011	1.99259
70	2.23119	2.14348	2.07369	2.01660	1.96888
80	2.21420	2.12632	2.05639	1.99912	1.95122
90	2.20106	2.11307	2.04299	1.98559	1.93757
100	2.19060	2.10252	2.03233	1.97483	1.92669
110	2.18208	2.09392	2.02365	1.96605	1.91783
120	2.17501	2.08677	2.01643	1.95877	1.91046
130	2.16904	2.08074	2.01033	1.95262	1.90425
140	2.16394	2.07559	2.00513	1.94735	1.89893
150	2.15952	2.07114	2.00063	1.94280	1.89433
160	2.15568	2.06724	1.99669	1.93882	1.89030
170	2.15227	2.06382	1.99322	1.93533	1.88677
180	2.14925	2.06077	1.99015	1.93220	1.88362
190	2.14657	2.05805	1.98740	1.92943	1.88082
200	2.14413	2.05559	1.98492	1.92693	1.87827
250	2.13494	2.04632	1.97556	1.91745	1.86870
1000	2.10756	2.01868	1.94763	1.88922	1.84008

Table 4: F - Values

Critical F Values (Upper 5% Level)

DF2	DF1 11	12	13	14	15
1	242.983	243.905	244.689	245.363	245.949
2	19.4049	19.4125	19.4189	19.4244	19.4291
3	8.76333	8.74464	8.72868	8.71490	8.70287
4	5.93581	5.91182	5.89124	5.87335	5.85785
5	4.70385	4.67775	4.65523	4.63577	4.61876
6	4.02745	3.99994	3.97636	3.95593	3.93806
7	3.60305	3.57470	3.55038	3.52927	3.51077
8	3.31295	3.28394	3.25903	3.23742	3.21840
9	3.10249	3.07296	3.04755	3.02547	3.00611
10	2.94296	2.91298	2.88717	2.86477	2.84502
11	2.81794	2.78758	2.76142	2.73865	2.71864
12	2.71733	2.68665	2.66019	2.63714	2.61686
13	2.63466	2.60366	2.57694	2.55364	2.53313
14	2.56550	2.53425	2.50726	2.48373	2.46302
15	2.50681	2.47532	2.44811	2.42437	2.40345
16	2.45638	2.42466	2.39725	2.37332	2.35225
17	2.41257	2.38066	2.35307	2.32895	2.30769
18	2.37417	2.34208	2.31431	2.29004	2.26862
19	2.34024	2.30797	2.28004	2.25562	2.23407
20	2.30999	2.27760	2.24952	2.22496	2.20328
21	2.28292	2.25036	2.22217	2.19747	2.17567
22	2.25852	2.22583	2.19752	2.17269	2.15079
23	2.23642	2.20361	2.17516	2.15024	2.12824
24	2.21631	2.18338	2.15482	2.12981	2.10768
25	2.19793	2.16489	2.13623	2.11111	2.08889
26	2.18107	2.14794	2.11917	2.09395	2.07166
27	2.16554	2.13230	2.10345	2.07815	2.05575
28	2.15120	2.11789	2.08894	2.06354	2.04107
29	2.13791	2.10451	2.07547	2.05000	2.02746
30	2.12556	2.09206	2.06296	2.03742	2.01480
31	2.11406	2.08048	2.05131	2.02569	2.00302
32	2.10333	2.06967	2.04042	2.01474	1.99199
33	2.09325	2.05955	2.03023	2.00448	1.98167
34	2.08382	2.05004	2.02067	1.99486	1.97199
35	2.07496	2.04111	2.01169	1.98581	1.96288
36	2.06661	2.03270	2.00321	1.97729	1.95431
37	2.05873	2.02477	1.99522	1.96927	1.94622
38	2.05129	2.01728	1.98767	1.96165	1.93858
39	2.04425	2.01018	1.98053	1.95445	1.93133
40	2.03758	2.00346	1.97376	1.94764	1.92446
41	2.03125	1.99708	1.96733	1.94116	1.91795
42	2.02523	1.99101	1.96122	1.93501	1.91175
43	2.01950	1.98524	1.95541	1.92915	1.90585
44	2.01405	1.97974	1.94986	1.92357	1.90024
45	2.00884	1.97450	1.94458	1.91825	1.89488
46	2.00387	1.96949	1.93953	1.91317	1.88975
47	1.99912	1.96470	1.93471	1.90830	1.88486
48	1.99458	1.96012	1.93009	1.90365	1.88018
49	1.99023	1.95573	1.92567	1.89920	1.87569
50	1.98606	1.95153	1.92143	1.89493	1.87138
60	1.95221	1.91740	1.88702	1.86024	1.83644
70	1.92829	1.89325	1.86266	1.83568	1.81168
80	1.91046	1.87527	1.84453	1.81738	1.79323
90	1.89667	1.86135	1.83047	1.80321	1.77894
100	1.88568	1.85025	1.81927	1.79191	1.76754
110	1.87673	1.84121	1.81014	1.78269	1.75823
120	1.86929	1.83370	1.80256	1.77504	1.75050
130	1.86301	1.82735	1.79615	1.76856	1.74397
140	1.85764	1.82192	1.79066	1.76302	1.73838
150	1.85300	1.81723	1.78592	1.75824	1.73354
160	1.84892	1.81313	1.78176	1.75404	1.72930
170	1.84534	1.80951	1.77813	1.75036	1.72559
180	1.84216	1.80629	1.77487	1.74708	1.72227
190	1.83933	1.80342	1.77197	1.74416	1.71932
200	1.83677	1.80083	1.76936	1.74150	1.71664
250	1.82708	1.79104	1.75946	1.73150	1.70655
1000	1.79816	1.76180	1.72990	1.70164	1.67637

Critical F Values (Upper 5% Level)

DF2	DF1 16	17	18	19	20
1	246.462	246.917	247.322	247.685	248.012
2	19.4333	19.4369	19.4402	19.4431	19.4457
3	8.69229	8.68291	8.67453	8.66701	8.66020
4	5.84412	5.83197	5.82112	5.81137	5.80256
5	4.60376	4.59045	4.57853	4.56782	4.55820
6	3.92233	3.90826	3.89571	3.88442	3.87419
7	3.49442	3.47988	3.46687	3.45514	3.44453
8	3.20163	3.18670	3.17332	3.16125	3.15036
9	2.98900	2.97370	2.96000	2.94765	2.93646
10	2.82757	2.81201	2.79806	2.78545	2.77402
11	2.70091	2.68512	2.67090	2.65808	2.64645
12	2.59889	2.58284	2.56843	2.55541	2.54360
13	2.51494	2.49868	2.48408	2.47088	2.45888
14	2.44464	2.42820	2.41342	2.40005	2.38791
15	2.38489	2.36830	2.35333	2.33985	2.32756
16	2.33349	2.31674	2.30164	2.28799	2.27557
17	2.28880	2.27189	2.25668	2.24289	2.23036
18	2.24959	2.23255	2.21720	2.20331	2.19067
19	2.21490	2.19773	2.18226	2.16828	2.15550
20	2.18399	2.16670	2.15113	2.13701	2.12416
21	2.15626	2.13887	2.12319	2.10898	2.09604
22	2.13128	2.11377	2.09800	2.08369	2.07066
23	2.10860	2.09101	2.07515	2.06076	2.04764
24	2.08796	2.07029	2.05433	2.03986	2.02666
25	2.06909	2.05133	2.03529	2.02074	2.00747
26	2.05178	2.03392	2.01781	2.00319	1.98985
27	2.03579	2.01787	2.00170	1.98697	1.97359
28	2.02103	2.00305	1.98679	1.97203	1.95856
29	2.00735	1.98929	1.97297	1.95816	1.94462
30	1.99462	1.97650	1.96012	1.94524	1.93165
31	1.98276	1.96457	1.94814	1.93320	1.91956
32	1.97168	1.95343	1.93694	1.92195	1.90826
33	1.96131	1.94300	1.92645	1.91141	1.89767
34	1.95157	1.93322	1.91660	1.90151	1.88774
35	1.94241	1.92400	1.90735	1.89221	1.87838
36	1.93378	1.91532	1.89863	1.88344	1.86956
37	1.92564	1.90715	1.89040	1.87514	1.86124
38	1.91794	1.89939	1.88260	1.86733	1.85337
39	1.91066	1.89206	1.87523	1.85992	1.84593
40	1.90377	1.88511	1.86824	1.85290	1.83887
41	1.89719	1.87852	1.86161	1.84622	1.83215
42	1.89095	1.87224	1.85530	1.83987	1.82577
43	1.88502	1.86627	1.84930	1.83383	1.81969
44	1.87937	1.86057	1.84356	1.82808	1.81390
45	1.87397	1.85514	1.83809	1.82257	1.80837
46	1.86881	1.84996	1.83287	1.81732	1.80310
47	1.86389	1.84499	1.82788	1.81230	1.79804
48	1.85917	1.84024	1.82310	1.80749	1.79320
49	1.85465	1.83570	1.81852	1.80288	1.78857
50	1.85032	1.83134	1.81413	1.79847	1.78412

DF2	DF1 30	40	50	60	70
60	1.64914	1.59427	1.55901	1.53431	1.51600
70	1.62205	1.56608	1.52996	1.50457	1.48569
80	1.60173	1.54489	1.50807	1.48212	1.46275
90	1.58594	1.52837	1.49098	1.46453	1.44478
100	1.57331	1.51513	1.47723	1.45039	1.43028
110	1.56297	1.50427	1.46595	1.43875	1.41835
120	1.55434	1.49520	1.45652	1.42901	1.40835
130	1.54705	1.48752	1.44852	1.42074	1.39984
140	1.54079	1.48092	1.44163	1.41362	1.39251
150	1.53537	1.47520	1.43566	1.40743	1.38613
160	1.53061	1.47018	1.43041	1.40199	1.38053
170	1.52643	1.46575	1.42578	1.39718	1.37557
180	1.52270	1.46180	1.42165	1.39290	1.37115
200	1.51636	1.45509	1.41462	1.38558	1.36359
250	1.50495	1.44297	1.40189	1.37234	1.34989
1000	1.47057	1.40629	1.36319	1.33183	1.30775

Table 5: z-Values (Standardized Normal Distribution): Density and Probabilities

z value	f(z) Density	Area −∞ to z	Area 0 to z	z value	f(z) Density	Area −∞ to z	Area 0 to z
0.00	0.39894	0.50000	0.00000	0.51	0.35029	0.69497	0.19497
0.01	0.39892	0.50399	0.00399	0.52	0.34849	0.69847	0.19847
0.02	0.39886	0.50798	0.00798	0.53	0.34667	0.70194	0.20194
0.03	0.39876	0.51197	0.01197	0.54	0.34482	0.70540	0.20540
0.04	0.39862	0.51595	0.01595	0.55	0.34294	0.70884	0.20884
0.05	0.39844	0.51994	0.01994	0.56	0.34105	0.71226	0.21226
0.06	0.39822	0.52392	0.02392	0.57	0.33912	0.71566	0.21566
0.07	0.39797	0.52790	0.02790	0.58	0.33718	0.71904	0.21904
0.08	0.39767	0.53188	0.03188	0.59	0.33521	0.72240	0.22240
0.09	0.39733	0.53586	0.03586	0.60	0.33322	0.72575	0.22575
0.10	0.39695	0.53983	0.03983	0.61	0.33121	0.72907	0.22907
0.11	0.39654	0.54380	0.04380	0.62	0.32918	0.73237	0.23237
0.12	0.39608	0.54776	0.04776	0.63	0.32713	0.73565	0.23565
0.13	0.39559	0.55172	0.05172	0.64	0.32506	0.73891	0.23891
0.14	0.39505	0.55567	0.05567	0.65	0.32297	0.74215	0.24215
0.15	0.39448	0.55962	0.05962	0.66	0.32086	0.74537	0.24537
0.16	0.39387	0.56356	0.06356	0.67	0.31874	0.74857	0.24857
0.17	0.39322	0.56749	0.06749	0.68	0.31659	0.75175	0.25175
0.18	0.39253	0.57142	0.07142	0.69	0.31443	0.75490	0.25490
0.19	0.39181	0.57535	0.07535	0.70	0.31225	0.75804	0.25804
0.20	0.39104	0.57926	0.07926	0.71	0.31006	0.76115	0.26115
0.21	0.39024	0.58317	0.08317	0.72	0.30785	0.76424	0.26424
0.22	0.38940	0.58706	0.08706	0.73	0.30563	0.76730	0.26730
0.23	0.38853	0.59095	0.09095	0.74	0.30339	0.77035	0.27035
0.24	0.38762	0.59483	0.09483	0.75	0.30114	0.77337	0.27337
0.25	0.38667	0.59871	0.09871	0.76	0.29887	0.77637	0.27637
0.26	0.38568	0.60257	0.10257	0.77	0.29659	0.77935	0.27935
0.27	0.38466	0.60642	0.10642	0.78	0.29431	0.78230	0.28230
0.28	0.38361	0.61026	0.11026	0.79	0.29200	0.78524	0.28524
0.29	0.38251	0.61409	0.11409	0.80	0.28969	0.78814	0.28814
0.30	0.38139	0.61791	0.11791	0.81	0.28737	0.79103	0.29103
0.31	0.38023	0.62172	0.12172	0.82	0.28504	0.79389	0.29389
0.32	0.37903	0.62552	0.12552	0.83	0.28269	0.79673	0.29673
0.33	0.37780	0.62930	0.12930	0.84	0.28034	0.79955	0.29955
0.34	0.37654	0.63307	0.13307	0.85	0.27798	0.80234	0.30234
0.35	0.37524	0.63683	0.13683	0.86	0.27562	0.80511	0.30511
0.36	0.37391	0.64058	0.14058	0.87	0.27324	0.80785	0.30785
0.37	0.37255	0.64431	0.14431	0.88	0.27086	0.81057	0.31057
0.38	0.37115	0.64803	0.14803	0.89	0.26848	0.81327	0.31327
0.39	0.36973	0.65173	0.15173	0.90	0.26609	0.81594	0.31594
0.40	0.36827	0.65542	0.15542	0.91	0.26369	0.81859	0.31859
0.41	0.36678	0.65910	0.15910	0.92	0.26129	0.82121	0.32121
0.42	0.36526	0.66276	0.16276	0.93	0.25888	0.82381	0.32381
0.43	0.36371	0.66640	0.16640	0.94	0.25647	0.82639	0.32639
0.44	0.36213	0.67003	0.17003	0.95	0.25406	0.82894	0.32894
0.45	0.36053	0.67364	0.17364	0.96	0.25164	0.83147	0.33147
0.46	0.35889	0.67724	0.17724	0.97	0.24923	0.83398	0.33398
0.47	0.35723	0.68082	0.18082	0.98	0.24681	0.83646	0.33646
0.48	0.35553	0.68439	0.18439	0.99	0.24439	0.83891	0.33891
0.49	0.35381	0.68793	0.18793	1.00	0.24197	0.84134	0.34134
0.50	0.35207	0.69146	0.19146				

Note: Mean $\mu = 0$, standard deviation $\sigma = 1$.

z-Values (Standardized Normal Distribution): Density and Probabilities (2)

z value	f(z) Density	Area −∞ to z	Area 0 to z	z value	f(z) Density	Area −∞ to z	Area 0 to z
1.01	0.23955	0.84375	0.34375	1.51	0.12758	0.93448	0.43448
1.02	0.23713	0.84614	0.34614	1.52	0.12566	0.93574	0.43574
1.03	0.23471	0.84849	0.34849	1.53	0.12376	0.93699	0.43699
1.04	0.23230	0.85083	0.35083	1.54	0.12188	0.93822	0.43822
1.05	0.22988	0.85314	0.35314	1.55	0.12001	0.93943	0.43943
1.06	0.22747	0.85543	0.35543	1.56	0.11816	0.94062	0.44062
1.07	0.22506	0.85769	0.35769	1.57	0.11632	0.94179	0.44179
1.08	0.22265	0.85993	0.35993	1.58	0.11450	0.94295	0.44295
1.09	0.22025	0.86214	0.36214	1.59	0.11270	0.94408	0.44408
1.10	0.21785	0.86433	0.36433	1.60	0.11092	0.94520	0.44520
1.11	0.21546	0.86650	0.36650	1.61	0.10915	0.94630	0.44630
1.12	0.21307	0.86864	0.36864	1.62	0.10741	0.94738	0.44738
1.13	0.21069	0.87076	0.37076	1.63	0.10567	0.94845	0.44845
1.14	0.20831	0.87286	0.37286	1.64	0.10396	0.94950	0.44950
1.15	0.20594	0.87493	0.37493	1.65	0.10226	0.95053	0.45053
1.16	0.20357	0.87698	0.37698	1.66	0.10059	0.95154	0.45154
1.17	0.20121	0.87900	0.37900	1.67	0.09893	0.95254	0.45254
1.18	0.19886	0.88100	0.38100	1.68	0.09728	0.95352	0.45352
1.19	0.19652	0.88298	0.38298	1.69	0.09566	0.95449	0.45449
1.20	0.19419	0.88493	0.38493	1.70	0.09405	0.95543	0.45543
1.21	0.19186	0.88686	0.38686	1.71	0.09246	0.95637	0.45637
1.22	0.18954	0.88877	0.38877	1.72	0.09089	0.95728	0.45728
1.23	0.18724	0.89065	0.39065	1.73	0.08933	0.95818	0.45818
1.24	0.18494	0.89251	0.39251	1.74	0.08780	0.95907	0.45907
1.25	0.18265	0.89435	0.39435	1.75	0.08628	0.95994	0.45994
1.26	0.18037	0.89617	0.39617	1.76	0.08478	0.96080	0.46080
1.27	0.17810	0.89796	0.39796	1.77	0.08329	0.96164	0.46164
1.28	0.17585	0.89973	0.39973	1.78	0.08183	0.96246	0.46246
1.29	0.17360	0.90147	0.40147	1.79	0.08038	0.96327	0.46327
1.30	0.17137	0.90320	0.40320	1.80	0.07895	0.96407	0.46407
1.31	0.16915	0.90490	0.40490	1.81	0.07754	0.96485	0.46485
1.32	0.16694	0.90658	0.40658	1.82	0.07614	0.96562	0.46562
1.33	0.16474	0.90824	0.40824	1.83	0.07477	0.96638	0.46638
1.34	0.16256	0.90988	0.40988	1.84	0.07341	0.96712	0.46712
1.35	0.16038	0.91149	0.41149	1.85	0.07206	0.96784	0.46784
1.36	0.15822	0.91308	0.41308	1.86	0.07074	0.96856	0.46856
1.37	0.15608	0.91466	0.41466	1.87	0.06943	0.96926	0.46926
1.38	0.15395	0.91621	0.41621	1.88	0.06814	0.96995	0.46995
1.39	0.15183	0.91774	0.41774	1.89	0.06687	0.97062	0.47062
1.40	0.14973	0.91924	0.41924	1.90	0.06562	0.97128	0.47128
1.41	0.14764	0.92073	0.42073	1.91	0.06438	0.97193	0.47193
1.42	0.14556	0.92220	0.42220	1.92	0.06316	0.97257	0.47257
1.43	0.14350	0.92364	0.42364	1.93	0.06195	0.97320	0.47320
1.44	0.14146	0.92507	0.42507	1.94	0.06077	0.97381	0.47381
1.45	0.13943	0.92647	0.42647	1.95	0.05959	0.97441	0.47441
1.46	0.13742	0.92785	0.42785	1.96	0.05844	0.97500	0.47500
1.47	0.13542	0.92922	0.42922	1.97	0.05730	0.97558	0.47558
1.48	0.13344	0.93056	0.43056	1.98	0.05618	0.97615	0.47615
1.49	0.13147	0.93189	0.43189	1.99	0.05508	0.97670	0.47670
1.50	0.12952	0.93319	0.43319	2.00	0.05399	0.97725	0.47725

z-Values (Standardized Normal Distribution): Density and Probabilities (3)

z value	f(z) Density	Area −∞ to z	Area 0 to z	z value	f(z) Density	Area −∞ to z	Area 0 to z
2.01	0.05292	0.97778	0.47778	2.51	0.01709	0.99396	0.49396
2.02	0.05186	0.97831	0.47831	2.52	0.01667	0.99413	0.49413
2.03	0.05082	0.97882	0.47882	2.53	0.01625	0.99430	0.49430
2.04	0.04980	0.97932	0.47932	2.54	0.01585	0.99446	0.49446
2.05	0.04879	0.97982	0.47982	2.55	0.01545	0.99461	0.49461
2.06	0.04780	0.98030	0.48030	2.56	0.01506	0.99477	0.49477
2.07	0.04682	0.98077	0.48077	2.57	0.01468	0.99492	0.49492
2.08	0.04586	0.98124	0.48124	2.58	0.01431	0.99506	0.49506
2.09	0.04491	0.98169	0.48169	2.59	0.01394	0.99520	0.49520
2.10	0.04398	0.98214	0.48214	2.60	0.01358	0.99534	0.49534
2.11	0.04307	0.98257	0.48257	2.61	0.01323	0.99547	0.49547
2.12	0.04217	0.98300	0.48300	2.62	0.01289	0.99560	0.49560
2.13	0.04128	0.98341	0.48341	2.63	0.01256	0.99573	0.49573
2.14	0.04041	0.98382	0.48382	2.64	0.01223	0.99585	0.49585
2.15	0.03955	0.98422	0.48422	2.65	0.01191	0.99598	0.49598
2.16	0.03871	0.98461	0.48461	2.66	0.01160	0.99609	0.49609
2.17	0.03788	0.98500	0.48500	2.67	0.01130	0.99621	0.49621
2.18	0.03706	0.98537	0.48537	2.68	0.01100	0.99632	0.49632
2.19	0.03626	0.98574	0.48574	2.69	0.01071	0.99643	0.49643
2.20	0.03547	0.98610	0.48610	2.70	0.01042	0.99653	0.49653
2.21	0.03470	0.98645	0.48645	2.71	0.01014	0.99664	0.49664
2.22	0.03394	0.98679	0.48679	2.72	0.00987	0.99674	0.49674
2.23	0.03319	0.98713	0.48713	2.73	0.00961	0.99683	0.49683
2.24	0.03246	0.98745	0.48745	2.74	0.00935	0.99693	0.49693
2.25	0.03174	0.98778	0.48778	2.75	0.00909	0.99702	0.49702
2.26	0.03103	0.98809	0.48809	2.76	0.00885	0.99711	0.49711
2.27	0.03034	0.98840	0.48840	2.77	0.00861	0.99720	0.49720
2.28	0.02965	0.98870	0.48870	2.78	0.00837	0.99728	0.49728
2.29	0.02898	0.98899	0.48899	2.79	0.00814	0.99736	0.49736
2.30	0.02833	0.98928	0.48928	2.80	0.00792	0.99744	0.49744
2.31	0.02768	0.98956	0.48956	2.81	0.00770	0.99752	0.49752
2.32	0.02705	0.98983	0.48983	2.82	0.00748	0.99760	0.49760
2.33	0.02643	0.99010	0.49010	2.83	0.00727	0.99767	0.49767
2.34	0.02582	0.99036	0.49036	2.84	0.00707	0.99774	0.49774
2.35	0.02522	0.99061	0.49061	2.85	0.00687	0.99781	0.49781
2.36	0.02463	0.99086	0.49086	2.86	0.00668	0.99788	0.49788
2.37	0.02406	0.99111	0.49111	2.87	0.00649	0.99795	0.49795
2.38	0.02349	0.99134	0.49134	2.88	0.00631	0.99801	0.49801
2.39	0.02294	0.99158	0.49158	2.89	0.00613	0.99807	0.49807
2.40	0.02239	0.99180	0.49180	2.90	0.00595	0.99813	0.49813
2.41	0.02186	0.99202	0.49202	2.91	0.00578	0.99819	0.49819
2.42	0.02134	0.99224	0.49224	2.92	0.00562	0.99825	0.49825
2.43	0.02083	0.99245	0.49245	2.93	0.00545	0.99831	0.49831
2.44	0.02033	0.99266	0.49266	2.94	0.00530	0.99836	0.49836
2.45	0.01984	0.99286	0.49286	2.95	0.00514	0.99841	0.49841
2.46	0.01936	0.99305	0.49305	2.96	0.00499	0.99846	0.49846
2.47	0.01888	0.99324	0.49324	2.97	0.00485	0.99851	0.49851
2.48	0.01842	0.99343	0.49343	2.98	0.00470	0.99856	0.49856
2.49	0.01797	0.99361	0.49361	2.99	0.00457	0.99861	0.49861
2.50	0.01753	0.99379	0.49379	3.00	0.00443	0.99865	0.49865

Note: Generated by a computer program.

Index

(fold)

(fold)

IRWIN

Please use this postage-paid form to report any errors that you find in these Guides. Be as specific as possible and note which changes should be made. We will do our best to address them in subsequent printings and future editions. Thank you.

Attention: C. Tuscher

Name_____School_____

Office Phone_____

Please fold and seal so that our address is visible.